PENGUIN BOOKS

THE RIGHT NATION

'To understand conservatism in the US, one should turn to the brilliant *The Right Nation*' Michael Burleigh, *Literary Review*

'The best book I have read recently about the US' David Aaronovitch, *Guardian*

'Elegantly written, comprehensive and scrupulously fair minded, *The Right Nation* is required reading for anybody who wants to understand the United States today' Walter Russell Mead

'Drawing on their extensive travels across the country and their wide reading in American history, they paint a convincing picture of where America is today, how it got there and where it is likely headed' Michael Barone, *US News & World Report*

'John Micklethwait and Adrian Wooldridge brilliantly explained why Bush and his ilk would win, before they did, in *The Right Nation*' Matt Ridley, *Daily Telegraph*, Books of the Year

'There is an Atlantic Right-wards shift, blowing across the democracies, which is far from over. Reading this book, you wonder whether the next British generation will be to the Right of today's thirtysomethings' Andrew Marr, *Daily Telegraph*

'An immensely knowledgeable description of the history and beliefs of modern American conservatism . . . the authors do an excellent job of analysing the different streams that have flowed together to make up modern American conservatism' Godfrey Hodgson, *Independent*

ABOUT THE AUTHORS

John Micklethwait is the U.S. editor for the *Economist* and Adrian Wooldridge is its Washington correspondent. They have written three previous books together. They were both educated at Oxford.

THE
RIGHT
NATION

WHY AMERICA IS
DIFFERENT

John Micklethwait AND Adrian Wooldridge

PENGUIN BOOKS

PENGUIN BOOKS

Published by the Penguin Group
Penguin Books Ltd, 80 Strand, London WC2R ORL, England
Penguin Group (USA), Inc., 375 Hudson Street, New York, New York 10014, USA
Penguin Group (Canada), 90 Eglinton Avenue East, Suite 700, Toronto, Ontario, Canada M4P 3YZ
(a division of Pearson Penguin Canada Inc.)
Penguin Ireland, 25 St Stephen's Green, Dublin 2, Ireland (a division of Penguin Books Ltd)
Penguin Group (Australia), 250 Camberwell Road, Camberwell, Victoria 3124, Australia
(a division of Pearson Australia Group Pty Ltd)
Penguin Books India Pvt Ltd, 11 Community Centre,
Panchsheel Park, New Delhi – 110 017, India
Penguin Group (NZ), cnr Airborne and Rosedale Roads, Albany,
Auckland 1310, New Zealand (a division of Pearson New Zealand Ltd)
Penguin Books (South Africa) (Pty) Ltd, 24 Sturdee Avenue, Rosebank 2196, Johannesburg, South Africa

Penguin Books Ltd, Registered Offices: 80 Strand, London WC2R ORL, England

www.penguin.com

First published in the United States of America by Penguin Group (USA) 2004
First published in Great Britain by Allen Lane 2004
Published with new material in Penguin Books 2005
1

Copyright © John Micklethwait and Adrian Wooldridge, 2004, 2005

Page 451 constitutes an extension of this copyright page

Maps drawn by Peter Winfield

Printed in England by Clays Ltd, St Ives plc

CONTENTS

THE RIGHT NATION

The Changing Geography of the Right Nation

States won by Richard Nixon, 1960

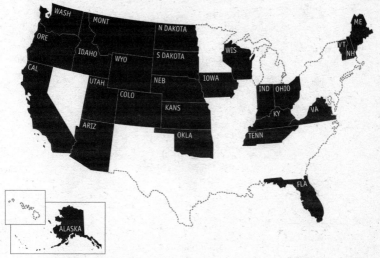

Richard Nixon in 1960 won 219 electoral college votes with 49.6 percent of the popular vote.

States won by George W. Bush, 2000

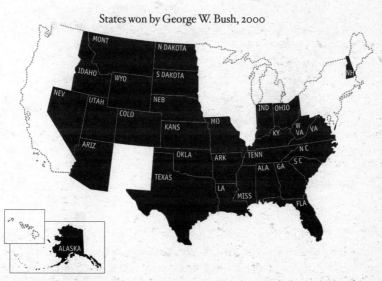

George W. Bush in 2000 won 271 electoral college votes with 47.9 percent of the popular vote.

CONSERVATISM OF HOUSE MEMBERS

Republicans 1972

Republicans 2002

Conservatism of members of the
U.S. House of Representatives as
rated by the American Conservative
Union (see Appendix, p. 399)

- 80–100
- 60–79
- 40–59
- 20–39
- 0–19

*no Democratic
congressmen

†no Republican
congressmen

**Vermont's congressman in
2002 is an Independent
who caucuses with the
Democrats.

Democrats 1972

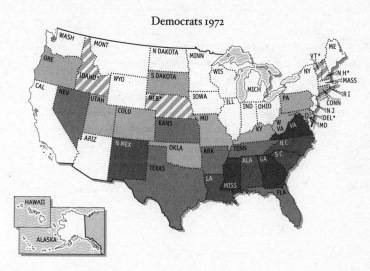

Democrats 2002

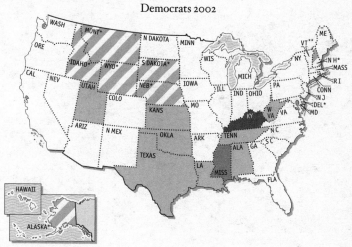

Source: American Conservative Union

INTRODUCTION

SITTING ON A SOFA with their plastic cups of coffee, Dustin and Maura look like a couple of twenty-somethings in a creative writing course: a sprawl of slightly scruffy sweatshirts, jeans and sneakers, Dustin in a baseball cap, Maura with her blond hair tied behind her head with a Native-American band. They both recently graduated from liberal-arts colleges on the East Coast, and they have traveled around most of Europe. Maura has worked for Habitat for Humanity in Malawi and done a spell at the European Parliament, and is about to start a job at a pharmaceuticals firm; Dustin interned at the White House, and is thinking about politics.

And those politics? Both are working for the Republican Party in Colorado Springs in 2002. Both are prolife "under any circumstances." Both immediately volunteer John Ashcroft, the fire-breathing attorney general, as someone they admire. Both support capital punishment and oppose gun control ("At college, people were like 'Why does anybody need guns?' and I was like 'Have you ever been to a ranch?'"). Both go to church every week. Both passionately support school vouchers. Both think government should be smaller and prison sentences tougher. Both regard the United Nations as a bit of a joke and support the decision to withdraw from the Kyoto Protocol. They dissent from the Right on some things—they dislike any intolerance toward gays, for example, and they were initially nervous about dealing with Saddam Hussein unilaterally, though they both eventually supported George W. Bush's decision to invade Iraq (Maura's fiancé, Jack, was among the troops). For Dustin and Maura, conservatism is a progressive creed. It is not about old people trying to cling to things, but about young people trying to change them. And that, they insist, is what America is all about too.

Few people in Colorado Springs would dispute that assertion. Nestled under Pike's Peak, the mountain that inspired "America the Beautiful," Colorado Springs is now one of America's most successful cities—the home of "Silicon Mountain" and much of the U.S. Olympics bureaucracy. It is also one of America's most conservative cities. Almost all the local politicians are Republicans; more Libertarians than Democrats ran for the local state assembly in 2002.

Colorado Springs has long had a military connection, and it remains a favorite place for old soldiers to retire. But in the past two decades, the town has added two rather more Evangelical strands of conservatism. First, it has spawned a tax-cutting movement, which in 1992 pushed through a Taxpayers' Bill of Rights that bans Colorado's politicians from increasing any tax without first getting the electorate's permission. Second, in 1991, the town's leaders, battling with a recession that had left it the "repossession capital of America," used $5 million worth of incentives to lure Focus on the Family, a Christian ministry founded by Jim Dobson, from California. There are now one hundred or so other Christian organizations in the town. As a charity, Focus, which employs 1,700 locals, is prohibited from direct involvement in party politics, but it is enormously influential in Republican circles. Each week, 8 million Americans tune in to broadcasts by Dobson, a former professor of child psychiatry who has also written a succession of best-selling books on Christian parenting. It is now de rigueur for Republican presidential candidates to make a pilgrimage to the Focus campus.

More liberal-minded Americans prefer to dismiss people like Dustin and Maura, and places like Colorado Springs, as belonging to the extreme fringe. So do Europeans, who are accustomed to visiting Manhattan, Boston and San Francisco. In fact, however, at least one in three Americans supports all the principles that Dustin and Maura believe in, and in many cases, such as the death penalty, taxes and tough sentences, Dustin and Maura stand firmly with the majority. Twice as many Americans describe themselves as "conservative" (41 percent) as describe themselves as "liberal" (19 percent). Wander around America—particularly Southern and Western America—and you'll find plenty of towns that feel like Colorado Springs. As Republicans never stop pointing out, the counties that voted for George W. Bush take up far more of the map than the ones that voted for Al Gore.

These places help to explain modern America. They explain why George

W. Bush is in the White House, why the Republican Party has won six of the past nine presidential elections and controls both houses of Congress, why every serious Democratic candidate for president supports mandatory sentencing and welfare reform, why the cultural capitals of Hollywood and Manhattan remain the exception and why the much disdained "flyover" land that lies between them is the rule.

This is not to say that America is on the verge of becoming a giant version of Colorado Springs. Politics is something of a tug of war, and there are millions of Americans trying to pull the country in exactly the opposite direction: witness the enormous groundswell of support on the Left for Howard Dean's presidential campaign. Maura, who now lives in Boulder, Colorado's most liberal town, spends a lot of her time arguing with friends about Iraq. America is more polarized than it has been for decades. Yet there is no doubt which pole is exerting the most force. The Right has been winning the tug of war and forcing its opponents in the Democratic Party to make compromises. All sorts of Bush haters—not just in liberal America but in Old Europe—might imagine that a Bush defeat in November 2004 would bring their nightmare to an end. But a Democratic president would still have to deal not just with the Republicans in Congress but with Colorado Springs, with Focus on the Family, with Dustin and Maura—with the huge part of America we call the Right Nation.

Indeed, places such as Colorado Springs help explain why America is so different from other rich countries. Look at most of the controversies that divide global opinion, and the United States comes down on the conservative side. America tolerates lower levels of government spending than other advanced countries, and far higher levels of inequality, at least in terms of wealth. One in six American households earned less than 35 percent of the median income in 2002; in Britain, one of Europe's more unequal countries, the proportion of similarly disadvantaged households is closer to one in twenty.[1] America is the only developed nation that does not have a full government-supported health-care system, and the only Western democracy that does not provide child support to all families. America is one of only two countries in the Organization of Economic Cooperation and Development that does not provide paid maternity leave—and the other country, Australia, is actively considering introducing it.

America upholds the right to bear arms, the death penalty and strict sentencing laws: its imprisonment rate is five times that of Britain, the toughest sentencer in Europe.[2] The United States is much more willing to contemplate the use of force in human affairs, even unilaterally, and much more wary of treaties than its allies. American citizens are far more religious than are European citizens, and far more traditional in their moral values. The United States is one of the few rich countries where abortion is a galvanizing political issue, and perhaps the only one where half the families regularly say grace before meals. It has taken a far tougher line on stem-cell research than almost any other country. Some of these positions are "Republican," but most of them enjoy broad-based support. Even taking into account Dean and all those liberals, America's center of gravity is to the right of Europe's.

AN IDEA WHOSE TIME HAD COME

"So inevitable and yet so completely unforeseen" was Alexis de Tocqueville's verdict on the French revolution. Much the same can be said of the conservative revolution that has changed America over the past half century. Fifty years ago, America lacked a real conservative ideology, let alone a cohesive Right Nation. The term "conservative" was largely absent from the American political lexicon, other than as an insult, introduced by the Democrats during the Depression, and vigorously warded off by Republicans like Herbert Hoover, who insisted he was a "true liberal." Many early conservative heroes, such as Albert Jay Nock, preferred "radical," "individualist" or even "anarchist." When Dwight Eisenhower came to power in 1952, the American Right was on the wane. Its two great ideas—laissez-faire at home and isolationism abroad—had been put to flames by the Great Depression and the Second World War. The Republican Party was in the hands of the Northeast's patrician establishment—the party of Henry Cabot Lodge, Nelson Rockefeller and a self-proclaimed "moderate progressive" senator, Prescott Bush, who would found a political dynasty. Eisenhower prided himself on being above ideology ("His smile was his philosophy," a contemporary observed), and he appointed Earl Warren, a notoriously liberal Republican, to the Supreme Court. Richard Nixon and Jack Kennedy ran on almost identical platforms in 1960.

In the 1960s, many American liberals thought that they stood a good chance of making their country a much more "European" nation. Support for the death penalty fell to just 43 percent in the mid-1960s. Republican legislators, including the patriarch of the Bush dynasty, hugged the middle ground, under the influence of "New Republican" ideas about the mixed economy. The Kennedy administration wore its civilized European values on its sleeve (literally so in the case of the haute-coutured first lady). The president liked to point out that he had spent a year at the London School of Economics as a student of a prominent Marxist, Harold Laski.[3] He also claimed that his favorite film was Alain Resnais's *Last Year at Marienbad.*

"These, without doubt, are the years of the liberal," John Kenneth Galbraith wrote, somewhat smugly, in 1964. "Almost everyone now so describes himself."[4] In the 1960s, American liberals advocated the creation of a European-style welfare state, particularly through Lyndon Johnson's Great Society program (the phrase, incidentally, was taken from the title of a book by a British socialist, Graham Wallas). They imposed greater restrictions on firearms and they mounted campaigns to outlaw executions, legalize abortion and introduce not just racial equality but positive discrimination in favor of minorities (or affirmative action), all of which were to bear fruit in the 1970s. The liberal elites of Boston and New York felt that they had a good chance of civilizing what some of them called "the Yahoos."

The Yahoos refused to be tamed. The first howl of fury from the Right Nation came with Barry Goldwater's presidential campaign in 1964, which by ordinary standards was a calamity. Goldwater lost to Lyndon Johnson by a greater margin than anyone before or since. Yet in the long run, Goldwater had an extraordinary influence on the Republican Party. The senator from Arizona shifted the balance of power in the party westward, to a region where the American dream was being refashioned by sunlight and open space. He did as much as anyone to redefine Republicanism as an anti-government philosophy: "I fear Washington and centralized government more than I do Moscow," he said—and this from a cold warrior who had once suggested lobbing a nuclear bomb into the men's room at the Kremlin.[5]

Goldwater's rise coincided with a growing intellectual ferment on the Right, a ferment that was transforming the "know-nothing" wing of the party into the know-it-all wing—of autodidacts poring over Friedrich Hayek, Milton Friedman and William F. Buckley's *National Review*.

This dynamism helped explain why in 1964 clever young Hillary Rodham was a Goldwater girl right down to her fake cowgirl outfit. But the other begetter of modern conservative America was the cause that she embraced when she left her suburban Chicago home for Wellesley College: the radicalization of the Democrats. This phenomenon was not just about Southern racism, though Johnson's prophecy, as he signed the Civil Rights Act in 1964, that he was "signing away the South for 50 years" proved accurate. Southern whites certainly rallied to the Republicans, but so did other blue-collar workers annoyed by the Democrats' lurch to the Left. The Great Society had failed to deliver on its promises. As Ronald Reagan put it, "liberals fought poverty and poverty won."

The tiny band of "Goldwater Democrats" in 1964 grew into the small army of Nixon Democrats in 1972 and the mighty horde of Reagan Democrats in 1980. The Republican Party, which had once been characterized by Northeastern gentility, acquired a more ideological edge and a Southern-fried flavor. Sun Belt Republicans have won six of the past nine presidential elections: two Californians (Nixon and Reagan) and two Texans (Bush père et fils). The American Conservative Union tracks voting records of the members of the House of Representatives on the basis of loyalty to the conservative cause. In 1972, the average score for the House Republicans was 63 percent; by 2002 it was 91 percent. (See Appendix.)

It is true that, over the same period, the Democrats had moved to the Left, with their average score dropping from 32 percent to 13 percent. But that is the result of a combination of gerrymandering (which increased the number of safe Democratic seats) and the loss of the party's Southern Dixiecrats. The average conservative score for the House as a whole increased from 45 percent to 53 percent. The Democrats succeeded at the presidential level only by adopting at least some of the values of the Right. Bill Clinton became something of a Sun Belt conservative himself: he not only approved of the death penalty, but he returned to Arkansas during the 1992 election campaign to preside over the execution of a mentally impaired black man, Ricky Ray Rector. The most successful Democratic politician since FDR declared both "the end of welfare as we know it" and "the end of big government." Today nobody thinks it odd that a Democratic candidate for governor should make a point of campaigning with a gun in her handbag (even though it happened in Alaska). As for looking across the Atlantic for inspiration, the leaders of the Right Nation these days regard "Old Europe" as a sinkhole to be avoided.

A DIFFERENT SORT OF CONSERVATISM

This book is both a portrait and an argument. The portrait is of Conservative America—the Right Nation. The argument is that this conservatism explains why America is different. Not only has America produced a far more potent conservative movement than anything available in other rich countries; America as a whole is a more conservative place. Americans might imagine that their politics is as varied as everybody else's, and in one way it is: as we shall see, the gap between Dennis Hastert, the Republican Speaker of the House, and Nancy Pelosi, the Democratic minority leader (and the districts they represent in suburban Illinois and San Francisco respectively), is immense. But the center of gravity of American opinion is much further to the right—and the whole world needs to understand what that means.

Most Americans still do not realize how extraordinary their brand of conservatism is. While the American Left—unions, academics, public-sector workers—have their equivalents overseas, Dustin, Maura, Focus on the Family, the angry taxpayers and the militant gun owners are distinctly American. For instance, there are hardly any conservative talk-radio shows in Europe and only a handful of Christian radio stations. When asked about similar creeds overseas, many American conservatives mention Margaret Thatcher. "Now she was a western Conservative," argues Bill Owens, Colorado's ambitious young governor. In fact, Thatcherism was a far less durable phenomenon than American conservatism, and one without much of a moral agenda. When Thatcher tried to invoke God (in a sermon to the

General Assembly of the Church of Scotland in 1988), she was ridiculed even by her own supporters. That would not have happened in America, where there are 200 Christian television channels, 1,500 Christian radio stations and a highly organized Christian Right. Sometimes religious Southerners enthusiastically mention Europe's Christian Democrats, unaware that the adjective is largely ancestral. "How Christian is your party?" one of our colleagues recently asked the chairman of one such European party. "Definitely post-Christian," came the reply.

In no other country is the Right defined so much by values rather than class. The best predictor of whether a white American votes Republican is not his or her income but how often he or she goes to church. In 2000 Bush won 79 percent of the votes of those whites who went to church more than once a week (and only 33 percent of those who never went); by contrast he won just 54 percent of the votes of those Americans who earned more than $100,000 a year.[6] Yet despite the importance of values, America has failed to produce a xenophobic "far Right" on anything like the same scale as Europe has. The closest equivalent to a European hard-Rightist is Pat Buchanan, and his political fortunes have waned rather than waxed. (The paleoconservative's sole contribution to the 2000 contest was to appear puzzlingly close to Al Gore on the Florida ballot paper, confusing a lot of elderly people in Palm Beach into voting for him.) In Colorado Springs, conservatives see immigrants mostly as potential recruits, rather than as diluters of the national spirit.

The exceptionalism of the American Right is partly a matter of its beliefs. The first two definitions of "conservative" offered by the *Concise Oxford Dictionary* are "adverse to rapid change" and "moderate, avoiding extremes." Neither of these seems a particularly good description of what is going on in America at the moment. "Conservatism"—no less than its foes "liberalism" or "communitarianism"—has become one of those words that are now as imprecise as they are emotionally charged. Open a newspaper and you can find the word used to describe Jacques Chirac, Trent Lott, the Mullah Omar and Vladimir Putin. Since time immemorial, conservatives have insisted that their deeply pragmatic creed cannot be ideologically pigeonholed.

But, in philosophical terms at least, classical conservatism does mean something. The creed of Edmund Burke, its most eloquent proponent, might be crudely reduced to six principles: a deep suspicion of the power of the state; a preference for liberty over equality; patriotism; a belief in established institutions and hierarchies; skepticism about the idea of progress; and elitism. Winston Churchill happily accepted these principles: he was devoted to nation and empire, disinclined to trust the lower orders with anything, hostile to the welfare state, worried about the diminution of liberty and, as he once remarked ruefully, "preferred the past to the present and the present to the future."[7]

To simplify a little, the exceptionalism of modern American conservatism lies in its exaggeration of the first three of Burke's principles and contradiction of the last three. The American Right exhibits a far deeper hostility toward the state than any other modern conservative party. How many European conservatives would display bumper stickers saying "I love my country but I hate my government"? How many would argue that we need to make government so small that it can be drowned in a bathtub?[8] The American Right is also more obsessed with personal liberty than any other conservative party, and prepared to tolerate an infinitely higher level of inequality. (One reason why Burke warmed to the American revolutionaries was that, unlike their dangerous French equivalents, the gentlemen rebels concentrated on freedom, not equality.) On patriotism, nobody can deny that conservatives everywhere tend to be a fairly nationalistic bunch. "Nations have characters," insisted Benjamin Disraeli, one of Britain's most reflective conservative statesmen, "and national character is precisely the quality which the new sect of statesmen in their schemes and speculations either deny or overlook."[9] Yet many European conservatives have accepted the idea that their nationality should be diluted in "schemes and speculations" like the European Union, and they are increasingly reconciled to dealing with national security on a multilateral basis. American conservatives clearly are not.

If the American Right was merely a more vigorous form of conservatism, then it would be a lot more predictable. In fact, the American Right takes a resolutely liberal approach to Burke's last three principles: hierarchy, pessimism and elitism. The heroes of modern American conservatism are not paternalist squires but rugged individualists who don't know their place: entrepreneurs who build mighty businesses out of nothing, settlers who move out West and, of course, the cowboy. There is a frontier spirit to the Right—unsurprisingly, since so much of its heartland is made up of new towns of one sort or another.

The geography of conservatism also helps to explain its optimism rather than pessimism. In the war between the Dynamo and the Virgin, as Henry Adams characterized the battle between progress and tradition, most American conservatives are on the side of the Dynamo. They think that the world offers all sorts of wonderful possibilities. And they feel that the only thing that is preventing people from attaining these possibilities is the dead liberal hand of the past. By contrast, Burke has been described flatteringly by European conservatives as a "prophet of the past." Spend any time with a group of Republicans, and their enthusiasm for the future can be positively exhausting.

As for elitism, rather than dreaming about creating an educated "clerisy" of clever rulers (as Coleridge and T. S. Eliot did), the Republicans ever since the 1960s have played the populist card. Richard Nixon saw himself as the champion of the "silent majority." In 1988 the aristocratic George H. W. Bush presented himself as a defender of all-American values against the Harvard Yard liberalism of Michael Dukakis. In 2000, George W. Bush, a president's son who was educated at Andover, Yale and Harvard Business School, played up his role as a down-to-earth Texan taking on the might of Washington. As a result, modern American conservatism has flourished not just in country clubs and boardrooms, but at the grass roots—on talk radio and at precinct meetings, and in revolts against high taxes, the regulation of firearms and other invidious attempts by liberal do-gooders to force honest Americans into some predetermined mold.

We hasten to add that there are numerous exceptions to this exceptionalism. Some religious conservatives would happily put the Good Book at the center of government. Visit a Southern landed aristocrat and you will hear familiar stories of military exploits, riding horses and ancestors killed in duels. Rather than emitting optimism, William Buckley founded the

National Review in 1955 with the intention of standing "athwart history, yelling 'Stop!'" It is hard to be more elitist or skeptical about progress than the "Straussians," a group of neoconservatives who take their inspiration from Leo Strauss, a German-born philosopher who spent his life agonizing about the degradations of modernity.

Henceforth, to avoid confusion, we will use the terms "conservative" and "liberal" in the American way—to mean right- and left-wing. All the same, the fact that the Right is such a broad church—that it includes a hefty dose of liberal heresy along with the traditionalism—yields both weaknesses and strengths. On the positive side, it helps to explain why it is such a big and vibrant movement. American conservatism cannot help but contain contradictions because it contains so many vital elements. There are thousands of conservative activists, hundreds of conservative think tanks, a small army of conservative intellectuals. One useful book of conservative experts, published by the Heritage Foundation, the movement's biggest think tank, is as thick as a telephone directory. Yet the broad church also means that people are often worshipping different gods.

Look at Colorado Springs and you'll find at least three competing forms of conservatism—the laissez-faire individualism of the tax cutters and the gun owners, the Christian moralism of Focus on the Family and the militaristic nationalism, represented by the neighboring Air Force Academy and the bumper stickers laughing at Saddam Hussein. But how can you trumpet a strong military and a vigorous foreign policy and then insist on small government? How can you celebrate individualism but then try to subject those individuals to the rule of God? Wherever you go in the Right Nation, you discover similar contradictions.

A MOVEMENT, NOT JUST A PARTY

At this point, it is worth emphasizing the gap between conservative America and America. Despite its celebration of populism, American conservatism is not as popular as it likes to think. The Right may be in the driver's seat and it may help to explain why the United States is different, but the Right is not the United States. In 2000 George W. Bush lost the popular vote for president by 500,000 votes. "I do not believe a majority of Americans shares our values," Paul Weyrich, the man who invented the Moral Majority, admitted during the Monica Lewinsky affair.[10] Jim Dobson of Focus on the Family may be able to remind 8 million Americans about the evils of homosexuality, but *Will & Grace,* a sitcom with several openly gay characters, is watched by 20 million people a week.

Hence the importance of the movement—and indeed of organizations like Focus and the Moral Majority: no matter how much they claim to represent the real America, conservatives have succeeded in part because, in a country where only half the electorate bothers to vote, they are better organized than other sorts of Americans. When Hillary Clinton talked about a vast right-wing conspiracy, conservative activists could complain about the tone of the charge much more than they could about its substance. There is far more cohesion to the conservative movement—not just at the local level but also at the national level—than most Americans realize.

Evidence of this organizing prowess is on display every Wednesday in Washington. The day begins at Grover Norquist's weekly breakfast meeting at his Americans for Tax Reform on L Street. This used to be a fairly eccentric affair: the unhygienic libertarian types who attended were known as "droolers." Nowadays, more than 100 people come, a third of them women. The activists include lobbyists from the National Rifle Association, Christian Coalition staffers, home schoolers, free-market fundamentalists, Orthodox Jews, Muslim business people, contrarian blacks, intellectuals from the Cato Institute, congressmen, senators, the odd visiting governor (including Bill Owens of Colorado) and, of course, a contingent from the White House. Karl Rove, George W. Bush's chief political advisor, makes a point of turning up several times a year.

The gathering is impeccably egalitarian. Conservative grandees such as Rove, Owens or Newt Gingrich sit next to student activists fresh off the Greyhound bus. The table is littered with cholesterol, carbohydrates and caffeine. Every available surface is piled high with conservative literature: flyers advertising upcoming events; issue papers and reports; op-eds from the *Wall Street Journal* and the *Washington Times;* booklets about government waste; the latest offerings from the American Enterprise Institute. Throughout the meeting people walk around the room handing out yet more material. Here are details on an attempt to raise taxes in Oregon: can anybody help stop it? Has anyone heard of the dastardly attempt to prevent Mars from being opened to private enterprise? Now is the time to nip it in the bud.[11]

Norquist's meeting ends promptly at 11:30. Many activists immediately jump into taxis to head for Capitol Hill and the Coalitions for America lunch meeting. This is a slightly smaller affair—a mere seventy to ninety people. It is more venerable, having been established by Paul Weyrich back in 1983. The participants are older, more likely to be wearing suits and more focused on the culture wars than low taxes. The table bearing the buffet is draped in red-white-and-blue crepe bunting. Most people have American flags pinned to their lapels. Before the meeting starts everyone turns to a flag in the corner of the room and repeats the pledge of allegiance. "Born and unborn" someone adds loudly as the pledge finishes.

The atmosphere here is more inquisitorial than at Norquist's meeting. Rather than a forum for activists and staffers to pool their plans, Weyrich's lunch gives leading politicians and people from the administration a chance to justify themselves to the assembled barons of the conservative movement. Weyrich, who also founded the Heritage Foundation, and now runs the Free Congress Foundation, presides over the meeting from a wheelchair. A congressman is hauled over the coals for pondering a run for the Senate and thereby losing a place on a key committee. Bullied about an upcoming vote on school vouchers in the District of Columbia, a senator promises to provide the names of his colleagues who might be "a little wobbly." The barons are clearly unhappy with the prescription-drug bill—one man describes it as a "monstrosity"—but a congressman justifies it as a political necessity, and one, moreover, that George W. Bush supports.

The lunch group is much more narrowly focused on religious and social issues than Norquist's group. The room bursts into spontaneous applause when somebody condemns a decision to remove the feeding tube from Terri Schindler Schiavo, a disabled patient in a Florida hospital, as "the *Roe v. Wade* of euthanasia"—and this, one participant groans, at a time when the enemy-combatant prisoners in Guantánamo Bay have gained an average of fifteen pounds because America is feeding them so well! For all that, the two meetings are pretty similar—from the high-cholesterol food to the blizzard of press releases that each issues. People at both meetings have no doubt that they belong to a coherent movement. They dismiss moderate Republicans as "establishment types," discuss who should be "our candidate" in forthcoming congressional races and seem resigned to the fact that their lives will be measured out in an unrelenting series of battles against liberal evils of one sort or another. Every piece of paper at the Weyrich meeting is also a call to arms. Two-thirds of all partial-birth abortions are committed in New Jersey! Half of all marriages end in divorce! *Girls Gone Wild* videos are for sale in supermarkets!

So far nobody has thought of establishing a teatime meeting, but many of the people who have been to the earlier meetings reassemble for drinks at Norquist's house in the evening. Some of them will reappear at various Dark Ages weekends (the conservative movement's answer to the Clintonian Renaissance weekends) or go on holiday together. One recent vacation: a *National Review* ocean cruise to celebrate the liberation of Grenada, hosted by Oliver North, the lieutenant colonel at the heart of the Iran-Contra affair; Wayne LaPierre, head of the National Rifle Association; and a couple of congressmen.

This is a group of people that eats, drinks, vacations and inevitably sleeps together. At first sight, there is nothing unusual in that—most political parties have their clubs, their meetings, their romances. But they do not have the same omnivorous reach, the same devotion to an agenda and the same sense of struggle. Other groups are usually just there for the inebriation and the interns. There are brief moments when such organizations come alive— Bill Clinton's tenure at the Democratic Leadership Council is a good example. But they do not last, and there is no uniting idea of a movement. Indeed, the movement that most resembles America's New Right in recent history is Europe's Old Left. It too had its agenda, its omnipresence, its zeal and its hinterland. And just as the Old Left, gathered together, was always in danger of self-parody (remember when feminists demanded to be called "wimmin" to avoid the word "man"?) so is the Right. Visit the annual Conservative Political Action Conference (CPAC), the Right's main beanfest held between the Republican conventions, and you'll discover fresh-faced young men buying George W. Bush dolls and queuing up at the Traditional Values Coalition to fling beanbags at grotesque trolls called "Hillary Clinton," "The Liberal Media" and "The Homosexual Agenda."

CONSERVATISM = AMERICANISM?

For the Right, the rise of conservatism is not a matter of political strategy and electoral opportunism; it goes to the heart of what it means to be an American—and what other countries lack. As Maura puts it, "People came to America to seek one basic thing, freedom, and conservatism has evolved with much of that freedom in mind."

Talk to reflective conservatives about what makes their country so special and they usually mention four things. The first is the constitution. That document's enduring power comes, it is said, from its realistic (that is, conservative) assessment of human nature. The founders recognized that human beings were not naturally good, and that the only way to prevent people from abusing power is to divide and dilute it. They also recognized individualistic and acquisitive instincts, and tried to create a framework in which people could pursue their natural desire to enrich themselves. Of course, claiming the constitution is on your side is the oldest trick in American politics, but it is noticeable how many nonconservatives have agreed that the constitution is one reason why socialism made so little progress in America.

The second feature is geography. In overcrowded Europe, people have been forced to share space and been persuaded to give up freedoms that Americans take for granted. America has enough space to give every household an acre of land and still only populate a twentieth of the continental United States (and that does not include Alaska).[12] This has allowed ordinary Americans to aspire to the sorts of luxuries that were long reserved for the rich in Europe—a large house, plenty of land, an inheritance to pass on to their children. The frontier may also have helped inure Americans to violence (although why similar conditions in Canada didn't have the same effect is one of the great conundrums of comparative history). America's frontiersmen relied on guns to tame the wild. They also resorted to the ultimate punishment—execution—to preserve a precarious order.

A third aspect of the United States is reinvention. The New World has always been able to summon up even newer worlds, reinforcing American exceptionalism in the process. Jobs and people have moved south and west in search of cheaper land and lighter regulation. A century ago, Maine had more congressmen than Texas, and Rhode Island had more than Florida; now the two Northeastern states have just eight compared with the Sun Belt duo's sixty-one. According to the Census Bureau, the country's population center is still moving south and west at the rate of three feet an hour, five miles a year.[13] Conservatism and growth seem to have gone together with Republicanism's flourishing first in suburbs, then in exurbs. In booming Sun Belt cities like Dallas, the mega-churches sprout up next to office blocks and strip malls.

A fourth feature is moralism. The Right Nation has also been a Righteous Nation. G. K. Chesterton famously said that America is a nation with the "soul of a church."[14] In a recent book, *Hellfire Nation,* James Morone, a political scientist at Brown University, points out that American history has been a succession of moralistic crusades—against witches, drinkers, fallen women, aliens, Communists and so on. These crusades are so powerful that they can even trump America's prejudice against big government, most notably with Prohibition. Moralism is not a monopoly of the Right: the war against slavery in the nineteenth century and in favor of civil rights in the twentieth were both conducted in quasireligious terms. But the tradition predisposes Americans to see the world in terms of individual virtue rather than in terms of the vast social forces that so preoccupy Europeans. "No man in this land suffers from poverty unless it is more than his fault," said Henry Ward Beecher, a nineteenth-century Congregational minister, "unless it is his *sin.*"[15] And it predisposes Americans to go out in pursuit of dragons to slay. Until the fall of the Berlin Wall, the Right Nation thought that it had a God-given task to redeem the world from the evils of communism—and to redeem America from any hint that it might slacken in this task. Now it is organizing around the struggle against terrorism.

For the Right, the battle against "Islamofascism," as the conservative Internet bloggers call it, is a battle of good against evil. The more other countries question America's war plan, the more the redeemer nation is convinced of its rightness. The Bush doctrine commits America to smiting terrorism for years, perhaps decades, to come. The underlying point has to do with certainty. For the Right, terrorism is a simple thing; for the rest of the world, it is a complex debate. One key strategist at the Republican National Committee puts it this way: "Our people, like the president, deal in absolutes. They [i.e., our European allies and the Democrats] are relativists."

This approach has a certain electoral simplicity: by putting the Axis of Evil into the slot left by the Evil Empire, George W. Bush has reunited the conservative movement. Yet for almost exactly the same reasons, the war against terrorism reinforces the differences between America and the rest of the world. America is trumpeting nationalism and pouring money into the military just when European countries are sublimating their national identities to the European Union and cutting back their armies. Europeans shake their heads at America's lack of sophistication, what they see as the inability to look at the social causes of terrorism, at the refusal to consult them before doing things. In two years, George W. Bush spent most of the goodwill generated after September 11 — largely by developing positions that play much better in Colorado Springs than they do in Paris or Tokyo.

This division was at its clearest in early 2003 during the arguments at the United Nations Security Council on whether to invade Iraq. George W. Bush's conclusion that the problem required "regime change" struck most Europeans as cowboy justice; for pretty much the same reason, it went down very well in conservative America. The division can also be seen in the feud over Israel, a country whose cause has been embraced with evangelical fervor by conservative America. (Hanan Ashrawi, a Palestinian moderate and, incidentally, a Christian, is feted in London or Paris; when she came to speak in Colorado Springs, she faced mass protests from the Religious Right.) And these individual battles about policy soon merge into deeper ones about culture and values: for instance, why should Europe hand over terrorist suspects to America when it worries that America's more punitive legal system will execute them or imprison them without any apparent hope of a proper trial?

THE EVER-RIGHTER NATION

What will become of the Right? It is worth admitting that the conservative movement's two main crusades—against big government and moral decay—have so far been more successful as rallying cries than as policies. The fact that virtually every American politician now attacks Washington has not stopped government from getting ever bigger (particularly under George W. Bush). Meanwhile, the news from the culture war is mixed. Young people may be more patriotic and less supportive of abortion than their baby-boomer teachers, but the antics portrayed on the *Girls Gone Wild* videos suggest, at the very least, that there is ground to be recovered. So far this century, the Supreme Court, which Democrats accuse of engineering the Bush putsch of 2000, has produced liberal decisions on gay rights, affirmative action and medical marijuana. And one reason there are so many Straussians in Washington, D.C., is because they find it so hard to get jobs in America's liberal universities.

So the Right is not necessarily winning on every front, but it is making the political weather now in the way that the Left did in the 1960s. We argue in this book that the stage is set for a possible realignment of American politics, to make the Republicans the natural party of government in the same way that the Democrats once were. This might seem far-fetched. George W. Bush won the 2000 election only by the narrowest margin, and his continuing problems with both Iraq and the American economy suggest that he could have problems getting reelected in November 2004. The GOP also has deeper problems to contend with. Time and again in this book we ponder whether the Republicans have become too Southern and too moralistic for their own electoral good.

Still, it is noticeable how much more the 2004 contest matters to the Democrats. The presidency represents their best chance of seizing meaningful power. The Republicans control both houses of Congress, most of the governorships (including those in America's four biggest states) and the majority of state legislatures. Despite some demographic trends that favor the Democrats, the Republicans seem to have more of the future on their side: they are the party of entrepreneurs rather than government employees, of growing suburbs rather than declining inner cities, of the expanding Southwest rather than the stagnant Northeast. Another Bush victory would cement their lock on power.

Moreover, Bush does not have to prevail in 2004 for America to remain in the thrall of the Right Nation. We argue in this book that a Democratic presidential victory in 2004 would barely change America's basically conservative stance. For the foreseeable future the Democrats will be a relatively conservative party by European standards. They rely for their cash almost as heavily on big business and wealthy individuals as the Republicans do. They cannot win an election unless they regain the "conservatives of the heart"; hence their current attempts to lure in the progun, prolife "NASCAR Democrats" of the South. A Democratic administration might try to reduce the use of the death penalty, but it is unlikely to push states to abolish it. It might restrict the use of guns, but it would not ban them. Overseas, a Democratic administration would probably support Ariel Sharon no less trenchantly and would surely have no chance of persuading Congress to ratify the Kyoto Protocol. America would still be different.

THE AMERICAN PARADOX

This book tries to paint a portrait of the conservative movement—of the people and institutions who have been responsible for pulling America to the right over the past thirty years. It introduces the leaders like Bill Owens, Grover Norquist and Ralph Reed, but also foot soldiers like Dustin and Maura and the people queuing up at the CPAC convention to buy Saddam Hussein toilet paper and "Pray for him" George W. Bush badges. It peers inside the think tanks and foundations in Washington, D.C., but it also describes the troops beyond the Beltway—the gun activists in Liberty Park in Washington State, the black voucher enthusiasts in Milwaukee, Wisconsin, the home schoolers in Virginia, the planned communities in Phoenix, Arizona.

These people are interesting in themselves (and have been written about far too little), but they also constitute a prism through which we try to examine why America is such a distinctive country. We will set the Right in a global context, detailing the ways in which America is so much more conservative than other advanced countries, and looking at the consequences of that conservatism for the rest of the world.

In this exercise, we may have many weaknesses, but we would like to claim one strength: we are not members of either of the two great political tribes that dominate the American commentariat. Throughout this book, we have tried to avoid using any of the jibes that are commonplace on both sides of the debate; after all, there is no shortage of people we can quote doing this. And we have also tried to avoid the same pressures when describing both the anti-Americanism in Europe and the anti-Europeanism in America. If you have come to the book hoping to be told that George Bush is a moronic, oil-obsessed cowboy or that the French are "cheese-eating surrender monkeys," then we hope that you paid for it before reaching this sentence.[16]

The paradox of the United States is that it is at once both the most admired country in the world and one of the most reviled; outside its borders, "America" has somehow become a code word for technological sophistication, meritocracy and opportunity as well as for primitive justice, imperialism and inequality. No coherent objective explanation exists as to why the hyperpower that most other governments want to emulate and befriend finds itself so often alone. This is a riddle to which everybody surely wants an answer. Whether we have found it or not is for you to judge.

PART I

HISTORY

CHAPTER I

FROM KENNEBUNKPORT
TO CRAWFORD

SIR LEWIS NAMIER, the great historian of English politics in the age of George III, once remarked that "English history, and especially English parliamentary history, is made by families rather than individuals."[1] The same could be said of American political history, especially in the age of George I and George II. There is no better introduction to the radical transformation of Republicanism in the past generation—from patrician to populist, from Northeastern to Southwestern, from pragmatic to ideological—than the radical transformation of Republicanism's current leading family, the Bushes.

GRANDFATHER PRESCOTT

The Bushes began political life as classic establishment Republicans: WASPs who summered in Kennebunkport, educated their children at boarding schools and the Ivy League and claimed family ties to the British royal family (Queen Elizabeth II is the thirteenth cousin of the first President Bush). George W.'s paternal great-grandfather, Samuel P. Bush, was a steel and railroad executive who became the first president of the National Association of Manufacturers and a founding member of the United States Chamber of Commerce.[2] His maternal great-grandfather, George Herbert Walker, was even grander. The cofounder of W. A. Harriman, Wall Street's oldest private investment bank, Walker's stature was summed up by his twin Manhattan addresses: his office at One Wall Street and his home at One Sutton Place.[3] There was certainly muck beneath this brass: both Walker and Bush had their share of Wall Street shenanigans and cozy government deals, but in the age of Rockefeller, Vanderbilt and Morgan such things were expected.[4]

The first family member to hold high political office was George W.'s grandfather, Prescott Bush. Prescott was the very image of a patrician: immensely tall, a gifted athlete and a stickler for proper behavior. Exactly the sort of chap you might expect to find in the marbled corridors of the Senate. At Yale, he excelled at golf, tennis and baseball, sang with the All-Time Whiffenpoof Quartet and joined the college's most exclusive secret society, the Skull and Bones. He married Walker's daughter, Dorothy, in 1921, and five years later joined W. A. Harriman, which in the next decade merged into Brown Brothers Harriman.

Prescott belonged firmly to the progressive wing of the GOP: liberal on domestic policies and internationalist on foreign affairs. He even sent his son George to Andover rather than his own school, St. George's, because he thought it was more modern. His liberalism cost him his first bid for a Senate seat in 1950. During the election campaign a radio broadcaster described him as "the president of the birth-control league."[5] This was a particularly incendiary accusation in Connecticut, which was then one of two states in the country that outlawed the sale of condoms. It also contained a grain of truth: Prescott was a member of Planned Parenthood and a friend of Estelle Griswold, the woman whose legal challenge to the state's ban on contraception later persuaded the Supreme Court to enshrine the right of sexual privacy in *Griswold v. Connecticut* (1965) and thus laid the foundation for *Roe v. Wade*. Anti-Bush leaflets appeared on every pew in every Catholic church in the state and Prescott was narrowly defeated.

Prescott eventually made it to the Senate in a special election in 1952 caused by the death of the sitting senator, and stood true to his brand of moderate Republicanism for two terms. He cosponsored the bill that created the Peace Corps and strongly supported civil rights, a higher minimum wage and larger immigration quotas. "Bush Says Tax Burden May Have to Be Bigger," reads one delightful newspaper headline from his Senate years.

Prescott beseeched his fellow senators to "have the courage to raise the required revenues by approving whatever levels of taxation may be necessary" to pay the nation's bills for defense, science and education.[6] Shortly after ill health forced Prescott to retire in 1962, he received an honorary law degree from his alma mater, Yale, alongside the young President Kennedy. The citation read: "You have served your country well and personified the best in both political parties."[7] For Prescott, partisanship was a dirty word.

The best linksman on the Hill, he frequently played golf with Eisenhower. A firm believer that "manners makyth man," he once took Joseph McCarthy to one side and lectured him for more than an hour on his boorish behavior.[8] His hostility to the radical Right was as much aesthetic as intellectual. When McCarthy came to Connecticut to address a Republican meeting, Prescott recoiled at the rowdy crowd: "I never saw such a wild bunch of monkeys in any meeting I ever attended."[9] At home he was such a stickler for standards that friends called him the "Ten Commandments Man."[10]

He insisted that his four sons and many grandsons wear jackets and ties at dinner, even at their summer home in Kennebunkport, and that none of them leave the house on Sunday. Relaxation was of a bracing kind—either hunting or playing sports with alarming enthusiasm. This was to prove a permanent trait, but much else was to change.

George H. W. and the move to Texas

Prescott's son, George Herbert Walker Bush, could easily have followed him into his world of East Coast privilege. He was educated at Andover and Yale, where he outstripped even his father, proving that he possessed a superabundance of character, athleticism and leadership. He married the eligible Barbara Pierce and was showered with offers of jobs on Wall Street when he graduated. A lifetime of lunches in the Partners' Room of Brown Brothers Harriman, with its deep maroon carpeting and dark wood paneling, was his for the asking.

Yet the young George H. W. was made of sterner stuff. He had joined the navy straight out of school, and had been shot down by the Japanese in 1944 and rescued by an American submarine, making him perhaps the country's youngest war hero. He wanted to make his career on the new American frontier. The day after he graduated from Yale in 1948 George climbed into his red Studebaker and drove to Odessa, West Texas, to take a job with Dresser Industries, which supplied parts for the state's booming oil industry.[11]

Bush was not exactly turning his back on his powerful family. Prescott Bush sat on the board of Dresser Industries, and warmly recommended his son for a job. Prescott had even given George his new car. All the same, Odessa was a godforsaken town—a scattering of oil jacks and tin-roofed warehouses in the middle of the vast West Texan wilderness. In gracious New Haven George had lived next door to the president of Yale University; in Odessa he and Barbara lived in a shotgun house next door to two prostitutes (a mother-daughter team, no less).[12] But, ugly as it might be, the town was booming. Odessa and its sister city, Midland, sat on top of the largest concentration of oil ever found in the continental United States. The wildcatters and roughnecks who arrived there every day were willing to endure anything—the tornadoes and sandstorms, the distance from civilization, the endless tedium, living in tent cities and chicken coops—in order to make themselves rich.

The Bushes soon moved from Odessa to Midland, a white-collar town twenty miles down the highway. They were not the only patrician family to seek their fortune in Midland. The town soon boasted Ivy League clubs and posh cocktail parties, and the hyperactive Bushes inevitably became pillars of the local establishment. But for all that, Midland was still an entrepreneurial frontier town. Its population tripled during the 1950s. Yalies and roughnecks worked side by side to carve a living out of the desert. George W. remembers an idyllic existence playing on unpaved streets. By the time the Bushes left for Houston in 1959, George H. W. had made his fortune—and was ready to turn to politics.

At the time, Republicanism was a minority creed in Texas. This, after all, was the state of Lyndon Johnson and Sam Rayburn, a Democratic stronghold since the Civil War and a place where Republicans were Yankee pirates. "I will never vote for the electors of a party which sent the carpetbagger and the scalawag to the prostrate South with saber and sword to crush the white civilization to the earth," Rayburn, the future Speaker of the U.S. House of

Representatives, once explained.[13] At the turn of the century, O. Henry, then a Texas newspaperman, wrote that "We have only two or three laws, such as against murdering witnesses and being caught stealing horses, and voting the Republican ticket." Up until the late 1950s, the only real politics in Texas revolved around Democratic primaries.

Yet if Texas was Democratic, it was also deeply conservative. The state is littered with monuments to the Confederate cause, such as a huge statue of Jefferson Davis in the grounds of the University of Texas's Austin campus and another edifice outside the State Capitol unapologetically lauding "those who died for states rights under the Constitution." Michael Lind, a Texas-born author, labels Texas a *Herrenvolk,* or master-race democracy, where, as he puts it, "the ethnic majority controls the government and uses it to repress ethnic, racial and religious minorities."[14] During the brief period of Reconstruction after the Civil War, some blacks actually held office in the legislature and there was even a Republican speaker. Once the federal troops left in 1876, white Democrats "reclaimed" the state, setting up a minimalist constitution (the legislature meets only once every two years) and repressing blacks. Waco was a breeding ground for the Ku Klux Klan in the early twentieth century.

There were other things to remind George H. W. that he was no longer in Connecticut. Texans were suspicious of Yankee banks and manufacturing. As one historian, T. R. Fehrenbach, puts it, "the majority of Texans tended to admire or envy a family that owned 100,000 acres more than one that produced two great surgeons, a fine musician or a new theory of relativity."[15] By 1950, landowners were raking in $500 million a year in oil royalties. Most of the Texan ruling class had the mentality of plantation owners: resources, including oil rights, were there to be extracted, immigrant labor was there to be used, power was there to be maintained, money was nothing to be ashamed of and liberalism was to be crushed.

From this perspective, George H. W.'s timing was propitious. True, his first notable foray into politics was to lose a hotly contested Senate seat to Ralph Yarborough in 1964, but he went on to win a seat in the House of Representatives in 1966. More broadly, his timing coincided with the beginnings of a tumultuous change in Texas politics—a revolution that began while

Kennedy was in the White House and was only completed in 2003 when the Republicans finally took control of the statehouse. The first chink of light shone in 1961, when a squabble between Democratic liberals and conservatives for Lyndon Johnson's vacant Senate seat allowed John Tower to become the state's first Republican senator since Reconstruction. Although Texans loyally voted for Johnson in 1964, Barry Goldwater's message plainly struck a chord with local conservatives.

This switch to the Republicans lasted decades rather than years. In 1964, Democrats had controlled all 31 seats in the state Senate, and all but one in the 150-strong House. In 1968, the Republicans could count only two state senators and eight members of the House. One of the eight, a twenty-five-year-old from Midland named Tom Craddick, who had been offered the seat by both parties, boldly told a Midland newspaper that the Republicans were the party of the future.[16] In fact, it would take him a decade to win any power in the House (he was eventually given the chairmanship of a committee). Many white Texans chose to stick with conservative Democrats rather than switch parties.

All the same, Craddick gradually won his bet. In many cases, the catalyst was race. No Democratic presidential candidate has won a majority of the white vote in Texas since Johnson's civil rights act. The burgeoning counterculture and the antiwar protests also alienated white conservatives. (Texas, militaristic as ever, contributed a disproportionate number of troops to Southeast Asia.) Demography was also on the GOP's side. The Democrats' power base was in the old Texas of agriculture and benevolent government, but tenant farmers were being squeezed out by the big estates: between 1930 and 1957, the number of tenants was halved while the average size of farms doubled. Meanwhile, in the new suburbs and corporate office parks, the Republican message of less government, lower taxes and strong families resounded with the new arrivals (at the height of the 1950s oil boom, more than a thousand people moved to Houston every week).

If the GOP changed Texas politics, Texas also changed the GOP—and the Bush family along with it. Texan Republicanism was very different from Prescott's country club creed: more antigovernment, more populist, more marinated in religion. Prescott had thought that McCarthy had no manners;

a group of Texas conservatives sent McCarthy a Cadillac as a wedding present. The question, still debated among Republicans to this day, is: How far did George H. W. embrace this new, brasher creed?

George H. W. has always had a reputation of being "somewhat to the center of center."[17] Many Texans mistook his East Coast politeness for wimpishness, dismissing him as a "clean-fingernails Republican" or, worse, "the sort of man who steps out of the shower to take a piss," as one of our colleagues was once told. In 1966, Yarborough derided him as a patrician Yankee, asking the oilmen in East Texas whether they were ready to vote for "a carpetbagger from Connecticut who is drilling oil for the Sheik of Kuwait."[18] When George eventually got himself elected to Congress, he made a name as a moderate on cultural issues. Wilbur Mills, the chairman of the House Ways and Means Committee, even nicknamed him "Rubbers" because of his enthusiasm for family planning.[19]

George H. W. climbed the Republican ladder by taking on the sort of institutional jobs that would have delighted his father—ambassador to the United Nations, party chairman, envoy to China and director of the CIA. In 1980, when he ran for president, he condemned Ronald Reagan's "supply-side" ideas as "voodoo economics"—and he was offered the vice presidency partly as a sop to what remained of the East Coast wing of the party. Despite eight years of loyal service to the Gipper, many conservatives only supported Bush's run for the presidency in 1988 on Reagan's say-so. Once president, he infuriated conservatives by raising taxes—and they struck back in the 1992 election by rallying to Pat Buchanan in the Republican primaries and encouraging Ross Perot, who made much of the fact that he was a more genuine Texan than the president, in the general election.

Yet he was clearly more conservative than his father was. Bush ran for that Senate seat in 1964 as a firm supporter of Goldwater conservatism—hardly Prescott's cup of tea. He denounced LBJ's civil rights bill, the Nuclear Test Ban Treaty, increases in foreign aid and "wildly spending money on anti-poverty programs." He even condemned Martin Luther King Jr. as a "militant" whose civil rights organization was bankrolled by the unions.[20] His style of campaigning was also a long way from Connecticut. Prescott had had members of the Yale Whiffenpoof Society sing at his rallies.[21] George was introduced by country music and the Bush Bluebonnet Belles, who sang: "The sun's gonna shine in the Senate some day / George Bush is going to chase those liberals away."[22]

Bush's rise through the institutions was not quite the pure patrician ascent it might seem: Nixon liked him because he was different from "the usual Ivy League bastards."[23] As a presidential candidate, Bush assiduously courted the Right. He employed Lee Atwater, a master of populist dirty tricks, as his campaign manager. He also flirted with the religious Right, inviting Jim and Tammy Faye Baker to the vice presidential mansion, appearing at Jerry Falwell's Liberty University and making a video about his "life-changing" conversion to Christianity. As president, Bush eventually endorsed stands on abortion that were, by some measures, to the right of those of his son. It was also George H. W. who recommended Barry Goldwater's *The Conscience of a Conservative* (1960) to his eldest son.

George W., eastern born, Texas bred

Nobody can deny that George W. Bush's career has retained some of his family's patrician heritage. Indeed, its early stages seemed to be a faded carbon copy of his father's: he went to Andover, where he was a cheerleader rather than a sports star, and scraped into Yale, where grandfather Prescott conveniently sat on the board of trustees. He was elected to a fraternity, Delta Kappa Epsilon, and to Skull and Bones. But it was plainly a less comfortable experience for him than for his father. George W. found Andover "cold and distant and difficult." At Yale, he had a couple of run-ins with the police, once when he stole a Christmas wreath from a local storefront and once when he and a group of friends tore down the Princeton goalposts after a football game. (One of the original drafts of his commencement address to his alma mater contained the following reminiscence: "It's great to return to New Haven. My car was followed all the way from the airport by a long line of police cars with slowly rotating lights. It was just like being an undergraduate again." Sadly, it was dropped.)[24]

It naturally suits the forty-third president to downplay his patrician education, to hint that he longed to be back among the people of Texas — away from the snobs and among decent patriots. However, even allowing for a bit of spin, it is clear that by the late 1960s a gulf was opening up between George W.'s Texan values and the sorts of things he found at Yale. This was not just because George W. was a rabble-rouser while his father was a natural prefect. It was because Yale had changed too. The campus had been radicalized by Vietnam. One of the pivotal moments of George W.'s university career came when he bumped into William Sloane Coffin, the university chaplain, shortly after his father had been defeated by Yarborough. Coffin had been tapped for Skull and Bones by George W.'s father, so the young Bush made a point of introducing himself to the chaplain. "I know your father," replied Coffin. "Frankly, he was beaten by a better man."[25]

A better man! The highest accolade in the Bush vocabulary is that somebody is "a good man." George H. W. Bush was the very model of a good man in his son's eyes: a man who had risked his life for his country, had made a fortune and was now risking his dignity in running for public office. And here was the chaplain of his old university implying that he was no better than a Southern racist. There were plenty of things that were pulling George W. Bush toward Sun Belt conservatism, but he was pushed too.

George W. encountered suspicion in Texas at first. In 1978 he decided to run for Congress from West Texas, telling friends who were surprised by his sudden interest in politics that he was terrified that under Jimmy Carter the "United States was heading for a European-style socialism."[26] But his Republican opponent in the primary, Jim Reese, secured Ronald Reagan's endorsement—a bitter slight to the Bush dynasty—and mailed out a letter expressing disappointment that Bush had "Rockefeller-type Republicans such as Karl Rove to help him run his campaign."[27] George W. managed to beat Reese but he was confronted by an even tougher opponent in the general election, a local Democrat named Kent Hance. Hance relentlessly typecast the young Bush as a Yankee carpetbagger with a fancy East Coast education and no roots in the local community—that he was "born with a silver boot up his ass," as one local put it.[28] Didn't Bush belong to something called the Skull and Bones Society? And wasn't his father a member of the Trilateral Commission, an organization that many farmers blamed for driving down agricultural prices?

Hance's job was made easier by the fact that Bush's list of donors read like a who's who of the Republican establishment, including the former defense secretary, Donald Rumsfeld. It was also made easier by George W.'s foolish decision to make a television advertisement of himself jogging. ("That might be a good ad for Highland Park or Houston," one commentator said, "but if a guy is jogging in Dimmitt, somebody is after him.") The caricature was so convincing that, during a set-piece debate between the two candidates, the moderator asked Bush to his face if he was a tool of a shadow government. Hance won the race easily.

During his unsuccessful campaign, George W. often said that he had only one regret—that he hadn't been born in Texas. But the more Texans got to know George W., the more they were willing to forgive him this one oversight. Texans can be made as well as born—the Lone Star State is after all a state of immigrants—and people soon realized that George W. was plainly a more authentic Texan than his father. While George H. W. had been chauffeur-driven to Greenwich Country Day School, wearing a uniform of sweater and knickerbockers, George W. walked or bicycled to a school where they taught Texas history in the fourth grade before they taught American history in the fifth.[29] He had no problems with the antigovernment populism of the state. He swapped his family's Episcopalianism for heart-on-the-sleeve Methodism. Increasingly, his father used his eldest son as his emissary to the conservative movement.

Ironically, the man who helped George W. conquer Texas was another out-of-state import, this time from Utah: Karl Rove. They are an odd couple. While Bush grew up as the apolitical son of a political dynasty, Rove was a political junkie. "When the president was growing up, he wanted to be Willie Mays," quipped Mark McKinnon, a Texas politico, referring to the great baseball player. "When Karl was growing up, he wanted to be senior advisor to the president."[30] Bush was the archetypal frat-boy, always the center of the crowd. Rove was the archetypal nerd, complete with spectacles, pocket protector and briefcase. He campaigned for Richard Nixon as a teenager, then joined the College Republicans at a time when American universities were erupting in anti-Vietnam protests. Lee Atwater, sensing a kindred spirit, invited him to Washington to work for the Republican National Committee, and in 1977, George H. W. lured him to Texas to work for his political action committee. Rove quickly turned himself into the most highly regarded Republican political consultant in the state.

Even a decade after Craddick had made his bet, Texas was not an obvious choice for a young Republican on the make: in 1977 the party held only 21 of the 181 seats in the legislature, and the young George W.'s first race in 1978 was hardly propitious. But Rove sensed which way the wind was blowing. He built up a peerless list of Republican donors and worked for all the state's leading Republicans: Phil Gramm, a former Democrat who was elected to the Senate seat as a Republican in 1984; Kay Bailey Hutchison, who captured the state's other Senate seat in 1993; Rick Perry, elected governor in 2000, and, of course, George W. All this was the political equivalent of buying shares in Microsoft when it first went public.

The sternest test of both George W.'s Texas credentials and Rove's politicking was the governor's race in 1994. The incumbent, Ann Richards, was an authentic Texan: a quick-witted woman whose Texanisms were collected in a book and who numbered Willie Nelson among her closest friends. She was a protégée of Barbara Jordan, the first black woman elected to Congress from the South, but she also had Republican-style hair, steely white and piled high on her head. She was responsible for the most damning condemnation of the senior Bush: "Poor George, he just can't help it," she told a rapt audience at the 1988 Democratic Convention. "He was born with a silver foot in his mouth." And she tried to do exactly the same to the son, calling him "Shrub," "Junior," "Prince George" and "the wind-up doll."

Yet Prescott's grandson succeeded in out-Texaning the daughter of the Texas dirt patch. Bush announced his candidacy with a hymn to the Lone Star State: "I view Texas as a way of life, a state of mind, a way to think. . . . I don't want Texas to be like California." He repeatedly conjured up the image of California to suggest that Richards was an effete liberal (and worse) out of touch with bedrock Texas values—and, surprisingly, he got plenty of help from the Richards campaign, whose leading donors fed this image and included Steven Spielberg, Annie Leibovitz, Robert Redford, Sharon Stone, Farrah Fawcett, Roseanne Arnold and Barbra Streisand. Bush's donors included Roger Staubach, the legendary Dallas Cowboys quarterback, and Mike Ditka, a football coach. Toward the end of the campaign Richards went on stage with Rosie O'Donnell in Dallas to celebrate abortion rights. On the same day, Bush was visiting tiny rural towns, dressed in eelskin boots and a Texas Farm Bureau jacket, accompanied by Billy Joe Dupree, a former Dallas Cowboys tight end, and the great Chuck Norris.

George W. even managed to use what he referred to as his "nomadic years" to his advantage. "Did I behave irresponsibly as a kid at times?" he asked inquisitive reporters. "Sure did. You bet." One of his father's problems was that he had been too good to be true: one of life's perpetual head boys. George W., who chewed tobacco well into the 1980s, was made of rougher stuff. Throughout the campaign against Ann Richards rumors circulated about his wild youth—about how he'd been arrested for drunk driving, experimented with drugs, knocked up this or that girl, got high at his father's inauguration. . . . With the exception of the drunk driving, these rumors were unproven, but they somehow succeeded in establishing George W. as more authentically Texan. "He understands Bubba because there is more Bubba in him," Rove once told reporters. "He is clearly the wild son."[31]

During the campaign George W. laid out his trademark "compassionate conservatism" theme. He supported increased funding for education. He argued that religious organizations could improve the delivery of welfare. "Government doesn't have a monopoly on compassion" was his mantra. He also had plenty of old-fashioned red meat for the hard Right: locking up juvenile offenders and allowing them to be tried as adults at age fourteen; supporting an antisodomy statute that gay leaders were trying to repeal; requiring teenage girls who wanted an abortion to get their parents' permission; making it legal to carry handguns; denying benefits to welfare recipients who had already had two children.

The result was a triumph: Bush won by 53 percent to 46 percent—the biggest margin in twenty years. Bush went on to demonstrate his Texas credentials all over again—this time not by defeating a Texas icon but by seducing one. In Texas, most of the real institutional power lies with the lieutenant governor. In 1994 the lieutenant governorship was held by an über-Texan who happened to be a Democrat. Bob Bullock was an ex-alcoholic who had been married five times (twice to the same woman) and who had once been a legendary hell-raiser. (On one occasion, after a night's drinking, Bullock climbed into the back of a parked car to catch a nap. He woke up to find the car on the move. He immediately thrust his hand over the seat to introduce himself to the driver: "Hi there!" he boomed. "I'm your secretary of state!")[32] Bullock had the power to destroy Bush's governorship. Why would this grizzly figure want to get along with a silver-spoon Republican? But Bush quickly won him over. Legend has it that in one exchange between the two, Bullock complained that "if you're going to fuck me, you're going to have to kiss me first." Bush immediately applied his lips to the cheek of the grizzled old pol.

By this stage, the Democratic Party that had ruled Texas for a century was crumbling. From 1965 to 1995 Texas experienced the country's biggest growth in Republican votes in House elections.[33] George W. and Rove set about destroying the few remaining bricks in the once grand edifice with relish. Even Kent Hance, the Democrat who had frustrated Bush's first bid for office, had switched to the Republican Party and bowed at the knee to his former opponent. In 1998, Bush won reelection with 68 percent of the vote, swamping his opponent by 1.4 million votes, and the state Senate finally fell into Republican hands. In 2002, the party won every statewide race, and it finally captured the Texas House. Craddick, the lone Republican from Midland, became the first Republican Speaker since a union soldier was removed at the end of Reconstruction.

When one of us interviewed George W. as governor in the late 1990s, it was clear that he was a different sort of Bush than his father and grandfather.[34] He might have been sitting behind a large mahogany desk that had been passed down to him by his father, but George W. talked a different, more colloquial language, beginning sentences with "Folks don't like . . ." and "Y'all might think that, but . . ."

On a small table behind the governor's desk he displayed a collection of family photographs. One faded black-and-white image of Prescott Bush showed him waving to an audience at a 1952 victory rally. Prescott's image now faced out onto a world that was different from anything he had known—a world in which a Bush wore cowboy boots, in which Barry Goldwater was regarded as a serious thinker, in which Mexico loomed larger than Europe, in which conservatism was treated as a radical movement for change. He would undoubtedly have been proud of his grandson, but he might have wondered: How on earth did the Republican Party change so much?

CHAPTER 2

THE CONSERVATIVE ROUT,
1952–1964

THE NEXT THREE CHAPTERS try to answer the question: How on earth has the Republican Party changed so much? Even the most optimistic conservative would have to concede that the rise of the Right over the past fifty years has hardly been a straightforward march toward the light. There have been dramatic interruptions—Watergate and Bill Clinton, to name but two—as well as time-consuming detours. But three themes nevertheless thread through this tale: demography, the footsoldiers and the intellectuals.

The Bushes were part of a vast army of Americans who sought their fortunes in the South and the West. This demographic revolution helped to refashion not just the nation but the Republican Party. The Sun Belt challenged the old Northeastern establishment with a rougher-edged conservative creed, and it also provided many of the Right's footsoldiers. These activists can be divided—very crudely—into two groups: social conservatives and antigovernment conservatives. While social conservatives (many of them from the South) wanted to get politicians to do the Lord's work, antigovernment conservatives (many of them from the West) simply wanted to get Washington out of their hair. If abortion was the rallying call of the social conservatives, taxes and guns were the starting point for the antigovernment brigade. The intellectuals reshaped the party just as dramatically as the footsoldiers. In 1952, conservatism was a fringe idea in American life. By the end of the century, it was a veritable encyclopedia of ideas about everything from judicial activism to rogue states.

THE IKE AGE

In 1952, the year that brought Prescott Bush to Washington, Dwight Eisenhower became the first Republican to win the presidency since Herbert Hoover in 1928. Ike beat Adlai Stevenson by a smashing margin of 55 percent to 45 percent and brought on his coattails Republican majorities in both houses of Congress (albeit a majority in the Senate that depended on the vice president's tie-breaking vote). He had all the personal prestige of the man who had led the Allied armies to victory in the Second World War.

Yet this Republican Caesar was no conservative partisan. Having spent almost his entire adult life working for the federal government, Ike had no time for radical ideology. The general sometimes described himself as a "progressive Republican"; he might just as well have been a "conservative Democrat."[1] In fact, before he accepted the Republican nomination in 1952, he had been implored by the Democrats to be their candidate. In 1956, when he again went on to beat Stevenson comfortably, one journalist even floated the idea of both parties nominating him. Eisenhower chose the Republicans because of personal connections as much as anything else. Lyndon Johnson, the new Democratic minority leader in the Senate, hailed Eisenhower's inaugural address as "a very good statement of Democratic programs of the last twenty years."[2]

Abroad, Ike favored containing the Red Menace, not rolling it back. At home, he didn't try to tear up the New Deal or reduce the tax burden. He declared that "gradually expanding federal government" was "the price of a rapidly expanding national growth."[3] "Should any political party attempt to abolish Social Security and eliminate labor laws and farm programs, you would not hear of that party again in our political history," he wrote to his brother Edgar, a rather more conservative figure. The number of Republicans who seriously supported such policies was negligible, he argued;

besides, they were "stupid."[4] His first recommendation to Congress was to establish a new cabinet department of Health, Education and Welfare;[5] and when the woman in charge of the new department, Oveta Culp Hobby, unveiled plans to trim spending on schools, Eisenhower let her have it with both barrels: "I am amazed at the thought of an education cut! This is the most important thing in society. Every liberal—including me—will disapprove."[6]

If Eisenhower had a philosophy, it was managerialism. He had risen to fame coordinating the Allied forces in Europe, and he liked the business world. He appointed the chairman of General Motors, Charles Wilson, as his defense secretary (giving rise to the quip that he had replaced the New Dealers with the car dealers).[7] Such corporate types saw no reason to rock the boat. Since Herbert Hoover's election in 1928, the federal workforce had swelled from 630,000 civilian employees to 2.5 million, and the annual federal budget had increased from $3.9 billion to $66.2 billion,[8] but such an increase in government did not seem to worry the car dealers.

Eisenhower also welcomed into his cabinet the same liberal establishment types that had served the Democrats. Henry Cabot Lodge, the very epitome of the Boston Brahmin, managed Ike's presidential campaign and subsequently served as American ambassador to the United Nations. The secretary of state, John Foster Dulles, was a firm believer in NATO, foreign aid and internationalism.

Eisenhower could afford to snub the Right because there wasn't much of a Right to bite back. Within the Republican Party, "Dewey Republicans," the faction that surrounded Ike, had largely outmaneuvered "Taft Republicans." The latter were led by Senator Robert Taft: "Mr. Republican," as he liked to be known, had been an uncompromising critic of the New Deal and NATO ("We have quietly adopted a tendency to interfere in the affairs of other nations," he complained in 1949, "to assume that we are a kind of demigod and Santa Claus to solve the problems of the world").[9] By contrast, the moderates, who took their name from Thomas Dewey, the patrician governor of New York, accepted the New Deal at home and relished internationalism abroad. For all Taft's clout in Congress, it was the Dewey Republicans who won every Republican presidential nomination from 1940 to 1960, provided the governors of the country's biggest states, including Pennsylvania and California, and controlled the major media organs of Republican opinion, such as *Time, Life* and the *New York Herald.* Their triumph seemed complete when Mr. Republican died in the first year of Eisenhower's presidency.

If the conservative movement did not have much bite in Congress, it had even less bark in the intellectual world. Liberals had eight weekly magazines to choose from. Conservatives, by contrast, had only one, *Human Events,* an eight-page newsletter that had been launched in 1944 with a readership of 127.[10] American academia was so uniformly liberal that one conservative foundation, the William Volker Fund, had to hire assistants to hunt for scholars who could be persuaded to receive its largesse.[11] The provisional title for *The Conservative Mind* (1953), Russell Kirk's path-breaking history of Anglo-American conservatism, was *The Conservative Rout.*

In contrast, liberals thought the world was their oyster. In *The Liberal Imagination* (1950), Lionel Trilling observed that "liberalism is not only the dominant, but even the sole, intellectual tradition" in the United States. The country possessed a conservative impulse, he admitted, but this expressed itself in "irritable mental gestures" rather than full-fledged ideas.[12] In *The Liberal Tradition in America* (1955), Louis Hartz went further. The lack of both a feudal aristocracy and a class-conscious working class meant that America was the world's purest example of a liberal society, he argued. The biggest problem for American liberalism was that it lacked a doughty conservative opponent.[13] In *The End of Ideology* (1960), Daniel Bell, who was then firmly in the liberal camp, argued that the fiery clash of Left and Right had been replaced by a cool debate about management techniques.

The absence of a coherent conservative movement meant that Americans who had the misfortune of suffering from Lionel Trilling's "conservative impulse" were a rather weak bunch. In particular, they tended to fall victim to one of three intellectual aberrations: paranoia, eccentricity and nostalgia.

Paranoia found plenty of outlets on the Right. The Reverend Billy James Hargis roamed the country in a customized Greyhound bus denouncing communism and treason. Kent Courtney, the founder of the Conservative Society of America, accused Barry Goldwater of being "tainted by socialism." Harold Lafayette Hunt, a billionaire oilman, notorious bigamist and prolific funder of right-wing causes, argued that people's voting power should be determined by their wealth (which gave him an awful lot of votes). In his privately published *The Invisible Government* he warned that a sinister conspiracy aimed "to convert America into a socialist state and then make it a unit in a one-world socialist system."

The paranoid element had been given a huge boost during the Truman presidency by a drama that proved that there was much to be paranoid about: the Alger Hiss affair. From the 1940s onward, the conservative cause had been strengthened by a growing band of disillusioned Marxist intellectuals. Reformed Trotskyites like the writer James Burnham were of a completely different caliber than the likes of Hargis and Hunt, but they also focused on the need for America to fight back harder against the Soviet threat, both abroad and at home. In August 1948, one of these angry ex-Communists, Whittaker Chambers, a senior editor at *Time,* told the House Un-American Activities Committee that one of his contacts in the 1930s had been a young State Department official named Alger Hiss. Hiss by now had just left the State Department, but he was a leading ornament of the Washington establishment—a delegate to the Yalta conference, president of the Carnegie Endowment for International Peace, a fixture at Georgetown dinner parties—and he immediately sued Chambers for libel. Liberal America closed ranks to defend the elegant Hiss against the decidedly inelegant Chambers. President Truman denounced the case as a "red herring." Eleanor Roosevelt insisted that Hiss must be the victim of a witch hunt led by a disgusting young Californian congressman, Richard Nixon. Then Chambers astonished the country by producing documentary proof that the two of them had spied for the Soviets in the 1930s. Hiss was tried for perjury, and in January 1950 he was sentenced to five years in prison.

The Hiss affair deepened conservative hostility to the liberal establishment. Why did Washington society turn against Chambers? And why could the secretary of state, Dean Acheson, say that he could not turn his back on Alger Hiss even after he had been convicted of spying for the Russians? In his powerful book, *Witness* (1952), Chambers raised a point that was to be developed by generations of conservative champions of the "silent majority":

> No feature of the Hiss Case is more obvious, or more troubling as history, than the jagged fissure, which it did not so much open as reveal, between the

plain men and women of the nation, and those who affected to act, think and speak for them. . . . It was the enlightened and the powerful, the clamorous proponents of the open mind and the common man, who snapped their minds shut in a pro-Hiss psychosis. . . .[14]

The Hiss drama set the stage for the man who came to symbolize right-wing paranoia in the 1950s: Senator Joseph McCarthy. "Tail-gunner Joe" was at the center of American politics from February 1950, when he traveled to Wheeling, West Virginia, to announce that he possessed the names of 205 Communist spies in the State Department, to December 1954, when the Senate voted, by a majority of two to one, to condemn his behavior. McCarthy, who had been elected senator for Wisconsin only in 1946, just before his fortieth birthday, won a huge following, with McCarthy clubs springing up spontaneously all across the country. Adlai Stevenson, the Democratic presidential candidate in 1952 and 1956 and the very embodiment of high-minded liberalism, wasn't exaggerating that much when he said that the Republican Party was one-half Eisenhower and one-half McCarthy.

An Irish Catholic who grew up on a small farm in the Midwest and attended Marquette, a Catholic university in Milwaukee, where he liked to box, McCarthy personified populist resentment against the liberal elite. He spoke like a longshoreman, dressed like a slob, drank like a fish and expressed the resentments of millions like him when he denounced the "privileged, sissified State Department," or when he savaged Dean Acheson as a "pompous diplomat" with striped pants, a lace handkerchief and a phony British accent, or when he accused George Marshall of being "part of a conspiracy so immense, an infamy so black, as to dwarf any in the history of man." "If you want to be against McCarthy, boys," he told a crowd of reporters, "you've got to be either a Communist or a cocksucker."[15] No wonder Prescott Bush found it necessary to give him a lecture about manners.

Not all McCarthy's fears were unfounded: it turned out that there were indeed some Communists in the State Department. But his wild indifference to detail, his menacing manner and growing alcoholism did his cause little good. Even Roy Cohn, his right-hand man, admitted that people might be put off by his "easily erupting temper, his menacing monotone, his unsmiling mien and his perpetual five o'clock shadow." By 1955, McCarthyism had devalued one of the Right's trump cards, anticommunism, and provided liberals with an enduring bogeyman.

Paranoia may have been the most conspicuous failing on the Right, but eccentricity was the more common malady. Albert Jay Nock, one of the postwar Right's few grand old men, was a self-styled aristocrat who loathed "our enemy, the state," as he titled one of his essays, and looked down on the common people. He regarded his fellow conservative intellectuals as a "remnant," isolated from the American mainstream—and dramatized his own isolation by wearing a cape, carrying a walking stick and calling his autobiography *Memoirs of a Superfluous Man* (1943). Nock accused his native country of possessing the moral code of the plunderer, and argued that the world's ideal society existed in, of all places, Belgium.

Another caped crusader was Ayn Rand, a Russian émigré who wrote a clutch of novels celebrating economic individualism. Rand is now a revered figure on the Right. Two of her novels, *The Fountainhead* (1943) and *Atlas Shrugged* (1957), have sold in the millions, and the fact that the chairman of the Federal Reserve, Alan Greenspan, was once a devotee has added to her status. But to many contemporaries, the cult that surrounded her seemed a bit weird. She envisaged a hyperminimalist state with no taxation and no traditions of any kind, least of all Christianity. She preached her philosophy of "objectivism" in a thick Russian accent, urged people to have as many orgasms as possible and dressed in a flowing black cape tied closed by a gold brooch in the shape of a dollar sign. "The cross is the symbol of torture," she explained to *Time* magazine. "I prefer the dollar sign, the symbol of free trade and therefore free minds."[16] *The Fountainhead* ends with a postapocalyptic moment when one of the novel's survivor-heroes blesses the desolate earth by tracing a dollar sign in the air. Rand believed firmly that people had a duty to smoke (because it represented man's taming of fire): the publishing party for *Atlas Shrugged* featured custom-made cigarettes embossed with little gold-leaf dollar signs. At her memorial service in 1982 a six-foot-high dollar sign was placed next to her open coffin and the room was filled with the strains of the song "It's a Long Way to Tipperary."[17]

Rand at least focused on the future. The third attribute of postwar conservatism was nostalgia. Richard Weaver, a Southerner who spent most of his academic life teaching English literature at the University of Chicago, was nicknamed "the St. Paul of the Agrarians." He was in love with the Old South and its world of feudal plantations, religious faith and gentlemanly ethics. In *The Southern Tradition at Bay* (published posthumously in 1968 but written in the 1940s as his dissertation), he claimed that the South was "the last nonmaterial civilization in the Western world," a society that had been "right without realizing the grounds of its rightness." He blamed the Civil War for spreading the barbarous code of free-market contract to the whole of the United States. His best-known book, *Ideas Have Consequences* (1948), began with the bold statement: "This is another book about the dissolution of the West." Things had started to go drastically wrong in the late fourteenth century, he argued, when man had abandoned his belief in transcendental values in favor of William of Occam's nominalism.

The dean of nostalgia was Russell Kirk, who tried to reinterpret Edmund Burke for Eisenhower's America. In *The Conservative Mind* (1953), his precocious masterpiece, Kirk argued that the American Revolution was a conservative project, based on a skeptical view of human nature and a reverence for tradition. Kirk duly won enthusiastic reviews from both the *New York Times* and *Time*, but, symptomatically, he was driven by some inner demon to marginalize himself from the mainstream. He spent his life living in Mecosta, Michigan (population 200), referred to himself as "the last bonnet laird of the stump country," and described the motor car, the very icon of American life, as a "mechanical Jacobin."[18] For Kirk, capitalism was just the Doppelganger of communism ("Rockefeller and Marx were merely two agents of the same social force"). Salvation was to be found in a fixed social hierarchy sanctioned by divine will. No wonder one critic accused Kirk of sounding like "a man born one hundred and fifty years too late and in the wrong country."[19]

What happened to transform this eccentric rabble into the champions of a conservative revolution? Three things were stirring under the surface of Eisenhower's America. The first was the arrival of a group of intellectual entrepreneurs. The second was the South's growing impatience with the Democratic Party. The third was the shift in America's center of gravity to the west. All these forces were brought together by Barry Goldwater.

PLACES TO THINK

The main sign that intellectual life on the Right was something more than a freak show was the increasing prominence of a group of free-market economists. That said, these economists drew their inspiration from an unlikely place—Austria. For the Austrian school, according to Ludwig von Mises, one of its founders, "the main issue is whether or not man should give away freedom, private initiative, and individual responsibility and surrender to the guardianship of a gigantic apparatus of compulsion and coercion, the socialist state."[20] The man who convinced many Americans that this was their battle too was a pupil of von Mises, Friedrich von Hayek. From the 1930s onward, Hayek mounted a full-frontal assault on the Keynesian orthodoxy that dominated academic economics, to the occasional irritation of Keynes himself. Hayek's polemical *Road to Serfdom* (1944), which argued that central planning is the thin end of the wedge of totalitarianism, became a best-seller in the United States, with *Reader's Digest* publishing a condensed version and Hayek giving lectures across the country. One early convert was a middle-aged Hollywood actor, Ronald Reagan. When Lee Edwards, one of the leading chroniclers of the conservative movement, visited the new governor of California in 1967, he was amazed to find that Ronald Reagan's bookshelves contained heavily annotated copies of books by Hayek and von Mises.[21]

Hayek also helped to build two of the enduring institutions of the Right—the Mount Pelerin Society, a conference for free-market enthusiasts (which revealingly was founded in Switzerland, not the United States, in 1947), and the Chicago School. Hayek moved to the University of Chicago in 1950, and, even though he belonged to the Committee on Social Thought, not the economics department, he helped to make the university the command center of his insurgency. The Chicago School challenged the idea that "We are all Keynesians now" (to quote one cover of *Time* magazine in 1965) and the notion that "the Soviet economy is proof that . . . a socialist command economy can function and even thrive" (to quote Paul Samuelson's standard textbook of the time). Chicago economists such as Milton Friedman insisted that government spending should be left to a tiny number of "public goods"—most notably defense—and that everything else should be left to the market.

The Chicago boys dripped with contempt for big-government interventionism. Look at rent control, they said. Could anyone devise a better way of reducing the amount of rentable property on the market than by limiting the amount that landlords were able to charge for their property? Like Hayek, Friedman raised these questions not just with his fellow academics but also with the man in the street. He wrote a column for *Newsweek,* feuded with John Kenneth Galbraith and produced a best-selling book, *Capitalism and Freedom,* in 1962.

By then, the Right had begun to accumulate a little more thinking space. In the early 1950s, conservative intellectuals were not stymied just by their eccentricities. What the free-marketers desperately needed, no less than reformed Communists like Burnham and traditionalists like Kirk, was more institutional heft: places to meet outside the dreaded "liberal" universities to discuss their ideas, platforms for them to promote themselves. These emerged in the mid-1950s in the shape of two reinvigorated think tanks and a new magazine.

The oldest conservative think tank in Washington had been founded in 1943 by a group of businessmen. The American Enterprise Association (as it was christened at birth) was a decidedly unglamorous affair—little more than a trade association that lobbied against wartime price controls and occasionally hired academics to produce reports. It was no match for the Brookings Institution, a much more middle-of-the-road think tank, with its generous budget, elegant premises and ability to combine an academic aura with close ties to the political establishment. In 1954 the association's president considered putting the organization out of its misery but instead recruited William Baroody, a young Chamber of Commerce economist, to run the place.

Baroody, the son of a poor Lebanese immigrant, proved to be a talented intellectual entrepreneur. His aim was to convert the American Enterprise Institute (as he later rechristened it) into a conservative "brain trust." He understood that there could be no conservative movement without conservative theory. He and Glenn Campbell, a Harvard-trained economist, worked tirelessly to assemble a stable of thoroughbred scholars, appointing Friedman and another free-market economist, Paul McCracken from the University of Illinois, as academic advisors. The logic was clear: if the Right was going to have a hard time getting its voice heard in universities, then it would invent conservative institutions of its own. And instead of teaching students, it would teach politicians.

Meanwhile, something similar was happening across the country at the Hoover Institution. Herbert Hoover had founded his think tank at Stanford University in 1919 to house the remarkable collection of documents he had scavenged as a famine-relief administrator in Europe. After losing office in 1932, Hoover pushed the think tank in a more conservative direction. He wanted to create an institution that was "free of the taint of 'left-wingers!'" and devoted to the great mission of demonstrating "the evils of the doctrines of Karl Marx." In 1960, the Hoover Institution appointed Baroody's partner, Glenn Campbell, as its director, and Campbell set about turning the Hoover tower into a lighthouse of conservatism in the surrounding sea of academic liberalism.

The most important platform for conservative ideas was the *National Review*. William F. Buckley brought three vital qualities to America's tiny conservative universe when he decided to found the *Review* in 1955. The first was his extraordinary self-belief. At the age of five Buckley had supposedly dashed off a letter to King George V caustically suggesting that His Majesty repay Great Britain's overdue war debts to the United States.[22] On graduating from Yale University he published a coruscating attack on his alma mater, *God and Man at Yale* (1951), for its hostility to both Christianity and capitalism. His second vital quality was a considerable private income from his father's oil business, and the third was a lively sense of humor that made his creed seem more human.

Buckley began the first issue of the *National Review* with a resounding statement of intent: the magazine "stands athwart history, yelling Stop, at a time when no one is inclined to do so, or to have much patience with those who do." Buckley wanted to halt the growing fashion for atheism and collectivism that he had diagnosed in *God and Man at Yale*. He also wanted to transform conservatism from a hubbub of regional doctrines—Southern conservatism, Midwestern conservatism, and so on—into a truly national doctrine, hence the title of his magazine. Buckley's pitch to potential funders was simple: the New Deal had been helped along by the *Nation* and the *New Republic*. Why not fund a magazine that promised to do the same thing for conservatism?[23] It was a pitch he had to make frequently because America's most pro-free-market publication started out as something of a commercial runt. It got going with only $100,000 from Buckley's father and relied on the generosity of donors. Yet the magazine eventually established itself as a presence in American life: its circulation shot up from 34,000 in 1960 to 90,000 in 1964.[24]

The *National Review* became the Right's debating chamber. Buckley succeeded in avoiding the hectoring tone that comes so easily to rebels. He published some established heavyweights: James Burnham wrote a toe-curling column called "the Third World War." Buckley also sought out younger writers such as Joan Didion and Garry Wills, who were both going through conservative phases. This helped inject a cosmopolitan edge to a movement that had too often been isolationist and philistine. The *National Review* didn't just attack the Left; it mauled "the irresponsible Right." Gerald Smith and his Nationalist Christian Crusade was an obvious target, but one of the best early articles was Whittaker Chambers's demolition of Ayn Rand's work as a heap of pretentious pagan nonsense. "From almost any page of *Atlas Shrugged*," he claimed, "a voice can be heard, from painful necessity, commanding: 'To a gas chamber—go.'"[25] (Rand responded by denouncing the *Review* as "the worst and most dangerous magazine in America.")[26]

Buckley tried to fashion a synthesis out of the three fractious components of 1950s conservatism: traditionalism, libertarianism and anticommunism. Isn't communism the biggest threat to the Western Judeo-Christian tradition? he asked. And isn't the free market better than government at promoting traditional moral standards? Buckley also sprinkled the nascent conservatism with a little glamour. William Rusher, the *Review*'s managing editor, once observed that "to the liberal intellectuals of the 1950s conservatism was not so much invisible as simply beneath notice."[27] Most conservatives were simply too dull to bother with. But Buckley was anything but dull. Suddenly, there was a conservative who could dash off books and duel with liberals on television before disappearing off to some nightclub. In 1960 he helped to found Young Americans for Freedom, a youth movement that spread like wildfire across the country. It added 5,400 new members in 1964 alone, at a time when the total membership of its more famous rival, the Students for a Democratic Society, was 1,500.

RUMBLINGS DOWN SOUTH

These intellectuals eventually provided the Right with its message and inspiration. But what about the footsoldiers? One reason the Right's impact was blunted was because its troops were divided between two parties. Conservatives in the Northeast and Midwest might regard their natural home as the Republican Party. But Southern conservatives belonged to the Democratic Party.

In 1950, the GOP had no senators from the South and only two congressmen in a Southern delegation of 105.[28] Over the previous fifty years, it had mustered only eighty victories in 2,565 congressional races—and fifty of these victories took place in just two districts in east Tennessee. The Republicans had alienated the region during the Civil War, and had been widely blamed for the Great Depression. "I've never seen such shitasses in my life," was Sam Rayburn's verdict in 1933, after meeting some Wall Street Republicans.[29] For their part, the Democrats had both defended Southern segregation and poured resources into the region through the New Deal, cajoling Northern taxpayers into paying for huge dams and roads. Trent Lott, growing up in Mississippi in the 1940s and 1950s, claims that he "never met a live Republican."[30]

Yet the South, in which the GOP's future leader in the Senate grew up, was changing. The postwar years saw huge internal migration, as blacks moved from the rural South to Northern inner cities, and whites moved down South looking for jobs or retirement homes. Southern governors started luring companies to their states with generous "economic development" packages. Air conditioning made the region's humidity more tolerable to nonnatives; and suburbanization began to erode some of the South's feudal ties.

None of this would have mattered without the civil rights movement. Southern whites remained loyal to the Democrats so long as the national party turned a blind eye to the region's racial practices. But a growing number of Northern Democrats found that bargain unacceptable. Strom Thurmond, then governor of South Carolina, walked out of the 1948 Democratic Convention after Northern delegates forced through a pledge "to eradicate all racial, religion and economic discrimination." Two weeks later he helped to form the States' Rights Party—the Dixiecrats—at a gathering in Birmingham, Alabama. Thurmond and his vice presidential candidate, Fielding Wright, the governor of Mississippi, declared that "we stand for the segregation of the races and the racial integrity of each race"—that is, for separate schools, separate lunch counters, separate bathrooms, for the entire machinery of Jim Crow segregation. Thurmond sent his Confederate-flag-waving audiences into a frenzy when he declared that "all the laws of Washington and all the bayonets of the Army cannot force the Negro into our homes, our schools, our churches." This was a little hypocritical since the governor had already sired an illegitimate child with a black maid, but in the 1948 national presidential election, candidate Thurmond succeeded in taking four states, Alabama, Mississippi and Louisiana as well as South Carolina, and the white Democratic vote declined dramatically. Almost three-quarters of white Southerners had voted for FDR in 1944; only about half voted for Truman four years later.[31]

Thurmond rejoined the Democratic Party in short order, but the seeds of doubt about Democratic perfidy had been planted in the hearts of many white Southerners. The big question for them was the nature of the Republican Party. After all, the most conspicuous Southern Republicans were the "black and tan" delegations—blacks who loyally trooped to Republican conventions and who received federal patronage whenever the GOP won the White House.[32] The Republican attitude to race could hardly be characterized as progressive in modern terms. The generally moderate Eisenhower, who had opposed Truman's order to desegregate the armed services in 1948, told Earl Warren that he could understand why Southerners would not want their "sweet little girls" to sit in school alongside "some big overgrown negro."[33] Nevertheless, throughout the 1950s the Republicans were consistently more liberal than the Democrats in votes on antilynching bills and other racially charged subjects. As late as 1962, when asked which party would "help Negroes get fair treatment in jobs," 22.7 percent of Americans said Democrats and 21.3 percent said Republicans, with the rest having no opinion.[34]

Two years later, the numbers had changed dramatically: by late 1964, 66 percent of voters reckoned the Democrats would help blacks find jobs, while only 7 percent plumped for the Republicans.[35] Two things explain this:

the Civil Rights Act of 1964 and Barry Goldwater. The Civil Rights Act was a monumental piece of social legislation which made illegal the entire structure of entrenched segregation in the South—from schools to lunch counters. The act was actually introduced by John F. Kennedy in June 1963, but, after his assassination, Johnson heroically pushed it through the Congress, despite a fierce filibuster from his fellow Southern Democrats. Willis Robertson, a senator from Virginia (and, incidentally, the father of televangelist Pat), waved a tiny Confederate flag as he spoke. For Thurmond, it was all too much. Defeated in his long battle with the national Democratic establishment, he defected into the waiting arms of the Republican Party.

In one way this was an odd choice. Firm support from the Rockefeller Republicans of the Northeast meant that the GOP provided bigger margins of support than the Democrats for both the Civil Rights Act and the 1965 Voting Rights Act.[36] But Thurmond did not join Nelson Rockefeller's party. He joined Barry Goldwater's.

GOLDWATER'S ACHIEVEMENT

The Republican candidate for president in 1964 was one of only eight Republican senators who voted against the Civil Rights Act. Goldwater made states' rights (which, as far as the South was concerned, meant the right to keep segregation) one of the centerpieces of his presidential campaign in 1964. This otherwise calamitous campaign collected 55 percent of the white Southern vote, carrying five states in the Deep South and winning an astonishing 87.1 percent of the vote in Mississippi. Indeed, if it hadn't been for Dixie, Goldwater would have carried only his native state of Arizona (where he scraped to victory by a meager 4,782 votes).

In an odd way, Goldwater's stance on civil rights was a microcosm of his contribution to the Right. In the short term, his opposition to equal rights for blacks only added to the idea that he was a bigoted nut. Outside the South, white voters backed the civil rights laws by enormous majorities. In the long term, however, he prepared the ground for the Republican Party's Southern strategy—partly because of his "principled" stand on states' rights but even more because of what the Democrats did with the landslide he precipitated.

In some right-wing circles these days, mentioning Barry Goldwater is rather like mentioning Bonnie Prince Charlie in Scotland: he was always the lad who was born to be king and unjustly deprived of the crown. Pat Buchanan has said that the Goldwater campaign was like "first love" for many conservatives, and indeed Goldwater was a rather dashing character. A good-looking, Thunderbird-driving fighter pilot, he took to the air whenever he could. During the convention at San Francisco's Cow Palace that nominated him, he crisscrossed the skies above the city. To his supporters, who included Joan Didion as well as Buchanan, he had the courage to defy the liberal orthodoxies of his time—to offer the voters "a choice, not an echo," as he liked to put it.

Yet, by any conventional standard, he was a calamitous presidential candidate. "Give me Barry. I won't even have to leave the Oval Office," quipped John Kennedy during a discussion of possible opponents in 1963.[37] At that time, Goldwater had looked like a longshot for the Republican nomination the next year. It was generally assumed that the task was Nelson Rockefeller's to inherit. In 1964, the *New York Times* even ventured that Rockefeller was in no more danger of losing the nomination than of going bankrupt. Goldwater's narrow victory at the convention was commonly attributed to two things. The first was Rockefeller's private life: he divorced his wife of thirty years in 1963 and rapidly married a recent divorcée known as "Happy." This scandalized many straitlaced Republicans, including Prescott Bush and provided Goldwaterites with a splendid slogan: "Do you want a leader or a lover in the White House?"[38] The second was organization. Goldwater's troops, choreographed by F. Clifton White, a former Cornell political science instructor, quietly took over the party's moribund machinery in the South and created machinery where none had previously existed in the West, flooding the Republican convention in San Francisco with Goldwater delegates. "What in God's name has happened to the Republican Party?" Henry Cabot Lodge exclaimed, leafing through the list of delegates: "I hardly know any of these people."[39]

Dumbfounded, Rockefeller complained that the Republican Party was "in real danger of subversion by a radical, well-financed and highly disciplined minority." Goldwaterites were "wholly alien to the broad middle course that accommodates the mainstream of Republican principle."[40]

More than eighty Eisenhower-era officials, seven of them with cabinet rank, signed a stinging letter to their party's candidate.[41] The Democratic governor of California, Edmund G. "Pat" Brown, smelled "the stench of fascism" in the air.[42] Goldwater's only foreign support came from pro-apartheid South Africans, Spanish monarchists and German neofascists. Only three newspapers endorsed him: the *Los Angeles Times* (then a very different paper from what it is today), the *Chicago Tribune* and the *Cincinnati Enquirer*.[43] The reliably Republican *Saturday Evening Post* editorialized: "Goldwater is a grotesque burlesque of the conservative he pretends to be. He is a wild man, a stray, an unprincipled and ruthless jujitsu artist like Joe McCarthy." "What would a Goldwater presidency be like?" *Time* magazine quipped. "Brief."[44]

It is no surprise that Goldwater's supporters felt that they were the victims of an establishment witch hunt. But as one of the great chroniclers of American politics, Theodore H. White, put it, covering Goldwater was like "shooting fish in a barrel."[45] His solution to the great nightmare of the time—nuclear holocaust—was to make such a war more thinkable, by perfecting a variety of "small, clean nuclear weapons" that could be used on the battlefield.[46] He was particularly keen on a portable nuclear device called the "Davy Crockett."[47] Asked during the California primary how he would block Communist supply lines along the border into South Vietnam, he suggested "defoliation of the forests by low-yield atomic weapons." No wonder the Democrats' famous "daisy ad" (which pictured a little girl counting the petals of a daisy while an adult voice counted down to the launch of a nuclear weapon) proved so devastating.

It wasn't just a question of extremism. Goldwater cheerfully broke all the basic rules of politics. He sometimes started speeches by listing all the people he didn't want to vote for him. (Top of the list: "the lazy, dole-happy people who want to feed on the fruits of somebody else's labor.") He told an audience in Texas that an aerospace contract should have gone to Boeing in Seattle rather than to a local company. He denounced Johnson's antipoverty program in poverty-stricken West Virginia.[48] He didn't so much touch the third rail of politics as impale himself upon it by dismissing Social Security as "free retirement." One fan came up with a soft drink called "Gold Water— The Right Drink for the Conservative Taste." The candidate, with characteristic political sensitivity, promptly spat it out. "This tastes like piss!" he spluttered. "I wouldn't drink it with gin."[49]

The election result was one of the most dramatic defeats in political history. Goldwater amassed 27 million votes to Johnson's 43 million. Johnson's victory, with 61 percent of the vote and forty-four states, was bigger even than FDR's record-setting victory in 1936. The Johnson tide washed away every time-honored Republican stronghold in the country—the industrial Midwest as well as New England, the Plains states as well as the Rocky Mountain states. In the House, the Republicans faced the largest Democratic majority since 1936; in the Senate, they were outnumbered two to one; in the state capitols, they held only seventeen of the country's fifty governorships.[50] In 1940, 38 percent of voters had described themselves as Republicans, compared with 42 percent who described themselves as Democrats; in Goldwater's *annus horribilis* the Republican number had fallen to 25 percent and the Democratic number had risen to 53 percent.[51]

Goldwater's defeat turned conservatives into pariahs. Theodore H. White tells a remarkable story about Goldwater's chief speechwriter, Karl Hess.[52] Chief speechwriters of losing campaigns usually find a safe berth somewhere in the party machinery, but not so Hess. First, he applied for positions with conservative senators and congressmen—the very politicians who had been cheering him on a few months before. Unwanted, he lowered his sights dramatically. Could he perhaps work the elevators in the Senate or the House? Still no luck. The apostle of the free market was reduced to the ranks of the unemployed. He enrolled in a night-school course in welding and eventually found a job working the night shift in a machine shop.

If Goldwater had only brought Southern whites into the Republican coalition, he would not have proved to be a transformative figure. But he also linked conservatism to a very different region—the booming West. Up until the 1950s the Republican Right had been dominated by solid Midwestern types like Taft. Goldwater, however, hailed from the emerging West where George H. W. Bush was making his living.[53] Goldwater's grandfather, a poor Jewish immigrant, had started Phoenix's largest department store. Goldwater saw the desert city grow from a small town of 30,000 people during his boyhood to a sprawling mass of 816,000 in 1963 and to 2 million in the

1980s. "Out here in the West and the Midwest, we're not constantly harassed by the fear of what might happen," Goldwater once said. "Sure there are risks, but we've always taken risks."[54] He was obsessed by new technology. Behind his house in Arizona rose a twenty-five-foot flagpole controlled by a photoelectric mechanism. As dawn rose over the desert, light activated the flagpole's motor, and the Stars and Stripes slid up the staff; as dusk gathered, the flag automatically descended.[55]

The senator found some of his most vociferous supporters in the thriving regions of the West: in the desert cities of Arizona, in the gigantic sprawl of Los Angeles and in the cookie-cutter towns of Orange County. These Westerners were natural individualists: people who lived in bungalows, not apartment blocks, and who relied on cars rather than public transport (though "relied on" is perhaps too weak a term to convey an attitude that often bordered on worship). They witnessed every day how "individual initiative made the desert bloom," in Goldwater's phrase. And they judged people usually by what they achieved rather than where they came from.[56]

Westerners combined this gut individualism with a powerful opposition to "the establishment." Many of these people had moved out West to escape from the tight little clubs that ran the East Coast business world, the trade-union machines that dominated blue-collar life and the ethnic bosses who ran urban politics. They resented the fact that the East Coast elite continued to exercise a disproportionate amount of power (with the federal government owning more than 40 percent of Arizona and 90 percent of Alaska). Economic vitality was rapidly moving away from the old establishment: New York's share of the country's banking resources were halved from 25 percent in 1945 to 12.5 percent in 1964.[57] By that year California's Bank of America was as big as the Rockefellers' Chase Manhattan. Yet the East Coast elite continued to ignore most of the country. "This continent tilts," observed Robert E. Smylie, the Republican governor of Idaho during the 1964 election, "but Easterners don't recognize it. You have an 'overflight' complex—you think the first stop after Idlewild [now John F. Kennedy International Airport] is Los Angeles."[58] How could they not applaud when Goldwater railed against big government or proclaimed that the country would be "better off if we could just saw off the eastern seaboard and let it float out to sea"?

The West was a breeding ground for all sorts of right-wing groups. Conservatives set up "Freedom Forum" bookshops that sold magnificently titled books such as *The Naked Communist, Masters of Deceit* and *You Can Trust the Communists (To Be Communists)* along with Bibles and American flags. They ran in school board races, offered their services to the Republican Party, joined any anticommunist society going and met for private screenings of *Communism on the Map* or *Operation Abolition*. They flocked to listen to right-wing speakers such as the Reverend Robert Schuller, a Southern Californian firebrand who warned that UNESCO meant "the complete destruction of the American way of life and the dethronement of true democratic freedom," and Fred Schwarz, a lay preacher from Australia who had given up his medical career to devote himself full-time to running his Christian Anti-Communism Crusade. Schwarz also set up a School of Anti-Communism: one session in the spring of 1961 attracted as many as seven thousand students, many of them excused from their regular classes by local school boards.[59]

If there was one book that every Western conservative bought, it was *The Conscience of a Conservative*. By the 1964 election, Goldwater's personal manifesto had sold 3.5 million copies. "I have little interest in streamlining government or in making it more efficient, for I mean to reduce its size," he wrote. "I do not undertake to promote welfare, for I propose to extend freedom. My aim is not to pass laws, but to repeal them." Goldwater did more than anyone else to put hostility to the growth of government at the heart of modern Republicanism. He happily called for the scrapping of popular middle-class entitlements, argued that federal spending on domestic programs should be reduced by 10 percent a year and championed the flat tax. This was all heady stuff for a presidential candidate—particularly in the middle of the 1960s.

All this points forward to Reaganism. The Gipper was a regular speaker at Schwarz's School of Anti-Communism, and one of his first ventures onto the national stage was to nominate Goldwater at the 1964 Republican Party convention in San Francisco. He carried forward the same ideas. As George Will once quipped, Goldwater did eventually win his presidential election—in 1980.

It was under Goldwater that the Right began to coalesce—as a minority, to be sure, but as a highly disciplined and determined one. In 1960, the

Nixon campaign attracted fewer than 50,000 individual contributors; Goldwater attracted 650,000. Goldwater marched into his doomed election with 3.9 million party volunteers, twice as many as worked for Johnson.[60] Car bumper stickers supporting Goldwater outnumbered those supporting Johnson by a ratio of ten to one. These Goldwaterites could sometimes go over the top, as when they howled Nelson Rockefeller off the stage at the 1964 convention, but they constituted a cadre of activists who relentlessly tilted the Republican Party rightward. Goldwater solidified the relationship between conservative footsoldiers and conservative intellectuals. William Buckley's brother-in-law, Brent Bozell, ghost-wrote Goldwater's *Conscience of a Conservative.* Goldwater's speech at the 1964 convention, in which he proclaimed that "extremism in the defense of liberty is no vice," was written by Harry Jaffe, one of the first disciples of Leo Strauss, who would become the neoconservatives' favorite philosopher. The *National Review* enthusiastically endorsed his candidacy, as did conservatives as different as Russell Kirk and Ayn Rand. William Baroody turned the American Enterprise Institute (AEI) into Goldwater's brain trust, persuading conservative intellectuals such as Milton Friedman, Robert Bork, William Rehnquist and the ominously named Warren Nutter to enlist in the Goldwater army.

THE RIGHT ELECTION TO LOSE

None of this prevented electoral catastrophe in November 1964. The problem was not just with Goldwater, dismal candidate though he was, but with the whole machinery of right-wing insurgency. Many of the people that the Right now hails as intellectual giants were widely dismissed at the time as eccentric pygmies. The Ivy League establishment looked down on "Chicago boys." The then-respected Robert Lekachman brusquely dismissed the Chicago School as nothing more than an "ingenious sect."[61] Some Keynesian economists successfully lobbied to get Friedman's *Capitalism and Freedom* purged from university libraries.[62] Rowland Evans and Robert Novak, then beginning their journalistic partnership, summed up respectable opinion when they wrote that the Goldwater campaign was run by "a group of little-known academicians and publicists loosely allied with an obscure tax-exempt educational foundation in Washington, D.C., called the American Enterprise Institute for Public Policy Research." And even some of Goldwater's most outspoken supporters harbored doubts about their hero's capacity to run the country. "What would happen if he were elected President of the United States?" *Time* magazine asked William Buckley. "That," Buckley replied, "might be a serious problem."[63]

The plain fact was that there were still far too many weirdos in the movement. Schwarz's School of Anti-Communism might be excused as merely overvigilant, but the John Birch Society, which also flourished in California's Orange County, suffered from an even more advanced case of paranoia than the McCarthyites. The organization was founded in 1958 by Robert Welch, a retired Massachusetts candy maker, who named it after a militaristic Protestant missionary who had been murdered by Chinese Communists. Welch set up the society during a three-day lecture he delivered in Indianapolis, and he ruled it with the iron hand of an autocrat. (The organization did have a governing council, but its sole purpose was to choose a new leader in the event that "the founder" was assassinated by Communists.) By the early 1960s, it had 25,000 members, including Fred Koch and Harry Bradley, industrialists who became two of the conservative movement's biggest benefactors, numerous city officials and John Rousselot, chairman of the congressional Republican freshmen caucus.

Conspiracy theories were the John Birch Society's lifeblood. Welch decided that Eisenhower was a "dedicated, conscious agent of the Communist conspiracy" and claimed that this assertion was based on "an accumulation of detailed evidence so extensive and so palpable that it seems to put this conviction beyond any reasonable doubt." Other "conspirators" included Allen Dulles, George Marshall and, it often seemed, half the entire population. And why not? How else could you explain how America had lost China and North Korea? Or why Alger Hiss had risen so far? Or why Castro had been allowed to seize Cuba? Or why government just kept on growing bigger? Opinion polls discovered that more than 5 percent of Americans broadly agreed with the society—a fairly remarkable number but hardly the basis for a popular revolt.[64]

However, the main barrier to the conservative movement was not so much the ravings of its lunatic fringe as the success of the status quo. Put Goldwater, Friedman or Buckley on a stage, and a minority would agree with everything that they said, but most listeners would shrug their shoulders. What was so wrong with America? The economy was booming. The government was solving social problems. Communism was being held at bay abroad. This faith was shaken in the next few years as the country began to spin out of control. The other handmaiden of modern conservatism was the man who thrashed Barry Goldwater at the polls—Lyndon Johnson.

CHAPTER 3

THE AGONY OF LIBERALISM, 1964-1988

SOMETIMES A SINGLE GESTURE can convey the essence of an entire philosophy. Visiting Providence, Rhode Island, during the 1964 election campaign, Lyndon Johnson was so overcome with emotion that he clambered onto the roof of his car and seized a bullhorn. "I just want to tell you this," the Democratic incumbent roared at the cheering crowd. "We're in favor of a lot of things and we're against mighty few."[1]

In the mid-1960s big-government liberalism was in a triumphant mood. Keynesian economists thought that they had discovered the secret of economic growth: all you needed to do was adjust a few economic indicators and, presto, the world would go on getting richer. More amazingly still, policy makers thought they had the power to cure social ills, from poverty to prejudice, and most Americans still trusted them to do so. One group of scientists, their expenses paid by the National Science Foundation, even began a research project aimed at controlling the weather.[2]

The victorious Johnson was determined to bring the country closer together. He wanted to promote national unity by building on thirty years of successful progressive policies, fighting poverty at home and containing communism abroad. Instead, he ended up doing the opposite—dividing the country and shattering the Roosevelt coalition. When Johnson left the White House in January 1969, he handed over the key to the Republicans.

Western conservatives—some admittedly more conservative and Western than others—held the White House for twenty of the next twenty-four years.

This period was as turbulent for the Right as for everyone else. In 1976, as the dust began to settle from the Watergate affair, many conservatives assumed that Republicanism was dead for a generation. Yet in most of the years between 1964 and 1980 the Right was generally gaining ground. This was a period when the footsoldiers in the South and West gradually became a more unified army, when the intellectuals began to shape policy and when demography continued to drag America in a Southwestern direction. All three forces came together in 1980 in the shape of Ronald Reagan—a man whose philosophy was exactly the opposite of Johnson's: government was the problem, not the solution.

VEERING OFF TO THE LEFT

In 1965 Johnson took up where he had left off in 1964. He added the Voting Rights Act to the Civil Rights Act. He unleashed his "all-out war on human poverty and unemployment in these United States." He extended the federal government's role in education (through the Head Start program of pre-school education), in higher culture (through the National Endowment for the Arts and the National Endowment for the Humanities) and in health care (through the enormous Medicare and Medicaid programs). "It is the Congress of accomplished hopes," Speaker John McCormack boasted. "It is the Congress of realized dreams."[3] Many of these Great Society programs were undoubtedly laudable, but even the best policies can have unintended consequences. The programs built up a dynamic of their own, throwing up bureaucratic empires, and stoking white resentment. And they relentlessly dragged the Democratic Party ever further from its centrist roots, swelling the "coalition of the fed-up" that had voted for Goldwater.

The Democrats' civil rights agenda rapidly broadened from guaranteeing basic rights to black citizens (such as the right to equal opportunity and to vote) to making amends for past injustices with preferential treatment. Johnson's "community action program," for instance, was supposed to help the poor help themselves, but in practice it often reinforced, rather than resolved, grievances by handing power in poor communities to professional protesters of the sort caricatured by Tom Wolfe in 1970 in "Mau-Mauing the Flak Catchers."[4] The growing radicalism of the ghetto further strained the Democratic coalition, particularly when riots engulfed Northern cities in the late 1960s. Half the party—urban radicals, intellectuals and blacks—seemed to feel that this was legitimate protest, and that the answer was more cash and more preferences. The other half—poor whites, suburbanites—disliked the collapse of order, and wondered why blacks should be given special treatment.

Meanwhile, traditional Democrats discovered another source of concern in the judiciary. The Warren Supreme Court progressively recast the law to give rights to all sorts of previously excluded groups—not just blacks but also women, homosexuals, the handicapped, prisoners, the mentally ill, even pornographers.[5] The Court found that criminal defendants were entitled to a wide range of constitutional protections: in came due process and the right to silence and a speedy trial; out went self-incrimination—and all of this at a time when the nation's crime rate was soaring. The Court barred prayer from public schools (in 1962); made the prosecution of obscenity much more difficult (in 1962 and again in 1964); and, thanks to Prescott Bush's friend Estelle Griswold, legalized the sale of contraceptive devices, including the birth-control pill (in 1965). Under Warren Burger, the Court banned the death penalty in 1972 on the ground that there was a "wanton and freakish" pattern to its application. Momentous though it was, the Roe v. Wade decision on abortion in 1973 was just one in a long succession of outrages for the "coalition of the fed-up."

For many working-class Americans in the big cities the biggest judicial outrage of all was court-ordered busing. Busing struck most ordinary people as both unfair and hypocritical: unfair because children were forced against their will to travel miles in order to achieve "racial balance"; hypocritical because the "liberal elites" that supported the policy usually sent their own children to private or suburban schools. When Senator Ted Kennedy tried to address an antibusing rally in Boston in 1974, an angry Irish-American crowd shouted him down and pursued the lion of liberalism with eggs and tomatoes when he took refuge in the Federal Building named after his brother. As Christopher Lasch put it, "so much for Camelot."[6]

Another divisive force was the antiwar movement. For many activists, the Vietnam War was the greatest evil of the day—and the counterculture was a natural accompaniment to a life of protest. For many rank-and-file Democrats, however, the antiwar movement was an abomination. What did the average workingman have in common with hippies who spent their time taking drugs and squandering their families' trust funds? Or with students who desecrated the American flag? The antiwar protesters, most of whom would be given student deferments rather than being sent to fight, were even more unpopular than the war itself.[7] Far too many of them seemed not just hostile to this or that American policy, but to America in general. The shooting of four students at Kent State in May 1970 may have inspired Neil Young to song, but a week later blue-collar America cheered when a group of hard-hat union construction workers in New York beat up a group of antiwar demonstrators.

The most visible symbol of the revolt within the Democratic Party was the governor of Alabama, George Wallace. In 1964, his attempt to get the Democratic nomination was easily repulsed by Johnson, but four years later Wallace ran as an independent, providing a voice for resentful whites everywhere, in Northern cities as well as the Southern countryside. His answer to a journalist's inquiry about the issues that would dominate the 1968 election gives a good sense of what was troubling white America at the time:

"Schools, that'll be one thing. By the fall of 1968, the people of Cleveland and Chicago and Gary and St. Louis will be so God-damned sick and tired of Federal interference in their local schools, they'll be ready to vote for Wallace by the thousand. The people don't like this triflin' with their children, tellin' 'em which teachers to have to teach in which schools, and bussing [sic] little boys and girls half across a city jus' to achieve 'the proper racial mix.' . . . I'll give you another big one for 1968: law and order. Crime in the streets. The people are going to be fed up with the sissy attitude of Lyndon Johnson and all the intellectual morons and theoreticians he has around him. They're fed up with a Supreme Court that . . . It's a sorry, lousy, no-account outfit. . . . Folks won't stand for it. . . ."[8]

Around 13.5 percent of the "folks" backed Wallace in the 1968 election, drawing enough Democratic votes from Hubert Humphrey to give Richard

Nixon victory. Yet the Democrats continued to move to the left. Radical liberals won the war for the soul of the Democratic Party, not least because of elaborate changes in the party's constitution that gave minorities extra delegates. The Irish machine politicians, trade-union bosses and Southern conservatives who had dominated the party for decades began to lose out to birds of a very different feather: antiwar protesters, feminists and environmentalists. The 1972 Democratic platform had separate planks on the rights of the poor, Native Americans, the physically disabled, the mentally retarded, the elderly, women, children and veterans. The platform devoted more attention to the restoration of constitutional rights to released convicts than to efforts to combat street violence.[9] The 1972 Democratic convention that nominated George McGovern was a world apart from the one that sent Johnson into battle against Goldwater in 1964. Reformism had mutated into radicalism, with something of an anti-American bent. Four-fifths of the delegates in 1972 had never attended a Democratic convention before. The place was full of postadolescents (two Arizona delegates had not even turned eighteen when they were selected). The entire event was chaos: the nominees did not manage to make their speeches until the small hours of the morning, robbing the party of its television audience. Many of the most important meetings still took place in smoke-filled rooms, but this time the smoke smelled rather different.

All the while, the country was falling apart. The Keynesian economists who claimed to have mastered the art of fine-tuning the economy to keep both inflation and unemployment low were flummoxed by "stagflation." The level of serious crime, which had remained stable throughout the 1950s, began to rise at a rate of almost 20 percent a year in the mid-1960s, and a disproportionate share of this crime—particularly violent crime—was committed by blacks. The black arrest rate for murder, for example, increased by over 130 percent in the 1960s. At the same time, the number of births to unmarried black women escalated, from 21.6 percent in 1960 to 34.9 percent in 1970.[10] The liberal elite that had seemed so self-confident just a few years earlier suddenly seemed powerless. They had no solution for the breakup of the family—other than more generous welfare payments. They had no solution to the problem of rising crime—other than more cash for rehabilitation and social science studies. The establishment increasingly lost the support of the public. In 1965, the proportion of the population who thought that the courts treated criminals "about right" or "too harshly" was 36 percent; by 1977 that number had fallen to a mere 11 percent.[11]

Worse, from the perspective of many conservatives, the cultural elite was happy to indulge this disorder. In August 1967, the *New York Review of Books* printed instructions on its cover telling readers how to make a Molotov cocktail. In 1970 Leonard Bernstein invited leaders of the Black Panthers to dinner. Hollywood too turned leftward. In 1965 the Oscar for best picture went to *The Sound of Music;* in 1969 it went to *Midnight Cowboy.*[12] In the film *Shampoo,* which came out in 1975 but is set on election night in 1968, the hero, played by Warren Beatty, has sex with his girlfriend, his girlfriend's best friend, the best friend's lover's wife and the lover's wife's daughter, and as Michael Elliott points out, "his behavior is not thought remarkable."[13]

Suddenly the conservative message—that government was the problem, not the solution—began to resonate. Back in 1964, 62 percent of Americans had trusted the government in Washington to do the right thing most of the time. That figure now went into relentless decline, eventually reaching 19 percent in 1994.[14]

THE FALSE DAWN: RICHARD NIXON

The man who transformed these inchoate resentments into Republican votes was a longstanding hero to many on the Right. Richard Nixon had a long history of anticommunism, both of the honorable variety (he played a leading role in exposing Alger Hiss's lies) and of the dishonorable sort (he ran a Red-baiting Senate campaign in California against Helen Gahagan Douglas in 1950, accusing the actress-turned-congresswoman of being "pink right down to her underwear"). Nixon hailed from the Sun Belt, just like Goldwater, and made no secret of his dislike of the East Coast establishment. Throughout his career he had repeatedly thrown bones to the conservative pack. He claimed to be an admirer of Russell Kirk,[15] and he was not above hinting that he shared many of the darker fantasies of the John Birchers and McCarthyites. "Isn't it wonderful," he said shortly after Eisenhower's election ended Dean Acheson's tenure at the State Department, "to have finally a secretary of state who's on our side of the table."[16]

Nixon campaigned as a conservative—and as a conservative, moreover, with a genius for harnessing populism to his cause. Before Nixon, populist revolts pitting the forgotten majority against the hard-faced elite had usually taken the form of economic sanctions against the rich. Nixon's genius was to pick up on George Wallace's insurgency in the Democratic Party and direct populism against cultural elites: against what Nixon saw as the effete snobs who controlled institutions like Harvard and the *Washington Post*. Nixon echoed Wallace in giving a new, pejorative meaning to the word "liberal," which, in Nixon's dictionary, meant a cosseted elitist who cared more about everybody else than about hard-working, straight, white Americans.

Nixon ruthlessly used cultural issues to drive a wedge between working-class Democrats and their increasingly liberal party. Liberal baiting was hardly a chore for Nixon: there was something about the envy-ridden Californian that sent liberals into a paroxysm of rage (and vice versa). He recruited the young Pat Buchanan to stir up populist prejudices, and he encouraged Spiro Agnew, his vice president, to let rip at "radiclibs" and the "nattering nabobs of negativism." Nixon was the first Republican president to win over a majority of working-class, Catholic and trade-union voters.

In 1968, the newly elected president duly gave the conservatives a little hope. He appointed some leading conservatives to his administration: Arthur Burns to the Federal Reserve Board, Warren Nutter to the Defense Department, Martin Anderson (author of *The Federal Bulldozer* and later a right-hand man to Ronald Reagan) to the White House staff. Even William Buckley received an appointment (albeit to an advisory commission to the United States Information Agency).

Yet there was more than one Richard Nixon: if the Californian campaigned as a conservative, he governed as a liberal. He gave two of the most prominent jobs in his administration to Harvard professors with close ties to Rockefeller Republicans and Kennedy Democrats—Henry Kissinger and Daniel Patrick Moynihan—and he boasted that his cabinet was less conservative than Eisenhower's.[17] Nixon shared Ike's Europe-first internationalism and his belief that the job of Republicans was to manage the New Deal better than the Democrats, but he took a more liberal stance on social issues. Nixon was far more concerned with black rights than Eisenhower, who seemed to assume that blacks should be content with second-class citizenship. Nixon was the first president to embrace affirmative action, mandating its extension to women as well as blacks. Both federal spending and federal regulation grew faster under Nixon than they had under Johnson. Social spending overtook defense spending for the first time. The number of pages of the *Federal Register* (the roster of federal rules and regulations) grew by 121 percent under Nixon compared with only 19 percent under Johnson. The Clean Air Act of 1970 was the most ambitious environmental measure yet produced. A year later, the president called for the passage of a comprehensive national health-insurance plan. For a while he became excited about providing all Americans with a minimum annual income. As Hugh Scott, the Democrats' leader in the Senate, crowed, "The conservatives get the rhetoric; we get the action."[18]

Much of this went down well with the American public, but for the right-wing intelligentsia, it was a calamity. Hard-liners moaned that Henry Kissinger practiced a brand of realpolitik that drained foreign policy of any moral content. What most of the world interpreted as smooth operating—disengaging America from Vietnam and striking a deal with China—they saw as appeasement. At home Nixon created a mass of new government agencies that conservatives would spend much of the next two decades trying to get rid of, such as the Environmental Protection Agency (EPA) and the Occupational Safety and Health Administration (OSHA). He particularly infuriated conservatives by creating the Cost of Living Council in 1971–73 to try to control prices and wages, in what was America's most concerted attempt to introduce state control of the economy since the Second World War. (The man Nixon put in charge of this quixotic venture was the then merely middle-aged Donald Rumsfeld.) On July 26, 1971, several prominent conservatives, including William Buckley and James Burnham, "suspended their support" for the administration.[19]

Those conservatives who stuck by the president soon ran into Watergate. They wasted a huge amount of political capital defending the indefensible. Similar to Joe McCarthy two decades before, Nixon brought out the worst in the conservative movement: its paranoia and self-pity, its obsession with conspiracies, its hatred of the establishment for no better reason than that it was the establishment. He saddled the Right with a reputation for sleaziness and skulduggery that took years to live down. And all for what? Nixon was not only guilty of breaking the law, he was, as far as policy was concerned, very much on the liberal rather than the conservative side.

Nixon's resignation in 1974 left the conservative movement in ruins. His successor, Gerald Ford, was a middle-of-the-road Republican—"Eisenhower without the medals." Ford infuriated the Right by appointing Goldwater's old foe, Nelson Rockefeller, as his vice president. ("I could hardly have been more upset if Ford had selected Teddy Kennedy," wrote Richard Viguerie, the conservative direct-mail king. "I immediately got on the phone and invited about fourteen conservative friends to dinner to talk about how we could stop Rockefeller.")[20] Ford's wife, Betty, angered conservatives still further with her outspoken support for abortion. The Right backed Ronald Reagan's cheeky attempt to grab the Republican nomination from Ford in 1976—and was promptly blamed when Ford lost a very close election to Jimmy Carter.

Even if Ford had been more sympathetic to "the movement," he would hardly have been in any position to feed it red meat. His job was to heal the country after the trauma of Watergate. In 1974 the proportion of the electorate who described themselves as Republicans fell to 20 percent.[21] Most Americans thought of the Republican Party as untrustworthy, incompetent and closely allied with big business.[22] Asked to name something good about the party, two-thirds of voters couldn't think of anything at all.[23] The Republican National Committee ran advertisements asking rather desperately, "When has it been easy to be a Republican?"[24] Some right-wingers considered abandoning the GOP for other political vehicles—perhaps a new party, perhaps even the Democratic Party. "In ten years," predicted Viguerie, "there won't be a dozen people in the country calling themselves Republicans."[25]

THE NEOCONSERVATIVES

How on earth did the Right conjure the Reagan presidency out of such a disaster? The answer once again can be found partly in the foibles of its opponents: Jimmy Carter's approval ratings eventually sank three points below even Nixon's on the eve of his resignation. But it had much more to do with the mounting backlash against liberalism—and with the determination of a ever larger band of conservatives to fashion that backlash into a coherent movement. The footsoldiers and intellectuals were beginning to come together.

For conservative intellectuals of all sorts, the excesses of the left in the 1960s and 1970s presented a golden opportunity. Buckley's *National Review* looked prescient rather than eccentric. Milton Friedman's once dangerously radical ideas attracted a growing crowd of admirers. From the 1970s onward Chicago School–trained economists won more Nobel prizes than economists from any other institution (even if the only country that seemed prepared to implement their ideas was Chile, an international pariah). However, the most important change on the intellectual Right was the defection of one group of liberal intellectuals, for whom the 1960s was a turning point.

The neoconservatives sprang from the very heart of Democratic America. Most of them lived in New York or Boston and most made their living in academia. But these were not traditional Harvard men, lantern-jawed and blue-blooded. Most of them were Jewish, virtually all of them the children of immigrants; some grew up in homes where Yiddish was spoken as much as English. The key members of the group—Irving Kristol, Daniel Bell, Seymour Martin Lipset and Nathan Glazer—all attended City College of New York together in the 1930s at a time when the college provided a first-rate education for New Yorkers who were too poor and too Jewish to attend the Ivy League. The neocons were modernists to a fault. They didn't go around expressing nostalgia for the lost glories of medieval Christendom, nineteenth-century capitalism or the Old South.[26] Most of them had been Marxists of one sort or another in their youth. But as they grew older they embraced old-fashioned liberalism—the liberalism of meritocratic values, reverence for high culture and a vigorous mixed economy. It was the betrayal of this liberalism (as they saw it) by the Left that then turned them into neocons.

The neocons hated what was happening to America's universities, the institutions that had lifted them out of the ghetto. How could the high priests of America's temples of reason stand idly by while students trashed university property? How could people who were supposed to care about intellectual standards agree to the introduction of quotas? Criticizing the war in Vietnam was all very well, but how could these overprivileged brats burn the American flag? How could they argue that America was always wrong and its critics always right? Knee-jerk anti-Americanism was particularly offensive to people whose families escaped the Holocaust only because they emigrated to America.

These thinkers provided an enormous boost to the Right. To begin with, they were cosmopolitan figures. Norman Podhoretz, was a protégé of Lionel Trilling, and studied under F. R. Leavis at Cambridge between 1950 and 1952. Kristol was based in London from 1953 to 1958 when he was coeditor of *Encounter*, and sent his son, Bill, to the French Lycée.[27] Crucially, the neocons spoke the language of social science. Conservatives had long insisted that government programs weakened the natural bonds of society, without ever being able to prove it. The neocons showed that social problems were much harder to understand than they appeared—and that social engineering of the Great Society sort was plagued by perverse consequences. Welfare payments can reinforce dependency. Preferential treatment may harm its supposed beneficiaries by shielding them from competition. Overzealous egalitarianism can undermine educational institutions such as New York's City College and reduce social mobility. The neocons were muckrakers of the Right, discrediting government just as the original muckrakers had discredited the robber barons.

The neocons also dwelt on the importance of the sort of informal institutions that other social scientists ignored. In 1965, a young official in the Department of Labor, Daniel Patrick Moynihan, caused a sensation with a paper—immediately dubbed the Moynihan Report, though his name did not appear on the original document—that suggested that the problems of the urban black poor stemmed, in large measure, from the collapse of the black family.[28] Other neocons showed that a society's "little platoons"—its voluntary institutions—are much more vital to its health than ambitious government programs. And they warned that disorder was a much bigger threat to social well-being than permissive liberals might imagine. In other words, they dressed traditional conservative insights in the language of social science.

The neocons did not need to win every argument. Merely by raising dissenting voices they punched a hole in the liberal establishment's claim to possess a monopoly on expertise.[29] Hitherto liberals had enjoyed perhaps the most valuable resource policy makers can possess: the impression that they represented objective scientific wisdom. This isn't just our opinion, they could argue; this is scientific orthodoxy. The neocons ended this convenient fiction.

The neocons also added a cutting edge to the Right's criticism of liberal foreign policy. One spur was the United Nations' growing hostility to Israel (which increased after Israel occupied Palestinian territory in the wake of the 1967 war). They also became increasingly convinced that the United States was losing the Cold War. Arms control was mutating into appeasement. The Soviet Union was building on communism's victory in Vietnam. The American establishment was paralyzed by "Vietnam syndrome." If the *National Review* broke the isolationists' grip on the Right, the neocons helped push the bulk of the movement far more firmly into the internationalist camp.

The moralistic approach to foreign policy had an intellectual godfather. As well as drawing on social science, the neoconservatives also looked to the insights of one of the most opaque political thinkers of the postwar era. Leo Strauss was in some ways an odd choice for the neoconservatives. He was an elitist political philosopher, who had little interest in the minutiae of social policy, and who spent his career at the University of Chicago rather than in the neocons' world of Boston, New York and Washington. Yet Strauss's impact is hard to exaggerate. Alongside Lionel Trilling, he was the main intellectual influence on Kristol, who credited Strauss with introducing him to "non-utopian politics," a politics based on helping you cope with the world as it is rather than creating a theoretical ideal.[30]

Strauss challenged some of America's most cherished assumptions about progress, democracy and the wisdom of the common man. He rejected the belief that the Enlightenment had improved the human condition; rather, he insisted that the main flourishing of great thought had been with the ancient Greeks. He encouraged his pupils to spend their lives poring over the great texts of the ancients—particularly the writings of Plato and Aristotle. This would allow them to look at the world through the other end of the telescope—not as moderns looking down on ancients but (if they studied hard) ancients looking at moderns.

Strauss insisted that the best way to save democracy from its more self-destructive tendencies was through an educated elite that could guide the masses. Straussianism, according to Milton Himmelfarb, Kristol's brother-in-law, was "an invitation to join those privileged few who, having ascended from the cave, gaze upon the sun with unhooded eyes, while yet mindful of those others below, in the dark."[31] Having no truck with the liberal fashion for moral relativism, Strauss used words that had long been banned from sophisticated discourse: such as "good" and "evil" and "virtue" and "vice." He argued that the measure of a healthy society was not how much freedom people enjoyed (the obsession of libertarians such as Hayek) but how virtuous its citizens were. Strauss thus reinforced the neoconservatives' growing conviction that what was wrong with America was not so much the lack of individual liberty but the destruction of individual virtue.

This might sound a little like William Buckley's creed. But Straussians owed their traditionalism to Athens rather than Rome. Buckley built his conservatism on his Catholic faith; the Straussians built theirs on ancient philosophy. They were for the most part agnostics when it came to religious faith—but agnostics who nevertheless believed that religion helped to promote social cohesion and social virtue. Their writings are littered with references to "noble myths." Religion might not be true, they seemed to be saying, but it can serve a useful social purpose in keeping society in order.

This willingness to accept "noble myths," as long as they helped the cause, helped to forge the neocons' reputation as Machiavellian string-pullers. Were they really that organized? There is certainly a danger in implying a cohesion to the movement's founders that never existed. In the 1960s, most of them were still Democrats: Moynihan would eventually become a Democratic senator from New York. On the other hand, one hallmark of the neocons was their ability to build a network of institutions that kept the conservative message alive in a largely liberal intellectual world. They tapped foundations, spawned organizations and established magazines. The *Public Interest,* a quarterly magazine that began appearing in April 1965, tried to deliver a heavy dose of "reality therapy" to the Great Society, and under Norman Podhoretz's editorship, *Commentary,* the monthly journal of the American Jewish Committee, crackled with articles with titles such as "The Limits of Social Policy," "Liberalism versus Liberal Education" and "Growth and Its Enemies."

The man who did most to transform neoconservatism from an impulse into a movement was Irving Kristol. A Trotskyite in his youth at City College, he started moving steadily to the right in 1942 (when he was in the army) and never really stopped. His career included a long stint as the coeditor of *Encounter,* a spell as a senior editor at Basic Books and a key role in setting up both the *Public Interest* and, a generation later, the *National Interest,* which focused on foreign affairs. Kristol combined a sharp intellect with a wry sense of humor (he once defined a liberal as someone who thinks that it's all right for an eighteen-year-old girl to perform in a pornographic film so long as she is paid the minimum wage) and a genius for networking and institution building. He established close relations with rich benefactors such as William Simon, Nixon's treasury secretary, and became such an important instigator of grants and fellowships that his fellow conservatives jokingly referred to him as the Godfather. Jude Wanniski, a supply-side economist, christened Kristol the "hidden hand" of the conservative movement.

THE THINK TANKS AND THE GIVERS

One place where the neocons and other conservative thinkers gathered was William Baroody's American Enterprise Institute. Baroody, however, had run into several obstacles to realizing his dream of turning the AEI into a conservative brain trust. His support for Goldwater had provoked (with a little nudging from Democrats in Congress) a two-year IRS investigation into the AEI's tax-exempt status. Once bitten meant twice shy, and for a time, Baroody's staff produced laboriously evenhanded analyses of congressional bills, and he made a point of recruiting as many liberals as possible. From the AEI's point of view, hiring former Democrats such as Irving Kristol or Jeane Kirkpatrick, a bright young expert on foreign affairs, looked admirably evenhanded.

As the 1970s wore on, the AEI became much closer to Baroody's dream. Its growing respectability partly stemmed from the realization that its ideas might actually be useful. In the 1960s, the AEI's deregulation-mad economists had been regarded as irresponsible anarchists, but by the late 1970s, even the Carter administration was deregulating the transport industry. The AEI's income soared from $900,000 in 1960 (less than a fifth of that of the Brookings Institution) to $9.7 million in 1980 ($500,000 more than that of the Brookings). By the late 1970s the AEI had forty-five full-time scholars in residence, many more adjunct scholars at various universities, four journals and a monthly television show. It was even grand enough to offer fellowships to Gerald Ford and Arthur Burns (the former Federal Reserve chairman). Baroody, alas, never saw his brain trust being used by a conservative administration. He died in 1980, having handed over control of the think tank to his son, Bill Jr., two years earlier (for all his worship of open market competition, the old man obviously had a blind spot about nepotism). It was a mark of his achievement that both Ford and Reagan addressed a memorial dinner for him.

By then the AEI was no longer alone in conservative circles. The Heritage Foundation opened its doors in 1973 and was a much less highfalutin affair than the AEI, with no pretensions to being "a university without students." Heritage was an advocacy organization, plain and simple, a well-informed pressure group committed to changing policy. The other prominent new arrival, the libertarian Cato Institute, which was founded in 1977 in San Francisco and moved to Washington, D.C., in 1982, was somewhere between the AEI and Heritage: it published big books and put on courses for students, but it also borrowed Heritage's idea of shortish policy papers.

This new network of thinkers owed much to five particularly generous benefactors, who were businessmen and trust funders so worried about the country's drift to the Left that they decided to build a conservative counterestablishment to haul it back to the right. The first of these Medici of the conservative Renaissance was Joseph Coors, a brewing heir who stumped up $250,000 in seed money for Heritage, and also helped found its sister organization, the Committee for the Survival of a Free Congress. Coors was prodded into action in 1971 by a 5,000-word memorandum from Lewis Powell, an old-style Southern Democratic attorney (and later Nixon appointee to the Supreme Court). Powell argued that capitalism was under broad attack from some of its most pampered products—the liberal intelligentsia.

He accused the business class not just of appeasing its critics, but also of financing their anticapitalist activities, and urged them to stand up more vigorously for their interests. Coors also put money into other conservative causes, including the Independence Institute, a Colorado think tank; Accuracy in Media, a watchdog organization set up to sniff out liberal bias; and any number of social conservative outfits.

If Coors gave by the six-pack, Richard Mellon Scaife gave by the case. Scaife was one of the heirs to the Mellon fortune. His early career hardly suggested an interest in conservative ideas. In the mid-1950s Yale University kicked the young hell-raiser out before he could complete his freshman year. A car accident soon followed that almost killed him and injured five members of his family. Still, as Scaife grew older, he grew wiser (at least if you measure wisdom by involvement in conservative causes). He was one of Barry Goldwater's earliest financial backers, and the shock of his hero's devastating defeat only convinced him that conservatism needed to match the enemy's intellectual firepower. When his mother died in 1965, Scaife began a long argument with his sister, who wanted to continue her mother's habit of spending the family fortune on art, family planning and the poor. In 1973 the reclusive Richard finally won the argument. His first contribution to Heritage was $900,000. In 1976, Heritage's third year in existence, he gave $420,000—which at the time was 42 percent of the foundation's entire income. The *Washington Post* has calculated that in the four decades after 1960 Scaife and his family's trust gave at least $340 million to conservative causes—or about $620 million in current dollars.[32]

The third benefactor was the Koch family. The patriarch, Fred, was an oil and gas entrepreneur who invented a way of making gasoline more efficiently, did battle with big oil and gradually built up a highly diversified energy company. Despite building fifteen refineries in Stalin's Russia (business is, after all, business), he became a founder-member of the John Birch Society. His sons, David and Charles Koch, became prolific givers to libertarian causes. David supported both drug liberalization and abortion rights, and ran for vice president on the Libertarian ticket in 1980. Charles cofounded the Cato Institute with Edward Crane in 1977. They also built up a network of fellowships, grants and scholarships to nurture libertarians in America's universities.

The fourth benefactor—and one which was particularly generous to academics and intellectuals—was the Lynde and Harry Bradley Foundation, set up by two brothers who had made their money in Allen-Bradley, a Milwaukee-based electronics company. Harry Bradley, like Robert Koch, was a committed John Bircher, and Robert Welch was a regular speaker at Allen-Bradley sales meetings in the late 1950s. Harry also provided the struggling young *National Review* with both money and articles, and tried to take over *Newsweek* to get a broader audience for his ideas. Though Harry died in 1965, his foundation continued to give away money. The foundation got a huge boost in 1985 when Rockwell International bought Allen-Bradley, pushing the foundation's assets above $260 million. In the same year it also hired a particularly energetic president, Michael Joyce, who was one of Irving Kristol's protégés.

The last of the Big Five, the John M. Olin Foundation, was established in 1953 by John Merrill Olin, another rich businessman obsessed with the growing threat to liberty. By the 1970s, Olin was focusing on the link between academic ideas and public policy. As well as supporting the influential law and economics program at the University of Chicago, and trying to encourage imitators elsewhere, the foundation helped fund think tanks and publications, such as *The Public Interest.* Olin was particularly generous to a handful of favored scholars such as Robert Bork (who now holds the Olin chair of legal studies at AEI) and Irving Kristol (who until recently held an Olin fellowship there too).

These five benefactors were not alone. Other big givers included the Smith Richardson Foundation and the Howard Pew Freedom Trust. More generally, virtually everybody with a corner office in corporate America in the 1970s was moaning about the same things: the economy was in the doldrums, America was losing its competitive edge abroad, they were being regulated "up to their necks," "the other side" was winning. In 1972, the heads of the 500 biggest companies established the Business Roundtable to lobby for their interests on trade-union rights, antitrust, deregulation and taxes.

Companies also began to coordinate their campaign contributions. In 1974, labor "political action committees" (PACs) outnumbered corporate PACs by 201 to 89. Two years later the ratio was reversed, with 433 corporate PACs and 224 labor ones, and by 1984 companies had a 4 to 1 advantage

(1,682 to 394).[33] The type of giving changed too. In 1974, virtually all of it went to buying favors for particular companies, but soon money was going to support general probusiness propaganda and legislation.[34] Companies and their foundations stumped up cash for television series, such as Milton Friedman's *Free to Choose* and Ben Wattenberg's *In Search of the Real America*, for educational materials to be used in classrooms, for dozens of professorships of private enterprise and for probusiness "issue advertising." Above all, corporate America embraced conservative think tanks.

By 1980 the American Enterprise Institute had more than 600 corporate sponsors, including the Lilly Endowment, the Ford Motor Company and Reader's Digest. Its board of trustees, headed by a vice chairman of Mobil, consisted almost entirely of corporate types; and a fund-raising committee included the heads or former heads of Citicorp, General Electric, General Motors and Chase Manhattan Bank. The Hoover Institution, which had been on the verge of bankruptcy in the early 1960s, had an annual budget of $8.4 million in 1983. About 40 percent of that money came from corporations and corporate foundations, and its board of overseers included David Packard (of Hewlett-Packard), another emerging Republican paymaster. In the same year the Heritage Foundation raised money from almost 100 corporations and foundations, and Irving Kristol's Institute of Educational Affairs had 145 corporate donors.

QUEEN PHYLLIS AND FIRST SECRETARY WEYRICH

The 1970s saw another regiment of the conservative army mustering. The "social conservatives" (dubbed "the new Right" at the time) make a slight mockery of our division between intellectuals and footsoldiers. Many of them were thinkers—or at least think tankers—but they were not exactly intellectuals in the manner of Kristol and his friends. On the whole, they were middlebrow and middle-class—people who were moved by gut issues like abortion, busing, gun control and quotas rather than the latest essays in *Commentary* and *Public Interest*. More to the point, they combined zealotry with a rare gift for organization.

One early exponent of this art was Phyllis Schlafly. The Boadicea of social conservatism was born in 1924. She got her first job after leaving graduate school with the AEI, ran unsuccessfully for Congress on the Republican ticket, chaired the Illinois Federation of Republican Women, helped her husband run a right-wing answer to the ACLU (a typical client was a farmer who refused to obey government quotas), hosted her own radio show, *Wake Up America,* and somehow managed to raise six children. Schlafly captured national attention in 1964 with her paean to Goldwaterism, *A Choice, Not an Echo,* and then secured her place in the conservative pantheon by organizing a large grassroots movement against a proposed Equal Rights Amendment to the constitution that feminists began touting in the late 1960s. Focusing her organization's paltry annual budget of $50,000 on key legislators in swing states, she trained housewives and mothers to appear on radio and television, to testify before legislative committees and to organize letter-writing campaigns. The ERA was never ratified and was eventually ditched in 1978.

If Schlafly was the warrior queen, Paul Weyrich was the Lenin of social conservatism—a revolutionary with a rare talent for organization. Weyrich, whose Free Congress lunch we visited in our introduction, was a working-class boy (his father tended boilers in a Catholic hospital in Racine, Wisconsin, for fifty years) who started his career in journalism and went to Washington in 1967 to work as press secretary for Gordon Allott, a Republican senator from Colorado. There he became convinced that the conservative movement needed to create an establishment of its own to counterbalance such liberal strongholds as the Brookings Institution. In 1971, Allott received an AEI analysis of the administration's plan to fund a supersonic transport plane. The analysis was thorough and well-balanced. It also arrived two days after Congress had voted against the project. Weyrich and another conservative Allott aide on the Hill, Edwin Feulner, were so infuriated by the poor timing that they decided to establish a think tank of their own—but one that would focus on changing laws rather than thinking great thoughts.

The Heritage Foundation was born in 1973. Its early years would have seemed familiar to Lenin struggling in Zurich. It had a staff of just nine (twelve if you counted the three dogs that one employee brought to work), its impact on the czars in Tip O'Neill's Congress seemed negligible and it went through three different heads in its first four years. But by the time Feulner took over as head in 1977, Heritage was beginning to take shape. As with the AEI, this was partly a matter of the ideological wind changing direction. But it also had a lot to do with the sprawling network of sister organizations that Weyrich and his friends were creating or encouraging.

Weyrich's logic was simple: the liberals had managed to dominate Washington by outorganizing the conservatives; now the conservatives must return the compliment. "If your enemy has weapons systems working and is killing you with them," he once explained, in typically bellicose language, "you'd better have weapons systems of your own."[35] He unashamedly modeled these institutions on liberal organizations. His Committee for the Survival of a Free Congress was founded in 1974 to rival the National Committee for an Effective Congress. His Senate Steering Committee was based on the Wednesday Club, a group of liberal Senate Republicans. The Conservative Caucus was modeled on the Democrats' Common Cause. By the late 1970s, the boot was on the other foot: Douglas Fraser, the president of the United Auto Workers, complained that conservatives were "out-lobbying, out-working, out-spending and out-hustling us and, unfortunately, at times they are out-thinking us."[36]

Weyrich may have been the first secretary of social conservatism, but there were other commissars. Richard Viguerie, a wiry Texas Catholic, was a direct-mail genius. His youthful political heroes had been "the two Macs," Douglas MacArthur and Joseph McCarthy, and he had no time for the old-line Republican establishment, longing instead, as his friend William Rusher put it, "for madder music and stronger wine."[37] By 1980 Viguerie's computers held the names of about 15 million contributors. Terry Dolan built up the National Conservative Political Action Committee so that by 1980 it vied with the conservative National Congressional Club for the title of the nation's largest political action committee.[38] The conservative House Republican Study Committee claimed the support of the majority of House Republicans.[39] There were institutions to help organize conservative programs in state legislatures (the American Legislative Exchange Council), influence the media (the National Journalism Center, Accuracy in Media) and pursue their issues in the courts (the National Legal Center for Public Interest). In short, a counterestablishment had been born.

At times the social conservatives overstepped the mark. Reading Viguerie's memoirs from the time (*The New Right: We're Ready to Lead*), an outsider could be forgiven for thinking that this was a slightly barmy sect. These were people who set up groups with names like the Truth Squad and the Committee for the Removal of the President (or CREEP II). But this cranky inventiveness also drove them to look well beyond the Republican Party for allies. In 1973, Viguerie agreed to retire George Wallace's debt from his 1972 presidential campaign in return for his list of donors. Two years later, he floated the idea of a Reagan-Wallace third-party ticket. And throughout the 1970s social conservatives and conservative Democrats joined forces to fight against abortion, liberal school textbooks, affirmative action, gay rights and busing.[40]

THE MORAL MAJORITY

The social conservatives found their most enthusiastic allies in what came to be called the Religious Right. Until the mid-1970s Christian Evangelicals had closer ties to the Democrats than to the Republicans. A majority of Evangelicals voted for Jimmy Carter in 1976. But the Evangelicals chafed at the Democrats' leftward drift. They were particularly incensed when, in 1978, Carter's director of the Internal Revenue Service threatened to deprive all private schools started after 1953 of their tax-deductible status on the grounds that they were presumed to be discriminatory. The majority of private schools in the South were Christian. When the Reverend Tim LaHaye, one of the founders of the Moral Majority, left Carter's office after a particularly unproductive meeting, he bowed his head and prayed: "God, we have got to get this man out of the White House and get someone in here who will be aggressive about bringing back traditional moral values."[41]

Carter had stirred up a formidable enemy. Evangelical religion was on the march. During the 1970s the Southern Baptist Convention's flock grew by

16 percent and that of the Assemblies of God by 70 percent; meanwhile, the United Presbyterian Church declined by 21 percent and the Episcopal Church by 15 percent. In 1980 the two dozen largest churches in America were almost all Evangelical. W. A. Criswell's First Baptist Church in Dallas had a well-equipped fitness center (with saunas, bowling alleys, racquetball courts and a skating rink), 21 choirs, a mission center, a school for 600 pupils, an FM radio station, an annual budget of $8 million and 23,000 members.[42] The Religious Right was as much an electronic community as a physical one. The audience for Evangelical television and radio programs grew from about 10 million in 1970 to perhaps 61 million a decade later. Pat Robertson's *700 Club* and Jerry Falwell's *Old-Time Gospel Hour* reached 15 million people each. The Christian Broadcasting Network was the fifth largest cable network in the country with 30 million subscribers.[43]

Evangelicals initially resisted the temptation to interfere in Caesar's world. In the early 1970s, ministers taught the importance of individual salvation, not collective action. "Preachers are not called to be politicians, but soul-winners," said Jerry Falwell.[44] But Falwell and his cohorts found themselves dragged deeper into politics, provoked, as they saw it, by the country's downward spiral. "Satan had mobilized his forces to destroy America," Falwell explained later. "God needed voices raised to save the nation from inner moral decay."[45]

Plenty of liberals whispered that the moral decay lay with people like Falwell and Robertson seeking fame and power in politics. Still, demand for Christian political action was clearly coming from the pews as well as the pulpits. The IRS decision about private school funding was the final straw for many. The IRS received more than 200,000 letters objecting to the change, more than it had received on any other ruling. The White House and Congress were inundated with mail. Conservative members of Congress held hearings and eventually blocked the new IRS guidelines.

In 1979, social conservatives and the Religious Right made their bond official when Falwell and Weyrich formed the Moral Majority, a term that Weyrich coined during the two men's first meeting. It is a sign of the Christian Right's determination to enter American politics that Evangelicals were willing to meet with a "Catholic" such as Weyrich (even if Weyrich was a

Greek Melkite Catholic rather than a Roman one). The Moral Majority rapidly emerged as a hard-line Christian voice on domestic issues like abortion, school prayer, women's rights and gay rights. Over the next ten years it would register some 2.5 million new voters. The Christian Right rapidly became to the Republicans what blacks had been to the Democrats: the people who could be counted on, who did the work of turning up at meetings, knocking on doors and getting voters to the polls. Many of these footsoldiers were recruited from the part of the country that used to be the Democrats' political parade ground.

THE SOUTHERN REVOLT

In 1972, a bushy-haired young Democratic activist from Yale Law School traveled down to Austin, Texas, to campaign for George McGovern. In the final month before the election, the campaign produced a rousing advertisement urging Texans to stand by the party of Sam Rayburn and LBJ—and to send donations to a post office box in Austin. Each day the activists trooped down to pick up their treasure hoard, only to discover that the box was empty. Eventually a single envelope appeared and was opened back at campaign headquarters. Inside was a piece of excrement-smeared toilet paper and a note explaining that this was what East Texans thought of George McGovern. Richard Nixon went on to win Texas with 67 percent of the vote. It is unlikely that Bill Clinton ever forgot the experience.[46]

The civil rights revolution turned the bulk of Southern whites into loyal Republicans when it came to presidential elections. Richard Nixon won landslide victories in every single Southern state. Southern conservatives also rallied to Reagan's attempt to depose Ford in 1976: a third of his convention delegates came from the South—more than from any other region.[47] But the Republican Party's breakthrough was much slower at the congressional level, and slower still in state politics. The Democratic Party buttressed its position by exploiting the power of incumbency (particularly by gerrymandering districts). It also outflanked the Republicans on the Right. In 1965 and 1970 the majority of Southern Democrats opposed the Voting

Rights Act. Jack Flynt, a Georgia Democrat, laughingly recalled that a Republican challenger once tried to "out-conservative" him: "No matter how hard he tried he couldn't out-conservative me. There just wasn't any room. If he got on the conservative side of me, he'd fall off into the air."[48]

The Democrats' defenses were not strong enough to protect North Carolina from Jesse Helms, however.[49] Helms, who started life as a Democrat, made his name in the state as a right-wing radio and television commentator who relentlessly denounced the "humbug" of "civil rights." In 1972, he ran as the Republican candidate for Senate. Helped by infighting among local Democratic politicians and Nixon's landslide victory over McGovern, Helms easily won over disillusioned Southern whites with his uncompromising views and "he's one of us" slogan; he took the seat by a 54 percent to 46 percent margin and went on to build a huge conservative organization in the state through his Congressional Club—an enormously successful political action committee that meant he never had to rely on his party for funds.

In the Senate, Helms, whose personal courtesy was exceeded only by his public vitriol, quickly displaced Strom Thurmond as Washington's prize example of Southern resistance: a Republican George Wallace, unafraid to express the most elemental views on race and international affairs. "Senator No" soon became the most consistent voice in the Senate for cutting domestic programs, increasing spending on defense, supporting "Christian" rather than "secular" values and doing battle with the evils of communism and the United Nations, which often seemed interchangeable. He supported the apartheid regime in South Africa and sympathized with dictatorships in Latin America. For better or worse, Helms had no interest whatsoever in diluting his beliefs, compromising with his critics or expanding his base of support: in five Senate races he never won more than 55 percent of the vote, despite usually outspending his opponents by huge margins. Unlike Thurmond, who made efforts to bring blacks into the party, Helms refused to make any attempt to come to terms with the civil rights revolution. He ruthlessly played the race card—opposing the idea of a holiday in memory of Martin Luther King Jr. and hinting that blacks were stealing white jobs—in order to polarize voters and attach the white majority to his cause. He was so successful at attracting white former Democrats that they became known as "Jessecrats."

It was hardly pretty, but Helms's brand of Southern Republicanism arguably stood out only because of his crudeness. He dared say out loud what many other Southern Republican politicians communicated through hints and omissions. They didn't spend a month filibustering Martin Luther King Jr.'s holiday (as Helms did when the bill was introduced in 1983); they just voted against it quietly or, like Reagan, talked about states' rights whenever they were in the region. The message got through to the Jessecrats just the same.

WESTWARD, HO

The 1970s were almost as much of a nightmare for the East Coast Republican establishment as they were for old-fashioned Democrats. It was not just Watergate and the defeat of Ford. The common rooms of the great universities, the editorial offices of the *New York Times,* the palatial New York premises of the Council on Foreign Relations—these used to be places for civilized debate between Republicans and Democrats. Now pragmatists like Kissinger and Ford found themselves accused of elitism, racism and imperialism, and many old-style establishment figures were either too cowed or too caught up in the general drift to the Left to defend them. Rockefeller Republicanism lost its brio.

On the other side of the country a new establishment was forming that did not lack for self-confidence. The West was full of successful people who had never given a damn about John Kenneth Galbraith or the Council on Foreign Relations in the first place: people who wanted to reinvent politics just as they had reinvented so many other aspects of American life (and indeed, in many cases, themselves). The West threw up an idiosyncratic conservative antiestablishment.[50] Reagan's kitchen cabinet was full of the sort of businessmen who would have had difficulty getting elected to the Knickerbocker Club and who would have counted an invitation from the Trilateral Commission as an insult: Holmes Tuttle, a car dealer from Los Angeles; Cy Rubel, a Texan oilman; the ubiquitous Joseph Coors; Henry Salvatori, an oil geologist; Walter Annenberg, a publisher; Charles Wick, a nursing home builder; and Justin Dart, a chain-drugstore owner. Many of them had backed Goldwater before turning to Reagan. Most of these men were not in the Rockefeller rank in terms of wealth, but they had more than enough money to spare.

It is fitting that this brand of conservatism marched back onto the national stage in the form of a tax revolt. By the late 1970s Californians were thoroughly fed up with their state's tax code. Property taxes were a particular bugbear: they had risen steeply with house prices at a time when the state government was cutting back on the amount of support it gave to local schools and community services. Middle-class Californians, particularly in Los Angeles, were paying ever more money to receive ever fewer services.

The driving force behind the tax revolt was Howard Jarvis, an idiosyncratic outsider whom the Right had alternately embraced as a hero and denounced as a traitor (he was suspected of pocketing some of the money he raised for Businessmen for Goldwater in 1964). In 1978 Jarvis hit on the idea of using the state's ballot system to reduce property taxes. Proposition 13 promised that all property would be taxed at a flat rate of 1 percent of its actual value, and that there could be no new taxes without further ballots. The entire California establishment lined up against the proposition—the chamber of commerce just as furiously as the labor unions, civil rights groups and public-sector employees.[51] All this counted for naught when set beside the army of angry suburbanites mobilized by Jarvis and Viguerie. The proposition passed by a margin of 65 percent to 35 percent.

Proposition 13 started a peasants' revolt that swept across the country— and indeed across the world. It reminded Americans that their country was founded by a tax revolt, and that politicians were the public's servants, not its masters. Over the next four years at least eighteen states voted for referenda to cut or limit taxes. Republican leaders took to flying around the country in a Boeing 727 nicknamed "The Republican Tax Clipper." Jimmy Carter was so worried by the suburban revolt that he agreed to sign a series of tax breaks, agonizing even as he put pen to paper that the changes would favor the rich. Across the Atlantic, the newly elected leader of Britain's Conservative Party, Margaret Thatcher, interpreted Proposition 13 as yet more proof that her hard-edged brand of conservatism could be sold to the voters. For the first time, the Right seemed to acquire the trappings of a global intellectual movement, with libertarian ideas ricocheting back and forth across the Atlantic.

It was hardly surprising that people in Britain were apoplectic at paying up to 97 percent of their income in taxes. But even in America, where rates never reached those levels, plenty of people were paying more tax than they ever had before. Inflation-generated "bracket creep" meant that millions of people were moving into higher tax brackets. In 1961, nearly nine in ten Americans basically paid a flat tax of 22 percent, but by the end of the 1970s only 55 percent had marginal tax rates below 23 percent.[52] In the same year as Proposition 13, two radical congressmen, Jack Kemp from Buffalo and William Roth from Delaware, dreamed up the Kemp-Roth bill, which proposed cutting tax rates by around 30 percent across the board. It failed to get through Congress, but it added yet more punch to antigovernment conservatism. Meanwhile, at the *Wall Street Journal,* Robert Bartley, the editor of the editorial pages, was giving plenty of space to "supply-side" economists like Arthur Laffer, Jude Wanniski and Robert Mundell, who argued that the best way to get the economy to grow was to cut taxes and government spending and let America's entrepreneurs do the work.

EUREKA: RONALD REAGAN

The conservative movement now had a flotilla of think tanks, an enthusiastic army of followers and a popular cause. All it needed was a charismatic pitchman to sell it to the American people. Ronald Reagan was the answer to years of prayers: a true believer by any standard and a charmer too. At the 1981 Gridiron Dinner in Washington, D.C. (two days before a madman tried to shoot him), Reagan quipped that "sometimes our right hand doesn't know what our far-right hand is doing."[53]

As Steven Hayward points out in *The Age of Reagan* (2001), the Gipper was one of a handful of American presidents who have been genuine outsiders, neither educated in the Ivy League nor nurtured by a big political machine. He went to tiny Eureka College, and he worked in an industry that the established political machines regarded as too silly to bother with.[54] He was also the first American president to embody Western conservatism. He kept a bronze saddle in the Oval Office, rejoiced in his Secret Service code name of Rawhide, spent almost a year of his presidency at his California ranch and—rather magnificently—rushed to appoint Malcolm Baldrige as his commerce secretary when he learned that Baldrige's hobby was roping cattle at rodeos.[55] Many things were a little odd about Reagan, not least his belief in space aliens and his refusal to admit he dyed his hair, but when Reagan presented himself as an outsider who knew little of the "puzzle palaces of the Potomac," he was not inventing things.

Reagan started life within the Democratic fold: a self-described "near hemophiliac liberal" who worshipped FDR and spent years as a trade union boss in Hollywood. But he moved steadily to the right in the 1950s and his speech supporting Goldwater's faltering campaign at the 1964 convention turned him overnight into a conservative hero (and earned considerable jealousy from Goldwater himself). Two years later Reagan shocked the political establishment by trouncing Edmund G. ("Pat") Brown for the governorship of California by almost a million votes, and turned out to be a surprisingly successful governor, combining hard-line rhetoric on student unrest with surprisingly liberal policies on the environment and abortion. Age could easily have ended his political ambitions had he not been willing to seize the moment. He broke his own eleventh commandment ("Thou shalt not speak ill of a fellow Republican") by challenging Gerald Ford for the nomination in 1976. By 1980 the aging screen actor could rely on the unbridled energies of the Republican Right.

Reagan was an archetypical Western conservative who believed in reducing the size of government and smiting communism wherever it lurked. But he had also been one of the few prominent non-Southern politicians to oppose both LBJ's Voting Rights Act and his Civil Rights Act, and he knew how to rope in Southern whites. (On Trent Lott's advice, Reagan launched his postconvention presidential campaign in Philadelphia, Mississippi—a town in which the local police had famously done little to investigate the murder of three civil rights workers.)[56] As for the Christian Right, the Hollywood divorcé convinced them that he was on their side, less through his actual positions on the culture wars than through his ability to reduce politics of all sorts to certain core principles. "There are simple answers," he liked to say, "just not easy ones."[57] This approach was particularly resonant in foreign policy, whose shortcomings Reagan blamed on "the fetish of complexity, the trick of making hard decisions harder to make—the art, finally, of rationalizing the non-decision."[58]

Yet if Reagan was a true believer, he was a true believer without the usual personality defects—a sectarian with an ecumenical style. Oliver Wendell Holmes's famous description of FDR—that he possessed a second-class mind but a first-class temperament—was equally true of FDR's lifelong admirer. Reagan was an optimist in a party that had acquired a habit of pessimism. He had no doubt that there was something buried deep in the American character that could pull the country out of any temporary funk, and he had a knack for using humor to defuse the conservative movement's biggest problem: the widespread fear that it was dominated by wild-eyed extremists. In the 1960s most conservatives went into paroxysms of rage when student radicals were mentioned. Governor Reagan quipped that they "act like Tarzan, look like Jane and smell like Cheetah."[59] He told audiences who were reeling from news of some student atrocity or other that he had had a terrible nightmare the previous night: he had inherited a laundromat in Berkeley. Or he joked that a liberal's idea of being tough on crime was to give longer suspended sentences. "Believe me," he liked to say, "*Bedtime for Bonzo* made more sense than what they were doing in Washington."

Were the American people ready for such a conservative figure? In 1980, the Rockefeller wing of the Republican Party worried that Reagan's candidacy would produce a disaster. The pollsters predicted a close election, but Reagan shook up politics by pulling "conservatives of the heart" into the Republican camp. In 1980, Reagan carried 44 states with a total of 489 electoral votes. The GOP also picked up 12 seats in the Senate—giving it a majority for the first time in a quarter of a century—and 33 seats in the House. In 1984, he clobbered Walter Mondale by 59 percent to 40 percent, gaining a majority in every region in the country, in every age group and in every occupational group except the unemployed.[60] Mondale got only 13 electoral votes, fewer than Strom Thurmond did in 1948 (39 votes) or George Wallace in 1968 (46): indeed the only candidate from a major party to do worse than Mondale was Alf Landon, who got 8 votes in 1936 against Reagan's hero, FDR.

For the Right, the Reagan era was the first time that one of their own was in the White House, a sensation that they did not have again until George W. Bush's administration. Norman Podhoretz boasted that not only were most of the upper echelon of Reagan's administration *Commentary* readers, but a few of them (including Jeane Kirkpatrick) were even *Commentary* writers. More than fifty of the members of the antidétente Committee on the Present Danger received appointments in the administration.[61] William Rusher gives the example of a few days in Reagan's timetable in early 1983: on February 21, he attended a large reception in Washington, D.C., for the *National Review,* declaring it his "favorite magazine"; two days later he gave James Burnham and Clare Boothe Luce medals of freedom; and three days after that he gave the speech at Terry Dolan's annual CPAC conference, something he had done eight times in the previous ten years.[62]

Reagan's record was not quite as perfect as conservative nostalgia suggests. His failure to cut public spending while cutting taxes increased the national debt by $1.5 trillion—and put a question mark over conservative stewardship of the economy that remains to this day. His administration was marred by a constant struggle between the Reaganauts and the pragmatists. Michael Deaver, a leading pragmatist, even went so far as to try to prevent the president from receiving *Human Events,* a magazine that he had subscribed to for years, but Reagan got around the fatwa by having the magazine delivered directly to the White House residence.[63] Reagan, who survived an assassination attempt only three months into his presidency, frequently gave the impression of being detached; this was an administration in which the first lady's astrologer was at times as much of an inspiration as Hayek. For all his overtures to the Christian Right, this easygoing divorcé did relatively little to help conservative cultural causes such as the antiabortion movement. "I don't give a damn about the right-to-lifers," Nancy Reagan once declared as she deleted a discussion of abortion from the 1987 State of the Union message.[64]

Some conservatives grumbled, but who on the Right could really doubt that Reagan's big successes—winning the Cold War, revitalizing the country's economy and restoring America's sense of pride—outweighed such failures? Reagan began his presidency by pulverizing organized labor, sacking more than ten thousand members of the air-traffic-controllers' union for striking (even though the union had been one of the few to support his presidential bid). He increased military spending by a third between 1981 and 1985. His tax cuts weakened the progressive principle, sending the top tax rate tumbling from 70 percent to 33 percent. He took the opportunity provided by Supreme Court Chief Justice Warren Burger's resignation in 1986 to remake the Court, elevating its most conservative member, William Rehnquist, to Chief Justice and naming another conservative, Antonin Scalia, to the resulting vacancy.

By the end of Reagan's term all the pieces on the Right seemed to be in place. Republicans had a lock on California and the West. The South was now Republican territory—undoubtedly in presidential elections and increasingly in congressional ones. Buoyed by these new recruits, the congressional Republican Party had become a more conservative outfit. Between 1972 and 1986 the average rating for Republican House members from the American Conservative Union increased from 63 percent to 75 percent.[65] The Religious Right was on the march. White ethnics in the North were ceasing to think of themselves as Democrats (one of Reagan's slogans for reelection in 1984 was "You haven't left the Democratic Party, the Democratic Party left you"). The American people seemed to be fully committed to small government. The Right had won the great foreign-policy argument of the Cold War. Who would have predicted that within four years that scruffy McGovernite from Arkansas would be sitting in the White House or that California would be a Democratic stronghold?

CHAPTER 4

THE FIFTY-FIFTY NATION,
1988–2000

IN THE 1990S, American conservatism met its nemesis in the shape of a charming baby boomer from Arkansas. It is hard to exaggerate how exciting Bill Clinton once seemed. One of us first encountered him at the fall meeting of the Democratic National Committee at the Biltmore Hotel in Los Angeles in October 1991. The event was, frankly, a chore. It was a hot day, and the prospect of meeting the Democratic presidential candidates was hardly enticing. Even though the economy was in the dumps, it seemed inevitable that George H. W. Bush, the victor of Desert Storm, would eventually romp home. That "inevitability" was one reason why the best-known Democrat, Mario Cuomo, hadn't made it to Los Angeles. The mood at the Biltmore was perfectly captured by two Southern journalists sweltering dismissively by a low-cal buffet. "I'm bored," the fatter of them announced. "Let's buzz Hillary."

Around the room small groups of their fellow scribes dutifully talked to the prospective candidates, but one group was already much bigger than the rest—and kept growing the more the candidate talked. You did not have to spend much time with Clinton to realize that he was a natural. There was the firm, long *Primary Colors* handshake, the immediate feeling of intimacy. There was also the fact that he really knew his stuff. Day care in Orange County, welfare reform in Minnesota, policing in Germany: the man had an encyclopedic knowledge of social policy. And as the ideas kept coming, you realized that this was not old-style liberalism. Clinton didn't want to expand welfare, he wanted to change it. He supported free trade adamantly, talked a tough line on foreign policy and favored the death penalty. Here, at last, was a Democrat—or rather a New Democrat—whom middle-class America could support.

Perhaps it was not hard for a young man full of ideas to shine when set against George Bush, a cold-warrior whose Cold War was over and who couldn't even order "a splash of coffee" without coming across as an out-of-touch patrician. That belies the big point about Clinton. The New Democrat at the Biltmore Hotel was as close to a conservative-killing machine as liberal America could produce: the best communicator of his age, with a Southern accent and a centrist message. To conservatives he soon became the devil incarnate—not just because his sins were so numerous but because he was so darned good at politics. Newt Gingrich once watched Clinton make a State of the Union speech and thought: "We're dead. There is no way we're going to beat this guy."[1] Despite a string of follies, both personal and political, Clinton left office with the best sustained job-approval ratings since JFK.

Clinton was not the only challenge the Right faced in the 1990s. Indeed, if American conservatives were not such a God-fearing bunch, they might have paused to wonder why the Almighty chose to hurl so many thunder-bolts in their direction in barely a dozen years. The fall of communism, welcome though it was, rid the conservative movement of the one thing that could always bind it together. The first Bush presidency ended in fratri-cidal chaos. Having twice imagined that they had changed American poli-tics for good—in 1968 and 1980—conservatives found that America was still a "fifty-fifty nation." All the talk was of swing voters—this was the decade when the soccer mom's SUV pulled up at the polling booth—and of establishment-busting candidates like Buchanan, Perot and John McCain.

But was it really such a disastrous time for the conservative movement? The decade ended with a far more conservative Bush in the White House and with the Republicans in control (albeit barely) of both houses of Con-gress. More important, the 1990s demonstrated the limits of liberalism.

Left-wing America was given the answer to all its prayers—the most talented politician in a generation, a long period of peace and prosperity, and a series of Republican blunders—and the agenda was still set by the Right. Clinton's big achievements—welfare reform, a balanced budget, a booming stockmarket and cutting 350,000 people from the federal payroll—would have delighted Ronald Reagan. Whenever Clinton veered to the left—over gays in the military, over health care—he was slapped down. And when his anointed successor, Al Gore, tried to rekindle liberal populism, he lost an unlosable election.

THE UNDERREACHING MR. BUSH

The dozen years between the first George Bush's run for the White House in 1988 and his son's in 2000 unfolded in a surprisingly musical form: four years of conservative underreach (the first Bush presidency); two years of liberal overreach (the first two years of Bill Clinton); two years of conservative overreach (the "Gingrich revolution"); then four years of liberal underreach (the second Clinton term).

There are two ways to look at the first Bush presidency. One is as an example of dutiful public service. A decent pragmatist shepherded the Atlantic Alliance through the traumatic end of the Cold War, punished Saddam Hussein by mobilizing the United Nations, moderated the excesses of the Reagan era and laid the groundwork for the long Clinton boom by making unpopular decisions. That view is the one that most Americans and Europeans now share,[2] and Bush's approval ratings have risen steadily since he left office. But it is decidedly not the view of the conservative movement.

With the son's installation in the White House in 2001, it was easy to forget how much the father was loathed by the Right. In 1988, Vice President Bush faced strong primary challenges from Pat Robertson, a champion of the Religious Right, and Pete DuPont and Jack Kemp, idealistic tax cutters. After Bush's defeat in 1992, many conservatives talked about "the Bush-Clinton years" as if they were part of the same ghastly drift. Here is Dick Armey, then a Republican congressman from Texas, looking back from 1995:

When Ronald Reagan left for California on January 20, 1989, George Bush was left with more assets than any president in history. A thriving economy. A world awakening to new freedom. Socialist ideas in disgrace . . . Seeing liberalism in its death throes, voters turned to George Bush [H. W.] and said, "Finish it off!" Instead, they got a reversal of the Reagan revolution.[3]

To Armey and his allies, the 1988 campaign made clear that Bush was no Ronald Reagan. When Bush was denounced as a wimp on the cover of *Newsweek* or dismissed as "every woman's first husband" on the late-night talk shows, the liberal media were merely saying publicly what many conservatives muttered privately. For a time it looked as if Michael Dukakis could take advantage of this.

If the Clinton at the Biltmore Hotel was the perfected Terminator, Dukakis was an earlier cyborg—a redesigned Democrat with vital bits missing. He was certainly a break from Walter Mondale, who had run as an unreconstructed New Dealer in 1984. Dukakis drew on the technocratic "neoliberal" ideas that Gary Hart had championed in 1984 (and would have tried to promote again in 1988 had he not been caught frolicking with an actress on a boat called *Monkey Business*). Neoliberalism was basically a creed aimed at suburban voters: it abandoned leftish stances on economic issues (Dukakis proposed no new taxes) but still took a "civilized" European approach to cultural issues like gun control, the environment and the death penalty. The efficient-looking governor of Massachusetts leaped to a big lead in the spring. When Grover Norquist, the antitax activist, turned up at his Harvard reunion, his liberal peers taunted him with the news that Bush was seventeen points behind.[4]

Bush's campaign manager, Lee Atwater, wore down the Dukakis advantage with a campaign, largely aimed at blue-collar voters, that focused on the downright un-American nature of this European approach. Dukakis, the Bush campaign roared, was a "card-carrying member of the ACLU [American Civil Liberties Union]," a man who let black rapists like Willie Horton out of prison early so they could add murder to their list of crimes and who was soft on defense (a message reinforced by pictures of Dukakis riding in a tank, looking nerdy). The old Reagan coalition duly rallied, with

Bush winning 81 percent of the votes of Evangelical Christians—more even than Reagan—and a majority of white male votes at all income levels.[5]

If Bush the candidate was prepared to fight like a Southern redneck, Bush the president preferred to govern like a Tory paternalist ("That's history," he said of Atwater's antics). Margaret Thatcher, who once famously told him, "You're not going to go wobbly on me now, George," immediately recognized Bush as a "wet"—a pragmatic toff for whom ideology mattered less than good government. All of a sudden, government was no longer the problem. In his first speech outside the White House grounds, Bush told a crowd of senior civil servants that they were one of the most important groups he would ever speak to: "Each of us is here because of a belief in public service as the highest and noblest calling."[6] The idea that Reagan's successor could hail government service as the highest calling was anathema to true believers.

There were other heresies too. What was this mantra about a "kinder, gentler nation"? Surely that endorsed the liberal calumny that the 1980s had been a decade of greed.[7] What was this promise to be the environmental president other than an endorsement of the libel that Reagan had trashed the wilderness? And abroad, rather than speeding up the fall of communism, Bush, in the neocons' view at least, preferred to slow it down: he carried on treating the enemy as the legitimate government even when it barely had control of its own streets. At home, Bush gave the impression to the Right that he regarded domestic policy as a Democratic fief. It was best either to leave things alone (his chief of staff, John Sununu, suggested at one point in 1991 that Congress "come together, adjourn and leave" because the White House did not have any bills to send up the Hill) or try to strike sensible compromises.[8] The Clean Air Act and the Americans with Disabilities Act infuriated the Right, not just because they expanded government but because they showed Bush's disdain for the "vision thing." "We don't have ideologies," one senior official told the *Washington Post,* "we have mortgages."

This message of pragmatism over principle was sent out even more emphatically at a personal level. There were small pockets of conservatism, notably the vice president's office, which was run by Irving Kristol's son Bill, and Jack Kemp's Department of Housing and Urban Development. In general, though, Bush tried to replace the glue of shared beliefs with that of dynastic loyalty. The key question was: What was your relationship with the president? At times this was comical. One of Bush's secretaries, Nancy Huang, was the daughter of the owner of the president's favorite Chinese restaurant in Houston.[9] Chase Untermeyer, who had himself served as an intern in Bush's congressional office back in the mid-1960s, was given the job of weeding out the Reaganites and replacing them with Bushies. The forms that job seekers had to fill out asked candidates to specify their "Bush experience."[10] No wonder the conservative intellectuals who graced the *Wall Street Journal*'s editorial page were so hard on Bush from the outset.

The footsoldiers also felt neglected. During the presidential campaign, Bush desperately courted the Right, promising not to raise taxes, speaking at Evangelical gatherings and talking about his own religious convictions. Then, with the election in the bag, he forgot all about them. In the Reagan era, the White House had created a Public Liaison office to reach out to conservative activists. Sununu quickly folded this into his empire and then reduced the number of officials in the office who dealt with conservatives to one, expanding the Public Liaison's outreach to include all interest groups, not just Republican ones.[11] By the time Sununu left office in the spring of 1992, conservatives were trading stories about being treated with disrespect: "I'm going to cut your balls off with a chainsaw," Sununu screamed at Richard Lesher when the Chamber of Commerce chief criticized the 1990 budget deal on a television show.[12]

If Bush failed to pay his dues to the conservatives, he was all too polite with the Democrat-controlled Congress. As a former congressman, Bush had a very high opinion of the institution, and he often presented himself more as a prime minister than a president. "I don't think about the word 'mandate,'" he said as president-elect. "I want to work with Congress to determine the will of the people." From the Right's perspective, Congress set the agenda of the Bush presidency far too often, and the president criticized his Democratic corulers far too little, despite, to conservative eyes, a rich field of targets, from Ted Kennedy's involvement in a Palm Beach rape case to a money-laundering scandal in the House post office.

The Right had a point. Bush's refusal to confront the Democrats turned out to be a classic story of short-term benefits and long-term disaster. Even though Bush's approval rating reached 91 percent (in the spring of 1991, as the returning troops marched past him down Pennsylvania Avenue), his chances of a second term were wrecked by two new political animals: a new breed of highly partisan Republican in Congress and a new breed of centrist Democrat in the country. These types were personified by two precocious young baby boomers—both intensely bright, both the products of broken homes, both sex obsessed—who would dominate politics for much of the 1990s.

NEWT AND BILL

Newt Gingrich first made his name in May 1984, when he was denounced by an enraged Tip O'Neill, the long-serving Speaker of the House. In an earlier late-night speech, the young Georgia congressman had taunted several Democrats, accusing them of being "blind to communism" and challenging them to respond. At the time, C-SPAN's cameras were allowed to show only the member speaking, so viewers had no way of knowing that none of Gingrich's victims were in the chamber. "It's the lowest thing I've seen in thirty-two years in Congress," fumed O'Neill—but in so doing he broke Congress's own rules of etiquette, and his words had to be excised from the *Congressional Record,* an indignity no Speaker had suffered since 1798.

For Gingrich, O'Neill's humiliation was a sign to redouble his efforts. Six years before, the idealistic former college professor had burst into Congress with the modest aims of taking the House back from the Democrats and overthrowing the "liberal welfare state." For Gingrich, momentum was everything. "I have enormous personal ambition," he explained in 1985. "I want to shift the entire planet. And I'm doing it."[13] Gingrich threw out ideas, memos, videotapes at an astonishing rate. He even took to ringing one Reagan official at 6:30 each morning in the belief that he could influence the White House's thinking for the rest of the day.[14]

In Gingrich's world, the Democrats were not just wrong; they were corrupt. Breaking the clubby rules of Congress, he called his opponents "stupid" and "immoral."[15] Gathering a group of fellow bomb throwers in the Conservative Opportunity Society, he hit on the idea of exploiting cable TV's C-SPAN, then ignored by most congresspeople because of its low ratings, as a medium to deliver a relentless series of short, sharp attacks on the Democrats—like the one that infuriated O'Neill. When O'Neill gave up the Speakership in 1987, Gingrich focused on exposing the sins of the new Speaker, Jim Wright. His evidence against Wright was slight, to put it mildly (Wright's worst sin seemed to be getting a special deal on a contract to write a book). Many Republicans urged Gingrich to stop digging, but in 1989 the House Ethics Committee indicted the Speaker on five counts, claiming he had broken fifty-nine House rules. Eventually, Wright was forced to resign— to the embarrassment of moderate Republicans and the complete jubilation of Gingrich's radicals.

Gingrich symbolized a new period of furious partisanship that underlined that the parties were no longer labels of convenience but of ideology. Between 1972 and 1986, the gulf between the two parties in the House (as measured by their average voting-record ratings from the American Conservative Union) had widened from 31 percentage points to 55. (See Appendix.) In the Reagan years, Democrats had forgotten all the old rules about civility in judicial appointments by lashing into Robert Bork, a conservative intellectual who was nominated by Reagan for the Supreme Court in 1987. Rather than questioning him politely, Ted Kennedy ranted about Bork ushering in a period of backstreet abortions. George Bush's attempts as president to be gentlemanly did nothing to prevent more "Borking." His first nominee for defense secretary, Senator John Tower, was accused of a string of minor personal misdemeanors by his former colleagues amid a "feeding frenzy" of often exaggerated press speculation.[16] The battle over Clarence Thomas, a black conservative whom Bush nominated to the Supreme Court in 1991, took the politics of personal destruction to new depths—particularly when Anita Hill, a young law professor, accused Thomas of making improper comments to her. Democrats leaked details about the judge renting pornographic videos, and conservatives smeared Hill in books and columns: the judge's accuser was "a little bit nutty and a little bit slutty," pronounced the *American Spectator* in March 1992 in an article the author, David Brock, later admitted was based on false information.[17]

But Bush's problems were as much with the Gingrichites as with the Democrats. The 1980s had seen a growing split in Republican ranks between pragmatic senators such as Bob Dole, who were prepared to raise taxes to reduce the deficit, and die-hard tax cutters. Bush had jumped from one side of the divide (denouncing Reagan's "voodoo economics" in the 1980 campaign) to the other ("Read my lips: No new taxes" in 1988). As president, he chose pragmatic economic advisors, such as Richard Darman and Nicholas Brady, who convinced him that the only way to get the economy back into shape was to cut the deficit.

On the morning of June 26, 1990, a routine-looking statement was pinned up on the White House bulletin board. The statement was the product of negotiations between the White House and the Democratic leadership in Congress, and it signaled that the two sides had agreed on a deficit-reform program that included "tax revenue increases."[18] By that afternoon, some ninety House Republicans had sent a letter to Bush vowing to vote against any such package. The White House bet that Gingrich's troops would fall in line, and unveiled a package raising $130 billion in new taxes over the next five years. But it was voted down, with 105 Gingrichites joining forces with left-wing Democrats who wanted even more redistribution. With Gingrich intransigent, the only way that the wretched Bush could get the bill passed was by luring in more Democrats with tax rises (including a hike in the income tax top rate from 28 percent to 31 percent). The president was furious with Gingrich; but many conservative footsoldiers regarded Bush's retreat on taxes as traitorous. As the economy worsened, they flocked to Pat Buchanan, a conservative commentator who mounted a pitchfork rebellion against King George.

Buchanan represented yet another growing faction in the fast-splintering coalition of the Right: the paleoconservatives. At home these traditionalists wanted lower taxes and a tougher stance in the culture war; abroad, the fiery former speechwriter offered a Taftian return to isolationism, protectionism and America-Firstism. With the Cold War over, he argued, America needed to keep out of imperial entanglements. "There are a lot of things worth fighting for," he said of the Gulf War, "but an extra 10 cents on a gallon of gasoline is not one of them."[19] Picking a fight with the neocons, Buchanan blamed the war on "the Israeli Defense Ministry and its amen corner in the United States."[20] This provoked charges of anti-Semitism, but Buchanan's angry nativism provided a convenient receptacle for conservative fury against the Bush administration and he won nearly 40 percent of the vote in the New Hampshire primary in January 1992, helping to set up Bush's defeat that November.

That defeat might still have been avoided if the Democrats had not begun to twist themselves into a credible shape. The Democratic Leadership Council (DLC) had been founded in 1985 by Al From, a clever young congressional aide, to prize the party away from the rainbow coalition of radical interest groups whom he dubbed "its new bosses."[21] From deliberately modeled his creation on conservative groups like Heritage; indeed, in 1989 the DLC spawned a think tank, the Progressive Policy Institute (PPI). Powered by smart young Democrats from the West and South, the DLC was initially shunned as being too white, too cerebral and too probusiness: "Democrats for the leisure class" in Jesse Jackson's acerbic phrase. But it won growing influence through the sheer clarity of its analysis.

The DLC took a different stance on cultural issues from neoliberals like Dukakis. Its members were hawkish on defense and asked tough questions about social policy. Could Democrats continue to accuse anybody who wanted black single mothers to take more responsibility for their children of being "racist"? Was the Democratic Party the party of the teachers' unions or of education? The PPI's first paper argued against a higher minimum wage and in favor of a larger earned-income tax credit.[22] In electoral terms, From was looking beyond soccer moms to Reagan Democrats—particularly white blue-collar workers in the Rust Belt, who even Democratic polls showed to be infuriated by liberal attempts to suck up to minorities.

Various Democrats, including Al Gore, had served as mouthpieces for the DLC's ideas, but from the moment Clinton became head of the organization in 1990, it was plain that he could sell its message better than anybody else could. Middle-class voters, Clinton kept on insisting to his party, "have not trusted us in national elections to defend our national interests abroad, to put their values into social policies at home, or to take their tax money and spend it with discipline."[23] Ever since 1972, when Richard Nixon had managed to frame the election as "square America versus radical America," the Democrats had been pitching their tent in radical America. The saxophone-playing Clinton was hardly a square, but neither could he be dismissed as a Dukakis. He attacked Bush for being too soft on China and Sister Souljah, a black activist, for being racist.

It is a mark of George H. W. Bush's lack of political touch that he failed to take Clinton seriously until it was too late. He once pointed toward his chair in the Oval Office and said, "Can you imagine Bill Clinton sitting there?" to the general mirth of his aides.[24] Interestingly, one person who was fully aware of Clinton's potential was Lee Atwater. In 1990, he hatched a plan to get Tommy Robinson, an Arkansas congressman, to run against Clinton for the governorship of Arkansas. ("We're going to throw everything we can at Clinton—drugs, women, whatever works," he is supposed to have said. "We may win or not, but we'll bust him up so bad he won't be able to run again for years.")[25] The plot went awry when Robinson failed to win the Republican nomination, but many conservatives think that Atwater, who died in March 1991, was the one man who could have kept Clinton out of the White House in 1992.

Certainly the Republicans tried. Throughout the election campaign, Clinton was fingered as a draft dodger, an adulterer, a dodgy real-estate investor and the husband of a divisive feminist. None of it worked. Clinton stuck to the economy, and Bush simply ran out of ideas. In April 1992, the Los Angeles riots prompted a slew of suggestions from Clinton and Gingrich, but none from the White House. Bush's own approval rating declined by 57 points between the Gulf War and the Republican Convention in Houston. That convention was an unadulterated disaster: voters saw the intolerant Right of the Republican Party in full cry, with Buchanan urging people to arm themselves for the coming cultural war and Pat Robertson railing against Clinton's deviant lifestyle. As the election drew near, one of us approached a collection of clean-cut young men emerging from an action film in Salt Lake City. Whom would they vote for? They paused. Eventually one of them, a veteran of the Gulf War, replied: "Bush, probably." When an incumbent Republican president can't inspire much enthusiasm from Steven Seagal–loving Mormon veterans, he is in trouble. George H. W. Bush duly suffered the fourth biggest decline in his share of the vote for any sitting president—and won just 168 electoral college votes, against Clinton's 370.

The result was a burst of cheering not just in Little Rock, where the Clintonites danced around to Fleetwood Mac's "Don't Stop (Thinking about Tomorrow)," but also in many parts of conservative America. By the end of the Bush presidency, conservative writers like George Will and Paul Gigot almost seemed to welcome a Republican defeat. "Oh yeah, man, it was fabulous," recalled Tom DeLay, the hard-line congressman from Sugarland, Texas, who had feared another "four years of misery."[26] At Heritage, a group of young conservatives called the Third Generation conducted a bizarre tribal rite: they filled a hall with like-minded people and entered bearing a plastic head of the deposed president on a platter with bloodred crepe paper.[27]

Had George H. W. Bush really ruined everything? The polling numbers suggest that he was beaten by two factors. The first was the economy, which grew more slowly under him than under any recent president. But this was hardly Bush's fault. In football terms, Reagan had given Bush "a hospital pass": Bush caught the presidency at the same time as a host of economic bad tidings arrived. In fact, many of the things that Bush did to tackle the deficit were sensible enough. The second factor was Ross Perot, a Texas businessman with a grudge against the Bush family and an obsession with that deficit. The diminutive Texan captured 19 million votes in 1992, the best showing by a third-party candidate since 1912.

There was another lesson lurking in the exit polls. Although Perot voters told pollsters that they preferred Clinton to Bush, it was Perot, not Clinton, who detached them from the Republican Party—and their main concerns, such as fiscal prudence and distrust of government, were conservative ones. Clinton was elected with 43 percent of the vote—the same proportion that the lackluster Dukakis had received. Despite all his attempts to reach out to blue-collar voters, Clinton won by hanging on to his base, while Perot divided the Reagan coalition. As Ronald Brownstein and Dan Balz point out in *Storming the Gates* (1996), Clinton's victory in 1992 was similar to Nixon's in 1968, when George Wallace split the Democratic base. To create anything more permanent, Clinton now had to follow Nixon's example and bring the Perot voters into his own coalition.[28]

CLINTON: LIBERAL OVERSTRETCH

Unfortunately for the Democrats, the new president set off in the opposite direction. Inexperienced and tired (he refused to take a break between the election and the inauguration), Clinton fell into three traps within days of his victory.

On November 11, the president-elect was asked whether he would fulfill a campaign promise to let gays serve openly in the military. One of the best wafflers in American politics gave a surprisingly direct answer—and just said yes. The result was a firestorm of criticism from nearly every American in uniform, from the chairman of the Joint Chiefs, Colin Powell, on down. Eventually, Clinton compromised and accepted a "Don't ask, don't tell" policy, but the damage had been done. Short of walking around the bowling alleys and bars of the Rust Belt with a sign proclaiming himself to be a "Faggot-loving draft dodger," Clinton could not have sent a clearer message to blue-collar voters that he was really Dukakis in disguise.

The idea that Clinton was a closet liberal was reinforced by his second mistake: an increasingly ridiculous search for a politically correct cabinet. An obvious gesture for a New Democrat would have been to recruit a few Republicans. Instead, Hillary Clinton oversaw an auction between left-wing interest groups, with great store being set on finding a female attorney general. The first two candidates were duly "Borked" by the vengeful Republicans, and the Clintons were saddled with Janet Reno, whose main qualification for the job, even Clintonites admitted, was her gender.

The last mistake was to woo the increasingly unpopular Democrats in Congress. Rather than trying to attract Republican moderates (there were probably ten senators and forty or so congresspeople who were there for the taking), Clinton became obsessed by keeping the Democrats together, which inevitably meant a more liberal stance. The sleek modernizer was now carrying a lot of old baggage. "We took Secretariat," lamented one DLC man, referring to the racehorse, "and hooked him to a fucking plow."[29]

To make things worse, the Republicans were bruising for a fight. In the Senate, Bob Dole announced that he was going to represent the 57 percent of the electorate who did not vote for Clinton—and promptly organized a successful filibuster of Clinton's economic stimulus plan. In the House, the Republican leadership was still nominally in the hands of Robert Michel, a moderate of the old school, but the momentum was with Gingrich. Shortly after the election, he summoned his team to a seminar where he laid out his ambitions on flipcharts:

Gingrich — primary mission.

Advocate of Civilization.

Definer of Civilization.

Teacher of the Rules of Civilization.

Arouser of those who Fan Civilization.

Organizer of the pro-civilization activists.

Leader (possibly) of the civilizing forces.

A universal rather than an optimal Mission.[30]

Together with Haley Barbour, the party's new chairman, Gingrich focused the Republican message in 1993 on disgust with Washington. Barbour quadrupled the party's direct-mail operation, soon discovering that the best way to raise money was to demonize the Clintons.

Clinton stirred up feelings of hatred in the Right Nation unseen since the McCarthy era. The pasting the president received daily from Robert Bartley's troops on the *Wall Street Journal*'s editorial page was of a completely different order from the gentle mockery of George H. W. Bush by Maureen Dowd in the *New York Times*. And the *Journal* was as nothing compared with talk radio or the *American Spectator*, where Richard Mellon Scaife financed a series of half-truthful articles about the Clintons' sex life and dodgy business dealings. Things got particularly out of hand after the suicide of White House counsel Vince Foster, a close friend of Hillary's, in July 1993, shortly after the publication of a *Journal* editorial trying to implicate him in skulduggery. Jerry Falwell sold 150,000 copies of *The Clinton Chronicles*, which claimed that Clinton had ordered the murder of people who might expose his role in a cocaine-smuggling operation.[31]

This was the conservative movement at its ugliest: so ghastly in fact that Clinton apologists have rushed to claim his presidency was hijacked by his enemies, that the national press was led astray by a "vast right-wing conspiracy" (in Hillary Clinton's phrase) into chasing a series of "pseudoscandals" (as Sidney Blumenthal, the president's often comically loyal assistant, still insists on calling the various escapades).[32] It was certainly not the media's finest hour, but, taken as a whole, the hijacking theory does not stand up for two reasons. First, behind most of the bigger stories there was usually some legitimate issue of sleaze or evasion. Was it presidential to start selling off nights in the Lincoln bedroom? Was it sensible to refuse the *Washington Post*'s request in 1993 to see documents on Whitewater, a property deal that involved the Clintons buying some land on what looked like generous terms (but proved not to be) in partnership with some shady Arkansas operators? Aides pleaded with Clinton to hand them over. The first lady said no, and the fuss continued.[33] The second reason why it is hard to blame the problems of the Clinton presidency on people like Scaife is that the sleaze would not have mattered if the president had gotten the governing bit right—which, for the first two years, he generally did not.

Whenever Clinton moved to the center he could still pull off real successes. By rooting his economic policy in cutting the deficit (and thus pleasing the bond market), Clinton paved the way for the later boom and budget surpluses. On the North American Free Trade Agreement (NAFTA), he reached out to the Republicans. In 1993, he assembled four former presidents outside the White House to defend the treaty. Having heard Clinton's pitch, George H. W. Bush gracefully admitted, "Now I know why he's inside looking out, and I'm outside looking in."[34] There were also incremental achievements that turned out to have big effects: for instance, Clinton forced through an earned-income tax credit, making it much more profitable for poor Americans to work than stay at home.

However, the general impression was of liberal overreach—and chaotic liberal overreach at that. By 1994, Clinton seemed incapable of getting bills through Congress. Campaign-finance reform was defeated. A crime bill finally passed, but not before the White House had suffered an embarrassing defeat at the hands of the National Rifle Association and not before it had gotten snared in an argument with the congressional black caucus about giving minority convicts on death row the right to challenge their sentences. But nothing symbolized the overreach better than health care.

The health-care reforms were supposed to be a perfect example of the new liberalism. They would solve the problem of rising health-care costs. They would make it easier for workers to change jobs. And at the same time, they would solve one of the gaping injustices in American society: the fact that more than 40 million Americans had no health-care coverage. Just as the New Deal had created a lasting constituency for Roosevelt's brand of liberalism, health-care reform would create a lasting constituency for Clinton's brand of government activism.[35]

That was the theory. The reality was "Hillary care." Even the most jaded Washingtonians had never seen anything quite like it. By the time the health-care task force run by the first lady and Ira Magaziner delivered its report, it had outdone all previous committees on every imaginable measure: size (it had five hundred full-time members and innumerable hangers-on); complexity (it was divided into fifteen "cluster groups" and thirty-four working groups); rigor (the heads of the working groups had their work reassessed by "auditors" and "contrarians"); and, not least, ambition. At the heart of the final 1,367-page plan stood a proposal to force businesses of all sorts to provide coverage for their employees through huge government-administered plans. Conservatives, egged on by furious small-businesspeople and the insurance industry, soon branded Hillary care a Soviet-style scheme to bring a seventh of the economy under government control. Ironically, the closest thing to an imaginative New Democratic solution was actually put forward by a Republican, John Chafee, who proposed giving individuals health-care tax credits which would work like vouchers. But the Democrats would not budge—and Hillary care duly passed away.

God's LA and Rush's dittoheads

By the 1994 midterm elections, Clinton had passed hardly any liberal legislation, but the mere fact that he tried both enraged and invigorated the conservative movement. Many of the new Republican footsoldiers were an intolerant lot—something Clinton would eventually learn to exploit—but they were also much more organized than ever before. And in a country where so few people could be bothered to turn up at the polls, that counted for a lot.

In some cases, the troops were new recruits. Hillary care, for instance, created a new conservative powerhouse in the form of the National Federation of Independent Businesses, (NFIB), a trade association representing 600,000 small businesses. Small businesses were the ones pumping out new jobs in the 1990s, and the Democrats had hoped to woo them, tagging the Republicans as the party of big business. Instead, Hillary care, which would have forced all businesses to purchase insurance for their workers, drove the NFIB deep into the conservative camp. It became a fiery part of the antiregulation, antitax coalition. A particular target was the tort system, which was naturally associated with the two lawyers in the White House: at one point in 1995, the NFIB generated 265,000 letters a week in support of a bill trying to limit private lawsuits.[36]

Clintonphobia also helped recharge some of the more established brigades on the Right. One might imagine that the 1990s—the era of the Columbine school shootings and the Waco siege—was a dismal decade for the National Rifle Association. But it did not feel that way inside the NRA. In 1991, control of the organization passed from Warren Cassidy, who had tried negotiating with gun-control advocates, to Wayne LaPierre, a hard-headed ideologue. LaPierre proceeded to prove that there was no better recipe for political success than sticking to your guns. He poured money into membership drives and rebuilding the NRA's lobbying machine on Capitol Hill. A particular spur for the NRA was the 1994 crime bill, which the organization fought with Rambo-like gusto. It cleverly changed its opposition from its standard "Guns don't kill people, people do" stance to fiscal probity: the bill had become stuffed with pork, argued the NRA, spreading the message by blast fax and talk radio. It secured the votes of enough rural Democrats for the House to defeat the bill in August 1994. Clinton still got a bill through limiting assault-weapon sales, but that only provided the NRA with a motive to fight all the harder for progun candidates that November, when it spent $3.4 million in targeted campaigns.[37]

In that election, seven in ten gun owners voted Republican. Indeed, the 1990s were a decade when the NRA's flirtation with the Republican Party turned serious. The percentage of the NRA's congressional campaign contributions going to Republicans rose from 61 percent in 1990 to 92 percent in 2000. This support was often embarrassing for the Republicans: George H. W. Bush resigned his life membership in 1995 in response to LaPierre's assertion that "if you have a [police] badge, you have the government's go-ahead to harass, intimidate and even murder law-abiding citizens." But when it came to trooping around precincts and rallying people to the conservative cause, the NRA showed a prowess second only to the Christian Right.

The Christian Right also found a new voice in the 1990s. At Bush's inaugural dinner in 1989, Pat Robertson found himself seated at the same table as a young man with the face of a choirboy but the political instinct of Lee Atwater.[38] Ralph Reed had first come to Washington as the executive director of the College Republicans in 1983, where he succeeded the considerably less fresh-faced Grover Norquist. Norquist claims that Reed was such a meticulous organizer that he even instructed young Republicans how to burn the Soviet flag correctly.[39] Although Reed was a committed Christian, it was harder to miss that he was a committed politician: chat with him and you were more likely to get preached to about polls than about pornography. In time, Republican leaders in Washington jokingly dubbed him God's LA (or legislative assistant). But Reed's real skill was as a grassroots organizer. In 1989, he convinced Robertson that he could turn the remnants of the evangelist's presidential bid into something considerably more potent than the Moral Majority, which had almost run out of steam. The Christian Coalition was born.

Working with his wife, Jo Ann, and a handful of volunteers, Reed built the coalition from the bottom up, getting people in churches to organize chapters and sign up the like-minded. He also stressed a broader agenda than the traditional hell-and-damnation stuff: "The pro-family movement must speak to the concerns of average voters in the areas of taxes, crime, government waste, health care and financial security."[40] True to this picture, the coalition's starting point was frequently schools: it convinced parents not just that their children were attending salons of liberal perversion but also that the Left was lowering academic standards. Protesting against soppy "outcomes-based education" and the like, the coalition targeted particular school districts for electoral raids. Reed, rather foolishly in retrospect, celebrated this stealth: "I paint my face and travel at night. You don't know it's over until you're in the body bag. You don't know until election night."[41]

It is a measure of Reed's organizing skill that by the end of 1990, the Christian Coalition had amassed 125 chapters with 57,000 members. By 1997 it had 2,000 chapters and 1.9 million members. In the 1994 election, Reed's troops helped man telephones for the Republicans, take people to the polls, organize registration drives and tell floating voters about the ungodly habits of the Clintons (only in America could a president who attended church every Sunday and began each of his weekly lunches with the vice president with a prayer be considered irreligious). The coalition distributed 33 million voter guides in 1994, and Republicans won most of the 120 close races where it had concentrated its attention. Exit polls in 1994 showed that 88 percent of churchgoing white Evangelicals cited "family values" as a major factor in how they voted.[42]

A remarkable number of these footsoldiers were now getting their news from one source, known universally as Rush. Until the 1990s it had been an article of faith in conservative circles that they could not get their message across. The liberal establishment completely dominated the television networks and most big-city newspapers, the *Wall Street Journal* being the honorable exception. To counter this, Paul Weyrich founded National Empowerment Television in April 1991—a sort of conservative *Wayne's World,* broadcast out of his office and staffed by Free Congress employees. It became a little more sophisticated when it was spun off as a freestanding organization, but the station nevertheless had a rather shopworn feel—the Cato Forum on libertarianism, the Family Research Council on families and the NRA on guns.

The big breakthrough came not with television but with talk radio—and Rush Limbaugh. A paunchy Missourian of Republican stock, Limbaugh achieved little in life until he was given a job reading the news at a Kansas City radio station. In 1984, a Sacramento radio station, which had recently fired its shock jock, took a flyer on him. Limbaugh tried something new. He had no guests; he just talked. He immediately showed that he had the same rare talent as P. J. O'Rourke: he could be amusing *and* right-wing. That is not to deny that Limbaugh could go over the top. There was nothing funny about calling the twelve-year-old Chelsea Clinton "the White House dog."[43] But his standard schtick was that of the ordinary guy dumbfounded by the crazy system. Why are we paying taxes to support so-called artists who dip crucifixes in urine? Why are university professors being paid to run conferences denouncing all men as rapists? Rush's followers were in such strong agreement with his arguments that they called themselves "dittoheads."

Rush provided these people with one of the most powerful resources in politics: knowledge that they were not alone. By the mid-1990s he was reaching 20 million people a week on 660 stations.

THINKING THE UNTHINKABLE

If Limbaugh provided the soundtrack to the Gingrich revolution, the music was being written in the American Enterprise Institute, Cato and the Manhattan Institute. You could argue that the Gingrich revolution came down to just one idea, summed up with characteristic punchiness by Dick Armey in *The Freedom Revolution* (1995): "The market is rational and government is dumb." That would understate both the complexity and the ferocity of the ideas that were circling on the Right.

The National Committee for Responsive Philanthropy, a leftish watchdog, has calculated that conservative think tanks spent $1 billion promoting conservative ideas in the 1990s. In the vanguard was the AEI, repowered by Chris DeMuth, an up-and-coming conservative who showed some of the same organizational talent as the first Baroody. In New York, the Manhattan Institute provided many of the ideas for Rudy Giuliani's no-nonsense mayorship. In Texas, George W. Bush, running for governor, was drawing on the "compassionate conservative" ideas of Marvin Olasky, an Evangelical Christian based in Texas (who had begun life as a New York Jewish Marxist), and Myron Magnet, a spectacularly sideburned scholar from the Manhattan Institute. A new generation of hyperactive neoconservatives emerged, many of them the offspring of the first generation (Michael Lind has dubbed them the "mini-cons"). For instance, after leaving the Bush White House, Bill Kristol spent a brief time surveying the Right for the Bradley Foundation; then he set up the Project for the Republican Future, a tiny think tank which distinguished itself as the most stubborn opponent of Hillary care (in her memoirs, the former first lady fingers Kristol as the man who turned her noble project into a partisan squabble).[44] He also founded the *Weekly Standard* (in 1996) and established another mini think tank with a foreign-policy bent, the Project for the New American Century.

We will save our main discussion of these organizations for Chapter 6, but one idea cannot wait until then: welfare reform. Welfare, broadly defined, can include everything from housing subsidies to food stamps; in the mid-1990s the government spent around $230 billion a year on various programs to help the needy, with nearly half that amount going to subsidized health care.[45] But the core welfare program that the politicians squabbled about was Aid to Families with Dependent Children, which distributed $12.5 billion in cash almost entirely to single mothers. In 1994, the program covered 14 million people in 5 million families. Nearly one in ten American children was on welfare, a disproportionate number of them black (40 percent) or Latino (20 percent).

Welfare had long been a hobbyhorse of the Right. In the 1980s, Ronald Reagan had protested about "welfare queens" exploiting a system that had been set up in 1935 to look after widows. Both Reagan and George H. W. Bush tried to make welfare recipients look for work, but they did not push hard. The cause of welfare reform was thus left to Republican governors in the states—notably Tommy Thompson in Wisconsin, who cut welfare payments and conducted various experiments (such as penalizing mothers who had more children while on welfare). In 1992, Clinton borrowed one of these ideas, suggesting a time limit for payments; after two years on the rolls mothers would have to take jobs—if necessary, ones provided by the state.

But there were much more aggressive ideas about "personal responsibility" floating around in Republican circles. Two prominent books in 1993 condemned the 1960s as the root of all evil—Myron Magnet's *The Dream and the Nightmare* and Marvin Olasky's *The Tragedy of American Compassion*. Bill Bennett, the first Bush's drug czar, offered *The De-Valuing of America: The Fight for Our Culture and Our Children* (1992) and then the best-selling *The Book of Virtues* (1993) (though it emerged much later that he plowed some of the proceeds unvirtuously into slot machines). Giuliani's zero-tolerance policing in New York, which focused on stopping petty crimes such as graffiti and panhandling in a belief they encouraged more serious felonies, drew heavily on the "Broken Windows" strategy originally outlined by George Kelling and James Q. Wilson.[46]

The man who had the sharpest impact on the welfare debate, however, was Charles Murray. Murray is best known for *The Bell Curve,* a 1994 best-seller that argued, among other things, that the gap in standardized test scores between different racial groups has a genetic component. But he first made his name as an expert on poverty. In *Losing Ground* (1984) he argued that the government was making the problem worse, and suggested, as a "thought experiment," that America simply get rid of the welfare system for people of working age. In October 1993, in a famous *Wall Street Journal* article, "The Coming White Underclass," he transformed the thought experiment into a policy proposal: the government should simply stop paying money to women who produced children out of wedlock.[47] Single-parent families were not viable economic units, so why on earth encourage them? Even though Murray cleverly focused on whites in his piece, it immediately provoked a storm of outrage. This was a far more dramatic assault on the Great Society than the original neocon rebellion. Daniel Patrick Moynihan, the man who had originally spotlighted the problem of the breakup of black families, still thought that government help was the answer. Murray was arguing not just that government social programs were inefficient, but that they were downright cruel and immoral. The question was whether the American public was really ready for this sort of thing.

GINGRICH: REPUBLICAN OVERSTRETCH

On its inauguration day in 1995, the 104th Congress met to choose a new Speaker. When Newt Gingrich's name was announced, he swept into the chamber and mounted the rostrum regally. "It's a whole Newt world," someone yelled.[48]

Republicans had not controlled the House for forty years. Gingrich had conjured up a victory out of nowhere. In November 1994, fifty-two Democrats, including Speaker Tom Foley, lost their seats in the House; another ten lost their seats in the Senate, handing control to the Republicans. And this time it was a thoroughly conservative victory, built on a conservative manifesto. The Contract with America, compiled by the congressional Republicans, was an extraordinary document—a list of ten policy proposals that received the support of more than three hundred GOP candidates and ended with the promise: "If we break this contract, throw us out."[49] The contract epitomized antigovernment conservatism. It included a balanced budget amendment, term limits and welfare reform. Gingrich's insistence on "60 percent issues," which easily commanded majority support, excluded more divisive social issues such as abortion and school prayer. The best the Christian Right got was a $500-per-child tax credit to help families.

By now, Speaker Gingrich saw himself as a Republican prime minister—not just the effective leader of his party in the lower House, but the ruler of the country. Republicans argued that Congress was resuming the role in shaping domestic policy that the framers of the constitution had envisaged. It certainly felt that way for the first three months of the Congress, with Gingrich holding press briefings every day, ushering bills into the House at a rapid clip and even forcing Clinton in April to lamely insist that the president was "relevant."

Nevertheless, Gingrich was overreaching himself. This time it was not a case of betraying promises: unlike Clinton, he certainly began governing as he promised. It was a case of misinterpreting his mandate. In November 1994, most Americans had voted against Bill Clinton, against a man who had $180 haircuts and a socialist wife, rather than in favor of conservative radicalism. The defanging of Gingrich over the next two years was in many ways the mirror-image of Clinton's debacle in 1992–94. He too ran into procedural challenges in Congress; he too faced questions about his personal ethics; he too was pilloried for his extremism; and he too was outmaneuvered by an effective political opposition.

In office Gingrich often behaved like a guerrilla leader who had spent years living off nuts and berries in the jungle only to gorge himself when the gates of the city were thrown open to him. The same man who had skewered Jim Wright over a book deal saw nothing wrong in accepting a $4 million advance for his memoirs from Rupert Murdoch (though in the end, after a huge outcry, nothing was signed). Gingrich's verbal diarrhea—his plans, his ideas, his management jargon (he broke everything down to VSTP—Vision, Strategy, Tactics, Projects)—was less than statesmanlike in government. One book of this period is called *Tell Newt to Shut Up* (1996).[50] But it could also have applied to many of his followers. Dick Armey, for instance, called Barney Frank, a gay congressman, "Barney Fag" on a radio station and told Hillary Clinton "reports of your charms are overrated." Although the House Republicans managed to pass nine out of ten parts of their contract, failing only on term limits, things slowed down in the Senate, which was run by Gingrich's old foe, Bob Dole. The upper chamber rejected the balanced-budget amendment, albeit by one vote; it also threw out plans to give states control over matters like school lunches. When the House Republicans came up with a plan to reduce increases in Medicare, the Democrats a little unfairly condemned them for "cutting" the program, and negotiations with the president about the budget stalled.

Having failed as a liberal president on the offense, Bill Clinton rediscovered his political flair on the defense. The turning point came on April 19, 1995, the day after his plea that the presidency was still relevant, when a right-wing extremist set off a bomb in Oklahoma City, killing 168 people. In a commencement speech at Michigan State University on May 5, Clinton tore into "the militias and all those who believe that the greatest threat to freedom comes from the government." In a passage that might have been aimed at the House Republicans, he warned: "There is nothing patriotic about hating your country, or pretending that you love your country but despise your government."[51]

Tacking to the center with the help of a new advisor, Dick Morris, Clinton followed a strategy of "triangulation" that was supposed to stress his independence from both Republicans and Democrats.[52] When it came to the budget, for instance, Clinton said he was in favor of spending cuts and a balanced budget (unlike his spendthrift party), but he also made a great show of fighting to protect Medicare (unlike those coldhearted Republicans). In the summer, everyone assumed a budget was just a matter of sorting out the details, but months drifted by in haggling. In October the government had to close down for lack of money, and it did again in December.

Gingrich's troops foolishly assumed that this would help them (after all, Clinton had vetoed the budget bills that would have kept government open). However, after twelve months of unrelenting government bashing by Gingrich, most Americans blamed the omnipresent House Speaker. Clinton's political sonar—his ability to say roughly what the American people wanted to hear—was returning. On the night of the government shutdown, he rounded on Armey: "If your budget passes, thousands of poor people are going to suffer because of your Medicaid cuts. I will never sign your Medicaid cuts. I don't care if I go down to 5 percent in the polls." The switch from Medicare to Medicaid was somewhat duplicitous, but it impressed everybody present, especially Al Gore, who muttered something about how they should make clear that they wouldn't give in even if Clinton's popularity went to zero. "Sorry, Al," Clinton replied. "If we hit 4 percent, we're caving."[53]

Whatever political sonar Gingrich had possessed was now turned off. In November, he complained to the press that he had been put in the back of Air Force One on the way back from Yitzhak Rabin's funeral, so the New York *Daily News* ran a cover with him as a crybaby. At the following year's Republican Convention in San Diego, Gingrich was reduced to delivering a brief lecture about the delights of beach volleyball.[54]

The biggest test of triangulation was welfare reform. Clinton vetoed the first two welfare bills from Congress because they were attached to the Medicaid reductions he disliked. In August 1996, the Republicans sent an unadulterated welfare-reform bill to the president—and dared him to sign it (if he balked, it would have provided ammunition for Dole's flagging presidential campaign). This was a much tougher bill than Clinton would have liked.[55] It even put a time limit on government support for poor single mothers. Citing evidence that 1 million children might go without food and shelter, the White House liberals, including his wife, urged him not to sign it; but the DLC crowd, including Gore, pushed in the other direction. Clinton signed it—and thus sealed one of the great conservative achievements of his presidency. By 2000, there were 7.5 million fewer people on welfare.

Even if Clinton had vetoed welfare reform, it would not have saved Dole in November 1996. The economy was on the president's side, and Clinton started raising and spending money early (thus putting off any pesky primary challenges). Dole faced a tough primary contest. Ross Perot popped up again to split the antigovernment vote, and, just like George Bush four years earlier, Dole looked too damned old. He had first gone into Kansas politics in the era of Robert Taft. A straight talker with a quick tongue, Dole could be an amusing man in private. A decade earlier or maybe even a decade later, his war record might have counted for more. Although the conservative movement rallied around Dole a little more loyally than they had around George H. W. Bush, the response was dutiful rather than emotional. Clinton stuck to a centrist message, embellished it in a series of small promises such as tax deductions for college tuition and kept a good distance from the Democrats in Congress. He swept to an easy victory, winning 379 electoral college votes, nine more than in 1992.

That said, the 1996 election was hardly a dramatic victory for liberalism. Bill Clinton won reelection with 49 percent of the vote—ten points less than Nixon and Reagan when they secured second terms. In the Senate, the Republicans gained two more seats, leaving them with a 55–45 majority—a fairly shocking figure when you consider that Clinton had inherited a Senate with 58 Democrats. In the House, the Democrats clawed back a few seats but the Republicans hung on to their majority. As Michael Barone concluded in his biennial review of the election in the *Almanac of American Politics,* 1996 merely reinforced the lessons of 1992 and 1994: that a New Democrat could beat an Old Republican at the presidential level and that New Republicans could beat Old Democrats at the House level.

Moreover, in ideological terms, Gingrich's two years of overreach produced far more red meat than Clinton's. In 1994–96, discretionary spending was cut for the first time since 1969.[56] And of course there was welfare reform. As Malcolm Gladwell pointed out in the *Washington Post,* Democrats barely put up a fight for one of the centerpieces of the New Deal: "The defenders of the old activism toward the poor surrendered willingly, with the shrugs and indifference of those who no longer believed what they stood for."[57] Intellectually, the momentum was still very much with the Right.

Dwight Clinton

During the middle of the 1993 budget battle, Clinton famously wailed that he did not want to be remembered as an "Eisenhower Republican."[58] In his second term, that is pretty much what he became—and America on the whole was mighty pleased with it.

The 1990s were a decade of extraordinary political turmoil: in 1992, George H. W. Bush's implosion left the GOP with its smallest share of the popular vote in eighty years. Two years later Bill Clinton presided over the worst performance of any incumbent party in nearly half a century. Clinton routed Bush by promising a more active government; Gingrich routed Clinton by promising a more limited one.[59] Yet after all this turmoil the fifty-fifty nation finally rediscovered its balance—in the form of a New Democratic president hemmed in on all sides by a Republican Congress. This was not so much "Tory men with Whig measures"—Disraeli's formula for an ideal government—as Democratic men with Republican measures.

There were two reasons why Clinton's second term seemed so insubstantial. The first is that it added little in the way of dramatic new laws. The main pieces of Clinton's legacy—NAFTA, welfare reform, deficit reduction—were all in place; he simply oversaw their fruition and the accompanying peace and prosperity. There was certainly more fiddling to be done, and Clinton began to carve out a minor new role for himself as a foreign policy president, trying to bring about peace in the Balkans, the Middle East and Northern Ireland.

One can make the argument—Joe Klein does it most elegantly in *The Natural*—that all the little things that Clinton achieved (the earned-income tax credits, the restrictions on gun sales, the environmental rules and so on) amount to a sort of big thing. But whatever this big thing was, it was not really a liberal big thing. A bit like Eisenhower, whose smile was his philosophy, Clinton became essentially what people wanted him to be—and in the "third way" he found a suitably capacious creed that suited this. In 1998, in the midst of the Lewinsky storm, Bill Clinton defined his presidency in the following terms:

> We have moved past the sterile debate of those who say that government is the enemy and those who say government is the answer. My fellow Americans, we have found a third way. We have the smallest government in 35 years, but the most progressive one. We have a smaller government but a stronger nation.[60]

The meaning of this passage depends on what is emphasized. Liberals might pick out the word "progressive," conservatives the words "stronger" and "small." Yet when you look at the substance, the conservatives had won most of the arguments. The deficit might have disappeared and the peace dividend might finally have been paid, but Clinton did not spend the surplus on great new liberal programs; instead, he hoarded it under the national mattress. There was certainly an increase in "interfering" regulation, and Clinton's trust busters took on Microsoft, but they took a laissez-faire attitude to the merger frenzy in the late 1990s. The first two-term Democrat for a generation seemed happy that his principal administrative legacy would be putting the federal government's books back in order—something that would have amazed FDR and LBJ, not to mention the bearded McGovernite who went down from Yale to Austin in 1972 to fight for the Great Society.

The other reason the second Clinton term seemed so insubstantial is, of course, Monica Lewinsky. Enough print has already been wasted on Clinton's affair with the intern, his denials of that affair and the Republicans' failed attempt to impeach the president without us adding a blow-by-blow account. Its genesis lay in Clinton's appointing an independent counsel to look into Whitewater shortly after he turned down the *Washington Post*'s request for documents. The first counsel, Robert Fiske, issued a preliminary report in June 1994 clearing the Clintons of some of the wilder charges, but he was replaced by Kenneth Starr, a much more fanatical figure. Clinton loyalists rightly point out that Starr, who had close ties to various conservative groups, steered the inquiry a long way away from its starting point. An investigation into a property deal in Arkansas ended up discussing a somewhat sordid but surely private series of sexual encounters in the Oval Office. The whole thing cost some $50 million without proving anything illegal. Conservatives retort that Starr caught the president in the most barefaced lie of our times ("I did not have sexual relations with that woman"); and Clinton's half-truths resulted in his being barred from practicing law in Arkansas.

In the longer term, the Lewinsky foolishness was a minisaga of overreach on both sides. In Bill Clinton's case, he thought once again he could get away with it (he would make the same mistake with his tawdry pardoning of Marc Rich on the last day of his presidency). In this he was plainly wrong. If Americans rallied around him, it was largely because they distrusted the Republicans even more. A generally successful president is now most often remembered, on late-night talk shows at least, in jokes about cigars and trying to redefine the word "is." He also damaged Al Gore: in 2000, voting patterns would closely follow people's approval ratings of Clinton, and George W. Bush would strike a chord with his talk about bringing dignity to the White House.

Yet if Clinton overreached, so too did conservatives. The extremism of the family-values wing of the Republican Party rallied Democrats to Clinton's cause and infuriated many independents. Was the attempt at impeachment really based on the high crimes and misdemeanors that the constitution demanded—or on just the political ambitions of the self-righteous Right? Many Americans found the hypocritical Puritanism of the Republicans even more stomach-turning than Clinton's exploits. Newt Gingrich, Henry Hyde and Bob Livingston had all led less than perfect lives; what were they doing calling for Clinton to go?

The impeachment hearings reinforced a wider fear that the Republicans had become an intolerant bunch—far too Southern and far too Evangelical. Independents liked their conservatism sunny-side up—the Reagan way. The disastrous Republican presidential conventions in 1992 and 1996 were remembered for the preening Christian Right and the ranting Pat Buchanan. Part of the success of the Contract with America lay in the fact that it eschewed religious causes, but it had not taken long for them to reappear. In May 1995, the Christian Coalition hosted a meeting called "Contract with the American Family," packed with Republican leaders, where Ralph Reed boasted: "We have finally gained what we have always sought: a place at the table, a sense of legitimacy and a voice in the conversation we call democracy."

This sort of talk certainly inspired some conservatives, particularly in the South, but it also frightened away independents, particularly the antigovernment cohorts who voted for Perot. Try as he might to soften Robertson's message, Reed was still under the command of a man who had sent out a fund-raising letter saying that feminists encouraged women "to leave their husbands, kill their children, practice witchcraft, destroy capitalism and become lesbians."[61] Throughout the 1990s, conservatives became more belligerent on the subject of abortion, turning on Colin Powell for his prochoice views when he was being touted as a potential Republican savior in 1996. In 1993, the same polls that showed Perot voters distrusting Washington and big government also showed them supporting abortion choice.[62] Nowhere did the Republicans' reputation for intolerance cost them more dearly than in the state that gave birth to Reagan's political career.

UNBUCKLING THE SUN BELT

Led by two Californians, Nixon and Reagan, the Republican Party had put together a highly successful coalition. The "Sun Belt Coalition" united the rapidly growing states of the South and West behind a common resentment of federal government—a resentment that was based on economics in the West and race in the South. This was an alliance that relied on both sides turning a blind eye to the other. Reagan, for instance, may have talked like a Southern moralist when he had to, but he lived like a Hollywood movie star. In the twelve years between Governor Reagan's signing of California's liberal abortion law in 1968 and his being elected president, 1,444,778 legal abortions were performed in the state.[63] But forgetting about such things had its political uses. In the 1990s California became unbuckled from the rest of the Republican Sun Belt—and the national party tilted too far away from Western individualism toward Southern moralism.

The Republicans discovered that the two cards that had served them so well in the South—race and religion—proved disastrous in the Golden State. Strangely, the man who is blamed for the race card was an embattled moderate. In the summer of 1991, just before Bill Clinton was charming people at the Biltmore in Los Angeles, Governor Pete Wilson went to a charity roast in Sacramento. Ross Johnson, the Republican leader in the Assembly, apologized for the absence of some of his colleagues, the diehard cavemen of Orange County. "They're out hunting spotted owls with AK-47s," Johnson explained to the governor, adding mischievously that the "owls tasted better over a redwood fire."[64] By then Wilson, a classic pragmatic Republican, was stuck in a full-blown war with his party's right wing—and not just over the environment. The cavemen had been suspicious of him when he was a U.S.

senator because he had supported abortion choice. They turned viciously against him in 1990 when he became governor and decided to raise taxes after discovering an appalling budget mess. Meanwhile, Democrats rallied behind Kathleen Brown, the state treasurer, who boasted a famous name (sister of Jerry, daughter of Pat), centrist politics and the comforting looks of a sitcom mom. California was in a mess: there were floods in the Central Valley in 1991 and riots in Los Angeles in 1992. By 1993, Brown enjoyed such a massive lead in the polls that Wilson supposedly considered not running.

Instead, he fought an unyielding rearguard action that focused on two issues—capital punishment and immigration. In particular, Wilson, who had long grumbled about the amount of money the state had to spend on illegal immigrants, supported Proposition 187, which sought to suspend welfare payments to illegal aliens. The result was a short-term success: white voters passed Proposition 187 (though it fell foul of the courts) and reelected Wilson comfortably in 1994. One in four Latinos actually supported the proposition. But the long-term cost to the Republicans of being identified with Proposition 187 in a state as multicultural as California proved immense. Two years later, Bob Dole managed to win only 6 percent of the Latino vote, compared with Ronald Reagan's 45 percent in 1984.

The point about supporting Proposition 187 so conspicuously was that it was unnecessary. By 1994, California's recovery was well under way, and Brown, whom one of us had foolishly bet money on becoming the first female president of America, proved a disappointing candidate (she couldn't seem to make up her mind even about the death penalty). In Texas, a state that is as Southern as it is Western, the Republicans, led by a young governor named Bush, were wooing Latinos, not vilifying them.

Not content with playing the race card badly, Republicans then proceeded to play an even worse hand with the morality card. In the 1990s, Evangelical Christians became ever more prominent in the state party. In 1994, *Campaigns & Elections,* an inside-the-Beltway magazine, listed California's Republican Party as one of eighteen state parties to be dominated by the Christian Right. It is hard to think of a state where this would go down worse. One reason Wilson was elected to both the U.S. Senate and the governor's mansion was that he was in favor of abortion choice; so was Richard

Riordan, a Republican who was elected mayor of Los Angeles in 1993. When one of Ralph Reed's stealth raids helped put conservative Christians in charge of the school board in Vista, rows soon broke out about pupils being taught creationism. In 1994 voters chucked out the stealthy Christians.

The Dixification of the party in such an easygoing state had dire electoral consequences. Consider the fate of two of the brighter young Republican stars, Dan Lungren and James Rogan. Lungren had deep roots in the California party (his father was Richard Nixon's physician). He had a meteoric career as a congressman, helping to write the Contract with America, and was then elected California's attorney general. There he excelled in locking people up and defending gun rights. This and his opposition to abortion got him through the 1998 gubernatorial primary, but in the general election Gray Davis, the Democratic candidate, demonized the doctor's son on the three "Southern" issues of abortion, the environment and handguns. Lungren lost by more than twenty points.

James Rogan was a more charismatic character than Lungren. The illegitimate child of a cocktail waitress and a barman, he was brought up by a succession of relatives in San Francisco's tougher districts before being returned to his mother (now burdened with an alcoholic husband and three more children). He dropped out of school and worked in a succession of odd jobs, including a three-day stint as a bouncer in a porn cinema. In the best American tradition, he turned his life around and fought his way up to become a successful Republican congressman for the twenty-seventh district, in the shadow of Southern California's San Gabriel Mountains. You might have imagined that a sense of tolerance for others' misdemeanors would have stayed with him. But in Congress, Rogan fell in with the party's Southern wing. His role as one of the House managers who tried to impeach Clinton turned him into a hero among national Republicans. Money and volunteers poured into his reelection campaign in 2000 from all over the country. But it turned him into a devil in his own backyard. The liberal employees of companies like DreamWorks, Disney and Warner Brothers, which all have their headquarters in his district, regarded his support for impeachment as evidence of mental derangement. Hollywood luminaries like David Geffen spent huge amounts of money opposing him. On the night of November 7,

2000, Bill Clinton supposedly took particular pleasure in the news that Rogan lost his congressional seat.

THE ACCIDENTAL PRESIDENT

However, there was not much more for Clinton to enjoy that night. Al Gore's defeat in the 2000 election is one of liberal America's horror stories. That is not just because the closest election in American history came down to a recount in Florida, which many liberals still fiercely contend was fixed. Nor is it because Gore won a majority of the popular vote only to be jilted by the electoral college. It is because, even allowing for these things, Gore lost an election that he should have won in a walk.

Clinton's capriciousness certainly made Gore vulnerable, but as Clinton boasted in his valedictory speech at the 2000 Democratic convention, his presidency had also seen the creation of 22 million jobs and the longest economic expansion in American history.[65] Gore was the perfect defender of that legacy. An early supporter of the DLC, he had helped sway Bill Clinton's mind on the budget deficit and welfare, and clobbered Ross Perot in a debate on NAFTA. He had a cause—the environment—that might lose him votes in car states but that gave him some credibility with the Left. Yet during the last two years of the Clinton presidency, Gore managed to throw away all his best cards. On the environment, he drifted to the Right (leaving room for Ralph Nader to run as a Green candidate). On pretty much everything else he drifted to the Left, campaigning as a champion of the people against the powerful. This populism never suited "Prince Albert." The son of Senator Gore had done most of his growing up in a smart Washington hotel, surrounded by aging politicians and groveling bellboys. He had floated his toy submarine in the Senate pool and sat on Richard Nixon's lap while the then–vice president was presiding over Congress. Gore always seemed to be introducing another Al Gore to the public: alongside Populist Al, fighting big business on behalf of working families, there was Internet Al, BlackBerry at his belt, Alpha Al, salivating for a taste of his opponents' internal organs and Prosperity Al promising "You ain't seen nothing yet."

Yet even in his populist incarnation, Gore didn't want to return to the big-government liberalism of LBJ. "I don't ever want to see another era of big government," he declared two weeks before the election. "In the tale of two candidates, I'm the one who believes in limited government, and I have believed in it long before it was fashionable to do so in the Democratic Party. I don't believe there's a government solution to every problem. I don't believe any government program can replace the responsibility of parents, the hard work of families or the innovation of industry."

Had Gore stuck to that message from the outset, he could have continued the Eisenhower Republicanism of Bill Clinton. But he did not. Instead, just enough voters in the right states decided to take a bet on George W. Bush. Bush was not a perfect candidate; despite a ton of money and the blessing of the conservative movement, he had nearly lost the nomination to John McCain after the senator from Arizona trounced him in the New Hampshire primary. Yet his malapropisms and rabbit-caught-in-the-headlights smirk helped hide a highly proficient machine politician. Bush stuck to the same five themes—taxes, education, Social Security, missile defense and Medicare—throughout the campaign. And while Al Gore knew a lot of things, Bush seemed much more comfortable in his own skin.

Amid all the hanging chads and squabbling lawyers, Bush certainly looked an Accidental President—or so *The Economist* dubbed him. But there was nothing accidental about his philosophy, which was straightforwardly conservative. That ideology certainly came in a much more tolerant wrapping than Americans had seen recently. This was a candidate with some of Reagan's easygoing nature, peddling "compassionate conservatism" and keeping off the subject of abortion. The scowling elderly white men of the Christian Right were given a back seat at the Philadelphia Convention. Instead, the Republicans presented a multicultural kaleidoscope. Pat Buchanan snarled that it was the "We Are the World Convention." But the independent Perot voters felt safe voting Republican again.

Bill Clinton's final hurrah was his address to the Democratic Convention in Los Angeles. It began with the camera following him through the bowels of the building as if he were a rock star. It ended with a paean to the country that had given so much to a poor white boy "born to a young widow on a stormy night in a small Southern town." Behind us sat an elderly black woman who whispered, "Sweet Lord, I'm going to miss that man." She was right in more ways than one. Liberal America had had its chance. With Bill Clinton, the end of the Cold War and the Internet economy, it had played its best cards—and achieved merely a sort of "conservatism lite." Now America had a conservative president. What would he do?

PART II

ANATOMY

CHAPTER 5

FOR TEXAS, BUSINESS AND GOD

FEW PEOPLE EXPECTED George W. Bush's presidency to be a study in conservatism. Bush had a pragmatist's pedigree. His father was an establishment Republican who surrounded himself with moderate realists such as Colin Powell, James Baker and Brent Scowcroft. George W. Bush hailed from the "sensible" gubernatorial wing of the party rather than the fire-breathing legislative branch: governors spend their time balancing budgets and building bridges rather than dreaming up schemes to send the handicapped into outer space (as Newt Gingrich once supposedly did). Throughout the presidential campaign, Bush dropped heavy hints that he was a moderate. He trumpeted "compassionate conservatism" (the idea apparently being that the liberal media would assume that "compassionate" was a code word for moderate, since a "fervent" conservative would by definition be heartless). He added some fudge about Republicans being a diverse lot to the antiabortion plank in the party platform. He argued in favor of "focused and energetic government."[1] He wanted to expand the Department of Education, even though one survey of delegates to the Republican convention in 2000 found that 79 percent of his troops wanted to get rid of it entirely.[2] Bush even found a good word for Lyndon Johnson and the 1960s: "My party has often pointed out the limits and flaws of the Great Society. But there were successes as well, and Medicare is one of them."[3]

There was a personal edge to this. Bush was frequently at odds with the Republican Right. He criticized Newt Gingrich for being too harsh and Robert Bork for being too pessimistic. The Right responded suspiciously. Dan Quayle ordered his staff never to utter the words "compassionate conservative": "This silly and insulting term was created by liberal Republicans and is nothing more than code for surrendering our values and principles." Pat Robertson denounced the 2000 Republican Convention, with its centrist posturing, as "Democrat lite."

It is true that just before the South Carolina primary in February 2000, Bush spoke at Bob Jones University, a place that banned interracial dating, in order to rally social conservatives and prevent John McCain repeating his victory in New Hampshire. And of course he promised an unfeasibly large tax cut. But most people assumed that this was just the sort of thing that a well-bred young patrician has to do in order to win the Republican nomination (Bush the father had also spoken at Bob Jones University, in 1988). How could a man who wanted to keep the National Endowment for the Arts really be a conservative?

There was another reason to expect moderation in 2000: Bush's extraordinarily narrow victory. He lost the popular vote, and carried Florida by only a few hundred votes—and then only after a 5-4 vote by the Republican-dominated Supreme Court ended the Florida recount. Surely anybody who had been through such an ordeal would approach the business of running the country with humility. Moderates—especially people around Colin Powell—thought it was they who had won the election, so they would control the president.[4]

Yet Bush's tenuous victory did not produce a tenuous presidency. From the very first the Bush White House proved to be both extraordinarily disciplined and surprisingly conservative. In barely six months Bush pushed through a highly ambitious agenda—the largest tax cut since Ronald Reagan, a sweeping reform of education and a rollback of regulations on business. He engineered the biggest shift of power from the congressional to the presidential branch in a generation, a change that started as soon as he came to office but gathered pace after the events of September 11, 2001. The accidental president turned into the most powerful president since Watergate had humbled the presidency in 1974.

How did George II succeed in turning himself into the king of Washington? His success was partly a testimony to two virtues that are often underestimated in politics: organization and experience. Unlike his more cerebral immediate predecessor, who would let meetings go on for hours if they were stimulating enough, Bush made it clear that he believed in order and discipline. He liked meetings to start and end on time, or even earlier. One of his top economic advisors once arrived five minutes early for a meeting only to discover the president's secretary looking anxious: the previous meeting had finished early, and the president had wanted to get on. The aide always arrived fifteen minutes early after that. Tony Blair has remarked to friends that when he talked to Bill Clinton, the two men were such ideological soul mates that they could finish each other's sentences, but when it came to getting clear answers and cast-iron commitments, he preferred dealing with Bush. Journalists have also noticed the difference. "They don't leak. They don't gossip. They don't stab each other in the back," David Brooks complained about the new White House. "It's a nightmare."[5] Bush liked to spend his evening with his wife and took breaks during the day. When a deranged man drew a gun near the White House early in the presidency, Dick Cheney was laboring away at his desk but Bush was in the gym. He told his aides that he saw no reason why a job in the White House was incompatible with a balanced home life.

The Bush administration could also draw on a wealth of experience. In 2000 there was general relief in Washington that the adults were back in charge and the ghosts of Monica Lewinsky, Marc Rich, Ken Starr and the rest of the Clinton specters could be laid to rest. Donald Rumsfeld had first arrived in Washington during the Nixon administration. He was Ford's chief of staff before handing the job to Dick Cheney. Colin Powell had been chairman of the Joint Chiefs of Staff under both the first Bush and Clinton.

The biggest reason for the new administration's surprising dynamism, however, was the fact that it had such a clear sense of direction. Bush's conservatism was certainly sharpened by September 11, but it was notable long before that. Dumping the Kyoto Protocol, losing the moderate Republican senator Jim Jeffords, pushing through the huge tax cut, getting rid of the ABM treaty: all this happened before the terrorist attacks.

What drove this conservatism? In Chapters 6, 7 and 8 we will look at the ways that different parts of the conservative movement have driven the Bush presidency, but let us start with the three much-caricatured influences that have shaped George W. Bush's personal conservatism: Texas, business and religion. These three things help to explain why Bush has been such a divisive figure in America, but the biggest gulf in comprehension comes between Bush and the outside world. It would be hard to invent a political leader whose three core values more perfectly typify the Right Nation that Europeans cannot understand.

YOU CAN TAKE THE MAN OUT OF TEXAS . . .

On the evening of his inauguration, the new president took his family to a black-tie-and-boots ball that featured live longhorn steers and ten thousand real or honorary Texans, including Senator Kay Bailey Hutchison dressed in red-and-gold ostrich cowboy boots.[6] "I don't care if you're Republican or Democrat," Bush told the guests. "It's sure great to be a Texan in Washington, D.C. I'm looking forward to some good common Texas sense."

George W. Bush had no shortage of Texas sense, good or otherwise, in his administration. His closest advisors have usually been Texans of one sort or another. Karl Rove made his career there. Karen Hughes, Bush's other consigliere, returned to Texas early because her husband and son were homesick. Other Texans in the administration include the commerce secretary, Don Evans, probably Bush's oldest friend, and Alberto Gonzales, the White House counsel and a former Texas secretary of state. In the months after the inauguration almost every car in the White House parking lot seemed to have a Texas license plate.

However, the influence of Texas on Bush has less to do with particular people than with a state of mind. From the beginning, Bush spent as much time as he could at his Texas ranch in Crawford, and he never tired of seeing the world in Texan terms. To people who wonder "What sort of place is Texas?" the simplest answer is that it is America exponentiated. Texas is America's America, or at least conservative America's America. Think of the characteristics, good and bad, that make America distinctive—its size and diversity, its optimism and self-confidence, its materialism and braggadocio, its incredible ability to make something out of nothing, its violence and religiosity—and you see them in their purest form in Texas.

Begin with its size. Texas is almost as big as Britain and France combined. One of the state's 254 counties is bigger than Prescott Bush's Connecticut. When he visited Israel, Bush was struck by the fact that Israel is only as wide as some Texas driveways are long. The state's size promotes a slash-and-burn attitude toward the environment, an attitude that is reinforced by the fact that so much of the state is physically nondescript, a collection of tedious plains, vast deserts and anonymous scrubland. Stephen Austin, an early colonizer, called Texas "a wild, howling, interminable solitude." The Gulf Coast is humid, mosquito-ridden and plagued by torrential rains. The west is desert. The border country is hardscrabble. The plains in the north are racked by winds. Texans have not always beautified their environment. Intensive cotton growing has ruined the soil of riverbeds, just as overgrazing has ruined the prairie soil. Oil speculators have left ghost towns and pools of pollution in their wake. This is a land that breeds a tough-minded respect for man's ability to master nature, the very opposite of the tender-minded environmentalism that flourishes in Europe's compact cities and beautiful countryside.

Size goes along with a swaggering boastfulness—a boastfulness, to some extent, encoded in the DNA of the United States. The prospectuses that persuaded Elizabethans to invest in the Massachusetts and Virginia companies were full of tall tales about the New World; so were the stories of gold in the West that started the wagon trains rolling. But on the East Coast this boastfulness was diluted long ago, in part by the desire to win the approval of "civilized" Old Europe. Texans do not feel very much deference to Old Europe. Whether they are sitting in the plush Driskill Hotel in Austin or some god-awful motel in Waco, Texans firmly maintain that they have the biggest-and-best-of-everything. This bragging does not always make other people love Texas, even in the West. (When, back in the early 1980s, one of us broke down in a car with Texas plates in southern Colorado, nobody stopped to help for what seemed like an eternity; the man who eventually did explained: "You should have had a sign saying you weren't from Texas.")

Yet Texans have a gift for turning their boasts into reality. They have managed to tame some of the most inhospitable territory in America with air conditioning, concrete and computer chips. A state that was once rural is now largely urban, home to three of the ten biggest cities in the country.

Texas's buccaneering capitalism has produced some extraordinary rags-to-riches stories: think of C. M. "Dad" Joiner, a seventy-one-year-old wild-catter who sank his last dollars into a makeshift drilling rig and hit oil at 3,600 feet down, or of the extraordinary Hunt silver dynasty that helped to gild the wilder fringes of American conservatism. It has also produced Potemkin companies, such as Enron, and a rather immature attitude to wealth. Michael Lind argues that the state's "gusher elite" practice a form of capitalism that is closer to gambling than to Max Weber's Protestant ethic. Texas is famous for its mega-mansions, Oil Barons' Ball and Neiman Marcus catalogue, which has offered such things as his and her giraffes and his and her submarines.[7] The state is also famous for speculative bubbles. The 1980s saw the pricking of no fewer than three—oil, property and the savings and loan industry. Today the state is struggling with the collapse of both Enron and the bursting of the high-tech bubble.

This boom-and-bust psychology also applies to government. Anyone who worries about George W. Bush's adventurous fiscal strategy of cutting taxes while increasing spending might look at what happened when he did the same thing in Texas. In the mid-1990s, he delivered both a big tax cut and plenty more spending, especially on education. By 2003, a fractious Texas legislature was trying to plug a $10 billion hole in the budget. Bush has taken his penchant for big political gambles to Washington. It is hard to think of any other president, with the possible exception of Ronald Reagan, who was so happy to take risks—from ripping up established arms-control treaties to invading Iraq. All Bush's gambles have had elements of calculation, but the general approach has been a brusque "Who dares, wins."

If Texas is generous to people who roll the dice and win, it is hard on the unfortunate. Texas is a land of low taxes, weak trade unions, a miserly public sector and a paltry welfare state, all of which ensure that plenty coexists with poverty. Houston's shimmering towers and gallerias sit next to unpaved streets and shotgun shacks; the city's world-class medical center sits on top of a health-care system that fails to reach the state's poorest citizens. The University of Texas boasts a star-studded faculty and the second largest endowment in the country after Harvard, with 2.1 million acres of rich oil-fields to its name. Yet the state of Texas also has some of the worst schools in the country.

As governor, George W. Bush certainly tried to improve the state's schools. But his attitude to the rest of this shriveled welfare state was to ask how it could be shrunk still further. He was much influenced by Marvin Olasky's argument that religious organizations were better at solving the problem of poverty than welfare bureaucracies because they tried to change people's hearts as well as give them money. Olasky's critics worried that some of the fundamentalist faith-based organizations that he admired were close to prison camps, with disobedient children forced to kneel for hours holding Bibles. They also pounced on his musing that the separation of church and state "maybe wasn't such a good idea."[8] Bush pushed ahead regardless. He was particularly ruthless in dismantling the ambitious program of drug and alcohol treatment set up in prisons by his predecessor, Ann Richards. Bush hadn't needed a twelve-step program to conquer his own drinking problem; he'd done it "the Republican way," as he liked to put it, with discipline and faith, and he wanted the state's prisoners to learn from their governor. He even handed over a wing of a Texas prison to Chuck Colson, a reformed Watergate villain who had done time himself. Colson's recipe might be termed total immersion in Evangelical Christianity: from dawn to dusk, inmates attended prayer meetings, Bible study and chapel.

Texas is steeped in military tradition as well as evangelism. The area around San Antonio is the embodiment of the military-industrial complex, with an army base, two air force bases, a huge army medical center, dozens of defense-related companies and thousands of veterans. Fort Hood, near Waco, is the army's second-largest base. The 16,000-acre Pantex plant in West Texas secretly assembled thousands of nuclear warheads during the Cold War, and is now being used to house what remains of America's nuclear arsenal.

Despite his cushy service in the Texas National Guard during the Vietnam War (keeping the skies of the Lone Star State safe from marauding

Louisianans), Bush has always reveled in the military. Did he ever look happier to be president than when he strode onto the deck of the U.S.S. *Abraham Lincoln* in an aviator's uniform (having just flown a warplane himself) to declare the end of major combat in the 2003 Iraq War? When he declared war on Iraq, there was no anguishing about ends and means: the decision made, he went out on the lawn to play with his dog. Davy Crockett and the rest of the Alamo band would have been proud of him.

Texas machismo is not limited to the military variety. Texas represents the confluence of the two most violent areas in the country: the South and the frontier. Tamed by gun-wielding cowboys, Texas is still thoroughly marinated in the gun culture. Even at Dell Computer, in liberal Austin, you find signs telling you where to leave your gun. This is a state where men who don't hunt are widely assumed to be homosexual (not that gay Texans don't do their bit to clobber wildlife) and where one person famously beat a murder rap by arguing that his victim "needed killin'." The state still has a much higher murder rate than other big states, despite the fact that 454 people are languishing on Texas's death row—13 percent of the nation's total.

Bush approached the subject of "criminals who needed killin'" with startling sangfroid: forty people were executed in his last year as governor alone. As for guns, he oversees an administration that goes huntin', shootin' and fishin' with an enthusiasm unseen outside the British upper classes. Bush is a keen fisherman, and a decent shot. One of his favorite spiritual advisors, James Robison, has an enthusiasm for blood sports that is reminiscent of one of Trollope's rural parsons. The magazines kept on *Air Force One* include *Bass Fishing, Fly Fisherman* and *Sporting News*. During one of Dick Cheney's prolonged absences in "an undisclosed location," the inhabitants of a small rural town were shocked to see the vice president, Secret Service detail in tow, on a hunting trip. During the row over Trent Lott's encomium to Strom Thurmond in December 2002, Karl Rove and Lott's successor, Bill Frist, had to call off a hunting trip with their boys, lest it be seen as a conspiracy. In most European countries, politicians point a gun at a fluffy-looking creature at the peril of their political careers. Not so in Texas, and not so in the Bush White House.

Once again, it comes back to a question of attitude. The phrase "Don't mess with Texas" is ubiquitous in the state; George Bush's foreign policy

might equally be summed up as "Don't mess with the U.S.A." The administration has always possessed a sort of Texas swagger—a deep self-belief and a
lack of concern about what fancy-pants East Coasters, let alone Europeans,
think about it. Meanwhile, outside America, the administration's Texas
license plate has prejudiced much of the rest of the world against it (not
unlike those Colorado drivers twenty years ago). It is not for nothing that
Bush is known as the Toxic Texan.

THE OTHER TEXAS: SUBSIDIES AND CRONIES

All this suggests that Texas has had a one-dimensional effect on the administration's conservatism, making it distrustful of government, foreigners and
do-gooding liberals. Yet the more you examine Texas, the more complicated
the state becomes. Texas is responsible for some of the administration's contradictions as well as its more obvious black-boots-and-Stetson attitude.

The most obvious contradiction involves government. Freedom-loving
Texans have taken all sorts of measures to tame the government beast. The
state legislature meets only once every two years for a 140-day session and
legislators are paid the nominal sum of $7,200 a year. The governor doesn't
even have the power to appoint his cabinet. The minimalist attitude to government is embodied in the Texas Rangers' motto: "One riot, one ranger."
Yet the Lone Star State owes as much to Washington, D.C., as anywhere else
in the country. The federal government's largesse helped transform a rural
backwater into a high-tech leviathan, starting with hydroelectric power in
the 1930s, intensifying with the space program in the 1960s and continuing
with today's huge military buildup. The reason the first word spoken on the
moon was "Houston" was Texas's skill at wielding political power.

Sam Rayburn, raised in hardscrabble Texas farm country along an unnav-
igable river, held the speakership of the U.S. Congress for twenty years—
longer than anybody else—and crafted much of the New Deal legislation.
Lyndon Johnson, from the backward Hill Country, was one of the most
powerful senators in American history. Between 1964 and 2000, this allegedly
antigovernment state produced three presidents (Johnson and the two
Bushes), two vice-presidential candidates (George H. W. Bush and Lloyd

Bentsen) and the most successful third-party candidate since Teddy Roosevelt (Ross Perot). Far from being free-market purists, Texas's Republican politicians have shown a genius for bringing home the bacon. Phil Gramm, a fiscal conservative who held LBJ's old Senate seat until 2003, liked to say "I'm carrying so much pork, I'm beginning to get trichinosis." He wouldn't vote for a program to manufacture cheese on the moon, he said, but if Congress ever approved of such an idea, he'd try to make sure that the milk came from Texas cows and that the "celestial navigation system" was developed in a Texas university.

The Bush administration has the same mixed feelings. George W. Bush is forever singing the praises of small government, but in reality, he has let government sprawl. Federal spending has increased not just on defense but on education and other social services—and at a far faster rate than under Bill Clinton. We will return to Bush's ominous weakness for big government in Chapter 10.

Some of the same mixed feelings crop up regarding individualism. For Texans, this sits at the heart of the state's character. Who but a larger-than-life individual would have the guts to keep drilling for oil into his seventies? The state's most successful politicians have all been outsized characters combining good ol' boy charm with cunning and eccentricity, people like Bob Bullock, Ross Perot and the great LBJ. But Texans also have a strong collectivist streak—a streak that can be seen in their obsessive loyalty to military regiments, football teams and fraternities, and in the intense rivalry between the state's two leading universities, the University of Texas and Texas A&M. For all its entrepreneurialism, the Texas business oligarchy is one of the clubbiest in the country, always working behind the scenes to conjure up a new sports center or museum. The state's business and political elites are hopelessly intertwined. Politicians have always had a habit of getting rich. LBJ somehow ended up owning the state's most lucrative media contracts. Perot was America's first welfare billionaire, thanks to a contract that allowed him to computerize the country's Social Security system. The oil and gas industry has been a master of crony capitalism.

Yet this clubbishness should not be mistaken for insularity. Economically, Texas has always been an export-based economy, first with cotton, then energy and now high-tech linking it to the global economy. This enthusiasm for openness has been reinforced by NAFTA, a project that was master-minded by Texans of both parties, notably Lloyd Bentsen and George H. W. Bush, and that has helped to transform the state's 1,250-mile border with Mexico from a potential problem into a huge opportunity. Seventy percent of America's exports to Mexico go through Texas. More than 3,000 *maquiladoras* have sprung up along the border, and twin towns such as El Paso–Juarez and Laredo–Nuevo Laredo exist in a mutually beneficial symbiosis. Some 9,000 trucks cross the World Trade Bridge between Laredo and its Mexican twin every day.

This openness is increasingly cultural as well as economic. Texas has a terrible tradition of racism, to be sure, but for most of the past two decades the accent has been on what even conservatives might call multiculturalism. In Laredo, newly rich Latinos put on debutante balls for their daughters, borrowing from an old Southern tradition. In Austin, Tejano musicians mix country and western with Mexican music. Certainly the Texas Republican Party has been far keener on immigrants than its California sibling. "Hell, if they'll walk across Big Bend, we want 'em," Bush said privately about illegal aliens.[9] Bush was a frequent visitor to Mexico and an enthusiastic, if less than perfect, speaker of Spanish. His first big initiative in the election year 2004 was to announce a plan to progressively "legalize" America's 10 million illegal aliens.

THE BUSINESS OF AMERICA IS BUSINESS

If Texas provides the best introduction to George W. Bush's conservatism, it is also worth drawing out two particular things that have always loomed large in his makeup: business and religion. God and Mammon have shaped both the substance and the style of the Bush presidency—though not always in the ways that its critics claim.

For many politicians, business is something you retire to. Not for George W. Bush. He was the first president with an MBA—from Harvard Business School, no less—and he appointed more CEOs to his cabinet than any other president. Bush has a gut belief in business. For him, business executives are the people who solve the world's problems and generate its wealth. Bush is a devotee of "management by objectives," a man who likes "to outline a clear vision and agenda," as he put it in his campaign autobiography, and then delegate the operational details to his subordinates.[10] In introducing his new appointees to the public, he never praises their academic credentials or their intellectual creativity. Instead, he harps on about their managerial experience. When he introduced Mel Martinez, his first secretary of housing, by saying that "He's an administrator. He's a good executive," he was not trying to damn with faint praise.

This enthusiasm for money makers is hardly surprising, coming from the great grandson of Samuel Bush and George Walker.[11] One of Bush's college friends recalled that Bush got excited only once about a political issue when he was at Yale in the late 1960s — an era that saw campuses across the country torn apart by the Vietnam War and the emerging counterculture. That was when some prospective change to the oil-depletion allowance threatened to harm the nation's oilmen.[12]

Here it is worth making a subtle distinction. Bush's enthusiasm has generally been for business, particularly big business, rather than for the free market. His own career was a textbook example of Texas crony capitalism, characterized by a succession of takeover deals in which outside investors with ties to his father periodically stepped in to save one floundering oil company after another. Arbusto Energy became Bush Exploration, which merged with Spectrum 7, which merged with Harken Energy. Bush's equity magically increased in value, despite a dismal oil market. Then in 1990 he sold 212,000 shares in Harken stock for $848,560 to pay for his investment in the Texas Rangers baseball team.[13] Construction of a spanking-new ballpark in Arlington was subsidized by an increase in the local city sales tax.[14]

This sort of buddy capitalism is hardly the stuff of Harvard Business School case studies. Yet Bush still saw himself as a businessman, and his base has always been the business class. Texas was an ideal state for such a politician because the state's campaign-finance laws place almost no limits on contributions. In his 1994 and 1998 gubernatorial campaigns, more than half the contributions came from corporate executives (including hefty contributions from Ken Lay, the boss of Enron). And he eventually used his business connections to create the most successful fund-raising machine in presidential history. In the 2000 election cycle Bush raised $191 million, compared with $133 million for the sitting vice president. His campaign got off to a flying start because of the generosity of 214 "Pioneers"—people who raised at least $100,000 for his election bid.[15] He eventually raised an astonishing $101 million from individual contributors, most of them businesspeople. Much has been made of the fact that Enron's political action committee was the largest donor to George W. Bush's presidential campaign. In truth, by 2000 Bush and Karl Rove had such a political hold over the Sun Belt business elite that it would have been far more remarkable had Texas's fastest-growing company *not* given a great deal of money. The three states that contributed most to the Bush presidential campaign were Texas, California and Florida. Bush outperformed Al Gore among businesspeople in almost every state in the country and in every industry sector. He even took twice as much money as Gore from one of the most socially liberal parts of the business world, the high-tech sector. Bush was the businessman's choice.

If the nursery of the Clinton administration was the university, the nursery of the Bush administration was the corporation. No president since Eisenhower has had more than one ex–chief executive in the cabinet, and Eisenhower had only two. Bush started with four: Dick Cheney (from Halliburton), Donald Rumsfeld (G. D. Searle and General Instruments), Don Evans (Tom Brown, a Denver-based oil and gas company) and Paul O'Neill (Alcoa). The Bush White House is a maze of business interests. Andrew Card, Bush's chief of staff, is a former General Motors executive who was also the car industry's chief lobbyist; the main recipient of car industry money in the 2000 electoral cycle was Senator Spencer Abraham, who became Bush's energy secretary. Ann Veneman, the low-profile agriculture secretary, sat on the board of Calgene, a pioneer in genetically modified food that was subsequently bought by Monsanto, a Missouri company with close connections to the former senator from Missouri and current attorney general, John Ashcroft. Even one of the most ivory tower members of the administration, Condoleezza Rice, sat on the boards of several big companies, including the Chevron Corporation, which named one of its super-tankers after her. Colin Powell is the first secretary of state with an MBA.

The Bush administration has systematically championed business-friendly policies, lifting taxes, rolling back regulations and generally trying to make life easier for business. The energy industry has been a huge winner.

Dick Cheney took almost all his advice for his energy policy from energy executives, including many from Enron. The administration also pushed relentlessly to allow drilling in the Alaska wilderness, a position that earned furious opposition from both environmentalists and Democrats.

Pandering to businesspeople is hardly new in American politics, but it is noticeable how many of the shakier periods of the Bush presidency have been produced by either pandering or the appearance of it. His decision to allow higher arsenic levels in drinking water set off an early round of accusations. His initial response to the collapse of Enron was particularly ill-judged: he tried to argue that it was just a case of a few bad apples; stood by his increasingly compromised choice as head of the Securities and Exchange Commission, Harvey Pitt (a corporate lawyer who kept on having to recuse himself from cases that involved his clients); ignored the accounting problems at Dick Cheney's alma mater, Halliburton; and resisted the Sarbanes-Oxley Act, which tried to improve corporate governance and sharpen up accounting practices.

A MAN OF GOD

During the 2000 election campaign George Bush was asked to name his favorite philosopher. "Jesus," came his unhesitating reply, "because he changed my heart." The fact of redemption is at the heart of George Bush's career, and the idea of redemption is at the heart of his politics. Bush has woven faith into his presidency more enthusiastically than any recent president. Ronald Reagan supported the church like a flying buttress, from the outside. Bush, a born-again Methodist, is more a pillar in the nave. The president has the enthusiasm of a convert—a convert whose life was once not only Godless but also rather directionless. Bush drank too much in his youth. He was overshadowed by his high-achieving father. And he could not seem to succeed at anything he tried. The turning point came in 1986 when Billy Graham visited his family and, as Bush puts it, "He led me to the path and I began walking." The man who frittered away the first forty years of his life gave up drinking and became a disciplined political machine. "Right now

I should be in a bar in Texas, not the Oval Office," he once told a group of religious leaders. "There is only one reason that I am in the Oval Office and not in a bar. I found faith. I found God. I am here because of the power of prayer."[16]

Bush starts each day kneeling in prayer and begins each cabinet meeting with a prayer. He reads a passage from the Bible every day. He also reads devotionals by the likes of Oswald Chambers, a Scottish-born theologian. Two of his earliest executive orders called for a national day of prayer and a religious war on want. Bush frequently speaks in religious terms, sometimes movingly so, sometimes disastrously so, as when he said that America would go on a "crusade" to hunt down its enemies (a statement that he immediately retracted). His chief speechwriter, Michael Gerson, is a master at translating Bush's religious sentiments into soaring prose with a seventeenth-century air.

"We're confident," Bush told the United Nations in November 2001, ". . . that history has an author who fills time and eternity with his purpose. We know that evil is real, but good will prevail against it."[17] He justified his $15 billion plan to fight global AIDS with similarly resonant phrases: "When we see a plague leaving graves and orphans across a continent, we must act. When we see the wounded traveler on the road to Jericho we will not— America will not—pass to the other side of the road."[18] And of course, he sees the war on terrorism as "a monumental struggle between good and evil." On September 11, 2001, he told the American people, "Today, our nation saw evil." In his State of the Union address on January 29, 2002, he referred to an "axis of evil." He frequently refers to terrorists as "the evil ones." It is hard to imagine another Western leader who would have framed the issue in quite this way. More often, though, the references to religion are hidden. Bruce Lincoln, a biblical scholar, looked at Bush's speech announcing the start of military action against Afghanistan: only 3 of his 970 words were unambiguously religious, but to the well-scriptured eye, the speech had plenty of biblical imagery and allusions from texts such as the Book of Revelation.[19]

The influence of religion also pervades the White House. The first words that David Frum heard on entering the White House to work as a speechwriter were "Missed you at Bible study."[20] Throughout his book on Bush, *The Right Man*, Frum, a worldly Jewish intellectual, is constantly being blindsided by worthy Evangelical Protestants. Bush people go to the White House with much the same reverence as they go to church. It is a place where ties and dark suits are always worn, where "damn" is considered a swearword, where voices are lowered, and where you take much the same vow as that of priest in the confessional—of perpetual silence.

Many of Bush's closest advisors have religious ties. Condoleezza Rice is a Presbyterian minister's daughter. Andrew Card is married to a Methodist minister. Karen Hughes is a Presbyterian elder who is nicknamed "the Prophet." Don Evans attended Bible study classes with Bush back in Midland. When Bush and his entourage found themselves spending Palm Sunday of 2002 on *Air Force One* (they were returning from a trip to El Salvador) some members of the cabinet suggested that they should hold an impromptu religious service. Before long forty officials were crammed into the plane's conference room. Rice, a talented musician, led the service. Hughes read the lesson. The entire affair ended with a spirited rendition of "Amazing Grace" and hugs and kisses all round as a sign of Christian fellowship.[21]

The White House has an official, Tim Goeglein, who is responsible for "Christian outreach"—that is, reminding Christian voters that the president shares their values. Bush has also given people from the Christian Right prominent roles in his administration. Kay Coles James, the director of the Office of Personnel Management, a position that oversees the entire federal workforce, is the former dean of the government school at Pat Robertson's Regent University and one of the country's most articulate opponents of abortion. Claude Allen and Wade Horn carry the banner of abstinence education and marriage promotion at the Department of Health and Human Services. And, of course, there is John Ashcroft. The attorney general holds the highest position ever held by a member of the Christian Right—and he holds it, moreover, in a Justice Department that inevitably deals with issues such as abortion, the death penalty, civil rights and the selection of judges. Ashcroft, the son and grandson of Pentecostal ministers, has no reservations about mixing religion and public life: he anoints himself with oil before important functions (his favorite brand is Crisco) and holds daily prayer sessions in his office in the Justice Department. In June 2003 he banned staff from having their own gay pride celebrations.

Yet if Bush is keen on mobilizing the Christian Right, he is usually careful not to be captured by it. Religion certainly pervades the Bush White House in much the same way as the Holy Spirit is supposed to infiltrate souls, but when it comes to shaping policy, godliness is a little less omnipresent. This is partly a matter of political strategy. Belief in God is a political advantage in a country where 85 percent of the people profess some sort of religious belief. But once that faith becomes too strident it quickly turns into a political liability. Banning abortion is no way to appeal to soccer moms. Nor is declaring that wives should submit to their husbands (as the Southern Baptist Convention did). For Karl Rove, one of the most uncomfortable moments during the 2000 Republican Convention occurred when the entire Texas delegation bowed their heads in prayer when a gay person addressed the audience.

Bush has devoted a great deal of energy to trying to broaden the definition of the Religious Right from Southern Evangelicals into something rather more ecumenical. (It is worth stressing that Bush is a Southern Methodist—fairly strong meat when set beside his father's Episcopalianism, but a lot milder than Jerry Falwell and the Southern Baptists.) His main quarry has been Roman Catholics, the biggest single religious group in the country and the most ripe for picking. Bush easily won the votes of a majority of religiously active Catholics in 2000, the best showing among them by a Republican presidential candidate since 1984. He has made a great show of visiting prominent Catholic institutions like the University of Notre Dame in Indiana. The White House has a weekly conference call with an informal group of Catholic advisors, and the Republican National Committee has revived a Catholic task force. Bush tries to include fashionable Catholic phrases, such as "the culture of life," in his speeches. And in Catholic circles at least, he plays down his party's antigovernment stance: Catholic voters are much more enthusiastic about government activism than are Southern Evangelicals. Bush's best chance of winning Pennsylvania and Michigan, which he narrowly lost in 2000, probably lies in seducing blue-collar Catholics.

Bush has also tried to reach out beyond Christians to other "people of faith." He has been particularly successful with Jews, though that is an incidental consequence of his foreign policy. Less noticed have been his attempts to woo Muslims. Soon after arriving at the White House, he invited a Muslim imam to the launch of his faith-based initiative program, appointed someone to work on "Arab-Muslim outreach," and has routinely added the word "mosques" to his lists of religious institutions. This rapprochement naturally took a battering after September 11, but Bush has still resisted demands from Protestant fundamentalists to make Muslim organizations ineligible for government grants.

What about his policies? The idea that Bush's religious beliefs have skewed his foreign policy is a complicated one, not least because it has gotten tangled up with all sorts of conspiracy theories about the neoconservatives (which we will deal with in Chapter 8). If you look at Bush's domestic policies, it is much easier to find the influence of hardheaded realpolitik than religious conviction.

The program that flowed most directly from Bush's religiosity—compassionate conservatism—unraveled quickly. The idea of "faith-based" solutions to problems that had eluded the welfare state offered a way of luring Catholics and blacks into the Republican coalition. But it fizzled out nevertheless. Part of the problem was Bush's choice of a leader: John DiIulio proved that a first-rate academic mind—he is a professor at the University of Pennsylvania—does not necessarily equip you to survive in the Machiavellian world of the West Wing. At the same time, plenty of people in Congress—not just liberals—objected to anything that encroached on the separation of church and state. Meanwhile, DiIulio managed to annoy white Evangelicals by directing money to black and Latino churches.[22] Bush and Rove retreated quickly, cutting a deal behind DiIulio's back that gave Protestant churches an exemption from federal hiring laws (which could have forced them to hire gay people). DiIulio resigned in August 2001, and the project was quietly shelved.

On abortion, one of Bush's first acts as president was to cut off funds for organizations providing abortions overseas. But that is now par for the course for any incoming Republican president, and is as much an excuse for doing nothing at home as it is an act of righteousness abroad. He deliberately used religious language in calling for a ban on cloning ("Life is a creation, not a commodity"), and he signed a bill banning partial-birth abortion in November 2003, putting an end to "a terrible form of violence." But most Americans are hostile to partial-birth abortion and nervous about cloning. When it came to stem-cell research, he certainly defied the biotechnology industry by imposing restrictions, but those restrictions were less fundamental than the Christian Right had hoped. He has nominated Evangelical Christians to judicial posts, but on the biggest question of all, appointing Supreme Court justices who would overturn *Roe v. Wade,* Bush reverts to waffling about appointing judges who will respect the Constitution.

By contrast, he has been much bolder in promoting Christian ideas where his religious principles are less likely to lose him votes—such as in the area of "abstinence education." Here he clearly understands the quip that a social conservative is a liberal with a daughter in high school. Bush has not just poured money into teaching teenagers the virtues of virginity, he has poured it into the most hard-line version of the creed—so-called SPRANS programs (Special Projects of Regional and National Significance), which teach that sex outside marriage is likely to have harmful psychological and physical effects and which refuse to promote condom use. Bush is keen on taking his message abroad. The Bush administration has earmarked for abstinence education a third of all the money that it has given for AIDS prevention in the developing world. This may prove disastrous: it has certainly provoked furor with aid institutions, but it did not cost Bush much at home. By contrast, when the Evangelicals tried to get China denied most-favored-nation trading status, Bush quickly sided with the business lobby.

Another example of Bush siding with the majority is gay marriage, though here he may be on more treacherous ground. By calling, in February 2004, for a constitutional amendment limiting marriage to heterosexual couples, the president in theory lined up with the two-thirds of Americans who oppose gay marriage. But the issue is more complicated than it first appears: Americans are much more tolerant of the idea of civil unions, which a federal marriage ban might disrupt, and many people even in the Republican Party dislike the idea of trying to change the constitution. In fact, Bush was pushed into action first by "activist judges" (as he always calls them) in Massachusetts ordering that state to start permitting gay marriages and then by the duly emboldened mayor of San Francisco, Gavin Newsom, issuing licenses to several thousand gay couples. With social conservatives up in arms, Bush had little alternative to backing the amendment, no doubt reasoning gloomily that the only politician who might have more to lose from the ker-fuffle than himself was John Kerry.

AN ALL-TOO-AMERICAN PRESIDENT

In all this delicate maneuvering, Bush is largely on ground that has been well-trodden by other Republican politicians who have hopscotched around abortion. More to the point, his religiosity does not seem odd in a country where 60 percent of the population think that God plays an important role in their lives, where 39 percent describe themselves as "born-again Christians," and where a third of registered voters are white Evangelical Protestants.[23] In the 1960s, Gallup found that 53 percent of Americans thought that churches should not be involved in politics. By 1996, 54 percent thought it fine for churches to talk about politics.[24]

It is hardly surprising that Bush's religiosity seems much odder in Europe, where only one in five people go to church regularly and born-again Christians are a tiny minority. Tony Blair, who is himself highly religious, reportedly didn't really know what to say when Bush asked him to kneel on the floor and pray with him. Alastair Campbell, Blair's thuggish former press secretary, once tried to scare off a *Vanity Fair* journalist from discussing the prime minister's religious faith with the riposte "We don't do God." George Bush very definitely does "do God."

Indeed, the closer you look at Bush's biography and beliefs—at his Texan-ness, at his admiration for business, at his religiosity—the more you realize the problem for those optimists who cling to the notion that the current rift in the transatlantic alliance is the temporary handiwork of an "atypical" president. For the Toxic Texan and Bible-thumping businessman who strikes Europeans as so odd does not seem odd at all to most American eyes. Bush may be more religious than many other Americans, but his religiosity is as all-American as his love of capitalism and his Texas twang. It is America that is exceptional, not its current president.

CHAPTER 6

THE *RIVE DROITE*

There is no such thing as spontaneous public opinion. It all has to be manufactured from a Center of Conviction and Energy. . . .[1]

ONE MIGHT IMAGINE that this quote came from Dick Cheney in one of his less guarded moments, or from Donald Rumsfeld muttering to a general about Iraq. In fact, the words come from Beatrice Webb, one of the founders of the Fabian Society. As the mouthpiece of British socialism at its most high-minded, the Fabian Society is hardly a name to conjure with in George W. Bush's Washington. Yet the society nevertheless provides a model for the way conservative ideas have influenced the Bush presidency.

The Fabians, a society of intellectuals, founded their organization in 1884. Their ranks included Sidney and Beatrice Webb, H. G. Wells and George Bernard Shaw. Their aim was to replace the "scramble for private gain" with "collective welfare," and their chosen technique was "permeation." They did not believe in overthrowing society, like the Marxists. They did not particularly care about winning elections, like the Labor Party they also helped found. Indeed, they tried not to tie themselves to one particular party. They hoped that socialism would come about gradually but relentlessly—by clothing collectivism in the garb of common sense and by extending government controls over one institution after another.

For the Fabians, the important thing was to change the climate of opinion so that whoever got into Parliament was marching to their tune. "Nothing in England is done without the consent of a small intellectual yet practical class in London, not 2,000 in number," Sidney Webb once observed. The society's primary aim was to influence that class, but it also made a point of shaping the minds of less important people. The Fabian pamphlet was one of their hallmarks; they established periodicals like the *New Statesman,* set the agenda on numerous parliamentary committees and founded the London School of Economics and Political Science.

The Fabians also helped to establish the idea that socialism was an exciting way of life, not just a political creed. They founded a network of "groups"— the women's group, the arts group, groups for education, biology and local government. One of the most successful of these was the "nursery," composed of bohemian young men and women who took that notorious roué H. G. Wells as their role model. The nursery had a strong social side. Edward Pease, the Fabian Society's secretary, described it thus: "Naturally the nursery is not exclusively devoted to economics and politics; picnics and dances also have their place. Some of the members eventually marry each other, and there is no better security for prolonged happiness in marriage than sympathy in regard to the larger issues of life."

The influence of the Fabians was long-lasting. Sidney Webb drafted clause 4 of the Labor Party constitution, which committed the party to "common ownership of the means of production, distribution and exchange." The Labor Party did not abolish clause 4 until the 1990s. Fabian institutions such as the London School of Economics churned out experts who believed in the magic power of bureaucracy; the *New Statesman* helped to shape the thinking of politicians for decades.

In some ways, the Fabians were a peculiarly British phenomenon. In others, Fabianism was a template for something that was much more universal. Across Europe groups of intellectuals helped to establish the idea that socialism was the wave of the future, and groups of activists helped to define socialism not just as a body of ideas but also as a community. The result of all these efforts was the "socialist movement": an ideology that was also a fraternity; a set of beliefs that could organize people's lives from the cradle to the grave; a faith that could exert a relentless pressure on moderates and extract a terrible revenge on traitors.

Pick up the memoirs of any left-wing European politician and you discover a tale of student radicalism, union meetings, incessant marches against the bomb, Vietnam and apartheid, lunches with the editors of *Le Monde* or the *Manchester Guardian,* composite resolutions at party meetings and a myriad of interminable meals where everybody present—politicians, journalists, unionists, academics, spouses or mistresses—thought they were part of the same cause. When François Mitterrand, Helmut Schmidt or Denis Healey got into government, they discovered that the ideals were often impracticable, and that they had to be shelved for the moment (and these betrayals usually inspired another generation to join the Left). But they were acutely conscious of the movement and of the importance of ideas. The *rive gauche* of the River Seine, the traditional haunt of Paris's left-wing intelligentsia, remains a potent force in French politics even today.

George W. Bush's presidency has the same relationship with the *rive droite.* Over the past thirty years the conservative movement has become an establishment. The Right may still think of itself as a scrawny underdog, snapping away at the forces of liberalism (that conviction is one source of its strength), but such a self-image is clearly mistaken. Those angry intellectuals, those improvised think tanks, those eccentric benefactors—the people whose stories we charted earlier in this book—are now as close to an establishment as the liberal hierarchy that John Kenneth Galbraith enthused about in the 1960s. They provide many of the Bush administration's policies, people and organization, and, through an increasingly vigorous conservative media, they have the ability to transmit their message across the country. Above all, they seem to have won the battle for ideas.

1150 SEVENTEENTH STREET

A good place to introduce this establishment is at 1150 Seventeenth Street, a standard-issue office building in downtown Washington, D.C. The address is a "Center of Conviction and Energy" if ever there was one; indeed, it contains more conservative brainpower than the average European country.

On the tenth, eleventh and twelfth floors, you find our old friend the American Enterprise Institute for Public Policy Research. For all its venerable history, the AEI is in its pomp at the moment. More than a dozen AEI veterans have had jobs in the George W. Bush administration, including Dick Cheney (whose wife is on the AEI board); Paul O'Neill, Bush's first treasury secretary; and Glenn Hubbard, his first chairman of the Council of Economic Advisors. Leon Kass is the head of Bush's Council on Bioethics. Larry Lindsey was head of the president's Council of Economic Advisors for Bush's first two years in office (and helped push through the tax cut of 2001). Kevin Hassett is one of the most forceful outside supporters of the administration's plans for cutting corporate taxes; he helped rewrite the 2003 tax cut. David Frum, the speechwriter who helped coin the phrase "axis of evil," is now at the AEI. Richard Perle, the former head of the Defense Policy Board, has been there for years. While one of us was interviewing Chris DeMuth, the AEI's president, two cabinet secretaries rang him up.

On the fifth floor sits the *Weekly Standard,* perhaps the most influential weekly magazine in George W. Bush's Washington. The magazine's circulation is relatively small: just 55,000, compared with 154,000 for the *National Review,* 85,000 for the *New Republic* and 127,000 for the *Nation.* Nevertheless, it easily passes the Webbs' test of reaching the "small intellectual yet practical class" that runs the country. Dick Cheney sends someone to pick up thirty copies of the magazine every Monday.[2] The *Standard* follows a long tradition of conservative magazines: it preaches the virtues of capitalism without actually making any money (it loses its proprietor, Rupert Murdoch, more than a million dollars a year). To its credit, the *Standard* has earned its influence the old-fashioned way—by dint of intellectual force rather than influence mongering. Bill Kristol, the *Standard*'s founding editor, is persona non grata with the Bushes, having crossed the family not once but twice—first by acting as a focus of conservative discontent within the first Bush administration (when he was Dan Quayle's chief of staff) and second by supporting John McCain for the Republican nomination. Yet every week the *Standard* is brimming with the sort of stuff that conservatives relish—from Max Boot urging America to take up the white man's burden (or words to that effect) to Christopher Caldwell anatomizing the spread of anti-Semitism in Europe.[3]

The AEI and the *Standard* are the flag bearers at 1150 Seventeenth Street, but they are not alone. Bill Kristol runs the Project for the New American Century out of his office. Also on the fifth floor, the Philanthropy Roundtable and *Philanthropy* tell rich conservatives how to give away their money. Founded by disaffected conservative benefactors in the late 1970s, the roundtable, which now boasts six hundred associates, sang the praises of voluntary organizations versus clumsy welfare bureaucracies long before George W. Bush came up with compassionate conservatism. The roundtable frequently joins forces with the Capital Research Center, located just around the corner, to harry liberal foundations about "donor intent": did the robber baron who established your foundation really want you to subsidize lesbian performance art?

The militaristic Webbs might well have appreciated the way that 1150 Seventeenth Street acted as an incubator for the Bush administration's Iraq policy: back on December 1, 1997, Bill Kristol and Robert Kagan cowrote a cover editorial for the *Standard* entitled "Saddam Must Go." In 1998 the Project for the New American Century dispatched a letter to Bill Clinton urging him to adopt a "full complement" of diplomatic and military measures to remove Saddam. The signatories included both Donald Rumsfeld and Paul Wolfowitz. Meanwhile, the AEI provided a perch for many of the most aggressive hawks, churned out pamphlets on democratizing the Middle East, and hosted meetings on rogue states. What could be more fitting than the fact that George W. Bush decided to commit himself to the goal of democratizing the Middle East at a huge AEI dinner in February 2003? A democratic Iraq, promised the president, "would serve as a dramatic and inspiring example of freedom for other nations in the region." The only bit of the president's speech that was greeted with stony silence was his tentative suggestion that, at some time, the Israelis should stop expanding settlements in Palestinian territory. The war against Saddam Hussein that 1150 Seventeenth Street had been urging for nearly a decade began just over two weeks later.

The R&D department

The existence of 1150 Seventeenth Street shows how much ideas have mattered in the Bush presidency. That is not to deny that the Bush White House is less cerebral than its predecessor. Under Bill Clinton, 1600 Pennsylvania

Avenue often felt more like a university common room than a government enterprise: it boasted six Rhodes Scholars (including the president), and a third of Clinton's 518 earliest appointees had attended Harvard or Yale. By contrast, only two of George W. Bush's original fourteen cabinet members had attended Ivy League universities as undergraduates; and, by any academic measure, there were no first-rate brains to set alongside Larry Summers or Robert Rubin.[4] Bush's favorite organ is the heart rather than the brain, and one of his least favorite people is Strobe Talbott, a Yale contemporary who spent his time foolishly studying books and attending lectures rather than bending his elbow with his fraternity brothers. By contrast, Clinton loved Talbott.

Yet from the first, Bush saw that conservative intellectuals could be useful—much in the same way that an R&D department is useful to a chief executive. His formative experience in Washington was to watch his father's administration disintegrating, in large part for want of "the vision thing." While Bush was governor of Texas, Karl Rove made sure that his boss was plugged into the national policy debate, introducing him to the writings of the venerable James Q. Wilson as well as of younger firebrands such as Marvin Olasky and Myron Magnet. On becoming president, Bush took care to sprinkle a few thinkers among the solid former CEOs: Condoleezza Rice was a provost of Stanford University; John DiIulio, who briefly ran his office of faith-based initiatives, is a leading social scientist (and a pupil of James Q. Wilson). The big ideas with which Bush launched his presidency—tax cuts, education reform, compassionate conservatism and missile defense—had all been fermenting for decades in different parts of the *rive droite*.

One barometer of the importance of ideas is the number of Straussians in George W. Bush's Washington. Every year some sixty of the followers of the philosopher get together for a Fourth of July picnic. Paul Wolfowitz, the deputy secretary of defense, was a pupil of one of Strauss's leading protégés, Allan Bloom (Wolfowitz even made an appearance in Saul Bellow's intellectual-worshipping novel about Bloom, *Ravelstein*). Other Straussians include Abram Shulsky, the director of the Pentagon's Office of Special Plans, John Walters, the drug czar, and Leon Kass, the head of the President's Council on Bioethics. Nobody would pretend that Bush, a man who regarded

Yale University as a drinking competition (which he damn-near won), spends his evenings reading Strauss's *Xenophon's Socratic Discourse*. But he knows the importance of people who do.

At the center of Bush's R&D department stand the right-wing think tanks. A short walk from Congress, the eight-story-high Heritage Foundation has an annual income of $30 million, employs around two hundred people and holds some seven hundred lectures, debates and conferences a year. In 2003 Heritage more than doubled the size of its Capitol Hill headquarters. Its new premises include apartments for interns and fellows, a 250-seat auditorium and a sports center—all to support what John Ashcroft calls the "wonderful work of truth that emanates from the Heritage Foundation." The Cato Institute preaches libertarianism from a striking glass building on the corner of Massachusetts and Tenth. The Center for Strategic and International Studies, which was founded by former AEI fellows, has had a hand in fashioning the Bush administration's foreign policy—as has Frank Gaffney's Center for Security Policy. The Ethics and Public Policy Center tries to bring "the Judeo-Christian moral tradition" to bear on political debate.

Heritage is not the only conservative institution to straddle the worlds of ideas and political action. On the tax-cutting Right, both Steve Moore's Club for Growth and Grover Norquist's Americans for Tax Reform act as sounding boards for concepts like the flat tax. The Institute for Justice, which George Will has described as "a merry band of libertarian litigators," campaigns in favor of school vouchers and against restrictions on local businesses.

The *rive droite* is not just a Washington affair. There are now about fifty conservative think tanks across the country (compared with just a handful of liberal ones). The Hudson Institute has offices in Indianapolis and in Madison, Wisconsin, as well as in Washington, D.C. It employs an eclectic mixture of libertarians and Straussians, and focuses on thinking about the future in unconventional ways. The grandest outside Washington, the Hoover Institution, boasts a staff of some 250 people and provides a home for George Shultz, Reagan's secretary of state, as well as for leading free-market economists such as Gary Becker and Milton Friedman (who, for some reason, has chosen to retire in San Francisco, the most liberal city in the country). Hoover produces widely read magazines such as the *Hoover Digest* and *Policy*

Review, and has its own television program, *Uncommon Knowledge.* The common room where the Hoover fellows gather for tea has a touch of Oxbridge about it: groups of tweed-jacketed gentlemen engaged in civilized—and sometimes animated—conversation. But anyone expecting the classic fare of the Oxbridge common room—lamentations about cuts in state funding and the iniquities of American imperialism—is in for a surprise. Hoover fellows will confess to you guiltily over their teacups that they are worried that school vouchers are a cop-out because they preserve some role for the state in education. They politely debate schemes for increasing the size of Bush's tax cut. Or they argue that America's military buildup needs to be much bigger to take into account the threat from China.

Other conservative think tanks operate on a more modest scale than Hoover; the Manhattan Institute, for instance, feels downright cramped. Each of them tends to have some quirk of its own. For example, many of the West Coast think tanks have a libertarian tone. The Milken Institute in Los Angeles, set up by the eponymous junk-bond king, is a hotbed of deregulation but has no time for social conservatism.

Another example is the Discovery Institute in Seattle, which was founded in 1990 by Bruce Chapman. A cerebral right-winger, who cowrote a book about the Republicans called *The Party That Lost Its Head* with George Gilder in 1966, Chapman ran the Census Bureau for a while before being drafted into the Reagan White House, where one of his jobs was to keep in contact with think tanks. When he left government, he initially found a perch at the Hudson Institute, and then tried to set up a Western version of Hudson in Seattle, before starting Discovery. The Discovery Institute, whose mission, "to make a positive vision of the future practical," sounds a little as if it comes from *Star Trek,* specializes in mixing futurism and the free market—a lifelong passion of Gilder, its most famous fellow. One big interest is transportation: the institute has been a proponent of a rail link connecting Seattle, Portland and Vancouver, B.C., and Chapman was one of the people Bush consulted about privatizing Amtrak. Discovery also has ideas about Western environmental issues (such as salmon and logging), tort reform and broadband deployment: it was a persistent critic of the antitrust suit brought against Microsoft.

For all its quirkiness, Discovery is clearly part of the conservative network. Its fellows are forever popping up in the *Wall Street Journal* and *National Review.* To keep up pressure on the administration about tax reform and telecom deregulation, it has formed a loose alliance with Cato, the Club for Growth and the National Center for Policy Analysis (a prominent proponent of privatization from Dallas), and taken its case directly to Karl Rove. In Washington State, it works closely with two other free-market think tanks, the Evergreen Freedom Foundation in the state capital, Olympia, and the Washington Policy Center (which Jack Kemp labeled "the Heritage Foundation of the Northwest"). Indeed, it is worth noting that Washington State, which voted for Al Gore in 2000 and has only two Republicans elected to statewide offices, probably devotes as many resources to producing conservative ideas as most European countries.

Discovery is also the leading proponent of an increasingly influential idea on the Right: "intelligent design." The intelligent design movement, according to Chapman, holds that "certain features of the universe and of living things are best explained by an intelligent cause, not as a part of an undirected process, such as natural selection." In other words, Darwinian theory does not wholly explain either the origin of life or the development of species. Chapman, a committed Christian, first got interested in the subject because of worries about free speech: in 1995 he rallied to the defense of a California science professor who was threatened with the sack merely for arguing that evolution does not explain everything. Most orthodox scientists dismiss intelligent design as upmarket creationism. But books and papers spew out of Discovery's Center for Science and Culture, and Chapman points to several victories in his battle against what he calls the neo-Darwinists. In October 2002, Ohio became the first state to establish science standards requiring students to "know how scientists continue to investigate and critically analyze aspects of evolutionary theory." A school district in Cobb County, Georgia, now urges teachers to discuss "disputed views" about evolution. Conservative Republicans also managed to squeeze a passage into the congressional conference report attached to the No Child Left Behind Act urging (though not forcing) schools to teach "the full range of scientific views."

The intelligent design movement is an example of the Right's grow-ing willingness to do battle with what it regards as the liberal "science establishment" on its own turf, using scientific research of its own. Right-wing think tanks have attacked scientific orthodoxy on stem cells, arguing that there is no need to harvest embryos, as it should be possible to extract stem cells from adults. They have also pored over the data on global warm-ing: Bjorn Lomborg, the author of *The Skeptical Environmentalist* (2001), an indictment of green overstatement, is a cult hero in places like the AEI and Discovery. There are also battles brewing on animal rights, euthanasia and the scientific origins of homosexuality. So far the science establishment has given little ground to the conservative upstarts, particularly on intelli-gent design. In Ohio, some scientists equated supporters of intelligent design with the Taliban. But the Right is clearly extending the battle of ideas into new territories, just as Milton Friedman and others did in economics forty years ago.

People and money

The conservative think tanks are incubators of people as well as ideas. Donald Rumsfeld and Condoleezza Rice are Hoover veterans. So are a quarter of the members of the Defense Policy Board. Elaine Chao, the Labor Department secretary, and Kay Coles James, the director of the Office of Personnel Man-agement, are Heritage alumni. Mitch Daniels, the former boss of the Office of Management and Budget, is a former president of the Hudson Institute. Elliott Abrams, George Bush's Middle East supremo, was a former head of the Ethics and Public Policy Center. The Center for Strategic and International Studies boasts so many top government officials that it was once nicknamed the "national security advisors' stud farm." Hundreds of lower-level adminis-tration employees cut their teeth in think tanks, where they were schooled by conservatives from previous administrations. Heritage employs Ed Meese, Reagan's attorney general, and Bill Bennett, his secretary of education. If "people are policy," as Edwin Feulner, the head of Heritage, likes to say, then the think tanks are becoming America's shadow government.

The think tanks also work as a general command center for the intellectual Right. Heritage runs an annual gathering which brings some 375 conservative policy groups from around the country together and allows them to swap ideas. Heritage's 2003 handbook of policy experts lists 2,200 people and 420 policy organizations, all eagerly waiting to be consulted. If this makes it sound as if there is some secret master plan behind this, in one way there is. Behind the right-wing think tanks, policy centers, university fellowships, highbrow quarterlies, student publications, television networks and radio programs sit a number of conservative foundations. The Big Five names — Scaife, Coors, Koch, Bradley and Olin — still matter, but they matter much less than they once did. The corporate giving that began in the 1970s continues: until recently, Ken Lay of Enron sat on the board of trustees of the AEI with his fellow energy boss, Dick Cheney. But the biggest change has been the growth of individual donors, pulled in by direct-mail shots. Heritage now has more than 200,000 individual contributors, who provide more than half of its money. The days when money from Richard Mellon Scaife accounted for 40 percent of its funding are long gone.

In America think tanks have taken over much of the policy making that is handled by political parties in other countries. To describe the Republican Party organization as intellectually barren would be a little unfair, but it mainly exists nowadays as a vehicle for raising and distributing campaign contributions. To the extent that the national party or its state equivalents have research departments, these are largely devoted to digging up stomach-churning stories about Democrats rather than, say, redefining the role of the state (its Democrat competitors are also prone to such muckraking). Meanwhile, every ambitious Republican in Congress is a semidetached policy entrepreneur looking for an idea that might make his or her reputation. They are normally strapped for time (all that fund-raising again), so what could be more sensible than to get think tanks to do their policy research for them? Moreover, the think tanks have become experts at exploiting the divisions of power in Washington. If an idea fails with the White House, you can try congressional bosses (as the *rive droite* did with welfare reform); if you run into opposition in the Senate, then lobby the president, as it did with the double taxation of dividends.

AT LONG LAST, RIGHT-WING MEDIA

In December 2002, something rather remarkable happened: Al Gore complained about the conservative bias of the American press. "The media is kind of weird these days on politics, and there are some major institutional voices that are, truthfully speaking, part and parcel of the Republican Party," Gore grumbled to the *New York Observer.* This complaint was sparked by the revelation that Roger Ailes, the head of television's Fox News, had sent memos to Karl Rove offering him advice in the wake of September 11.

For decades conservatives have complained that it was impossible to get their message heard on television. Under George W. Bush, Fox News came of age, replacing CNN (or the Clinton News Network, as conservatives called it) in 2002 as the most popular news channel and giving the conservative movement a completely new way to spread ideas. The cable news channel was actually born back in 1996. Rupert Murdoch, the network's owner, spotted that the leftward tilt of most news stations created an opening on the right with the "dittoheads" who listened to Rush Limbaugh. Ailes, who had worked both in the first Bush's White House and as a producer of Limbaugh's radio show, came up with an enormously successful formula. Emphasize talking heads (who are cheap) rather than foreign reporting (which is expensive). Emphasize controversy—preferably by getting the talking heads to wrestle with each other intellectually. And drive the liberal establishment mad by calling the whole thing "fair and balanced."

The Rush Limbaugh of Fox News is Bill O'Reilly. *The O'Reilly Factor* is cable's top-rated news show: the appetite for O'Reilly's brand of populist outrage is so huge that he now does a daily radio program as well. Every night on the *Factor* O'Reilly confronts some hapless representative of the liberal establishment—a bearded professor who hasn't quite realized the 1960s are over; a peace protestor with an earring and a ponytail—and then proceeds to harangue them about the absurdity of their views. (Why these people keep accepting his invitation is one of the great mysteries of our age.)

O'Reilly resolutely maintains that he is "apolitical," a spokesman for ordinary people disgusted by the entire establishment. In fact, he is a classic populist conservative: a product of the Irish lower-middle class (or working class, if you believe O'Reilly's downwardly mobile version of his origins) who resented the way that the liberal elites treated people like him as pawns in their affirmative-action and busing schemes. He keeps a doormat with Hillary Clinton's face on it beneath his desk, and proudly maintains that his is the "only show from a working-class point of view."[5]

Fox's mantra—"We Report. You Decide."—may be the best joke in American journalism. The network is often at its best when it is at its most shamelessly partisan: one morning show in 2003 began with a horrified discussion about the bias of the *New York Times* (the paper's television reviewer had recently revealed his outrageous liberal bias by accusing Fox of being conservative). The next segment dealt with protests against the Dixie Chicks, a country group that had been rude about George W. Bush. The Fox presenter, in no way letting politics interfere with the network's cultural coverage, immediately announced her intention to burn all her Dixie Chicks CDs.

The war against terrorism has brought out either the best or the worst in Fox, depending on your point of view. One of the correspondents, Geraldo Rivera, bought a gun and proclaimed his keenness to kill Osama bin Laden.[6] During an antiwar demonstration in New York City, Fox's electronic ticker tape read: "Attention, protesters: The Michael Moore Fan Club meets Thursday at a phone booth at Sixth Avenue and Fiftieth Street."[7] In one delightful scene from a protest in France, a Fox reporter, asked to explain the large number of people on the streets, looked confused for a while before confiding to the folks back home: "Many of these people are Communists."

Fox has given conservatives a TV station that they can leave on in the background. The Heritage Foundation had to warn its staffers to stop watching so much Fox News on their computers, lest the computer system crash. During the 2000 Florida recount Trent Lott confessed, "If it hadn't been for Fox, I don't know what I would have done for the news." George W. Bush even praised Tony Snow (who had worked for his father before becoming a Fox News anchorman) in a specially taped tribute to Snow's Sunday morning show in April 2000. "If I go on the Fox network," Newt Gingrich, a Fox News commentator, told the *New Yorker,* "no question that people in the administration see that. If there is one channel on in a Washington office that I visit, it's usually Fox." The Bush administration regularly sends its heavyweights to Fox to talk to the faithful, correctly gambling that the bigger broadcast networks will be forced to show highlights of Colin Powell or Dick Cheney.

One point that should not be underestimated about Fox is that, for all its partisanship, much of its political reporting is first-rate. Ailes is careful to balance blondes with big hair and a poor knowledge of French politics with highbrow commentators such as Fred Barnes and Charles Krauthammer. Its main political anchor, Brit Hume, is one of the smartest commentators on American politics. The network makes a habit of covering the big set pieces of American politics unusually well. Its coverage of the 2002 midterm elections, which featured Michael Barone and Barnes, was significantly better than that of its rivals.

Another weapon that has emerged for the Right under George W. Bush is the Internet blog. Unlike Fox News, the blog (a combination of "web" and "log") is a completely spontaneous phenomenon. The creators work mostly for a pittance. They acquire their following by word of mouth—and a click of the mouse—rather than by advertising. But they have already metastasized into an Internet phenomenon that wields enormous power. They comment on the news, provide Internet links to interesting items from the world's newspapers and draw on the brainpower of their readership, which also stretches around the world.

Blog sites are hardly a preserve of the conservative movement. Many bloggers are left-wing, and the two leading right-wing bloggers are hardly stereotypical conservatives. Andrew Sullivan, a former editor of the *New Republic* (and a friend of ours) is a leading gay writer; Glen Reynolds ("InstaPundit") is a libertarian law professor at the University of Tennessee. Still, as with talk radio, the blogosphere seems to suit the Right better than the Left. Sullivan and Reynolds earned the nickname "warbloggers" because their Internet sites took off in the aftermath of September 11, howling about peaceniks and anti-Semitism. Much of the bloggers' energy is devoted to exposing shoddy "liberal" reporting for mainstream newspapers and television stations, most notably the *New York Times*. The bloggers played an incendiary role in the firing of Howell Raines, the paper's executive editor.

Conservative ideas have also advanced in a lower-tech form of distribution: the big superstores like Wal-Mart. Many of the big chains are based in the South, and have provided a helping hand to some conservative products while shielding the citizens of the Right Nation from tawdry liberalism. Wal-Mart helped launch *VeggieTales,* a Christian cartoon series featuring talking vegetables. The store accounted for a quarter of its sales.[8] The *Left Behind* series, Christian books about Armageddon, also took off there. By contrast, *Maxim,* Eminem and Sheryl Crow have all been given the boot for being, respectively, too titillating, too crude and too close to the bone (Crow sang a song about Wal-Mart selling guns).

Even with the world's biggest retailer doing its bit for them, are the conservative media happy? Not at all. A persistent theme of Rush, Bill, Sean et al. remains that they are an endangered minority. Right-wing books depicting the one-sidedness of the media soar to the top of the best-seller list— books such as Bernard Goldberg's *Bias: A CBS Insider Exposes How the Media Distort the News* and Ann Coulter's *Slander: Liberal Lies About the American Right.* Gore's accusation in 2002 only provoked more howls of protest: surely any fool could see that the number of important liberal newspapers and television channels massively outnumbered right-wing ones. On the other hand, there is plainly more balance than there once was. These days left-wingers can toss off instant bestsellers about the way that the Right has hijacked the media too: witness Al Franken's *Lies and the Lying Liars Who Tell Them: A Fair and Balanced Look at the Right* (2003). At the very least, Fox and the bloggers have evened up the competition. There seem to be more right-wing columnists than ever before: the days when George Will and William Safire and the editorial board of the *Wall Street Journal* were the token conservatives are gone. Names like Krauthammer, Barone, Brooks, Kristol, Boot and Frum now appear on op-ed pages across the country.

WHY THE RIGHT WON

It is hard to exaggerate the degree to which the *rive droite* has won the battle for ideas in Washington. The right-wing think tanks are now a resource for both sides of the political spectrum. In 2002 several Democrats (including one of Bill Clinton's former right-hand men, Rahm Emanuel) turned up at Heritage's orientation session for new members of Congress. Visit a

Democratic senator's office and you are as likely to find copies of *Policy Review* and the *Weekly Standard* as the *New York Review of Books* and the *Nation.* Politicians go where the ideas are.

Why are conservative ideas so much to the fore? The capital, after all, supports a flotilla of liberal think tanks and liberal magazines. The big conservative foundations are minnows compared with liberal behemoths like the Ford, Rockefeller and MacArthur foundations. Bradley gives out less money in a year than Ford does in a month. Liberal America has first call on the country's paper of record, the *New York Times,* most of its network news organizations and America's giant universities. Put simply, there is more brainpower on the Left, more money and more resources. Yet the Left does not exercise the same influence as the Right, either in coming up with specific policies or in changing the general climate of opinion.

This is partly a function of power, of course. With a Republican White House and Congress, it is harder for liberals to make their thoughts known. Most conservatives would claim that it is also a reflection of the ideas offered. Despite their partisanship, they have a point. For better or worse, most of the more interesting ideas of the past two decades have come from the Right (just as in the Webbs' day they came from the Left). If conservative ideas weren't more vibrant than liberal ones, then George Bush would probably not be in the White House, American troops would not be in Baghdad and we would certainly not be writing this book.

But the *rive droite*'s preeminence also has to do with focus and commitment. The conservative foundations know exactly what they want—to change the world in a conservative direction. And they know exactly how they want to achieve their aim—by bringing their ideas to bear on policy making. Their liberal rivals are woollier. The Ford Foundation stands "to strengthen democratic values, reduce poverty and injustice, promote international cooperation and advance human achievement." All these are noble aims, but they could justify virtually any sort of program. The liberal foundations still contest part of the public-policy arena, but they push much of their energy into "grassroots organizations" and "community projects" of one sort or another, many of them overseas. Ford has thirteen offices in the Third World busy on projects such as helping the villagers of Chattis Mauja in Nepal "gain access to a canal planning process." This benevolence might well do far more good for the world than sponsoring a debate at the AEI on "The Future of Iran: Mullahcracy, Democracy, and the War on Terror," but it makes for a less focused movement.

The conservatives also bring an impressive degree of commitment to their cause. Cast your mind back to 1973 when the Heritage Foundation was created. Who but the loyalest of the loyal would want to brave the derision of their friends to work in a conservative think tank? Even now that these pioneers are rich and powerful, there is something endearingly rabid and unhygienic about many conservative think tankers. Old Prescott Bush would have felt at home in the Brookings Institution or the Council on Foreign Relations; if he woke up in a Cato seminar on "Saying Yes: In Defense of Drug Use" (the title of a talk by Jacob Sullum on May 29, 2003), he might feel like informing the police. The conservative media have the same sense of focus and commitment. "The conservative press is self-consciously conservative and self-consciously part of the team," Grover Norquist argues. "The liberal press is much larger, but at the same time it sees itself as the establishment press. So it's conflicted. Sometimes it thinks it needs to be critical of both sides."[9] Conservative pundits happily give addresses at social events hosted by, say, the Competitive Enterprise Institute, or turn up at Norquist's Wednesday morning meeting not as neutral observers but as participants.

In the same sort of spirit, conservative think tanks are also more hardheaded than liberal rivals. Many liberal and centrist foundations give the impression that they have been captured by people who run foundations for a living. The foundations exist to support their staffs—particularly the great and the good who sit on their boards. By contrast, conservative think tanks increasingly run themselves as businesses whose product is furthering the conservative revolution. One of the first things that Michael Joyce did when he took over the Bradley Foundation in 1985 was to tell conservatives that they could not expect his organization's cash as an entitlement.

The leader of this managerial revolution is the Heritage Foundation. Ed Feulner sold Heritage's flagship *Policy Review* to the Hoover Institution for no better reason than he thought the money could be better spent elsewhere. As for marketing, Heritage is as passionate about selling conservative ideas as Coca-Cola is about selling fizzy drinks. It invented two-page briefs for busy congresspeople. It hand-delivers its studies to members of Congress and heads of executive departments. It has a stock of colored index cards stating conservative positions in pithy phrases, a godsend to congressmen who get invited onto talk shows. One reason you see so many Democrats guiltily consulting Heritage's handbooks is because they are extremely user-friendly.

According to Eric Alterman, Heritage's computers are stocked with the names of more than 3,500 journalists, organized by specialty. Staffers even telephone reporters to make sure that they have what they need. Heritage provides convenient two-page synopses for all its studies and does its best to turn them into op-ed pieces. The think tank maintains two television studios. It also maintains a web site, Townhall.com, which provides a daily collection of conservative articles and has all sorts of convenient links which allow you to discover everything from upcoming conservative events to Heritage's position on euthanasia.

Heritage also illustrates another feature of the *rive droite:* the Right is unusually good at "covering the waterfront." There is an odd sort of synergy between Heritage's scrappy approach and the more cerebral work at the AEI. The AEI allows intellectuals to think grand thoughts: you can talk to John Lott about guns (his attitude is best captured in the title of one of his books, *More Guns, Less Crime*) or to Christina Hoff Sommers about "sexism" in schools (she thinks boys rather than girls get the worse deal in schools). Heritage is much more focused on the grittier business of Congress. This allows for a two-pronged assault on liberal orthodoxy. The AEI softens up the liberal establishment with long-range bombing; Heritage then sends in the ground troops to capture the territory and convert it into a conservative fief.

A NEW ESTABLISHMENT

Another way of looking at this is that, under George W. Bush, the conservatives have finally become an establishment. It is partly a matter of age.

People like Ed Feulner at Heritage and Chris DeMuth at the AEI, both of whom have been fixtures in Washington since the 1970s, are now just as much a part of the permanent Washington ruling class as the pooh-bahs of the liberal establishment. The angry young men are now grandees living in domestic splendor, and going to dinner at the White House.

Like any establishment, the conservative one provides a clear ladder. A conservative thinker can now spend his or her entire life in the movement's warm embrace, starting as a student working on a campus newspaper funded by one of the foundations, becoming a young intern at Heritage and ending up as a senior fellow at AEI, with diversions to the University of Chicago, a regional think tank and a spell in a Republican administration on the way. At each stage, options open up. Are you a student interested in economics? The Institute for Humane Studies at George Mason University runs weeklong programs to introduce star students to free-market ideas. Are you a neoconservative? Then your first port of call is the Bradley Foundation, but maybe you should pop into the AEI, and somebody should be able to get you an introduction at the *Standard*. A party loyalist? Then Scaife is for you, and there will probably be a perch for you at Heritage. A libertarian? Then you need to get in touch with the Kochs, and there are plenty of people at Cato and Hoover who can help you. The *rive droite* provides fame and riches for its most successful members: columns in the newspapers, regular appearances on Fox, generous fees for giving speeches to conservative audiences.

One example of the establishment's embrace is provided by Dinesh D'Souza. D'Souza, a native of India, arrived in the United States in 1978 and attended Dartmouth College, where he acted as the founding editor of the *Dartmouth Review,* a conservative newspaper that was funded in part by Irving Kristol's Institute of Educational Affairs. He burnished his conservative credentials by writing a biography of Jerry Falwell, doing a stint as a policy analyst in the Reagan administration and briefly acting as editor of the Heritage Foundation's *Policy Review.* He spent the 1990s at the American Enterprise Institute as an Olin scholar, where he wrote books on the evils of liberal universities and affirmative action and the virtues of Ronald Reagan—all before his fortieth birthday. D'Souza is now ensconced on the West Coast at the Hoover Institution, where he continues to be a prolific author.

This new establishment has much the same weaknesses that its liberal equivalent developed in the 1960s and 1970s. One is bias. Zealotry may provide intellectual fire, but it does not always combine with objectivity. Critics whisper that the conservative think tankers have become more interested in peddling ideology than in generating new ideas. The AEI and Cato might just get away with regarding themselves as "universities without students," but isn't Heritage just a peddler of the White House line? Many "studies" are nothing more than weapons in an ideological war. Certainly the centrist Brookings Institution has been better at resisting this sense of ideological déjà vu than the conservative organizations. Brookings has broken with liberal orthodoxy on school choice, at least in the sense of entertaining the idea that vouchers might be a good thing.[10] Heritage has seldom surprised people with similar ideological heterodoxy.

The other big danger for the *rive droite* is introversion. People who spend their lives in think tanks tend to get addicted to radicalism for its own sake. Asking a think tanker whether you need a dramatic solution to a problem is rather like asking a barber whether you need a haircut. The *rive droite* seems to egg on extremism. Papers arguing for bringing free enterprise to outer space, abolishing government departments or toppling Saudi Arabia attract more attention than the nuts-and-bolts questions of fixing American schools, hospitals and government services. The left-wing intelligentsia lost its grip in the 1960s because it became fixated with Vietnam and failed to notice what was going on in American streets. The same might happen with the current right-wing intelligentsia's fascination with the Middle East.

For the moment, though, the *rive droite* is firmly in control. The best measure of this is the fact that liberals are now trying to build their own version. Thirty years ago, when Paul Weyrich founded the Heritage Foundation, he consciously modeled his conservative counterestablishment on the liberal establishment; now liberals are returning the compliment. John Podesta, Bill Clinton's last White House chief of staff, created a new liberal think tank, the Center for American Progress, that is supposed to be a mirror image of the Heritage Foundation. Leading Democratic politicians have no doubt that such an institution is sorely needed to bring a bit of focus and forward thinking to the gaggle of interest groups that dominate the party.

There is no doubt that the Democrats sorely need some "new intellectual capital," as Hillary Clinton has been frank enough to admit.[11] Yet the conservatives' advantage lies in more than just ideas. It also lies in the armies of footsoldiers who labor out in the country. The same people who send Heritage checks go to Republican precinct meetings, lobby on behalf of the NRA and attend the annual right-to-life march in Washington, D.C. It is to these footsoldiers that we now turn.

CHAPTER 7

THE BRAWN

I DON'T KNOW what effect these men will have upon the enemy," the Duke of Wellington is supposed to have said, surveying his army before the Battle of Waterloo. "But, by God, they frighten me." If George W. Bush had visited the 2003 Conservative Political Action Conference (CPAC), he might well have said the same thing.

CPAC is an annual event, organized by the American Conservative Union. In 2003 it gathered together more than 4,000 conservative activists—1,700 of them college students—for a weekend in the no-man's-land of Arlington, Virginia, to listen to Dick Cheney, Katherine Harris and other heroes of the movement speak from a stage draped in red, white and blue and backed by eighteen American flags. The sessions included "Islam: Religion of Peace?" and "Myths, Lies and Terror: The Growing Threat of Radical Environmentalism." The fresh-faced delegates wore "Fry Mumia" T-shirts, held up posters saying "Give war a chance: peace through superior firepower," sported badges saying "Fight crime—shoot back" and bought George W. Bush dolls which intoned presidential classics such as "We're working hard to put food on your family." One of the most popular exhibits was a model of the Counter-Clinton Library, which members of the vast right-wing conspiracy intend to build within walking distance of the Clinton Library in Little Rock, Arkansas, and which will boast the Hillary Hall of Shame, the Clinton

Casualties, the Grifters' Gallery and the Department of Domestic "Affairs." Less amusingly, one man did brisk trade in "No Muslims = No terrorism" stickers until the vice president's office asked him to stop.

In politics, brains without brawn can get you only so far. The conservative think tanks sit on top of a muscle-bound body of conservative activists: the members of CPAC, and the hundreds of thousands of other footsoldiers around the country who think like them, are the people who knock on doors, sign petitions, telephone radio shows and, crucially, attend precinct meetings. A good chunk of this muscle is devoted not just to beating up the Democratic Party but to keeping the Republican Party in line. The Bush White House is acutely aware of the demands on these footsoldiers. It has point people who devote much of their time to pursuing the aims of different parts of the Republican constituency (or at least keeping them happy). And scrutinizing the scrutinizers is Karl Rove.

Few political operatives have enjoyed such a close relationship with the president as Rove enjoys with Bush. Bush thinks so much of his consigliere that he has bestowed on him not one but two nicknames: "Boy Genius" and "Turdblossom." Rove also straddles two roles. In the past, there have been policy makers who have been unusually close to presidents—Harry Hopkins lived in FDR's White House for long periods of time—but they have had relatively little to do with the dirty business of choosing political candidates and electoral politics. On the other side of the fence, there have been political consultants, like Lee Atwater and Bill Clinton's James Carville, who have kept away from the minutiae of policy making. Rove does both. His fingerprints can be found on all Bush's most controversial decisions, from the fudge over stem-cell research to the imposition of steel tariffs. At the same time, he is the de facto head of the Republican National Committee, vetter in chief of Republican candidates and the main link to the conservative movement.

Rove has an encyclopedic knowledge of that movement. It is amazing how many of the footsoldiers wandering around the hinterland of the Right Nation have had direct contact with Rove. One young CPAC activist boasted to a group of friends that he had Rove's cell phone number in the same sort of excited tones that other students might use to boast of having Britney Spears's.

Rove's job is complicated by the extraordinary variety of these activists. Visit CPAC and you can find booths advertising everything from monarchy to anarchy. The activists' loyalty is usually not so much to "conservatism" as such as to one of a thousand different causes—for example, keeping the Confederate flag, banning abortion or cutting the capital gains tax. The parallel that springs to mind is, once again, of an army—but this time of a medieval army. As king, George W. Bush may place his standard in the center of the line, but most of his troops wear the livery of other causes.

Those troops can be loosely divided into two main groups: rebels against government and social conservatives. The rebels want to limit Washington's hold over their lives, guns and wallets. The social conservatives want to reverse what they see as cultural decline and social disintegration. By and large, Rove and Bush have managed to keep both of these groups happy (though both the antigovernment wing and the social conservatives have sometimes been restless). Yet it is also plain that both groups take a much more extreme view of the world than Bush does. The Toxic Texan might seem like a right-wing extremist in Paris, France; in Paris, Texas, however, he can seem like a bit of a wuss.

SMALLER GOVERNMENT NOW

Hostility to government is arguably the American Right's ruling passion. This hostility takes many forms: from deranged survivalists living in caves surrounded by automatic weapons and army rations to discussion groups poring over Robert Nozick's *Anarchy, State and Utopia.* In the Clinton years the paranoids sometimes threatened to get the upper hand. Under Bush, the mood is much calmer.

On the face of it, this is bizarre—because if you hate government, then you should really hate a president who fed steroids to the monster. Bush has allowed government spending to rocket skyward, introduced steel tariffs, created 20,000 federal employees by "federalizing" airport security, signed the biggest farm bill on record, supported a ban on assault weapons and, as conservatives see it, infringed on their First Amendment rights by signing a "liberal" campaign-finance law. How has the White House avoided a full-scale revolt?

One answer is that the Right has become a little less paranoid. Even before Bush's election, some antigovernment conservatives realized that things had gotten out of hand. The Oklahoma City bombing gave many people pause for thought; Newt Gingrich's speakership suggested the limits of rage as a political strategy. After September 11, even gun enthusiasts in Montana realized that the balance between security and liberty needed to be adjusted in the direction of security. The underlying answer, though, is that the antigovernment platoons still count Bush as "one of us." He has achieved this by sometimes throwing them red meat to gnaw on, but more often by hinting that he is just about to. This applies to each of the three biggest groups of antigovernment conservatives: antitax crusaders, gun-rights activists and property-rights activists.

The antitax Right—the wing of the party that revolted against George H. W. Bush—has been given more red meat than most. George W. Bush established his credentials with two massive tax cuts in 2001 and 2003 and a smaller stimulus package in 2002. His administration has worked closely with two Washington pressure groups: Grover Norquist's Americans for Tax Reform (whose Wednesday morning meeting we described in our introduction) and Steve Moore's Club for Growth. The ties with these groups are personal and organizational as well as ideological. Rove and Norquist have been friends for years. Rove has helped raise money for ATR, and makes a point of attending Norquist's Wednesday meeting several times a year. The two men have collaborated on everything from building antitax movements in marginal states like West Virginia, Missouri and North Carolina to recruiting ethnic minorities. For instance, Rove has lent his support to the Islamic Free Market Institute, an organization that Norquist established in 1998 to bring Muslims into the Republican fold. Norquist reportedly helped to convince Rove that eliminating dividend taxation, a tax change that would hand a huge sum of money to rich Americans, could also be a popular cause, since 50 percent of Americans and 70 percent of voters own stock shares.

The tactical links extend to legislation. Just before Congress broke for Easter in 2003, two moderate Republican senators, Olympia Snowe of Maine and George Voinovich of Ohio, worried by the prospect of even bigger budget deficits, forced Congress to halve the second big Bush tax cut, chopping it down to a mere $350 billion over ten years. Bush took his message to the country, sending out officials to twenty-six states to push for a tax cut of at least $550 billion. Moore and Norquist's footsoldiers also got to work. They derided the idea that the moderates stood for fiscal rectitude: didn't Olympia Snowe have an almost Democratic enthusiasm for government spending? They also came up with an ingenious wheeze to get around the $350 billion restriction. The restriction applied only to the amount that was filibuster-proof (i.e., that could be passed with a simple fifty-one-vote majority in the Senate, rather than needing sixty senators). They pointed out that the special resolution also allowed for more than a trillion dollars of non–filibuster-proof tax cuts. Why not put the popular bits of the tax cut, such as increasing the child-tax credit, into this second category? Surely sixty senators would then vote for it? The $350 billion figure could thus be used for Bush's more controversial elimination of dividend taxes. This plotting was only half successful, but it showed the tactical savvy that the tax-cutting Right has at its disposal.

This sort of politicking is mimicked in state capitals. Opposition to taxes is one of the best ways to unite any local Republican Party, no matter how dysfunctional. It also lures in entrepreneurs. Although the Bush White House is stuffed with big-business types, Rove has also made a point of wooing people from small businesses. Few organizations have been courted as avidly as the National Federation of Independent Businesses. As we saw in Chapter 4, the NFIB has been a reliable opponent of both government spending and regulation ever since "Hillary care" in 1994. It is a much more fiery outfit than any of its big-business peers, ranking some 7,500 candidates in state and local elections. The organization, which represents 600,000 small businesses, has proved to be a loyal Bush ally on almost every issue from deregulation to tort reform to getting rid of the "death tax." The White House makes a point of wheeling out NFIB members whenever the president speaks about the economy.

GUNS 'N' VOTES

The second group of antigovernment conservatives marches under the banner of gun rights. The four-million-strong National Rifle Association vies with the American Association of Retired Persons (AARP) for the title of the most successful lobbying group in the country. The organization possesses all the accoutrements of modern influence peddling: a state-of-the-art office on Capitol Hill, a telemarketing department and a high-profile head in the form of Wayne LaPierre. But its most important resource is the commitment of its membership. The NRA has a million precinct-level political organizers all around the country. At elections 95 percent of its rank and file can be relied upon to vote in a country where 50 percent is a high turnout. This means that the organization can easily make all the difference in close races—and its position has become even more important in view of the decline of the Christian Coalition. Meanwhile, it has reinforced its ties with the wider conservative world by appointing Grover Norquist and David Keene (the head of the American Conservative Union) to its board of directors.

LaPierre described the 2000 election as the most important election in the history of the Second Amendment. The Clinton administration had shut the organization out of the White House for eight years and supported bans on assault weapons and restrictions on handguns, and the NRA feared that Al Gore would speed up Clinton's incremental assaults on gun rights, eventually tilting the balance of the Supreme Court against the Second Amendment. (In fact, Gore's position was relatively typical for an ambitious Southern Democrat. He supported gun rights as a young congressman from rural Tennessee, then endorsed various forms of gun control as he moved up the Democratic hierarchy and, finally, with the Democratic nomination in the bag, tried to woo white working-class male votes in *Deerhunter* states by waffling about gun rights.) The NRA did not trust Gore for a second, but George W. Bush was seen as having an exemplary record. He had signed two progun measures into law in Texas—one allowing people to carry concealed weapons and the other making it harder for local governments to file lawsuits against gun manufacturers. LaPierre acted as a cochair of a Republican National Committee gala that raised more than $21.3 million toward Bush's election. The NRA played a leading role in defeating Gore in at least three states—Arkansas, Tennessee and West Virginia.

What sort of return is the organization getting for all this investment? During the 2000 election campaign, the NRA's vice president, Kayne Robinson, made the disastrous mistake of being caught on videotape boasting that "if we win, we'll have a president . . . a president where we work out of his office . . . unbelievably friendly relations." Ever since then, the Bush administration has been careful to keep its distance from the organization. Nobody from the NRA was given a senior position in the White House. Bush has provided lukewarm support for allowing pilots to carry concealed weapons (an NRA hobbyhorse since September 11) and he has not retreated from his pledge to sign the assault weapons ban, a position that delights America's soccer moms as much as it outrages hard-core gun activists.

For all that, it would be a mistake to conclude that the NRA wasted its time. The gun lobby has warded off its biggest nightmare: a Supreme Court willing to overturn the Second Amendment. It has also strengthened its sway over the Republican majority in the House. The Bush administration has promised to support the NRA's main legislative priority: a law to shield gunmakers and dealers from lawsuits. Even Bush's promise to sign an assault-weapons ban is something of a pantomime. House Majority Leader Tom DeLay has promised not to bring the legislation to the floor, citing a lack of enthusiasm in the congressional Republican caucus, and Bush is refusing to put any pressure on his fellow Republicans to change their minds. The result is a perfect political compromise for the Republicans, with Bush winning points with moderate voters by boasting about his willingness to get rid of assault weapons, and with DeLay shoring up support among gun owners by making sure that no such bill ever reaches the president's desk.

The NRA is particularly delighted with Bush's choice for attorney general, describing John Ashcroft, who had been the top recipient of NRA money in his failed Senate bid in 2000, as "a breath of fresh air" after the dismal years of Janet Reno. In May 2002 the Justice Department, in a reversal of decades of official doctrine, argued before the Supreme Court that the Second Amendment protects the rights of individuals to carry guns rather than only a collective right of the states to organize militias.[1] Dozens of people across the country have already cited this interpretation of the Second Amendment to challenge their gun convictions. Ashcroft has tried to have records on gun sales in federal databases destroyed after twenty-four hours, and has tried to ban the FBI from using those records in its terrorism investigations—both astonishing policies in the wake of September 11.

He has also refused to support a reauthorization of the ban on assault weapons, a retreat from the position he supported during his confirmation hearing.

LIBERTY PARK

We have already remarked that George W. Bush's army consists of troops who wear the livery of other causes, such as the NRA. But the feudal analogy can be pressed further still. The NRA itself brings to Bush's standard not just its own troops but a loose collection of kinsmen from around the country.

Liberty Park is one of many small office blocks in Bellevue, a prosperous suburb of Seattle. It houses a couple of spin-offs from Microsoft, which is ten minutes up the road. A sharp-eyed observer, drawing up in the parking lot, might spot the "More guns, less crime" bumper stickers, but it is really only when you get inside the offices that you realize what Liberty Park is all about. In one office, volunteers in the Citizens Committee of the Right to Keep and Bear Arms organize a mass mailing flogging progun paraphernalia, including yet more bumper stickers ("The Second Amendment is Homeland Security," "Don't bother me: I'm reloading"). The committee is an offshoot of the Second Amendment Foundation, but Liberty Park also houses the Center for the Defense of Free Enterprise and various service agencies for libertarian and conservative causes that organize direct-mail campaigns, telemarketing and advertising.

Liberty Park is largely the creation of Alan Gottlieb. His empire also includes a national talk-radio network with more than a hundred affiliated stations, a variety of book imprints and several progun lobbying groups in Sacramento, New York State and Washington, D.C. The annual budget of these organizations is more than $10 million. Gottlieb also sits on the board of the American Conservative Union, which runs CPAC.

Sitting in his chaotic office, beneath a rather remarkable contraption—part mop, part gun and wholly camouflaged—that goes by the name of "an assault mop," Gottlieb admits that he was a slightly unlikely gun nut. A Jewish kid who was born in Los Angeles but grew up in New York, he annoyed his Democratic parents by working for John Lindsay's Republican campaign for mayor of New York in 1965, though he immediately regretted not supporting William F. Buckley's quixotic conservative challenge and became active in Buckley's Young Americans for Freedom. He got interested in the gun issue largely from a libertarian point of view. In 1974, furious with Nixon for introducing wage controls, cross with the NRA for being complacent and with only $500 to his name, Gottlieb set up the Second Amendment Foundation in a ramshackle office in Seattle. The 650,000-strong foundation regards itself primarily as an educational and legal defense organization, but it has taken a more aggressive line than the much bigger NRA, pioneering the use of direct mail for gun causes.

Liberty Park also illustrates another of the Right's characteristics: its foot-soldiers' willingness to fight under several different colors at once. Most gun enthusiasts take a dim view of taxes. They also support the property rights of Western ranchers (just as most ranchers support the gun lobby)—which is why in the office next to Gottlieb sits Ron Arnold and the Center for the Defense of Free Enterprise. Gottlieb set up this property-rights group in the 1970s, but by his own admission it really got going only when Arnold became involved in 1984. Arnold, a former Boeing manager, says he was an activist in the Sierra Club while it was still a "conservation" movement. But when it became an "environmentalist" movement in the 1970s (which he defines as "devoted to the hatred of capitalism"), he switched sides. Ever since then, he has been wrestling with zoning laws, the Endangered Species Act, the Clean Water Act, the Forest Service and various efforts by federal landowners to increase the government's power over ranchers.

Arnold's Center, which now has 15,000 members, is part of another mustering on the antigovernment Right. The property-rights movement amalgamates a variety of interests: ranchers and farmers (particularly in the West), off-road enthusiasts who want to take their vehicles into national parks, big logging companies, fishermen and miners. All these people are united by a common resentment of the fact that the government owns so much of the land in the West. And all of them fear that distant bureaucrats are willing to trample over their rights at the behest of city-dwelling environmentalists. Some property-rights people want to privatize public lands; most of them just want increased access, more generous compensation for landowners who are prevented from developing their own property by environmental rules and a rollback of government regulation—particularly of bans on mining and logging. The image of hard-working rural Americans locked in a life-or-death struggle with urban environmentalists who care more about spotted owls than about rural workers has proved to be an enormous vote winner for the Republicans throughout the West.

Just like gun owners, the property-rights people have their own constitutional amendment (the fifth, which not only guarantees the right to remain silent but also limits government's power of eminent domain) and their own network of organizations and activists. Stewards of the Range brings together ranching interests. The Mountain States Legal Foundation provides lawyers. The Competitive Enterprise Institute is a loud voice in Washington, D.C. The Political Economy Research Center in Bozeman, Montana, universally known as PERC, provides intellectual ammunition, making the case for free-market environmentalism. On the other hand, the libertarian Right is not completely united on the subject of property rights. Arnold still snorts about the Cato Institute, which he feels focuses far too much on ranchers' "subsidized" water. For the Western property-rights movement, the idea that an individual can own private property on public land is an inalienable canon.

Environmentalists dismiss the property-rights movement as a tool of big business. Some of the early cases were certainly fought on behalf of big logging and mining companies. For the most part, however, it is a genuinely bottom-up affair, with most of the activists spurred into action by some perceived injustice or another. The movement's best-known activist, Chuck Cushman, started the American Land Rights Association in 1978, after the National Park Service tried to slap a compulsory purchase order on his cabin in Yosemite. His group now has 26,000 members. The movement's current poster boy, Wayne Hage, is a Nevada rancher who is fighting to get compensation for ancient water rights that the federal government snatched from him twenty years ago. ("Why are you doing this?" Hage asked two Forest Service agents when he came across them while moving cattle. "Because that is what we were ordered to do," replied the faceless minions.)

In his first term, George W. Bush has done just enough to keep the Western property-rights movement on his side. So far he has not introduced any dramatic changes in the law. But Gale Norton, secretary of the interior, Richard Pombo, the Republican chairman of the House Resources Committee, and Mike Leavitt, Bush's second EPA chief (who replaced Christine Todd Whitman), are sympathetic to the cause. Bush has put the brakes on "the Clinton environmentalist bandwagon," creating fewer new national parks, allowing snowmobiles to creep back into Yellowstone, trying to open up the Arctic Refuge to oil drilling and encouraging the Pentagon to get an exemption from the Endangered Species Act (to let the armed forces use its ranges more freely). These were not exactly victories for property rights, but they were defeats for green causes, which for many Westerners amounts to the same thing.

WITH GOD ON MY SIDE

For Bush and Rove, one advantage of dealing with antigovernment conservatives like the ones gathered in Liberty Park is that, for all their stridency, they understand that politics is the art of the possible. Many of them are businesspeople, and businesspeople are by their nature deal makers. Gottlieb and Arnold, for instance, could hardly be described as delirious about the Bush presidency. Gottlieb is worried about the growth in government in the wake of September 11: he would much rather that new government entities have "sunset" dates, forcing Congress to consider their abolition. He is also cross that the Right has allowed John Ashcroft to pry into people's lives so freely. At the same time he understands the pressure that Bush is under to keep the Republican Party together—just as Arnold sees the need to secure moderate votes from environmentalists on the other side of America. In the 2004 election, the footsoldiers from Liberty Park will happily fight alongside the NRA in the Bush army.

Social conservatives, by contrast, are absolutists. They rally behind two causes that are sacred to them: "life" (which must be saved from abortionists) and "family" (which must be saved from gays). If you believe that life is sacred, you still regard abortion as murder even if it is performed on a mother who has been raped. If you believe that homosexuality is sinful, you cannot strike a deal letting gay people have civil unions but not full marriages.

To make matters worse for Bush, these social issues are exactly the ones that alienate many swing voters, particularly suburban women. It may be hard to appear to be too antigovernment in America (though Newt Gingrich somehow managed it); it is, however, easy to appear too conservative on, say, abortion and gay rights, as Republicans discovered in California in the 1990s. All this has made the social conservatives a much trickier group for the Bush White House to keep on its side. Bush's relationship with social conservatives has been like a troubled marriage: tantrums and tearful apologies, long sulks and periodic fireworks, trial separations and loving affirmations that they can't live without each other.

One tantrum occurred in April 2003 over the White House reaction to comments made by a leading social conservative, Rick Santorum. In an interview, the third-ranking Republican in the Senate linked gay sex to bigamy, polygamy, incest and adultery, asserted that sodomy was "antithetical" to a healthy family and declared, "I have no problem with homosexuality. I have a problem with homosexual acts." Santorum was merely expressing Republican orthodoxy: the party platform goes out of its way to define marriage in a way that rules out gay unions. Yet when he received a predictable roasting in what Republicans call the liberal media, the Bush White House hardly rushed to defend him. This infuriated social conservatives. Phyllis Schlafly described the establishment's defense as "limp." Paul Weyrich characterized it as "tepid."

Part of their anger was cumulative. The social conservatives were terrified that the Republican establishment was preparing to sell them down the river on gay marriage, all because of Bush's need to attract moderate voters. Even before Santorum opened his mouth, social conservatives had been fuming about a secret meeting in March 2003 between Marc Racicot, the Republican Party chairman, and Human Rights Campaign, a gay lobbying group. All this was part of a worrying trend, in their view: the son of Rubbers Bush refusing to back society's most fundamental institution. Hadn't he quietly purged the 2000 convention in Philadelphia of antihomosexual rhetoric? Hadn't he appointed several openly gay people to his administration, including one ambassador and two successive heads of the Office of National AIDS Policy?

After the Santorum incident, leading social conservatives met Racicot to make their unhappiness clear, and extracted a promise from him to meet with a group of "reformed" ex-gays. But the faithful were still edgy. Gary Bauer thundered that the "grass roots will not stand for continued ambivalence on these moral issues." His successor as head of the Family Research Council, Kenneth Connor, proclaimed that "a house divided against itself cannot stand." The Reverend Don Wildmon, who owns nearly two hundred radio stations, declared that if the Republicans continued to court gays, "We will walk."

Naturally, social conservatives were relieved when Bush eventually called for a constitutional amendment to ban gay marriage. Yet that has not stopped them worrying about other betrayals. Why has he called Islam a peaceful religion? Why has he called for a Palestinian state in what social conservatives call Judea? They remain petrified that Bush might appoint a moderate, such as Alberto Gonzales, to the Supreme Court if any of the current justices retire. "We will not put up with another [David] Souter," says Phyllis Schlafly, referring to a judge appointed by George H. W. Bush in 1990 who has since taken a liberal line on most subjects, not least of which is abortion. "How do you pronounce Souter in Spanish?" runs a conservative joke: "Gonzales."

The irony in this is that social conservatives freely admit that Bush is the best president they have had. This is partly because they genuinely think that he is "one of them"—a righteous man. Throughout his presidency, Bush has enjoyed astronomically high approval ratings among Christian conservatives. Doug Wead, an Evangelical who has worked with both Bush presidents, put it this way during a PBS *Frontline* documentary on the 2000 campaign:

> Every subculture has its own language and its own inflection. Even, sometimes, it's the emphasis of a syllable in a word, or you could have one word out of order, and instantly you recognize somebody from your own subculture. And the Evangelical subculture is no different. When G.W. meets with Evangelical Christians, they know within minutes that he's one of theirs.[2]

For all his snappishness about Bush's failure to back Santorum, Weyrich readily admits that the president's record on social issues is even better than the sainted Ronald Reagan's. As we mentioned in Chapter 5, Bush has given the social Right a lot to be happy with: abstinence education, a signature on a ban on partial-birth abortion, a cloning ban, a half victory on stem cells and so on. They just want much more.

This is why dealing with social conservatives presents such a difficult balancing act for the White House. On the one hand, Bush and Rove are acutely aware of the costs of seeming intolerant on abortion and homosexuality. They have also seen, in Arnold Schwarzenegger's victory in California, the immense possibility of big-tent Republicanism: a progay, prochoice Republican swept to victory in a state the party had written off. On the other hand, social conservatives can do enormous damage to George W. Bush's cause if they don't turn up at the polls. When the Republicans pored over the 2000 election results, they discovered one horrifying statistic: some 4 million Christian conservatives who voted in 1996 failed to vote in 2000. The return of these Christian conservatives to the fold in 2002 helped the Republicans pick up vital Senate seats in Georgia and Missouri.

INSIDE THE TENT

The White House also has another challenge to consider. The Christian Right is no longer a group of outsiders who simply troop to the polling booths on election day: they are very much inside the Republican tent. There has been something of a changing of the guard in the Christian conservative hierarchy. A general air of tiredness has settled over some of the more familiar parts of the Christian Right: after several years of intense activism, some of the leading Evangelicals are finally running out of energy and ideas — and are being replaced by new institutions and leaders.

The best-known organization on the Christian Right remains the Christian Coalition. The organization that Ralph Reed built still has close relations with several congressional leaders, notably Tom DeLay and Rick Santorum. In 2000, it distributed some 70 million voter guides, filled the airwaves with pro-Bush broadcasts and helped to stop the McCain insurgency. Yet the Coalition has been going through a difficult time since Reed left in September 1997. Its claim that it still has almost 2 million members is almost certainly an exaggeration: other data suggest that the figure is no more than 400,000. The Coalition's political contributions fell from a record $26.5 million in 1996 to an estimated $3 million in 2000. The organization has cut staff, dropped its minority outreach program, the Samaritan Project, and endured a bout of legal trouble, with black employees claiming that the Coalition's leaders were "uncomfortable" when blacks joined prayer sessions. The annual meeting in Washington, D.C., in 2002 was a lackluster affair: even the decision to cosponsor the conference with a famous televangelist, Joyce Meyer, was not enough to fill all the seats. The only thing that got the faithful going was a foreign cause—Israel.

The Christian Coalition's problems find echoes across the rest of the religious Right. The semiretirement of Ralph Reed and Gary Bauer has deprived the movement of articulate advocates. The nonretirement of its old warhorses Pat Robertson and Jerry Falwell has limited the movement's appeal. Robertson and Falwell did the Christian Right little good when they said, after September 11, that God had allowed the terrorist attacks to happen because the United States had become a nation of abortion, homosexuality and secular values.

In fact, however, the Christian Right is not so much fading away as metamorphosing. The footsoldiers are abandoning old banners and regrouping around new ones. Perhaps the most important is Focus on the Family, the Colorado Springs group that we mentioned in our introduction. Focus is neither as well-known as the Christian Coalition nor as overtly political, but it has a better record of preserving its influence. The organization was founded in 1977 by Jim Dobson. Back then, Dobson was an obscure academic—a tenured professor of pediatrics at the University of Southern California School of Medicine, with a textbook on developmental difficulties and a string of academic articles to his name. Then he published *Dare to Discipline,* a guide for parents that has since sold more than 3 million copies. A score of books have followed, most of them on the subject of raising children in an uncongenial world, and Dobson has expanded Focus into an organization with more than $130 million in annual revenues. His broadcasts, books and videos reach an audience of 22 million in America and perhaps 200 million worldwide. Focus's eighty-one-acre "campus" in Colorado Springs is so big that it has its own zip code and entrance off the freeway.

Dobson is not as much of a political animal as, say, Ralph Reed. People at Focus's headquarters are leery of politics (and not just because IRS rules forbid them from participating directly in politics). Dobson repeatedly tells his supporters that their first obligation is to their church. Only about 5 percent of Focus's $130 million annual budget is devoted to public policy. Focus's people say that things like abortion should be moral issues, not political ones. Yet Dobson's fundamental beliefs—that the family is the building block of any healthy society and that there are powerful forces at work in America ranged against it—inevitably force him to take a stand on abortion and other politically charged issues, such as homosexuality, cloning and school prayer. For instance, in August 2003, during the row over whether Alabama's chief justice, Roy Moore, should be allowed to keep a monument carved with the Ten Commandments on public display in the state judiciary building, Dobson visited Montgomery to offer his support, calling Moore's battle "a struggle against judicial tyranny."[3] Focus's web site posted a "Ten Commandments Action Center," explaining how people could get involved.[4]

Dobson has huge sway within the GOP. He helped establish the Family Research Council to lobby for "traditional family values" in Washington, D.C., for example; it now has 450,000 members. One example of this muscle came in 2002, when the business wing of the Republican Party tried to reform America's bankruptcy laws. Charles Schumer, a Democratic senator from New York, cunningly attached a provision designed to crack down on antiabortion protesters. Many Republicans in Congress were initially happy to tolerate this, but Tom Minnery, Focus's political director, set to work explaining Dobson's displeasure to Congress. Dobson himself denounced efforts by Tom DeLay to bring the bill to the House floor for a vote. Focus urged people to contact their congressmen and DeLay in particular. The bill was scrapped. In 2003 Focus's president, Donald Paul Hodel (who, incidentally, served in the Reagan cabinet), wrote a letter to the *Weekly Standard* complaining about a book review which had urged Evangelicals to draw a line between religion and politics. "The fact is," wrote Hodel, "without the hard work and votes of millions of Christians, there would be no Republican majority in both Houses of Congress, no Bush presidencies, few Republican governors and a small handful of state houses in Republican hands."[5]

Focus has also had an effect in the local Republican Party. Focus members do not stop being Christian conservatives when they go home at night; they reappear at local precinct meetings in a personal capacity (as they have every right to do). Minnery, for instance, was the vice chairman of the Republican Party in El Paso County (which includes Colorado Springs) in 1997–99. "For better or worse, in the mid-1990s, the Christian Right took over many of our precincts," says one prominent local Republican, who deals with Focus and its people on a regular basis. Precinct meetings are the core of any party; they are often tedious and sparsely attended. But the activists who bother to turn up get to choose the delegates to go to the state and county caucuses, who in turn select candidates for the primaries. Gradually, most of the local Republican politicians around Colorado Springs have ended up being "three Rs" (radical, religious and Right), or at least knowing how to mouth the words from the same prayerbook. By contrast, moderate RINOs (Republicans in Name Only), who have taken moderate positions on issues like gay rights and abortion, have had a tough time of it. Two particular targets were Mary Lou Makepeace, who was the mayor of Colorado Springs until 2002, and Marcy Morrison, a local state assemblywoman. Back in 1998 Morrison was forced to collect signatures by petition to get her name on the ballot because she knew that she would never get the necessary support from the caucus.

This Christian "takeover" should not be exaggerated. Makepeace and Morrison repulsed most of their challengers, though a worn-out Morrison has retreated to the mayorship of Manitou Springs, Colorado Springs's slightly more bohemian neighbor. But what happened in Colorado Springs now seems to be happening across the country. For most of the past thirty years, religious conservatives have usually been outsiders. Now they are taking their talent for grassroots organization to precinct meetings and the like inside the party. According to a study in the magazine *Campaigns & Elections,* Christian conservatives now exercise either "strong" or "moderate" influence in forty-four Republican state committees, compared with thirty-one committees in 1994, the last time the survey was conducted. They are weak in only six states, all in the Northeast.[6] It is no accident that Ralph Reed reemerged as head of the Georgia Republican Party.

This immersion within the party may cause the White House all sorts of headaches, but it is fundamentally a vote of confidence in Bush. In the past, Republican leaders have appealed to religious conservatives through the medium of their leaders, but Bush appeals to them directly—as one of their own number rather than as the head of a party that happens to be aligned with them. Christian publications and broadcasts routinely shower his leadership with praise. Religious leaders treat his election as an act of providence. The Internet boasts several sites offering prayers for the president's success.

PATRICK HENRY COLLEGE

Some conservatives have a foot in both the main conservative camps: they seem to be driven by suspicion of government and belief in God to equal degrees. The footsoldiers who best exhibit this are the homeschoolers—the people who don't trust the state to give their children a godly education.

The homeschooling movement is one of conservative America's most extraordinary success stories. When Ronald Reagan came to power in 1981 it was illegal for parents to teach their own children in most states: they had to go to school. Today it is a legal right in all fifty states—and only twenty-eight require homeschooled children to undergo some kind of official evaluation. Thirteen states simply demand that parents inform officials that they are going to teach their children at home. In Texas, a parent doesn't have to tell anyone anything.

According to the most recent Department of Education survey (in 1999), only 850,000 children are being homeschooled. The Home School Legal Defense Association (HSLDA) estimates the number of homeschooled children at about 2 million—or 4 percent of the school-aged population (considerably more than are attending charter schools or participating in voucher experiments). The chances are that the HSLDA number is closer to the truth. Rod Paige, the education secretary, uses the 2 million figure, and despite homeschoolers' resistance to answering government surveys, there is a wealth of anecdotal evidence that homeschooling is increasing rapidly. The market for teaching materials for homeschoolers is worth at least $850 million a year. More than three-quarters of universities now have policies for dealing with homeschooled children. Support networks have sprung up in hundreds of towns and cities across the country to allow parents to do everything from establishing science labs to forming sports teams and defending their rights and reputations: when J. C. Penney started selling a T-shirt in 2001 that declared "Home Skooled" next to a picture of a trailer home, the volume of complaints was so huge that the store immediately yanked the garment. And as with all conservative subcultures, news spreads quickly about prodigious accomplishments: a family with three homeschooled children at Harvard; a homeschooler with a best-selling novel; first, second and third place in the 2000 National Spelling Bee.

The rise of homeschooling is extraordinary for two reasons. First, it requires an enormous investment of time and effort. Homeschoolers give up a free public education that they have paid for with their tax dollars. They usually give up the chance of a second income as well, because one parent (usually the mother) has to stay at home to educate the children. And that is before you factor in the cost of educational materials. Second, homeschooling represents a remarkable rejection of the power of the state. Ever since developed countries began to introduce compulsory mass education 150 years ago, sociologists such as Emile Durkheim and Max Weber have regarded the state's domination of education as a natural corollary of "modernization." Yet in the most advanced country on the planet, some 2 million parents insist that education ought to be the work of the family.

It would be a mistake to present all homeschoolers as religious conservatives. One of the first advocates of homeschooling, John Holt, was a left-winger who regarded schools as instruments of the bureaucratic-industrial complex. Woodstock, New York, continues to be a center of homeschooling as well as tie-dyed T-shirts. There is a lively subdivision of the homeschool movement called "unschooling," which argues that children should more or less be left to educate themselves. And there are also plenty of "mainstream" parents, including a growing number of urban blacks, who seem to have decided that American public schools are too violent and disorganized for their children.

Yet the Praetorian guard of the homeschooling movement comes from the Christian Right. Social conservatives began to look at homeschooling seriously in the 1970s after the Supreme Court banned school prayer. Ever since the 1980s, they have provided homeschooling with political muscle. Christian conservatives not only fume that the public schools teach secular permissiveness, they also claim they can offer better education at home. One-to-one tuition enables children—*their* children—to go at their own pace rather than at a pace set for the convenience of teaching unions. And children can be taught proper subjects based on the Judeo-Christian tradition of learning—rather than politically correct flimflam. One growing fashion among Christian homeschoolers is to return to the classical notion of the *trivium,* with its three stages of grammar, dialectic and rhetoric (which also requires children to learn Greek and Latin). Meanwhile, the Internet makes it ever easier to get hold of teaching materials and to create virtual communities that swap information.

Yet the movement has been much less coordinated than this might imply—bottom-up rather than top-down and driven by a jumble of motives. For instance, Michael Smith, the head of the Home School Legal Defense Association, first got interested in homeschooling because he was worried that his young son was floundering in kindergarten. He was commuting to his law offices in downtown Los Angeles one morning, listening to James Dobson's radio program, when he heard one of Dobson's guests, Raymond Moore, talk about homeschooling. That drive-time radio program changed Smith's life. He started to homeschool his own children and became involved in the wider homeschooling movement, helping to defend homeschoolers who were being "persecuted" by the California authorities. (His first case featured a five-year-old who was being homeschooled because her school punished her for saying grace silently before a meal.) He cofounded the HSLDA in 1983 to act as "an equivalent of the ACLU" for homeschoolers.

Smith's office is now sited at a symbol of the conservative homeschooling movement's increasing ambition: its first university. Patrick Henry College was founded only in 2000, but it already boasts 242 students, 12 faculty members, 6,000 donors, some handsome redbrick buildings and ambitious plans to expand its undergraduate school to 1,600 and to add a law school of 400. Michael Farris, the college's founder and an erstwhile Republican candidate for lieutenant governor in Virginia, defines the college's mission as training "dedicated Christian men and women who will lead the nation and shape the culture." More than 80 percent of its students have been homeschooled.

Patrick Henry College is dedicated to two of the Right's great passions: "Christ and liberty." Its walls are covered with portraits of the Founding Fathers, and the dormitories are named after their houses (Monticello, Mount Vernon, and so on). Although there is a lively debate between the college's Jeffersonians and Hamiltonians about exactly how small the government should be, the college's conception of the role of government is clearly tiny by modern standards. The college gets no government support whatsoever. Yet religion is also omnipresent. The ubiquitous pictures of the Founding Fathers often show them in prayer: Washington on bended knee at Valley Forge, for example. The college has copies of the first prayer ever said in Congress. One of the campus roads is called Covenant Drive. Everybody in the college, including faculty, students and staff, is obliged to "give testimony of personal salvation through Christ alone." The professors all sign a "Comprehensive Statement of Biblical Worldview" that, among other things, emphasizes the literal truth of the virgin birth and the creationists' account of the origin of the universe. Drink and tobacco are banned on campus. Courtship is tightly regulated: male students must call a girl's father to get permission to arrange a date and must involve the family as the relationship progresses. Farris, a father of ten, describes the place as "a refuge from sex, drugs and rock 'n' roll. Well, at least sex and drugs." Students attend chapel every day.

At times it seems as if the mission of Patrick Henry College is to revive an entire country. "Just as your parents' calling was to turn around a generation for Christ," Farris tells his charges, "your calling is to turn our nation back to a godly foundation." The college is supposed to produce not just good Christians but people who will help the Right's values triumph in the wider political culture. Patrick Henry College's demanding curriculum is modeled on that "of the founders' generation," including philosophy, logic, a foreign language, history, biblical studies, economics, literature, sciences, Euclidian geometry and classical Greek or Latin.

The students practice confronting "alternative worldviews." "I do not want a graduate's first encounter with nihilism or materialism to be at a banquet on Capitol Hill surrounded by atheists and worldly antagonists," says Robert Stacey, chairman of the government department. Students have been dispatched to work as interns in Karl Rove's office and on Capitol Hill, and one graduate now works in Paul Bremer's office in Iraq. The college is also looking at setting up a film school, having already brought in members of a Christian screenwriters' group in Hollywood to teach a class in screenwriting.

Despite this abiding sense of mission, the students are far from being stereotypical social conservatives. For instance, Steven, who was homeschooled in Midland, Texas, litters his conversation with references to Michel Foucault and literary theory, and he is so worried about his home state's "overapplication" of the death penalty that he wants to get a job with an organization that wants to reform—but not abolish—the death penalty. Several students admit to being puzzled by much of George W. Bush's foreign policy. They are also remarkably friendly toward "secular Europe." Europe and America are both heirs to Western civilization, they say. The two continents can learn from each other by bringing different perspectives to bear on problems. Transatlantic differences are a source of strength, they argue, not of division.

Yet the students are clearly part of George W. Bush's army: dressed in sneakers and track suits and occasionally muttering about French deconstruction, they are nevertheless marching in the Right direction. There is a general feeling that Bush's relationship with Christ gives him the capacity to make the right decisions. "I just like the guy," explains Abigail, who thanks God that George W. Bush was in office on September 11. Kristen hopes to work for the Bush reelection campaign in 2004, and in the longer term she plans to focus on foreign policy. She also believes that Christians have opted out of the debate, lazily deciding that the United Nations should be abolished or just left to the liberal elite. She thinks that Christians should use their God-given talents to reshape global institutions in the same way they have remolded domestic policy. "I hope to take my relationship with Christ a step further," she says, "to influence policy in a more direct manner."

The relationship between the homeschooling movement and the conservative movement has deepened in recent years—spurred on in part by the way that the teachers' unions have sided with the Democrats. The most committed advocates of homeschooling on Capitol Hill are all Christian conservatives. Senator Rick Santorum is homeschooling his children (or at least his wife is). Colorado's Marilyn Musgrove, another homeschooler, sponsored a bill to clear up various legal confusions about grants and scholarships for homeschooled children. Bill Bennett, Reagan's education secretary, has even ventured that "maybe we should subcontract all of public education to homeschoolers." During the 2000 campaign, Bush said that "In Texas we view homeschooling as something to be respected—and something to be protected. Respected for the energy and commitment of loving mothers and fathers. Protected from the interference of government." As president, he has held several receptions for homeschooled children in the White House.

Just as with Liberty Park and Focus on the Family, there is no shortage of evidence of Patrick Henry College's links to the wider conservative movement. There are signed photographs of George Bush and Dick Cheney, and signed Christmas cards from George and Laura Bush. Ian Slatter, the college's press officer, used to work for the *Weekly Standard*. Paul Bonicelli, the college's academic dean, displays a *National Review* cover showing John Ashcroft with devil's horns under the slogan "every liberal's favorite devil" and the picture signed by the devil himself (Ashcroft's wife is on Patrick Henry's board of directors). And there is no doubt which way most of the students at Patrick Henry College are going to vote. The HSLDA calculates that homeschooled children are more politically active than their peers: 74 percent of homeschooled children aged eighteen to twenty-four vote in elections compared with just 29 percent in that age bracket in the general population. Homeschoolers are also significantly more likely to contribute to political campaigns and to work for candidates.

THE VAST RIGHT-WING CONSPIRACY?

Was Hillary Clinton right to talk about a vast right-wing conspiracy? A look at the conservative movement's brains and brawn suggests that she was correct—but not quite in the way she intended.

Certainly, the idea that the Right is a cohesive army is nonsense. If George W. Bush is an accidental president, then the army that gathers around his flag is something of an accidental coalition. "General" Rove has to work extremely hard just to make sure that most of it turns up for battle. The Right happily comes together to persecute the Clintons or to growl at Osama bin Laden, but its denizens differ on much else. What do antigovernment types who simply want to be left to themselves have in common with Christian ayatollahs who want to inject government into the most intimate aspects of people's lives? Some people on the Right are hippies with an impressive appetite for marijuana and firearms. Others are fearsome moralists who dislike anything that smacks of the 1960s. And many are beyond characterization. The man at the center of Hillary's great conspiracy, Richard Mellon Scaife, supports abortion rights and believes in restrictions on both immigration and trade.[7] And that is before you start on the personal feuds—McCain versus Bush, Kristol versus Norquist and so on. Many commentators expect that the Right will crack up over the next few years because of these extraordinary internal contradictions.

Yet the Right is much more cohesive than logic suggests. In part this is a matter of personnel. The same names keep recurring in the world of the Right. The American Conservative Union's board includes Grover Norquist from Americans for Tax Reform, Wayne LaPierre of the NRA, Morton Blackwell of the Leadership Institute and Alan Gottlieb from Liberty Park. Ralph Reed, Karl Rove, Lee Atwater, Terry Dolan and Grover Norquist all cut their political teeth with the College Republicans. And this overlap continues at the local level, as we saw at Liberty Park. David Low, the great Australian cartoonist, once said that when he first arrived in Britain, he felt a little like the British infantryman in China who could not tell whether he had seen one Chinaman a hundred times or a hundred Chinamen once.[8] The same could be said about the young people at the CPAC convention.

Another piece of evidence is the way that these organizations can work together with impressive smoothness. During the antiglobalization riot in Seattle in 1999, protesters boasted about how they had used the Internet to pioneer a new political technique: "swarming" their opponent through countless small organizations. The Right has been doing this for years—using direct mail, blast faxes, talk radio and now e-mail to attack or support this piece of legislation or that. Both Hillary Clinton and Marcy Morrison in Colorado were swarmed remorselessly.

Some detect a deeper ideological bond keeping the Right Nation together. Hillary Clinton insists the binding force is hatred of progress: "I do believe there was, and still is, an interlocking network of groups and individuals who want to turn the clock back on many of the advances our country has made, from civil rights and women's rights to consumer and environmental regulation."[9] From the other side, Grover Norquist likes to call the Republican coalition a "leave us alone coalition." Businesses dislike government taxes and regulations, he argues; Christians dislike government regulation of schools—so isn't it natural for them to march arm in arm?

It is not surprising that ideologues like Norquist and Clinton should keep on returning to ideology. But the argument does not hold water. Is John Ashcroft a "leave us alone" type? Something even more important than ideology holds the Right together: culture. The coalition is more sociologically coherent than one might imagine. Gun ownership is much more common among Evangelical Christians than it is, say, among university professors. Nearly half of small business owners consider themselves born-again Christians.[10] Antitax advocates and members of the Christian Coalition are both enthusiastic listeners to talk radio. Back in the 1960s, Jewish urban intellectuals and Southern moralists had little in common. They may still be odd bedfellows but, over time, they have discovered things to talk about: the tragedy of family breakdown, the evils of Yasser Arafat and Hillary Clinton.

"Culture" might sound a little vague, but it stands out a mile at Patrick Henry College and Liberty Park. And in elections it can be crucial. The Right Nation relies on rallying like-minded people around culturally charged questions of one sort or another. These questions sometimes seem opaque and sometimes downright silly but they all boil down to one bigger question: "Are you one of us, or one of them?" Look, for instance, at the 2002 elections in Georgia. There the Republicans not only captured a Senate seat, dispatching Max Cleland, whom most experts had deemed safe (he was a moderate Democrat who lost both his legs and his right arm in Vietnam), they also managed to unseat the even safer-looking Roy Barnes, a Democratic governor whom many had begun to see as presidential material. In both cases, the Republicans replaced them with relatively unknown local figures—a state senator, Sonny Perdue (who had far less money than Barnes but is now the state's first Republican governor since 1872), and Saxby Chambliss, a local congressman. And in both cases, the Republicans' attacks had more to do with culture than position papers.

Ralph Reed demolished Cleland by focusing on national security, accusing him of standing in the way of a new homeland security bill. The pitch was sometimes crude: the Chambliss campaign ran an ad showing pictures of Osama bin Laden, Saddam Hussein and Max Cleland, saying that Cleland "voted against the President's vital homeland security efforts eleven times." But the main argument was subtler, and less about votes than about values. "Look," Reed's people argued, "Cleland is an admirable man, but he sadly does not 'get' the danger the country faces—unlike Chambliss, who is chairman of the House committee on terrorism." George W. Bush came down to Georgia to ram the point home, and conservative white Southerners somewhat reluctantly agreed.

With Governor Barnes, the Republicans focused on another culturally charged issue: the flag. Under pressure from black Democrats, Barnes had pushed through a redrawn version of the state flag, with a much smaller version of the Confederate battle cross. Most Georgians were happy with this compromise (there had been talk of an NAACP boycott of the state), but rural whites were not; organizations like the Sons of Confederate Veterans saw the old flag as part of their heritage. "If I had thought it would mean this, I would have picked my own damn cotton," read one bumper sticker. Reed threw all his energies to getting out the rural white vote: precincts were organized, the NRA mobilized, Evangelical churches prompted and so forth. On a rain-spattered election day, volunteers stood at crossroads holding signs showing the Confederate flag and urging their neighbors to "Boot Barnes." The Democrats, by contrast, failed to get out the black vote. Barnes was brought down by the ground war.

A conspiracy at work? It was certainly highly organized. But in the end it was not about General Rove giving orders from the White House. It was about something more elemental: reminding conservatives of the heart why they hate the other side.

CHAPTER 8

WITH US OR AGAINST US: THE RIGHT AND THE WAR AGAINST TERROR

I N   H I S   A C C E P T A N C E   S P E E C H   to the Republican National Convention in Philadelphia on August 3, 2000, George W. Bush focused on a subject that was bound to delight his audience: his disappointment with the Clinton administration. They had so much promise, he said. But to what purpose?[1]

On September 10, 2001, you could have said the same thing about the Bush administration. It had certainly exceeded expectations to begin with: there had been the glory days of the tax cut and the education bill. But there was a growing sense of disappointment about the administration, particularly among the intellectuals and footsoldiers. Bush's agenda now seemed to be shrinking to injunctions to be good to your neighbors ("communities of compassion") and fudging difficult decisions on stem-cell research. One of his biggest ideas, compassionate conservatism, had fizzled. Conservatives were beginning to resort to the classic last-ditch defense of all Republican administrations: that merely by existing, by not being the other side, Bush was holding up the relentless advance of the liberal state. The Republicans had already lost control of the Senate, thanks to the defection of Jim Jeffords. There were worries about the midterm elections in 2002.

There were also worries about the man. Bush had surpassed many people's expectations, but the word "great" was seldom used to describe him, even on the Right. On the morning of September 11 he was engaged in one of the classic pastimes of a small-bore presidency—reading to fourth-graders in a schoolroom in Florida. And in the immediate aftermath of the attacks, he looked too small for the job. The rhetoric was hesitant; the words did not come easily, as they surely would have from Ronald Reagan or Bill Clinton. Bush took too long to get back to the White House and his team produced a lame story about there being a direct threat to *Air Force One*. In his generally sympathetic book about Bush, Frank Bruni of the *New York Times* describes his own doubts:

> In many regards the Bush I knew did not seem to be built for what lay ahead. The Bush I knew was part scamp and part bumbler, a timeless fraternity boy and heedless cut-up, a weekday gym rat and weekend napster, an adult with an inner child that often brimmed to the surface or burst through.[2]

Yet within a few days both the president and his presidency were transformed. The weekend napster acquired real grit and determination. Not only had he inherited a challenge as big as anything that America had faced since the Cuban Missile Crisis, he also had the purpose that his presidency had so long missed.

September 11 certainly had an effect on the domestic presidency: it changed the nature of the debates about immigration, taxes, security and much more. But the big change came in foreign policy. In the second presidential debate in Winston-Salem in 2000, Bush had warned: "If we are an arrogant nation, they will resent us. If we are a humble nation, but strong, they will welcome us." Four years later, he was talked of as an "imperial president," changing regimes, dispensing with allies, pronouncing radical new theories of preemption. Some of this stridency was inevitable: a giant nation had been bloodied and demanded revenge. Bill Clinton tells his friends that he would have removed the Taliban from Afghanistan. But Bush went much further than that. Bush's response to September 11 was not really a measured one; it was an exceptionally ambitious, radical response. In particular, it was an exceptionally neoconservative one.

ONE YEAR IN THIRD PLACE

Nowadays the idea that America has a neoconservative foreign policy is commonplace. Yet until September 11, the neoconservatives were junior members of the Bush team. Only about twenty of them found their way into the administration in 2001. The highest-ranking was Paul Wolfowitz, the deputy secretary of defense. Other prominent figures included Douglas Feith, number three at the Pentagon; Lewis "Scooter" Libby, Dick Cheney's chief of staff and a Wolfowitz protégé; and John Bolton, who, despite exhibiting a profound distrust of arms control, was put in charge of it at the State Department. Jim Woolsey, Richard Perle and Ken Adelman all found places on Rumsfeld's Defense Policy Board—but so did several dozen other people. The neocons were not CEOs-cum-bureaucrats like Cheney and Rumsfeld. They were not part of the Texas mafia like Karen Hughes and Karl Rove. They were usually Jews in a party that had traditionally been a bastion of gentiles. They were intellectuals and professionals—the sort of people who earned postgraduate degrees from venerable universities, forged careers in think tanks, academia and intellectual magazines and spent quite a lot of time disagreeing with one another. They were not natural comrades of a president who judged people by the content of their hearts rather than the quality of their minds.

It is notable that many leading neoconservatives—including Bill Kristol of the *Weekly Standard*—sided with John McCain rather than Bush in the 2000 Republican primaries. McCain was not perfect from their point of view—he didn't want to impose trade sanctions on China, for example[3]—but he nevertheless preached a brand of national-greatness conservatism that took rogue states and weapons of mass destruction deadly seriously. Kristol and his allies feared that Bush would be too much like his father, who had aborted the first Gulf War before Saddam had been destroyed, forced Israel into the Oslo peace process and employed a succession of Republican realists such as Colin Powell, Brent Scowcroft and James Baker (who was famously supposed to have said, "Fuck the Jews. They don't vote for us anyway").

During the election campaign, George W. Bush sided with the realist faction in the Republican Party. He sang the praises of a "humble but strong" foreign policy and criticized one of the key tenets of neoconservative philosophy: intervening in trouble spots such as the Balkans. Bush's knowledge of foreign affairs left something to be desired: he had traveled outside the country astonishingly little given his lineage, he referred to the Greeks (superbly) as Grecians and he flunked an admittedly tricky pop quiz. Having failed to name the ruler of Pakistan, Bush tried to turn the tables by asking the interviewer whether he knew the name of the foreign minister of Mexico. "No sir," said the reporter, "but I would say to that: I'm not running to be president of the United States."[4]

Wolfowitz was one of the early "Vulcans," as candidate Bush's foreign-policy team was known as, but Bush's most important tutor on foreign affairs was Condoleezza Rice, a woman who shared his interests in sports, exercise and religion. Rice's main concern was the great powers—particularly the great power that she knew best, Russia. She took a dim view of nation building, pouring scorn on the idea of "the Eighty-second Airborne escorting kids to kindergarten."[5] Even Dick Cheney, who arguably became the neocons' most powerful backer, differed from them on all sorts of vital issues. As defense secretary under the first President Bush, he had supported the decision to leave Saddam in place in 1991, a decision that neoconservatives regarded as an unforgivable error. He was on record as being critical of Israel and its settlement policies and, unlike Kristol et al., he did not want America to intervene in the Balkans.

The neoconservatives had even less influence in the Pentagon and the State Department than in the White House. Military types regarded the neocons as the worst sort of civilian meddlers: spindly intellectuals who had never been in battle themselves (most of the neocons had run away from Vietnam even faster than Bush) and yet who wanted to send American troops to war all over the world. Over at State, professional diplomats loathed the neocons' black-and-white view of the world and their penchant for rhetorical bomb throwing, and the new boss, Colin Powell, was very much on the left of the Republican Party—a supporter of affirmative action, international institutions and military caution, all the things that the neoconservatives disliked.

Ivo Daalder, a former member of Clinton's National Security Council who is now at the Brookings Institution, has divided the people jostling for influence around Bush into three categories: "democratic imperialists" like the neocons; "doveish pragmatists" like Powell; and "assertive nationalists" like Cheney, Rumsfeld and Rice, who agreed with the neocons about America's need to look after its own interests more aggressively but who had no patience with nation building, spreading democracy and the like.[6] Until September 11, the neocons were the weakest of the three groups. The assertive nationalists made sure that Bush's foreign policy had a much harder conservative edge than many Europeans liked: witness the way that the ABM treaty and the Kyoto Protocol were brusquely dispensed with. America was throwing its weight around (that phrase "Don't mess with Texas" comes to mind again), but the accent was usually on disengagement rather than regime change. The Texas tone was softened by the fact that Colin Powell won a number of these diplomatic tussles—including on Iraq, where America agreed to join the rest of the UN Security Council in a new round of "smart" sanctions.

This balance seemed to suit George W. Bush. He would certainly have loved to dispose of Saddam Hussein, if an easy chance presented itself (Paul O'Neill claims the idea was discussed only ten days after the inauguration)[7] and he developed an early distrust of both multilateral organizations and the French. But like most of conservative America, he regarded the Middle East as a rats' nest and nation building as a fool's game. As for terrorism, spies on both sides of the Atlantic insist that there was no real change from the Clinton administration's stance: bin Laden was regarded as a danger but not a priority. Bush's emphasis was on domestic policy. He was desperate not to repeat his father's mistake of getting too entangled in the outside world. Asked about the neocons in one TV interview in early 2001, Dick Cheney replied, "Oh, they have to sell magazines. We have to govern." [8]

In the immediate aftermath of September 11, most foreign-policy observers expected Bush to stick to assertive nationalism. America's wrath against the evildoers would be mighty, but the war against terrorism would probably be a limited affair. Powell calmly slapped down Wolfowitz when he declared at a press conference three days after September 11, that America's policy was "ending states who sponsor terrorism." Wolfowitz could speak for himself, Powell told reporters, but America's goal was ending terrorism, nothing more.[9] In fact, the next two years were to prove Wolfowitz right.

THE NEOCON CABAL

By April 2003, the neoconservative agenda had been made flesh and blood. What only two years previously had been hot air in the American Enterprise Institute was reality in the streets of Kabul and Baghdad. Saddam and the Taliban had been deposed; Syria and Iran were on the watch list; Yasser Arafat had been sidelined. "A Bush doctrine," hailed by the neocons as rivaling the Truman doctrine in its "audacity, success and revolutionary nature," had been launched.[10] The National Security Strategy of 2002 codified an explicit policy of preemption and called for "encouraging free and open societies on every continent." In the arguments about Iraq, Bush eventually decided to ignore the two neocon bêtes noires, the UN and Old Europe. If it had not been for Bush's keenness to create a Palestinian state, the joy at 1150 Seventeenth Street might have been truly unconfined.

How on earth had this revolution happened? The first and least convincing explanation comes from the Left (particularly in Europe): that a ruthless cabal hijacked foreign policy from a weak president. The second comes from the neocons themselves, who regard their rise as a matter of logic: they had foreseen a world of terrorism and knew how to deal with it. But in our opinion a third factor was the most important: after September 11, the neocon message, for better or worse, struck a mighty chord with the rest of the Right Nation. A neoconservative foreign policy soon became a conservative one.

Let's begin with the first theory, that the neoconservatives somehow launched a coup in the White House. An extraordinary well-organized and ruthless clique, goes the argument, had been dreaming about regime change in the Middle East for years. They seized on the disaster of September 11 to push American foreign policy in a radical new direction. "Neo-conservatives," Lord Jopling, a former British cabinet minister, told the British House of Lords on March 18, 2003, "have a stranglehold on the Pentagon and seem, as well, to have a compliant arm-lock on the president himself." The House of Lords was also informed by Baroness Shirley Williams (who was then married to a prominent Harvard political scientist, the late Richard Neustadt) that the Bush administration's policy is "propelled to some extent by what I can only describe as a fundamentalist Christian and fundamentalist Jewish drive that is almost as powerful as fundamentalist Islam itself."[11] A member of the French parliament quoted his country's foreign minister, Dominique de Villepin, as saying, "The hawks in the U.S. administration are in the hands of Sharon."[12] The novelist John le Carré has referred to a neocon junta seizing power in Washington and "limiting human rights to an extent that is quite unimaginable." He has also compared himself to the Jewish diarist Victor Klemperer, who hid from the Nazis in a cellar in Dresden waiting for the good Germans to return: "I'm waiting for the real Americans to come back."[13]

In the United States, Pat Buchanan founded a magazine, the *American Conservative,* to publicize his view that the neoconservatives had hijacked both the conservative movement and American foreign policy. Their goal was profoundly antithetical to America's best conservative traditions, he insisted: to turn a republic into an empire and to subordinate America's interests to Israel's. Michael Lind, who sometimes depicts himself as a reformed neocon (and who was the managing editor of the *National Interest* in 1991–93), takes a slightly more subtle line: "The neocons took advantage of Bush's ignorance and inexperience. . . . [Bush] seems genuinely to believe that there was an imminent threat from Saddam Hussein's 'weapons of mass destruction,' something the leading neocons say in public but are far too intelligent to believe themselves."[14]

Is there any truth in this? Like all the best conspiracy theories, the neoconservative coup theory contains elements of truth—but elements that are twisted together to create a misleading picture. The first element of truth is that the neocons are a distinctive clique—a group of people who share similar beliefs and lifestyles. Wolfowitz is a noted academic. Feith, Libby and Bolton are all lawyers. They work for the same think tanks (AEI is their favorite) and write for the same magazines (particularly the *Weekly Standard*). They are usually strong supporters not just of Israel but also of the hard-line Likud Party in Israel, home of Benjamin Netanyahu and Ariel Sharon. In 1996, Perle, together with Feith and David Wurmser, helped to write "A Clean Break," a report for a Likud think tank suggesting that Israel should take a more preemptive approach to its security—by, for instance, "removing Saddam Hussein from power," "containing Syria" and sidelining Arafat.[15]

Then there are all the social ties. Studying the neocons is like studying the Bloomsbury group in Britain or any other upper-crust literary set. Everyone seems to have been to school together, live next door to each other, belong to the same clubs, write papers together, or be related to each other. True, to the best of our knowledge, the neocons sleep with each other less indiscriminately than Virginia Woolf and her chums did. Yet you can play the same parlor game of social connections. You can start with Wolfowitz and discover that he, Perle and Woolsey are all friends, all disciples of the nuclear theorist (and supposed model for Dr. Strangelove) Albert Wohlstetter and all live in Chevy Chase, Maryland. You can start with Elliot Abrams (Bush's point man on the Middle East) and discover that he is Norman Podhoretz's son-in-law, and that he, like Perle and Frank Gaffney of the Center for Security Policy, all worked for Henry "Scoop" Jackson, a hard-line Democratic senator.[16] Or you can try linking the Cheneys to the group by pointing to Lynne's work at the AEI and the fact that they celebrate their wedding anniversary with the Adelmans.[17] Quite simply, there is enough stuff there to keep a conspiracy theorist going for years.

The current generation of neocons is the intellectual (and in many cases the biological) progeny of the disillusioned Democrats who founded neoconservatism in the 1960s. But there are also big differences. Few of the younger neocons had any roots in the Democratic Party in the way that the first generation did (though Perle enjoys reminding people that he is a registered Democrat). Most of them are the products of privileged upbringing and polished education in the Ivy League. Rather than seeing themselves as half conservatives, like the first neocons, those of the current generation see themselves as hyperconservatives, insisting that their party should be driven by principle, not expediency.

This brings us to the next truth. The neocons are indeed a cabal with a mission. At home, they want to reform welfare and get rid of affirmative action. Abroad, it comes down to two things: asserting American power in a more unilateral way, shorn of the pragmatic (and, in their view, enfeebling) entanglements of multilateralism, and using that power to redraw the map of the world and spread liberal democracy—particularly in the Middle East. During his time in the Carter administration, the young Paul Wolfowitz wrote a paper warning about Iraq. In 1992, as undersecretary of defense for policy, he produced another paper making the case both for preemptive strikes and for increasing America's military superiority. This was deemed so radical that his boss, Dick Cheney, was ordered to rewrite it. On September 15, 2001, at the first strategy meeting after the terrorist attacks, Wolfowitz was back again, insisting that Iraq be considered a target alongside Afghanistan, and saying that there was a 10 percent to 50 percent chance that Saddam had been involved in the attack. (Two days later Bush agreed to let the Pentagon planners look at Iraq, but said his "first-things-first administration" would concentrate on Afghanistan.)[18]

What about the accusation that the neoconservatives are ruthless about achieving their goals? Here again the critics have a point. The neoconservatives have been remarkably successful at stealing the conservative limelight. They are the dominant voice in the AEI, the Hudson Institute and the Manhattan Institute. They are in charge of several of the most important conservative foundations, including the Bradley and the Olin. They have received financial support from two powerful media barons, Rupert Murdoch and Conrad Black. Murdoch's News Corporation owns both the *Weekly Standard* and the *New York Post* (where Norman Podhoretz's son, John, is a prominent columnist). Conrad Black (whose now troubled Hollinger empire includes the *Jerusalem Post*) funds the *National Interest* and the *New York Sun*. The *Wall Street Journal*'s editorial page regularly runs op-eds by leading neoconservatives such as Max Boot (who used to be deputy editor of the page before becoming an Olin Fellow at the Council on Foreign Relations).

The neocons are also highly successful practitioners of Washington power politics. Many have been insiders for decades. Wolfowitz has worked for every president except Clinton since the Nixon era: it is hard to come up with a country in the world that he does not know his way around. Bill Kristol turned a fairly risible job in the first Bush administration—chief of staff to Dan Quayle—into a platform for the Right's discontent with the older Bush's middle-of-the-road policies. In terms of bureaucratic intrigue, though, it is hard to beat Richard Perle.

Clever, courteous and (if he is on your side) extremely amusing, Perle is an expert at steering both journalists and other politicians. When he worked for Scoop Jackson in the 1970s, he was the subject of a 3,700-word profile in the *Washington Post,* a highly unusual accolade for a staffer. Under Reagan, the "prince of darkness" was the Defense Department's sole representative when the Gipper and Gorbachev met in Reykjavik in 1986 to discuss arms control. Soon afterward he was paid $300,000 by Random House to write *Hard Line* (1992), a roman à clef about politics. In one passage he explained how a shadowy operator could accumulate so much power in Washington: "Knowledge was power. The more you knew, the more you could use what you knew to expand your empire or advance your political agenda—or both." Under George W. Bush, Perle occupied a shadow world between the government and private life. As chairman of the Defense Policy Board (until 2003, when he was forced to resign the chairmanship—though not his membership— after a dispute over conflict of interest) he was of the administration but not in it. This gave him the freedom he needed to clear a trail that more accountable politicians like Rumsfeld and Wolfowitz could then follow. One of the few times he was reined in was when he gave an interview about the composition of postconflict Iraq nine months ahead of the war (and from the garden of his house in France, at a time when the White House was sweltering).

There is nobody who unnerves European diplomats more than Perle. His specialty is to present liberals' worst fears about American foreign policy as if they are universally acknowledged facts. On the eve of Bush's 2002 State of the Union address, in a briefing for journalists that included a large number of Europeans, he explained that Bush had ditched Clinton's failed ideas about "globalism" in favor of the admirable principle of the "Wild West posse": America's job, Perle explained to the horrified listeners from *Le Monde* and German television, was to round up a few allies and then ride out and get the bad guys. After the Iraq War was over, he was among the first to admit that weapons of mass destruction had merely been a casus belli (the real aim being regime change), and he liked telling his European friends that American foreign policy could be summed up in two words: "Who's next?"

An independent president

So the neocons are clever, resourceful people with a clear goal. But none of this proves the hijacking charge. In the end, the neoconservatives serve at the behest of the president, not the other way around. They may provide clever advice, but they do not make the final decisions. Most of Bush's critics, particularly in Europe, are so committed to the idea that he is a muddle-headed buffoon that they are constantly on the lookout for his brain—whether in Karl Rove's head, or in the vice president's office, or in a neoconservative cabal. But the truth is rather more prosaic.

Throughout his career, Bush has used people and ideas to solve specific problems. "I may not be able to tell you exactly the nuances of the East Timorian situation," he said during the election campaign, "but I'll ask Condi Rice or I'll ask Paul Wolfowitz or I'll ask Dick Cheney. I'll ask people who've had experience."[19] He is relaxed about subcontracting the execution of a strategy—he seemed happy to leave the prosecution of both the Afghan and Iraq wars to the Defense Department; however, he makes sure that the big decisions are his alone, as even Dick Cheney discovered to his cost in August 2002 when he derided the idea that the United States would seek another Iraq resolution at the UN. Moreover, Bush has always been loath to let himself be identified with one particular faction or idea. He made a big personal investment in compassionate conservatism, a subject that was close to his heart as well as central to his presidential campaign in 2000. But when John DiIulio's faith-based initiatives no longer looked practical, "the whole compassion thing," as one White House insider calls it, was quietly dropped.

Arguably the best way to think of Bush's relationship with the neocons is in business terms. If a CEO concludes that a particular group of employees has produced a successful solution to a particular crisis, that does not mean that he is going to offer them a seat on the board. With the exception of Wolfowitz, who remains merely the number two in the Pentagon, the "board" of the Bush administration includes no full-fledged neocons in the democratic-imperialist mode.

Look closely at many of the administration's policies that are supposed to reveal the hidden hands of the neocon puppet masters and you'll find other motives. For instance, when Bush called for Yasser Arafat to be removed in 2002, many Europeans suspected that the neocons were pulling his strings to help the Likud Party: Arafat was, after all, the acknowledged (and elected) leader of his people. In fact, Bush's reasons seem to have been as much practical and personal as ideological. The president, who takes trust extremely seriously, was furious that Arafat had personally lied about a shipment of explosives from Iran. "You can't make a peace deal with that guy," Bush told his fellow diners at the White House Correspondents Dinner. "He screwed President Clinton."[20] Once the Palestinians sidelined Arafat and made Mahmoud Abbas their prime minister, Bush returned to the peace process and forced the Israelis to attend a peace summit at Sharm el-Sheik in June 2003. Although that effort failed, he stuck to the idea that the Palestinians should get a viable state. Given that most neocons dream about pushing the Palestinians into Jordan and regard the road map as a "sorry resurrection" of the hated Oslo peace process,[21] Bush's Middle East policy is still some distance from the neocons' script; they are held in balance by Colin Powell at the State Department, whose position on Israel has been strengthened by the influence of Tony Blair.

It is certainly true that this balance still leaves Bush's Middle East policy heavily biased toward Israel—and indeed toward hard-liners such as Ariel Sharon. But again that can hardly be blamed on the neocons. Strong support for Israel is not just a neoconservative cause. America—particularly conservative America—supports Israel emphatically, and that support has grown in the wake of September 11. In April 2002, a Gallup poll found Republicans split 68 percent to 8 percent in favor of Israel over the Palestinians, while the Democrats, who include most Jewish voters, were split 45 percent to 21 percent. David Frum, Bush's neocon speechwriter, quotes his master asking Rove, "What do you think our folks think of the Israeli-Palestinian conflict?" "They think that it's part of your war on terror," came the reply.[22]

This underlines our point. The policies that Bush followed after September 11 were no longer just neoconservative policies. They had become conservative policies—policies that resonated throughout the Right Nation. Who opposed the war in Iraq? Certainly not Colin Powell, who fronted the administration's policy throughout. Henry Kissinger, that supposed grand master of amoral realpolitik, stood foursquare behind the White House. America's neoconservative foreign policy was not so much a question of conversion, let alone hijacking. Rather, the views of one hitherto eccentric part of the coalition suddenly coincided with the movement as a whole. The neocons were not so much conspirators, operating under cover of night, as articulators, saying out in the open what so many conservatives privately found themselves thinking. After September 11, the neocon solution seemed, to conservatives at least, to be the American solution.

THE RIGHT SIDE OF NEOCONSERVATISM

The neoconservative view of the world can be divided into three parts: first, a pessimistic diagnosis, and then two radical solutions—one, a brutally realistic championing of American unilateralism, and the other, a surprisingly optimistic view of the moral imperative of spreading American values, particularly in the Middle East. The rest of the Right Nation rapidly fell in line behind the pessimistic diagnosis and the unilateralist response; it also at one point of the Iraq frenzy embraced the more dreamy creed of transformation, but not for very long.

First, the diagnosis. In the 1990s the neocons had never placed much stock in all the "globaloney" about the global village being united by a web of trade and treaties. Instead, they started from the assumption that the world was an exceedingly dangerous place. They saw nation-states locked in a Hobbesian struggle for advantage. They detected the forces of disorder and anarchy everywhere: governments collapsing or colluding with terrorists and drug traffickers; megacities pullulating with unemployed and directionless young men; religious fanatics using mosques and madrassas to find new converts; immigrants fleeing the world of disorder only to bring religious extremism into the heart of the West's great cities. The neocons also had a longstanding preoccupation with weapons of mass destruction. For most politicians, the NPT, the ABM, SALT and the other chunks in the alphabet soup of WMD were tedious extras to their trade—the sort of thing that Kissinger brought up at the end of international conferences—but people like Perle and Wolfowitz had long been missile junkies. Wolfowitz's first stint in Washington, D.C., back in 1969, involved helping to defend Nixon's plan to build an antiballistic missile system. Look, retorted the neocons to the "End of History" crowd, the globalization and technology that you celebrate are also putting devastating firepower in the hands of terrorists and rogue states. It is getting ever easier to produce nuclear bombs, ever easier to pack extraordinary destruction into a tiny briefcase, ever easier to turn the mundane tools of commerce, be they airplanes or computer systems, into weapons of destruction.

The neocons had no doubts about who would have to police this dangerous world. The United States was now living in a "unipolar world" (a phrase coined by a neoconservative commentator, Charles Krauthammer, in 1991). By 2002, America's military budget was bigger than that of the next fourteen countries combined. In the most high-tech aspects of space-based warfare, America was off the European radar screen. Even in the ordinary world of hardware, the gap is gigantic. Why should a country that has eighty-seven C17 transport planes bother to haggle with Western Europe, which can muster just four in total?[23]

This worldview had always struck a chord with the assertive nationalists. Bush's inner circle had always agreed with the neoconservatives about the dangerous nature of the world—and the importance of meeting danger with military might. In his campaign autobiography Bush noted that "this is still a world of terror and missiles and madmen."[24] Wolfowitz's radical Defense Planning Guidance, the 1992 plan that had been quietly buried, had actually been drafted for Dick Cheney. September 11 seems to have had a particularly dramatic effect on the vice president: he immediately started to speculate how much worse it would have been if weapons of mass destruction had been used. Rumsfeld had a similar reaction: he now tells friends that he starts every day wondering how a catastrophic terrorist attack on the United States can be averted, and he too has a history of worrying about weapons of mass destruction. In 1998 he headed a commission, which included Wolfowitz, that warned that a rogue nation might have the ability to hit the United States with a missile within the next five years (a third of the time then estimated by the CIA).[25] The same commission later warned of a "space Pearl Harbor" in which America's enemies might disable its satellites: hence the need for America to pursue "the weaponization of space, sooner rather than later."[26] In his speech accepting Bush's invitation to be his defense secretary, Rumsfeld argued that his main task would be to "transform" the military so that it was better able to deal with the twin threats of rogue states and unconventional weapons.

THE BUSH DOCTRINE

The neocons' gloomy view of the world led to their first solution—the need for America to take a more unilateralist course. This preference was widely shared on the Right; indeed, the neocons were arguably only adding fancy theories to things that Bush and Cheney felt in their gut. International treaties and bureaucracies, argued the neocons, might be fine for a regional power like the European Union that has spent the past fifty years trying to deepen an economic alliance into a political one, but for the United States they were more often encumbrances. America has interests and obligations that the lesser powers do not. Why should a country that is responsible for policing the North Korean border, with its million land mines, tie itself down by signing the anti–land-mine treaty? Besides, why did the world's foremost democracy need to get legitimacy from a body like the United Nations, which let Cuba onto its human-rights commission?

For the neocons, September 11 was horrific proof of their point. Treaties had done little to deter rogue regimes like the Taliban and nothing to stop fanatics like Osama bin Laden. The only realistic way to deal with bin Laden was for America to eliminate him with its own military might, preferably by preempting action rather than responding to it. The neocons pointed to Israel's successful preemptive strike on an Iraqi nuclear reactor at Osirak in June 1981 before it could make weapons as an example of how to nip a problem in the bud. As for the idea that you needed United Nations approval for such actions, that was a mere pantomime. The "sole source of legitimacy for the United States," a senior neocon in the administration reminded one group of horrified Europeans in 2003, is "our constitution. Period."

Most of Bush's inner circle would not have put it quite that bluntly to their allies, even in private. But any reservations the assertive nationalists like Cheney and Rumsfeld felt about unilateralism disappeared on September 11. America relied on a coalition of the willing to dispatch the Taliban in Afghanistan, brushing aside NATO's offer to help. In the summer of 2002, the White House formalized its position, first in a speech by Bush to the graduates at West Point on June 1, and then in a new National Security Strategy that was unveiled in September. Both made it clear that America had moved firmly away from old-fashioned notions like the balance of power. Under the Bush Doctrine, America's security relied on being an unchallenged hegemon—comfortably more powerful than any other power. The National Security Strategy of 2002 undertook that American forces "will be strong enough to dissuade potential adversaries from pursuing a military buildup in the hope of surpassing, or equaling, the power of the United States." This imbalance would not only scare off attackers, it would also allow America to shape the peace, thus "making the destabilizing arms races of other eras pointless, and limiting rivalries to trade and other pursuits of peace," as Bush told the graduates at West Point.

It was not just a matter of shrugging off international shackles. The Bush Doctrine made it clear that America's policy would often be one of preemption rather than containment and deterrence. Those Cold War strategies, Bush told the West Pointers, still apply "in some cases," but "new threats require new thinking." He explained, "If we wait for threats to fully materialize we will have waited too long."[27] He continued, "We must take the battle to the enemy, disrupt his plans and confront the worst threats before they emerge."

As with so many things in diplomacy, it is possible to claim that there were precedents for this. The National Security Strategy points out that "the United States has long maintained the option of preemptive actions." People trace the idea all the way back to a statement by Daniel Webster, secretary of state in 1841, that preemptive attacks could be justified if there was "a necessity of self defense, instant, overwhelming, leaving no choice of means and no moment for deliberation."[28] Similarly, America did not suddenly stop working through multilateral organizations in 2002. Yet, by any reasonable standard, the Bush Doctrine was a dramatic break from the past—not just from Clinton's globalism but from the old Republican idea of foreign policy. Eisenhower, for instance, had denounced "a preventive war" as "an impossibility," and Truman had written that "you don't 'prevent' anything by war other than peace."[29] Thirteen days after his West Point speech, Bush happily talked about "our *new* strategy of preemption" at a fund-raising dinner in Texas.[30]

Once again, Europeans jumped to the conclusion that the neocons had hijacked America's foreign policy. Yet the plain fact is that this more vigorously unilateralist approach came as music to the ears of conservative America. Most obviously, these were policies that Cheney and Rumsfeld had long championed: if assertive nationalism is about anything, it is about using American power to crush potential threats, preferably before they emerge. More broadly, the Bush Doctrine echoed two themes that had been popular on the Right for decades, particularly in the Sun Belt. The first was the importance of taking the gloves off. Conservatives had been as shaken as anyone by America's humiliation in Vietnam. But they had drawn the opposite conclusion from their liberal counterparts—not that America had plunged blindly into an unwinnable war but that it had failed to push hard enough for victory. Remember Barry Goldwater's enthusiasm for using "low-yield" nuclear weapons in Southeast Asia. The second was the limited value of multilateral organizations. The Far Right had long railed against the United Nations as an organ of world government, but many mainstream Republicans (as well as some Democrats like Patrick Moynihan) had begun to balk at the UN's general flakiness. Jesse Helms won widespread applause on the Right when he made reform a condition of U.S. funding of the UN.

In the period after September 11, these resentments came bubbling to the surface. As far as the Right Nation was concerned, only two things mattered. The first was that America was in danger. The mainland had been attacked; now it faced the prospect of the same attackers having weapons of mass destruction. The second was that America was now engaged in another battle between good and evil. Here, once again, the neocons found their message reverberating with the footsoldiers. In contrast, most intellectuals in both America and Europe are nervous about moral absolutes, preferring to see the world in shades of gray. After September 11, liberal academics looked for reasons to explain al-Qaeda: Was it the product of racism? Of economic injustice? Of American policies in the Middle East? On the other hand, the neocons, offspring of refugees from Nazism and Communism, had always maintained that evil existed in the world, and despised anybody who merely tried to explain it rather than fight it. They rushed to portray September 11 as the result of a marriage between religious fanaticism and totalitarianism. They talked about "Islamofascism" and "evil."

This delighted the wider conservative movement. Christian conservatives had no doubt that the felling of the twin towers was the devil's work.

Ayn Rand, 1945

Southern Democrats at their Dixiecrat convention in Birmingham, Alabama, 1948

A babysitting operation to allow mothers to vote for Eisenhower in the 1952 Massachusetts Republican Primary. In the general election, he won a larger majority among women than among men.

Prescott Bush smartens up Richard Nixon, 1953.

Friedrich Hayek, 1960

William F. Buckley, Jr., and the
National Review, 1958

Robert Welch, the founder of the John Birch Society, 1966

*The Barry Goldwater whom Hillary Rodham
and Joan Didion fell for*

Campaign buttons, 1964: Goldwater lost by a landslide.

Phyllis Schlafly on the warpath, 1978

Californians celebrate the first returns from Proposition 13 in 1978.

Irving Kristol, 1976

Paul Weyrich

Rev. Jerry Falwell and Senator Jesse Helms at a ceremony to support School Prayer Day, 1982

President Ronald Reagan examines his new life-membership card from the National Rifle Association, 1983.

Grover Norquist in Afghanistan

Karl Rove showing his political direct-marketing data in his Austin office, 1985

Ralph Reed and Pat Robinson at a Christian Coalition convention, 1994

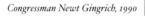

Congressman Newt Gingrich, 1990

Bill Clinton speaks, George H.W. Bush scratches, listens and wonders, 1992

The Right Nation howling at Clinton only one year into his presidency

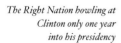

Governor Bush prepares for government.

Karl Rove, Mark McKinnon and Karen Hughes just after the South Carolina primary, 2000

George W. Bush conducting a prayer before a cabinet meeting

Colin Powell and Condoleezza Rice at Buckingham Palace, 2003

Patrick Henry College, a university for homeschoolers

John Ashcroft, listening to George Bush at the American Enterprise Institute dinner in February 2003, having just sung the National Anthem

Tom DeLay, the House Majority Whip; Dennis Hastert, the House Speaker; and Nancy Pelosi, the House Minority Leader; outside the White House, March 2003

The annual march to protest the Roe v. Wade *decision by the Supreme Court, 2004*

The *Wall Street Journal,* Rush Limbaugh and the blondes on Fox News queued up to denounce "sophisticated" explanations of terrorism as the fruit of poverty or oppression as so much poppycock. Wasn't bin Laden a multi-millionaire? Wasn't Saudi Arabia the world's single biggest source of oil? As for the idea that Israel might in any way be responsible for Arab discontent, the Right hit the roof (particularly when Palestinians, showing their usual flair for making their case to the American people, continued to use the same modus operandi as bin Laden: suicide bombers).

Indeed, this reinforced one of the strangest marriages in the conservative movement. The Religious Right had been pro-Israel since at least the 1970s. Evangelicals believe that the Second Coming will take place in Israel—and that it will be preceded by the conversion of the Jews to Christianity; thus, both the Jews and Israel need to be saved in order to fulfill their dual roles in Christian eschatology. The highlight of the Christian Coalition's 2002 conference was a rally for Israel. Fundamentalist congregations spend millions to subsidize Jewish settlements. Go to fundamentalist churches and you will find prayers to let Israel keep the biblical lands of Judea and Samaria.

You might think that, as secular intellectuals, the neocons would have found this eschatological brew a bit strong for their tastes, and that, as Jews, they would balk at being assigned to a bit role in the Christian revelation. But the neocons have always been remarkably good at biting their lips on these subjects, treating Christian fundamentalism as something of a Straussian "noble myth"—it might be nonsense, but it advances the conservative cause. Sometimes they break ranks—Bill Kristol supported John McCain's attempt to end the Religious Right's stranglehold on the GOP—but his father's infinite tolerance for the Religious Right's peccadilloes was a much more typical neoconservative position. In one essay, Irving Kristol praised the Religious Right for its vital role in creating the Reagan majority—and conveniently forgot to mention the fact that Pat Robertson had said some pretty terrible things about the Jews.[31]

The diplomatic maneuvering in the winter of 2002–03 that preceded the Iraq War only strengthened the relationship between the neocons and the rest of the conservative movement. This was partly because the Bush administration did nothing to squash the idea that Saddam Hussein had a hand in September 11 (a myth that the majority of Americans believed well into

2003). But for the most part it was because of mounting frustration across conservative America with the machinery of multilateralism. Most conservatives looked at the diplomatic maneuvering that preceded the war and concluded that the neoconservatives had been right all along. The United Nations was less a parliament of man devoted to the common good than an arena in which rival nation-states pursued their national interests. Bush secured a unanimous first resolution, 1441, from the Security Council on November 8, 2002, giving Iraq a final warning. But when, at Tony Blair's insistence, he tried throughout February 2003, to get an unambiguous second resolution passed authorizing force, he found himself confronted by "an axis of weasel," as the *New York Post* termed it, led by France, Russia and Germany.

In fact, the opposition to the second resolution went considerably beyond these three countries. America failed to get support from traditional allies like Mexico and Chile and never came close to getting the nine votes needed on the Security Council (an early sign, critics argued, that there was a cost to unilateralism). But the Right Nation fixated on France, spurred on by Chirac's threat on March 10, 2003, to veto a second resolution "whatever the circumstances." To conservative America, this seemed motivated neither by high principle nor a desire to produce a negotiated settlement but by the simple fact that France's interests in the region were different from America's. Fox News, Rush Limbaugh and the rest of them pointed out that the French were huge investors in Saddam's regime, and that France had long cherished a dream of acting as a counterweight to American power. French fries were renamed freedom fries; sales of French wine plummeted. What about the fact that most people in most other countries backed the French line? Well, that just proved how insidious the French were.

This triumphal moralism soared again once the fighting started in Iraq on March 19, 2003. America "liberated" the Iraqis from a monstrous regime in short order. The fact that America did it by itself (well, with some British help) underlined the awesomeness of American military might. America had already conquered Afghanistan, a country that had defeated both the British and Soviet empires. Now it crushed Saddam in three weeks, without incurring any of the disasters that the antiwar movement had confidently predicted. America lost fewer than sixty people, excluding friendly fire and accidents. Once Baghdad had fallen, Bush assigned the United Nations a bit part in the reconstruction of Iraq.

THE ACCIDENTAL IMPERIALIST

Thus far, the neocons had the rest of the conservative movement firmly behind them. Rather then reacting with alarm to Bush's new "neocon" policies of unilateralism and preemption, the footsoldiers were relieved that they had finally found a set of ideas they agreed with. For the Right Nation, the analogy was not *The Manchurian Candidate* but *Harry Potter.* The weedy boy in glasses suddenly comes up with the plan that saves the whole school. But the second "transformative" part of the neocons' solution—not just exercising American power but spreading its values—was always going to be a tougher sell.

The neoconservatives had long believed that American power needed to be tied to American principles: that America had a duty to spread its ideals and values around the world. It should forget about the grubby compromises of realpolitik (once again Jacques Chirac is usually cited). America should instead link military strength to moral clarity by championing the eternal values of freedom and democracy. This was not just the right thing to do, argued the neocons, it was also the sensible thing to do. The policy of propping up corrupt kleptocracies in the Middle East had helped to generate a seething resentment of the West. Democratization might produce instability in the short term, but in the long term it would produce a far more stable and trouble-free world. This meant that at the very least, America needed to democratize Iraq as well as depose Saddam. America might also need to move on to Iran, Syria and Saudi Arabia.

There were plenty of people in neoconservative circles who were so keen on spreading American values that they would even contemplate an old European sin, imperialism. A dozen years ago, the idea of a Pax Americana was a minority dream. "Why deny it? Why be embarrassed by it?" pleaded Krauthammer back in 1991. By the time of the Iraq War, the atmosphere had changed considerably. Some neocons, such as Robert Kagan, preferred the term "hegemony" (meaning that you merely control other people's foreign policies, not their whole states), but others became explicit imperialists. As Max Boot, one of Robert Bartley's protégés from the *Wall Street Journal*, wrote in the *Weekly Standard* in October 2001, "Afghanistan and other troubled lands today cry out for the sort of enlightened foreign administration once provided by self-confident Englishmen in jodhpurs and pith helmets."[32] In July 2003, he argued in the *Financial Times* that America needed a colonial office (adding, with a Perlish flourish, that you would have to come up with some meaningless politically correct title).[33]

In retrospect, the Bush administration went a surprisingly long way toward buying this idea. Imperialism was a departure from the sort of "humble" foreign policy Bush had outlined in his campaign. At West Point, he denounced the idea: "We don't seek an empire. Our nation is committed to freedom for ourselves and for others." Yet by May 2003 the Bush administration was—broadly speaking—acting in an imperial way, setting up satrapies of sorts in Iraq and Afghanistan, and asserting that it had the right—nay, the moral obligation—to apply its own values around the world, to "extend the peace by encouraging free and open societies on every continent," as Bush told the West Pointers. "Some worry that it is somehow undiplomatic or impolite to speak the language of right and wrong. I disagree."

The crucial thing that seemed to have won over Bush—along with Cheney, Rice and Rumsfeld—was the idea, embraced soon after September 11, that the war against terrorism had to be directed against states as well as terrorists. Once Cheney and Rumsfeld had been persuaded of the importance of toppling the terror masters, it was a relatively short step to persuading them that America had an obligation to rebuild these failed states. What else could they have done? Leaving Afghanistan and Iraq in ruins would have been an insult to Cheney's pragmatism; these countries had to be rebuilt in order to stop them from falling by the wayside. By 2003, Cheney was certainly happy using the word "empire" in sympathetic company.

Yet it soon emerged that the assertive nationalists' ideas about nation building fell a long way short of those advocated by the neocons. Afghanistan already provided a fairly clear example of the modesty of the Bush administration's concept of nation building. America handed most of the country back to warlords, ignoring the fact that many of them ran the country's heroin business, and left a smallish garrison. In contrast, in 1995 America, Britain and France put 60,000 peacekeepers into Bosnia once war had ended; in Afghanistan, a country twelve times the size and with seven times as many people, there were, by 2003, only around 5,000 troops helping to keep the peace, and another 12,000 looking for bin Laden. Fixated by Iraq, the neocons somehow managed to ignore this, explaining Afghanistan away as a medieval aberration. The real test of nation building would come in the Middle East—and here Bush had committed himself to democratizing the region, most notably in his speech to the AEI a few weeks before the Iraq War began. Yet fairly soon after Saddam was toppled, the gap between "democratic imperialism" and "assertive nationalism" began to emerge again.

Wolfowitz et al. may have been committed to the transformation of the Middle East as a noble long-term project, but this grated on the more cautious instincts of most other people on the Right. During the 2000 presidential campaign Bush had criticized Bill Clinton's foreign policy for being too wishy-washy—as driven by vague idealism rather than a clear set of objectives. "Rarely has our military been so freely used—an average of one deployment every nine weeks in the last few years," he complained. Guided by Rice, Bush was particularly hard on the Clinton administration for using troops to build nations rather than for their proper function—"to fight and win wars."[34] This skeptical strain in Republican thinking soon reasserted itself. Cheney and particularly Rumsfeld saw nation building as a more temporary measure than the neoconservatives did. Naturally, America needed to tidy up Iraq, and, naturally, it would labor mightily to promote friendlier regimes in the region, but it needed to establish its priorities and guard against mission creep.

The problems America encountered in Iraq in the summer of 2003 sharpened the divide between Bush's core advisors and the neocons. For the assertive nationalists, every American body bag and every dollar spent showed the danger of foreign entanglements. It soon became plain that the Iraqis were more ambivalent about the American presence than the neocons had envisaged. Stuck in their compounds in Baghdad, American troops, who had little training or aptitude for peacekeeping, began to send furious letters and e-mails back home, complaining about their delayed returns. In the summer of 2003 there were even protests by army wives in Texas. Support for the war in Iraq gradually declined; by September 2003 only half of the U.S. population thought it had been a good idea.

The neocons had an explanation for the sluggishness in Iraq: America was being nowhere near ambitious enough. The main target of the *Weekly Standard*'s fury was Rumsfeld, who was left in charge of Iraq after Saddam fell. Apparently buoyed by the success of his "lean" techniques in warfare (he had routed Saddam with fewer troops than many Pentagon generals had demanded), Rumsfeld set about nation building on the cheap too, with merely 150,000 troops. Rumsfeld's gamble was not helped by certain tactical mistakes — notably the tragic willingness, after such a surgical war, to let the liberated Iraqis loot so much of their infrastructure. The neoconservatives were not alone in their complaints about America's refusal to commit enough resources to Iraq. The British were complaining about the same thing.

The neocons may have had logic on their side, but they had lost conservative America — at least in terms of an open-ended commitment to transforming the Middle East. By the autumn of 2003, the polls still showed Republicans loyally backing the Iraq War, and also being prepared to stick it out. While 58 percent of Democrats wanted the troops to come home as soon as possible, only 20 percent of Republicans did.[35] But there was little enthusiasm for moving on to other countries, and there was also a clear demand for limits both on time and resources. In Congress, Republicans began to rebel over giving Iraq money, insisting it should be in the form of loans. The question was no longer Richard Perle's "Who's next?" but "How can we get out of this?"

In September 2003, just after a Congressional Budget Office report revealed that the army could not sustain an Iraqi occupation force beyond March 2004 without keeping its own soldiers there for longer than a year, Bush changed tack, though hardly in the way that the neocons wanted. He went back to the hated United Nations to ask for more help, and he moved control of Iraq from Rumsfeld at the Pentagon to Rice at the NSC. Bush had changed his mind after he was confronted in early September by Powell and a posse of generals, who explained that without foreign help, America would get into a quagmire. Rice, so often the swing voter in Bush's foreign policy court, was also plainly reverting to some of her earlier doubts about nation building (the Eighty-second Airborne apparently could help take kids to school but for no more than one semester). She immediately backed Powell, who already had the support of Tony Blair, by then under considerable pressure in Britain for having sided with America so unquestioningly.

The capture of Saddam Hussein in December, followed quickly by Libya's decision to come clean about its nuclear program, provided a valuable fillip for the White House. Yet as Bush's presidency entered its fourth year, the main battle within the administration was once again between the doveish pragmatists and the assertive nationalists. Of course, when it came to the bully pulpit, Bush continued to press the case for changing the Middle East. For instance, in November 2003 he delivered an even sterner warning to Egypt and Saudi Arabia than he had at the AEI at the beginning of the year, arguing that "for too long many people in that region have been victims and subjects; they deserve to be active citizens." Yet his rhetoric came unaccompanied by any commitment to increasing troop levels in Iraq, and the most common theme in his speeches was an angry insistence that America "would not cut and run." Iraq had become a tough slog, which he would see out.

As for the neocons, they seemed slightly defensive. They found themselves accused of having deliberately constructed a "noble myth" about weapons of mass destruction in order to justify their plans for reordering the Middle East, with some of their more Machiavellian utterings being held against them. ("One of the main teachings of Strauss," Bill Kristol once mused, "is that all politics are limited and none is really based on the truth.") But the neocons' real embarrassment was the ugly collision between their vision of transformation and the messy reality of Iraq. Nothing illustrated this better than an impromptu interview with Wolfowitz shortly after his hotel in Baghdad had been bombed in October 2003. He still spoke optimistically about the prospects in Iraq, but he was visibly shaken. A new book from Frum and Perle, *An End to Evil: How to Win the War on Terrorism,* published at the turn of the year, still packed in a lot of dramatic proposals, such as blockading North Korea and throwing Syria out of Lebanon, but spent much of the time settling scores with the State Department.[36] The *Weekly Standard* and the AEI fumed about the lack of progress, but the White House did not seem to be listening quite so intently.

It was not just a question of the neocons losing ground at court. From the point of view of future escapades, a number of huge holes had appeared in moral imperialism. Most obviously, conservative America has discovered the limits of its power: it had more than enough strength to smite its enemies, but rebuilding them required foreign help. And many countries, still smarting from the arguments about Iraq, were ill inclined to give that help— reflecting what Joseph Nye, the dean of the Kennedy School at Harvard, and other veteran observers of diplomacy had long warned, that aggressive unilateralism would harm America's "soft power."[37] In September 2001, the world had rallied to America, with even *Le Monde* proclaiming "We are all Americans now." By June 2003, an eleven-nation survey of eleven thousand people by the BBC (which included not just America itself but three of its closest allies, Israel, Britain and Canada) found that most people thought that America was a much bigger threat to global security than China, Iran, Syria, Russia or France. The United States tied with North Korea (though in South Korea, Bush was seen as posing a far greater danger than Kim Jong Il). The only force considered more dangerous than the Bush administration was al-Qaeda.[38] As for the cost of poor diplomacy, even traditional conservative critics of Old Europe, such as Max Boot, threw their hands up in dismay when in December 2003 Wolfowitz released a "boneheaded" memorandum pointedly excluding companies from Canada, France, Germany, China and Russia from reconstruction contracts in Iraq.[39] It was not just that Wolfowitz granted those famous multinationals from Rwanda, Uzbekistan and the Marshall Islands a ringside seat at the bidding, nor even that France, Canada and Germany had committed troops to Afghanistan. The memorandum appeared at exactly the same time that the Bush administration was trying to persuade France, Germany and Russia to forgive old Iraqi debts. For better or worse, a great deal of American soft capital had been spent.

Meanwhile, the doctrine of preemption had been undermined by the failure to find any weapons of mass destruction worthy of the name. Conservative America was prepared to believe that Bush's assertions about Iraq's weapons had been honest mistakes, based on faulty intelligence (though the Democrats and most of the rest of the world were far less forgiving). However, as a host of conservative commentators pointed out, the standards of proof for any future preemptive venture—for instance, against Iran's "nuclear weapons" or Syria's "chemical weapons"—had risen enormously. "Preemption presupposes the ability to know things," observed George Will, "to know about threats with a degree of certainty not requisite for decisions less momentous than those waging war."[40] And America's allies were even more circumspect. Even in those triumphant moments after the end of the war, when Richard Perle was asking "Who's next?" the Blair government went out of its way to stress the differences between Bashar Assad of Syria and Saddam Hussein. Britain had been prepared to bomb Iraq for nearly a decade; Assad had recently been to tea with the queen.

Indeed, the dream of transforming the Middle East began to melt away. It was not just that rebuilding civil society in Iraq proved to be devilishly difficult, despite the country's much-vaunted oil wealth and educated population. As the power of local Shia clerics such as Grand Ayatollah Ali al-Sistani grew, it soon became clear that a "democratic Iraq" would have a strong Islamic tinge and a marked anti-American bias. There was a straightforward contradiction between the pessimism of the neocons' diagnosis (the world is a much more dangerous place than you think) and the optimism of their trust in transformation. The first generation of neocon intellectuals made their reputations by demonstrating "the limits of social policy"—the inability of bureaucrats to deliver on their promises to reduce poverty or improve education. Why should government be any more omnipotent when it is wearing a military uniform in far-off Iraq?

Doubts about America's transformative mission reached even the American Enterprise Institute. Asked about conservative America's enthusiasm for "moral imperialism" in August 2003, Jeane Kirkpatrick, the grand old lady of conservative diplomacy, looked down the corridor and snorted, "I don't think there is one scintilla of evidence that such an idea is taken seriously anywhere outside a few places in Washington, D.C."[41] Taken at face value, a fully moral foreign policy would have America picking more fights with China (many neocons, remember, were against normalizing trade relations). It would also have the United States tackling North Korea, where strangely enough America desperately needed China's help. And how exactly should this new democratizing America deal with some of its less savory allies in the war against terror, such as Pakistan and Russia? To many foreign observers, the neocons seemed interested only in democratizing countries that could threaten Israel. And, on that subject, Europeans were far less inclined than Wolfowitz and Perle to see Israel as a standard-bearer of American-style democracy. Outside America, the neocons' symbol of "democracy in the Middle East" was increasingly compared to South Africa under apartheid.

MAD, BAD AND DANGEROUS TO KNOW

So the neoconservatives have clearly overreached, even when it comes to keeping the Right Nation behind them. But it would be wrong to end without noting how much they have changed American foreign policy. In the wake of the Second World War, Dean Acheson (who nicely entitled his memoirs *Present at the Creation*) masterminded the creation of an establishment that dominated American foreign policy for half a century, complete with an establishment style (gentlemanly and pro-European) and an establishment doctrine (containment). In the wake of the terrorist attacks of September 11 George Bush began to create a new foreign policy establishment, and the neoconservatives are firmly part of it. Their role may be exaggerated both by themselves and their enemies, but conservative America has plainly moved in their direction. The Bush doctrine is still being tinkered with, yet by any reasonable standard, America is now more committed to a unilateral course, more willing to intervene abroad, more willing to look at the world through moralistic eyes.

Those Europeans who think that the neoconservatives tricked their way into the heart of conservative America have got things topsy-turvy. The reason why the neoconservatives proved so influential was not because they deceived their fellow conservatives but because they succeeded in translating some of conservative America's deepest passions into a theory of foreign policy. That suggests that the neoconservatives were both less and more influential than Europeans imagine. They were less influential because they were simply putting into words what the rest of the Right Nation felt in its heart. But they were more influential because they helped to shape America's response to a cataclysmic event. The neoconservative moment will resound for many years to come.

PART III

PROPHECY

CHAPTER 9

THE ROAD AHEAD:
THE PATH TO
REPUBLICAN HEGEMONY?

I T I S N O S U R P R I S E T H A T William McKinley lacks a place in the Republican pantheon alongside Theodore Roosevelt and Ronald Reagan. McKinley was a dull man who is best remembered for being assassinated. As president, he was widely regarded as little more than a tool of Marcus Alonzo Hanna, an Ohio pig-iron magnate turned political boss. He was succeeded by the far more charismatic Theodore Roosevelt.

Still, dull men can make history just as much as flashy ones: the fact remains that McKinley ushered in a political revolution. Beginning with the 1896 election, the party won seven of the next nine presidential contests, and its dominance was ended only by the Great Depression. With the exception of Woodrow Wilson, who won only because of a split in the GOP, Republican presidents held sway until the arrival of another Roosevelt in 1932.

McKinley saw that the GOP's future lay in joining itself hip and thigh with the new industrial order. The party needed to forget about the Civil War—still the Old Guard's obsession—and to focus instead on hitching itself to the forces that were reshaping America. He deepened the party's links with the robber barons. He also reached out to the new working class—particularly to the millions of immigrants who were flooding into the country. McKinley understood that a business-based party can thrive in a democratic society—and that gigantic business fortunes can also mean better lives for ordinary people.

The 1896 election that brought McKinley to power was arguably the first modern election campaign. Hanna mobilized the entire Republican establishment behind McKinley—and raised an unheard-of $3.5 million in the bargain. The GOP blanketed the country's booming cities with millions of election pamphlets in a dozen languages. It was all too much for Teddy Roosevelt, who complained that Hanna advertised McKinley like a patent medicine, but it nevertheless created an air of predetermination about GOP victory. The 1896 election was also the first clear-cut fight between conservatism and radicalism since the Civil War. William Jennings Bryan identified the Democrats firmly with agrarian populism. ("You shall not press down upon the brow of labor this crown of thorns," Bryan told a mesmerized Democratic Convention. "You shall not crucify mankind upon a cross of gold.") The election divided the country along cultural lines. The Democrats carried the old Confederacy and most of the far West. McKinley took the East Coast and the Midwest and won a conclusive victory by 7.1 million votes to 6.5 million. Bryan's Democratic Party was reduced to being the voice of the old agrarian order railing against the new industrial age. McKinley identified the Republicans with the rising industrial elite—and thereby ushered in the longest period of Republican hegemony in American history.

At least until now. The Republicans have already occupied the White House for twenty-four out of the past thirty-six years. Now they have control of Congress, and George W. Bush and Karl Rove are determined to realign American politics to establish another period of Republican hegemony. Indeed, McKinley is something of a hobbyhorse for Rove. Bush's advisor deliberately introduced the twenty-fifth president into the 2000 election, comparing the contest to that of 1896 and even borrowing Hanna's idea of a "front-porch campaign," shepherding Republican dignitaries from all around the country to Austin to kiss the governor's ring—just as they had journeyed to Ohio a century before.[1] Of course, the 2000 election was hardly a conclusive victory, like 1896, but Rove has stuck to that task, gradually trying to broaden the Republican coalition in the same way that Hanna did. Almost everything that Rove has been involved in—from pushing steel tariffs to limiting stem-cell research to fighting for the elimination of dividend taxes—has been subordinate to this great project.

Will he succeed? In one sense, of course, he does not need to. A Democratic victory in 2004 would still leave America a conservative country, certainly when set beside its allies (a point we reiterate in the last part of this book). As we write, the 2004 election looks set to be a close-run thing. Nevertheless, the material is there for Rove to get his realignment. In this chapter we will compare the underlying strengths of the Republican Party with those of the Democrats. In the next chapter we will examine the Republicans' capacity to trip themselves up. Then we will look at the warriors who are advancing the conservative cause "behind enemy lines"—Republicans operating deep in Democratic territory.

THE SHORT-TERM VIEW

Any judgment about the relative strengths of the Republicans and Democrats has to take into account a combination of short-term maneuvering (the ups and downs of a particular presidency) and long-term positioning (the broad trends favoring either party). In general, the Republicans seem to have a narrow advantage in both.

On the face of it, there are two good reasons for being skeptical of the idea that we are experiencing a realignment similar to that following 1896. The first is the prospect of another close election in 2004—and the possibility of George W. Bush losing it. Even if all the tectonic forces in American society, from suburbanization to the growth in stock ownership, are shifting in his direction, any incumbent can still lose an election if the economy is sickly and a war is going badly—and the president is held to be responsible for both. Even with Saddam in American custody, Iraq still looks something of a mess—albeit one that is unlikely to cost Bush the election by itself. On the economy, Bush has certainly made mistakes in his handling of the government's finances, but it is hard to blame him for the downturn caused by the bursting of the bubble economy. Bush has tried to stimulate a recovery through fiscal measures, notably his tax cuts, and letting the dollar unofficially drift, while at the Federal Reserve Alan Greenspan has cut interest rates. Yet it has still been hard to create jobs, largely because the American economy has become so darned productive: companies are getting by with fewer people. In the longer term this is good news for America, but it will hardly help Bush in 2004. As long as productivity growth continues to zip along at more than 3 percent (and it has been higher than that), the economy will need to expand by well over 4 percent to have much impact on jobs. Incredibly, it achieved that pace in the second half of 2003, but as this book went to press, it still looked likely that Bush would have to go into the 2004 election having overseen the disappearance of around 2 million jobs: not a particularly helpful environment in which to win an election, let alone force a realignment.

The second reason for caution about realignment is the 2000 election. Whatever realignment means, it surely does not mean winning the White House with a minority of the popular vote—and only on the say-so of the Supreme Court. If a few hundred voters in Florida had changed their minds— or arguably even placed their votes where they intended—then President Gore would now be contemplating a fourth successive Democratic term in the White House.

But wait a moment. The very closeness of the 2000 election is itself a sign of something. By rights, Bush should never have come close to beating a sitting vice president. The country was enjoying one of the longest periods of peace and prosperity in its history. At the American Political Science Association's annual meeting three months before the election, six professors deployed the most sophisticated statistical models in the business to declare that Gore would fulfill his lifelong ambition of becoming president—with anywhere between 52.9 percent and 60 percent of the vote. All the standard formulas: the misery index; the incumbent president's approval rating; the history of "in" parties since the Second World War in presidential elections where the second-quarter domestic product growth topped 2 percent; the ratio of sunbeams to the square root of pi—everything pointed to a Gore landslide. James Campbell, a professor at the State University of New York at Buffalo who sported an ALPHA MALES FOR BUSH button, lamented that his vote would be wasted because his man wasn't going to win.

The fact that the Republicans could win in 2000 even when all the circumstances were ripe for a Democratic victory clearly raised the prospect that a sea change was under way. Needless to say, the psephologists claimed that there was nothing wrong with their *underlying* models: the results didn't reflect any deep trend but rather a series of one-offs: Monica Lewinsky had a far greater effect than she should have had; Gore was a peculiarly poor candidate. Perhaps. But if you look at the results carefully, they contain some gold dust for Republicans. Although Bush polled 540,000 fewer votes than Gore nationally, he outpolled Gore in 237 of the now redistricted 435 House districts and in thirty out of the fifty states, including 22 of the 34 Senate seats that are at stake in 2004.[2]

Since then history has been even kinder to the Republicans. In the midterm elections the Republicans succeeded in consolidating their position. It is highly unusual for the president's party to gain seats halfway through a presidency: the last time this happened in the House was in 1934 under FDR. But in 2002 the Republicans recaptured control of the Senate, picked up seats in Congress and held off the expected Democratic advance on the governors' mansions. The popular vote in the House of Representatives was split 51 percent Republican and 46 percent Democratic—an apparently clear break with the fifty-fifty nation. Republicans also gained 105 seats in state assemblies and 36 seats in state senates, giving them the first majority of state legislators since 1952. And in 2003, they picked up three governorships—in California, Kentucky and Mississippi (while losing Louisiana)—giving them twenty-eight in all. There was even a sign that the Democrats' traditional advantage in party registration that stretches back to the New Deal might have ended: in 2003, for only the second time in seventy-five years, there were slightly more registered Republicans than Democrats.[3]

Once again, it is possible to attribute these triumphs to special circumstances. Even Republicans admit that Arnold Schwarzenegger's election was a California peculiarity; in the Kentucky and Mississippi gubernatorial contests, local issues also were at the fore. As for the apparent sea change in 2002, that contest, argue the Democrats, took place at a time when George W. Bush's approval ratings were still "abnormally" high following September 11. Besides, the margin was still fairly narrow: with a swing of a mere 94,000 votes out of 75.7 million cast, Democrats would now control both the House and Senate.[4]

Still, as David Broder has pointed out, there is an ominous parallel for the Democrats in all this with Bush's record in Texas.[5] Bush was not expected to win the governorship in 1994, yet thereafter everything has gone the Republicans' way there. Bush will certainly never be able to turn America into Texas writ large. Yet there is a real chance that his accidental victory in 2000 may come to be seen as the beginning of a prolonged period of Republican dominance. Indeed, if you consider the current state of play from the perspective of a pessimistic Democrat, the 2004 presidential election can seem perilously close to a last chance to stop a period of Republican hegemony.

THROUGH A GLASS, DARKLY

One reason the Democrats are so fixated on the presidential campaign this year is that it represents the best chance they have of wresting power from the Republicans. Thanks to another bout of redistricting (which has given them another five seats in Texas alone), Republicans should hang on to the House; things look tighter in the Senate, where elections happen in a six-year cycle, but the Democrats are defending more vulnerable seats than the Republicans are. The Republicans, as we have mentioned, have more governorships and more state legislators. No wonder the Democrats are terrified that a second Bush presidency will be able to shift the judiciary to the Right and lay waste to the remnants of the Great Society.

One reason to be frightened is organization. The Bush White House is the most formidable money-raising machine in American political history. In the 2000–02 electoral cycle, the Republican Party raised $441 million in federally regulated contributions, compared with just $217 million for the Democrats.[6] Throughout 2003 Bush raised more money than all the Democratic presidential candidates combined (and had to spend very little of it). And the political flair goes deeper than just fund-raising. Under Clinton, Democrats used to reassure themselves that most of the political smarts were on their side, but this Bush White House is a long way from the first Bush's amateurish affair. It has stocked its communications department with people from network television with deep expertise in lighting, camera angles and the rest of it.[7] The attention to detail is meticulous. During one Bush speech in Indianapolis to promote his tax cuts, White House aides asked people in the crowd behind him to take off their ties so they would look more like the regular folk who were supposed to profit from the tax cuts. During another (at Mount Rushmore), the White House positioned the platform for television crews off to one side so that the cameras were forced to film the president in profile, unwittingly placing him among the four presidents carved in stone. Rove's people do not always get it right: Bush's speech on the USS *Abraham Lincoln* on May 1, 2003, where he declared the military phase of the Iraq War to be over, may have been beautifully choreographed (from his *Top Gun* landing to making sure that his speech coincided with "magic hour light" to cast a golden glow on the victorious leader), but the "Mission Accomplished" message proved hopelessly premature. Yet this seems to have been a momentary blip: the president's Thanksgiving visit to the troops in Iraq later that year was an impressive coup de théâtre.

The Democratic Party has traditionally had a big enough advantage in getting out the vote to justify adding a couple of points to their polling numbers, according to Larry Sabato, a political scientist at the University of Virginia. The party is concentrated in cities, where it is easier to organize people. And it is linked to a large number of well-manned and highly motivated organizations such as the AFL-CIO, the teachers' unions, the NAACP, black churches and various liberal pressure groups. All this means ready access to elbow grease and shoe leather.

Up until 2002 it looked as if the Democrats were destined to deepen this advantage. Both the Democratic National Committee and the AFL-CIO dramatically improved their get-out-the-vote operation throughout the 1990s. Union members, who account for 14 percent of the country's workforce, increased their share of votes cast from 23 percent in 1996 to 26 percent in 2000. At the same time the Republicans' favorite solution to the problem of getting people to vote—pouring money into television advertising—suffered from the law of diminishing returns, as the impact of advertising was diluted by the remote control, the multiplication of television channels and growing hostility to negative advertising. The 2000 election was a case in point. Bush enjoyed a solid five-point advantage in the week before the election, but the Democrats obliterated the lead with an extraordinary blitz of activity in the three days running up to the election. Republicans claim that in thirty-seven of the forty-one states where reliable data exist, Bush's actual vote fell short of his support in the last poll taken before the election.

Since then, the Republican National Committee has concentrated on improving its ground war. It established a "seventy-two-hour task force" to learn from the Democrats' success in those vital three days in 2000 and began to test-market its ideas. For instance, the RNC found a 3 percent increase in turnout when precinct workers "flushed" Republicans to the polls just before election day, and a 5 percent increase when volunteers, rather than hired callers, manned the telephones. In addition, Tom DeLay, then the House majority whip, created his own Strategic Task Force to Organize and Mobilize People (STOMP). In the 2002 election the RNC and STOMP sent trained activists to at least thirty congressional and Senate races across the country; they in turn mobilized volunteers to identify likely Republican voters and get them to the polls on election day. The results were impressive. In Georgia, Ralph Reed assembled an army of three thousand volunteers to target six hundred precincts in the last six weeks (the Republicans also sent out 5.2 million bits of paper).[8] In Colorado, senior Republicans claim that a last-ninety-six-hour push helped not only to save Wayne Allard's Senate seat, but to win a bitterly contested congressional seat and to move a couple of local races. In 2004, the Republicans will devote even more resources to the ground war, with computers identifying nonvoters in Republican neighborhoods (so activists can be sent to flush them out), organizations such as Generation-GOP motivating the youth vote, party workers being sent to naturalization ceremonies and even schemes to make sure that businesspeople who are traveling on election day vote by mail. Matthew Dowd, the president's pollster, says that all this could expand the Republican voter pool by as many as 3 million votes.[9] This may or not be true, but it is hard to call the Republicans complacent.

The two deeper reasons why the Democrats feel so defensive will be familiar from our history chapters: ideas and footsoldiers. Some of the ideas emanating from the *rive droite* may be far-fetched. Still more may be shop-soiled. Yet the Right clearly has more intellectual vitality than the Left—at least when it comes to suggesting practical policies. It is getting ever harder for the Democrats to proclaim themselves to be the party of progress when so many of the ideas are coming from the other side.

The Democratic Party's problems with its footsoldiers are even more severe. The party is still coming to terms with the breakup of the New Deal coalition that Franklin Roosevelt knitted together so brilliantly: Northern white working-class "ethnics" (as the descendants of European immigrants are known), Southern whites, racial minorities and intellectuals. The Democrats can still lay claim to most intellectuals (or at least the ones based in the universities). They have a firm grip on blacks and baby-boom women and an advantage for the moment with Latinos. But the Southern whites have jumped ship—and the Democrats are desperately struggling to hold on to white ethnics in the industrial states.

Here it is worth reintroducing an electoral stereotype. Like that other mythical swing voter, the soccer mom, "Joe Sixpack" is hard to be precise about, but you know him when you see him. He is a white, working-class man who never finished college (if he even started), and is often enamored of cheap canned beer, pretzels and televised sports. He doesn't necessarily carry a union card anymore, and sometimes works in services rather than manufacturing, but he still plays an electorally pivotal role in the industrial states of the Midwest and the Northeast. In the 1960s, Joe was a New Deal Democrat, bound to the cause by his union membership and by his absolute conviction that the Democrats were the party of the working man. However, first Richard Nixon and then, especially, Ronald Reagan succeeded in persuading Joe that he had little in common with the "liberal elite" who had taken over the Democratic Party. He sided with George H. W. Bush over Michael Dukakis from Harvard Yard, but then Bill Clinton and Ross Perot tempted some of Joe's friends away from the GOP. In 2000, enough white ethnics voted for George W. Bush to allow him to carry industrial states such as Ohio and West Virginia. The president has since spent a huge amount of time visiting Pennsylvania, which Gore won in 2000.

The Democrats have two ways of reeling Joe back to his home in 2004. One is the economy. Joe, usually one of the earliest to get laid off in any recession, votes with his wallet. In 2004, the sluggish economy (and the jobs lost in it) is sure to drive at least some white ethnics back to the Democrats. For instance, Bush will do very well to hang on to West Virginia in 2004. But the deeper tie—that old idea of class solidarity—looks ever more frayed. The Republicans have often managed to convince Joe that in America, class is not a question of money but of values. They have repeatedly found noneconomic issues to win over white Rust Belt males: abortion (Joe is often a Catholic), crime (he's pro–death penalty), gay marriage (nothing against them, but no thank you) and guns (remember *The Deerhunter*). And they are still doing so—not least because the Democratic Party is usually led by upper-middle-class, college-educated liberals, just the sort of people who get up Joe Sixpack's nose.

For instance, in August 2003 six of the nine Democratic hopefuls descended on the Teamsters Local 238 hall in Cedar Rapids, Iowa—downwind of the acrid stench of roasted maize from a local "corn sweeteners" plant—and proceeded to humble themselves, stressing working-class solidarity that was often not there to be stressed. "Lemme tell ya," thundered the Swiss-boarding-school-educated John Kerry to his "brothers and sisters," no doubt trying to forget his faux pas a few days earlier in Philadelphia when he ordered Swiss cheese with his cheesesteak. Howard Dean, the son of a Wall Streeter, bounded up to the microphone to the sound of Springsteen's hard-times anthem "Born in the USA." A quick scan of the parking lot by one of our colleagues revealed that one of only two Dean campaign stickers was attached to a minivan with a Minnesota license plate and a ski rack—hardly the sport of choice for teamsters.[10] The only first-division candidate who blended in was Dick Gephardt.

Gephardt may have come from a union family, yet his 2004 bid showed the fraying links between the old Democratic machine and organized labor. Back in 1988, he won the Iowa caucuses with plenty of union support. This time, he had to watch while most of the bigger unions, particularly those from the service and public sectors, endorsed Dean (who as a young Yalie had been ski-bumming in Vail while Gephardt, the teamster's son, had been struggling to become an alderman in St. Louis). Gephardt still picked up some old blue-collar unions, but that did not stop him from finishing a humiliating fourth in the Iowa caucuses in January 2004—and quitting the race.

Unions may be disproportionately good vote-gathering machines, but they are still in retreat—particularly the industrial unions whose cause Gephardt had faithfully served. In 1960, 40 percent of the American workforce was unionized; now just 13.5 percent is (compared with a European average of 43 percent). The figure for white males has dropped from 24 percent in 1983 to 14.8 percent in 2001.[11] Rather than being the backbone of American industry, unions are disproportionately creatures of the public sector. Teachers now matter more than car workers do—and Joe Sixpack has never felt much solidarity with teachers. Walter Mondale ran the perfect old-style New Deal campaign in 1984, endorsed by every union in America; he lost by a landslide.

Of all the elements gnawing away at the ties between working-class America and the New Deal, nothing is more savage than time. In 2002 only 8 percent of voters were old enough to have any direct experience of the 1930s.[12] An experience that shaped politics for decades—that persuaded intellectuals to embrace government and convinced politicians that their highest calling was to prevent a repetition of the Great Depression—is now a fading memory. There is little feeling that today's prosperity owes a debt to Roosevelt's activism all those years ago. In Tennessee, another state Gore lost in 2000, people no longer talk lovingly of the Tennessee Valley Authority (which Gore's father helped mold) as an engine for social change; they talk about it as an electricity supplier that needs to sharpen up its business model, clean up its power stations and lower its prices.

The point here is not to claim that working-class Americans are natural Republicans. It is to underline that they are no longer rock-solid Democrats. Come November 2004, Joe Sixpack may side with the Democrats, angry about the economy or Iraq or whatever, but the Democrats cannot take him for granted. In this, as in most other forms of short-term maneuvering, the Democrats are still mostly on the defensive.

Todo el día en español

This is no doubt gratifying to Republicans. Yet a realignment of the sort that Karl Rove is plotting requires more than just a weakening of your opponent's political coalition. It requires demographic and social trends to move in your direction. Here, at least at first sight, the Democrats have a much more compelling case to make.

This optimism is rooted in demography. In *The Emerging Democratic Majority* (2002), John Judis and Ruy Teixeira, a journalist and a psephologist, respectively, argue that three groups in particular are pushing America toward a "progressive centrist" future. The first is women, who supported Al Gore by 54 to 43 percent in 2000, and particularly the ever-growing number of well-educated working women.[13] We will deal with them more fully in Chapter 13. The other two groups are professionals and Latinos, both of whom tend to vote Democratic and both of whom look set to make up an ever bigger share of the electorate. Judis and Teixeira maintain that the more America becomes a multiethnic and postindustrial society, the more the Democrats will prosper. This is McKinley in reverse: the Republicans may win the odd election but the broad sweep of history is on the Democratic side.

One reason to take this argument seriously is the number of clever Republicans who do. Bill Owens, the governor of Colorado, worries that the collapse of his party in California in the 1990s could be repeated in much of the West; the Republicans need to be much more assiduous in courting minorities, professionals and women, and to curb any reputation for intolerance. This White House has been unusually keen to court Latinos, even producing a Spanish version of its web site. Yet the Judis-Teixeira view of the world ("All in all, demography is moving toward a Democratic majority") seems to us to be wrong on two counts. First, it is far too clear-cut and deterministic when both Latinos and professionals are changing fast; second, it omits other, nondemographic, social trends, especially those to do with values, which are moving in the Republican direction.

Consider the Latinos. Any Republican who feels bullish about his party's future should take a leisurely drive along one of America's most famous streets. Sunset Boulevard snakes away from the Pacific Ocean into the hills of rich West Los Angeles, one of the bastions of American liberalism. Then comes the garish Sunset Strip, where the blonde-studded billboards indicate that all is not going John Ashcroft's way in the culture war. But the harshest lesson is to be found farther down the boulevard. As Sunset works its way through Hollywood, you pass through a sort of no-man's-land—

or should it be everyman's land?—where El Pollo Loco, Hoy's Wok and a restaurant called Uzbekistan nestle beside Burger King. Gradually the number of Spanish signs increases. Television stations point out that they broadcast *"todo el día en español."* As you near Dodger Stadium, most dry cleaners and hairdressers have become *lavanderías* and *peluquerías*—although some shop signs mix the languages, as in *"Bonita y* Cheap." At the very end of Sunset lie two surprises. The first is a brief spell in Chinatown: suddenly Asian schoolchildren replace Hispanic ones, and Spanish signs give way to Chinese ones. The second is that soon afterward Sunset metamorphoses into Cesar Chavez Avenue, in honor of the late leader of the Latino farm workers' movement.

This journey down Sunset is far from exceptional. Some Angelenos would say that Wilshire or Olympic boulevards offer an even more cosmopolitan hodge-podge. In Chicago, Fullerton Avenue begins in rich, white Lincoln Park but soon takes you on a global walkabout through different parts of Eastern Europe and Latin America. In Queens, New York, you can take a similarly multicultural ride on the number 7 subway train above Roosevelt Avenue. Levittown, New York, the quintessential American suburb, boasts a Turkish mosque. In Orange County, California, the home of John Wayne Airport, the first two children to be born this millennium were Cambodian-American and Mexican-American. Back in 1950, America was 89 percent white and 10 percent black. Other races hardly made an appearance. Today blacks make up 12.7 percent of the total—less than Latinos at 14 percent. If current trends continue, Latinos will shortly be the majority in Los Angeles County. In twenty years, they will dominate Texas and California. By 2050, one in four of the 400 million people who will then be living in the United States will be Latino—and if you add Asians, their joint share will be one in three.

Demography gives Democrats hope. Although they are not always the most conscientious voters, hyphenated Americans increased their share of the voting electorate from about a tenth in 1972 to almost a fifth in 2000—and could make up nearly a quarter by 2010.[14] So far these new minorities have overwhelmingly supported the Democrats. The only big exception has been Cuban-Americans, who have stuck by the Republicans in the belief that they will take a harsher line with Fidel Castro.

We think this picture may begin to change. The big question about the Latinos is whether they will end up voting more like blacks or Italian-Americans. Blacks have stuck loyally to the Democratic cause, but most immigrant groups become more Republican the longer they stay in the country. They move to the suburbs, losing contact with the Democratic Party's great urban political machines. They start their own businesses, making them more receptive to the Republican Party's antiregulation message. All these things seem to be happening to Latinos as well. One analysis of Latino voting in ten states in the 2002 election found that about a third of Latinos plumped for Republican Senate candidates and almost half for Republican governors.[15] George Bush won 43 percent of the Latino vote in Texas in 2000. The great exception remains California, where Latinos were driven firmly into the arms of the Democratic Party not by underlying social trends but by Pete Wilson's colossal political blunder in supporting Proposition 187, which sought to deny state benefits to illegal immigrants. "We were being called lazy and loafers," says Gregory Rodriguez, a Los Angeles–based writer. "There is no more antiwelfare voter than a Mexican immigrant."[16]

This sort of comment underlines another claim made by Republican optimists: that Latinos are worthy strivers—hard-working, God-fearing, family-oriented and upwardly mobile. They have the highest male workforce participation rate of any measured group—and one of the lowest incidences of trade union membership and welfare dependency (only 17 percent of immigrant Latinos in poverty collect welfare, compared with 50 percent of poor whites and 65 percent of poor blacks).[17] Latinos are arguably the most family-oriented ethnic group in American society. They also have a marked propensity to start their own businesses and buy their own homes—both incubators of Republicanism. Rodriguez, who did a detailed study of Latinos in the five-county L.A. area in the 1990s, argues that the most common experience is one of upward mobility into the middle class. The study shows that in 1990 U.S.-born Latinos had four times as many households in the middle-class as in poverty and that about 50 percent of U.S.-born Latinos had household incomes above the local average. The percentage of Latino immigrants in poverty declines sharply the longer they stay in the United States—and the percentage who own their homes rises sharply.

Within twenty years of arriving in the country, half of Latinos own their own homes.[18]

This is not to say that Latinos are likely to move en masse into the Republican fold. The flow of poor South American immigrants into low-paying jobs will always provide a flow of recruits into the Democratic Party. Nevertheless, the likelihood is that the Latino vote will split increasingly along class lines, as the more established Latinos follow the pattern of Italian-Americans. There is no reason why the Republicans cannot make inroads into the Latinos provided they don't shoot themselves in the foot by supporting restrictive policies on immigration. Bush, who won one in three Latino votes in 2000 (compared with Bob Dole's one in five in 1996), is certainly aware of this. He floated the idea of a comprehensive guest-worker program early in his presidency, but the idea was scuttled by security concerns after September 11. In January 2004, he returned to the subject, proposing giving temporary legal status to the 8 million–10 million illegal immigrants in America (half of whom are from Mexico). The move, which was broadly welcomed by the Mexican government, will probably help the Republicans win Latino votes in swing states like Florida, New Mexico and Nevada.

Even in California, all is not lost with Latinos. We will discuss the 2003 California recall in more detail later in the chapter, but it is worth noting that Arnold Schwarzenegger picked up nearly one in three Latino votes cast. That may not look like a lot, until you take into account the fact that he was running against the highest-ranking Latino in California politics, the Democratic lieutenant governor, Cruz Bustamante, who received 51 percent of the Latino vote. Schwarzenegger came under heavy fire from the Democratic establishment for having voted for Proposition 187 and for having Pete Wilson as his campaign manager. He was even brutally disinvited from the annual Mexican parade in Los Angeles. Yet in his ham-fisted way, Schwarzenegger persisted, reiterating the idea that he too had once been a penniless immigrant, stressing his support for affirmative action and even praising Mexico as a great place to make movies. Although his support among Latinos was lower than among whites (among whom he won 52 percent of the vote), it was also markedly above that of blacks, from whom he got only

17 percent. Even in California, Latinos are clearly detachable from the Democrats in a way that blacks are not.

PROFESSIONAL ANGST

What about the other Judis-Teixeira group: professionals? Professionals, once a bulwark of the Republican Party, have been generally Democratic since 1988. Like Latinos, they too are a rising proportion of the population, growing from 7 percent of the workforce in the 1950s to 15 percent today; they also have a higher turnout than any other occupational group, making up 21 percent of the voting electorate nationally, and a quarter in many Northeastern states.[19] Judis and Teixeira point out that America's megalopolises—the regions that include San Francisco, Chicago and New York and employ most of the country's creative talent—are more likely to vote Democratic than Republican. The tone of these areas, they argue, is set by socially liberal knowledge-workers whose influence stretches far beyond their bohemian clusters.

It is certainly true that Bill Clinton did particularly well in such places during the 1990s. But does this have any long-term significance? A poll of 1,225 likely 2004 voters conducted by one of Clinton's best number crunchers, Mark Penn, for the Democratic Leadership Council in June and July 2003, found a very different picture.[20] Professionals were highly suspicious of the Democratic Party for being too much in favor of big government and too dominated by interest groups. They thought that Republicans had the best policies by a margin of 21 percent. Suburbanites plumped for Republican policies by a margin of 15 percent; white-collar workers did so by a margin of 29 percent. These categories are imperfect and overlapping, of course, but they hardly show that suburbanization and employment in service industries are a blessing for the Democrats.

One big problem with the Judis-Teixeira argument about professionals is that it ignores the importance of the life cycle in changing people's political allegiances. People usually become more conservative when they get married and have children. The Republican message of lower taxes and a more punitive attitude to crime may not resonate with young professionals living a Seinfeld-like existence in Manhattan or San Francisco. But it rings much truer when you have children and move to the commuter belt. Penn's poll gave the Republicans a 19-point advantage among married voters with children. Bill Clinton was the only Democrat in living memory to win this group (he carried them by 7 points in 1996). But since then old suspicions about the Democrats have returned. George Bush carried the group by 15 points in 2000.

If Sunset Boulevard foretells one future for the country, other bits of Southern California foretell a different, far more Republican-friendly future. Drive to the eastern end of the Los Angeles basin, beyond Latino East Los Angeles, to the area of family homes, sprawling car dealerships, nondescript strip malls and low-slung office parks known locally as the Inland Empire and you discover a very different world. The area's population grew from 1.6 million in 1980 to 3.2 million in 2000, making it one of the fastest-growing places in the country. The Census Bureau predicts that the Inland Empire will double in the next two decades, gaining more people than all but five states.[21] The bulk of this growth has been driven by young families (many of them Latino and Asian) who are fleeing Los Angeles, worried about its failing schools and high housing prices. The Inland Empire boasts one of the highest percentages of "married with children" households in the nation, and it is overwhelmingly Republican territory, with three of the four districts in the region in GOP hands.

It is true that the most ethnically diverse of the four districts, the forty-third, where 77 percent of the inhabitants are minorities, is the Democratic one. On the other hand, its congressman, Joe Baca, has one of the most conservative voting records in California's congressional delegation. The Republicans have a firm grip on the forty-second district, where Latinos make up a quarter of the population and Asians a sixth. The local congressman is a conservative Republican, Gary Miller, and his district voted 59 percent for Bush in the 2000 election. That may be because ethnic diversity matters less than the fact that the district (which includes Richard Nixon's home town, Yorba Linda) is littered with small businesses and boasts the highest percentage of married couples in the state.

Needless to say, the suburbs of Southern California rallied to Schwarzenegger—as they have done to other moderate Republicans. And this, remember, is California—the very belly of the Democratic beast. In most of the rest of the West or the South, the suburbs are presumed to be Republican-leaning. Meanwhile, in New York State, generally regarded as another Democratic stronghold, suburban voters have rallied to support Republican candidates, particularly moderate ones. Witness the ease with which George Pataki has won two terms as governor there.

THE REPUBLICAN CASE

The Inland Empire proves that demography is not destiny. Any Democrat who thinks that the party can project Bill Clinton's spectacular performance among both professionals and Latinos into the indefinite future is talking baloney. Meanwhile, conservatives, notably Michael Barone, the editor of the *Almanac of American Politics,* point to other social trends and aspirations that are pushing people in the GOP's direction.[22] Our impression is that the Republicans are more in tune than the Democrats with four of the most basic American passions—for business, property, choice and, most especially, national security.

America is, above all, a business civilization. The country creates proportionately more businesses than any other country in the world, and accords businesspeople much higher status. America's probusiness prejudices seem to have easily survived both a ballooning of inequality and a plague of corporate scandals, with CEOs rigging the system, duping their shareholders and robbing their employees. An astonishing 31 percent of Americans think that they will be rich one day, many dream of starting their own companies and they have a generally high opinion of their own employers.[23] The Republicans' record as a probusiness party is hardly perfect (they are too often more concerned with pandering to existing businesses than with promoting competition) but they are generally more probusiness than the Democrats on everything from regulation to trade to tort reform. They have the firm support of America's business lobbies, both big and small.

The Republicans' second advantage is closely related to the first: property. Disraeli once remarked that the British Tory Party's best chance of success lay in creating a "property-owning democracy." The same is true of today's Republican Party. Barone points out that America has witnessed a revolution in one sort of property ownership: share ownership. "In just 10 years time the electorate has changed from one in which a huge majority of voters were non-investors to one in which a substantial majority were investors."[24] More investors means more people with a stake in corporate America who will be skeptical about business bashing—something that probably did not help Al Gore's "the people vs. the powerful" campaign in 2000. More investors also means more people prepared to consider one of the Republican Party's signature issues—privatizing Social Security—on its merits. Democrats claim that Social Security is the third rail of American politics, too dangerous too touch, and Bush has certainly been nervous about approaching it. But young people in particular are quite keen on reform. In the summer of 2002, in the middle of one of the biggest corporate scandals in American history, a Cato Institute/Zogby International poll found that more than 68 percent of likely voters favored "changing the Social Security system to give younger workers the choice to invest a portion of their Social Security taxes through individual accounts."[25] The GOP has the chance of creating a virtuous circle, with Social Security privatization creating more investors and a growth in the number of investors reducing hostility to a further reduction in the role of government.

The third advantage is one that many Democrats like to claim as their own: choice. Here, however, we are talking about something other than abortion. The first industrial age was an age of giant organizations and standardized production. Henry Ford told his customers that they could have cars in any color so long as it was black; Walter Reuther organized the union members he represented as if they were cogs in a huge political machine. The information age is surely different. Four out of every five new jobs in America is created by a small business. Modern America is the world of narrowcast rather than broadcast, of the remote control, of the Google search engine, of the individualized mobile phone. When people feel free to choose the shape of their noses or even the sex of their babies, they are unlikely to want to accept a set menu of services from any government. With the notable exception of abortion, the Republicans give the impression that they are more comfortable with choice than the Democrats. The one argument for the Bush tax cuts that has remained constant is that people should be able to decide what to do with their own money. Conservative policies on education, Medicare and Social Security all try to give voters more choice over the use of public funds. The Democrats, on the other hand, are against both school choice and the partial privatization of Social Security.

THE GUN AND THE BALLOT BOX

The GOP's strongest card of all is national security. The Republicans may not always have played this card adroitly since September 11, but they seem to have seized control of an issue that served them so well from 1968 to 1988. In those two decades only the calamity of Watergate managed to dislodge the Republicans briefly from the White House—and Jimmy Carter's hapless presidency duly reinforced popular fears about the Democrats' robustness.

September 11 has allowed the Republicans to reassert their traditional advantage with a vengeance. Americans once more feel immensely vulnerable—more vulnerable to immediate attack, perhaps, than they felt during the Communist era. Patriotism has soared, with polls showing nine in ten Americans feeling very proud to be Americans, and Republicans even prouder than Democrats.[26] It is unlikely that Bush will ever regain his post–September 11 glow (when his job-approval ratings remained high for a longer sustained period than for any other president since polling began in 1935). But for the foreseeable future, Americans are unlikely to punish anybody who is overzealous about national security. Soccer moms have become security moms. Go back to Penn's poll in July 2003—a time of near-daily casualties in Iraq, continual assertions from the Democrats that George W. Bush exaggerated the threat posed by Saddam Hussein and Bush's own approval numbers slipping to around 50 percent. The polls showed that Americans favored the Republicans by 28 percentage points on terrorism, 33 points on homeland security and 35 points on national security. This advantage shows some signs of being durable. In January 2004, an ABC News/*Washington Post* poll found voters preferring Bush over a theoretical Democrat by 29 percentage points on terrorism and 20 points on Iraq.[27] Moreover, whenever the Republicans have played the national-security card forcibly—as they did against Senator Max Cleland in Georgia in 2002—they have usually prevailed. They will play it repeatedly in the 2004 campaign, even timing their own convention around the September 11 anniversary.

By selecting John Kerry, a much-decorated Vietnam War hero, as their candidate for 2004, the Democrats plainly think they have found a shield against the Republican onslaught. Kerry doesn't hesitate to bring up his war record, implicitly contrasting his decision to serve in Vietnam with George W. Bush's decision to join the National Guard, and he is certainly in a better position to ward off Republican taunts about being weak on defense than, say, Howard Dean. But biography is not everything: McGovern was a war hero too. Even in early March, when Kerry led Bush in the polls on every single domestic issue, he still lagged the president on questions to do with the war on terror, and Kerry's various "flip-flops" on defense-related issues were coming under attack. More generally, the Democrats have yet to find a clear voice on national security. During the 2002 election the Democrats tried to change the subject to domestic issues, particularly education and Medicare. The congressional vote authorizing war in Iraq saw the party split down the middle (a split that reflected the division among Democratic activists and funders).

It is possible that national security may even eliminate one of the Republicans' biggest liabilities—the sense that their values are in retreat. The shame of the Vietnam War has been replaced by the trauma of September 11. The stories are not of soldiers massacring civilians but of firefighters rushing into burning buildings, of the passengers on Flight 93 who revolted against their hijackers. Todd Beamer, the man who recited the Lord's Prayer with an air-phone operator before ending the call with the words "Let's roll," has become a national icon. It would be facile to say that Beamer will turn young Americans into Republicans, but it is hard to imagine there will be no effect at all. The Left already seems slightly spooked by the prospect. Katha Pollitt, a columnist for the *Nation,* revealed the incomprehension of aging leftists when she described an argument with her thirteen-year-old daughter, who attends a high school a few blocks away from the World Trade Center. Her daughter wanted to fly the American flag. Her mother objected. "Definitely not, I say: the flag stands for jingoism and vengeance and war."[28] The old Bob Dylan line about not criticizing what you can't understand may be coming full circle.

It would be bold to claim that all this amounts to an automatic Republican ascendancy or that the kind of full-scale transformation that began under McKinley (or that Rove and Bush achieved in Texas) is now under way. Still, the idea that the Republicans will become the default party of government at the national level if Bush somehow struggles through the 2004 election is not an outrageous one. After all, they already have a pretty firm lock on both houses of Congress. It does not seem unnatural for such a conservative nation to vote for the more conservative of the two parties. The question is whether the Republicans can keep themselves in shape to take advantage of that prejudice — and that is certainly not a foregone conclusion.

CHAPTER 10

HOW IT COULD GO WRONG: TOO SOUTHERN, TOO GREEDY AND TOO CONTRADICTORY

ON DECEMBER 5, 2002, the Senate threw a party for Strom Thurmond's hundredth (and last) birthday. This was a remarkable event by any standard. Thurmond was the Senate's longest serving member ever and its first centenarian. He was born before either television or Soviet communism—and yet he was still in the saddle, still helping to shape the fate of the world's only remaining superpower. The event was naturally taken up with comments on Thurmond's extraordinary life force—and his legendary eye for the ladies. Ol' Strom married his second wife, a twenty-two-year-old former Miss South Carolina, when he was sixty-six. The happy couple went on to have four children. He remained flirtatious well into his nineties, despite his gruesome-looking hair transplant. "When he dies," a fellow senator once remarked, "they'll have to beat his pecker down with a baseball bat to close the coffin lid."[1]

Soon the old goat's birthday party became famous for a different reason. Trent Lott, the new Republican majority leader, fresh from the success of the 2002 election, was one of the speakers who paid tribute to Thurmond's long career. Lott had no shortage of material, given his subject's extraordinary life, but he decided to praise Thurmond for running as a segregationist presidential candidate in 1948. "I want to say this about my state," announced the senator from Mississippi. "When Strom Thurmond ran for president, we voted for him. We're proud of it. And if the rest of the country had followed our lead, we wouldn't have had all these problems over all these years, either."

Lott later claimed that he was making a point about states' rights, but to any reasonable listener the implication was pretty clear: America would have been better off if it had kept Jim Crow. For a couple of days, it looked as if Lott might get away with it. The mainstream press buried the story, but an odd alliance of black activists and conservative bloggers forced it onto the front pages. The White House, in effect, disowned him, and the hapless Lott was reduced to appearing on Black Entertainment Television to proclaim that he had always been a supporter of affirmative action—a belief he had mysteriously kept to himself. He eventually resigned as majority leader, and had to watch a more telegenic Southerner, Bill Frist, take over the leadership of the new Republican Senate.

For many Republicans, Lott was a ghastly reminder of their party's racist past. Lott, it emerged, had spent much of his career flirting with the demons of the Old South. As a student at Ole Miss in Oxford, Mississippi, he led a campaign against the integration of his fraternity. Well into his Senate career, he gave speeches to the Council of Conservative Citizens, an organization formed to succeed the segregationist White Citizens' Councils of the 1960s: "The people in this room stand for the right principles and the right philosophy," he told a gathering in Greenwood, Mississippi, in 1992.[2]

Lott was the Republican Party's nasty little secret brought to blow-dried life (his hair, incidentally, is almost as extraordinary as Thurmond's was). But look a little closer at Strom's birthday party, and the picture of conservative America becomes a little less ghastly. If Lott's speech was a sign of how little had changed for a few Republicans, his prompt removal showed how much had changed for the party in general. Whatever his faults, George W. Bush has been far more reluctant to play the race card than his predecessors (including his father) had been. Indeed, he has tried hard to put a multicultural face on his party, in everything from the Philadelphia convention to his multihued cabinet.

The Lott affair is a microcosm of the state of the Republican Party: it suggests both the depth of its problems and its capacity to deal with them. The party's real challenge is not the supposed fixed loyalties of this or that demographic group; it is the party's own profile and politics—its capacity for extremism and intolerance, its contradictions, its weakness for various vested interests, its sheer boneheaded ability to screw things up. None of these things will probably matter in the 2004 election as much as the state of the American economy, but they will make a big difference to how the Republican Party fares in the longer term. How could things go wrong? We will move on to two problems in a moment: the Republicans' sloppiness with government spending and the continuing danger, exemplified by Lott, of seeming intolerant. But we will begin with the challenge for any Republican leadership of "managing the mob"—somehow keeping this sprawling, feuding party together and preventing it from gobbling up its leader.

MANAGING THE MOB

Imagine for a moment you are George W. Bush. As you stare at your political empire, you wonder at the absurdity of the Republican coalition. How on earth have you managed to persuade Colin Powell and Tom DeLay to fight in the same colors? What exactly are the neoconservatives doing, bedding down with the fundamentalists? Do Olympia Snowe and Ann Coulter have anything in common? Would Arnold Schwarzenegger and Pat Robertson like to share a taxi home?

Contradictions are inevitable in any national party in a country as big as America. H. L. Mencken once remarked that the Democratic Party consisted of "gangs of natural enemies in a precarious state of symbiosis." And many of the Republicans' contradictions merely reflect their success in assembling such a broad coalition. One is reminded of the old Walt Whitman line about his contradictions being proof of his enormity.[3] Most Democrats would be delighted to have the Republicans' "problem" of having too many white Southerners in their party. All the same, these contradictions are a problem when it comes to policy. Look at almost any subject and you can find a debate raging. One group of Republican lawyers thinks that the best way to defeat liberal judges (particularly on abortion) is to assert the primacy of the legislative branch, for instance. But another faction supports activist judges against the legislature, provided of course that they strictly enforce the constitution on things like guns and property rights.

Rather than detailing every split in the Republican ranks, we will concentrate on three overlapping contradictions: the ideological split between libertarians and traditionalists; the social split between religious conservatives and the business community; and the logical tension between free-market principles and the heartland's values.

As we explained in our introduction, modern American conservatism is a different beast from traditional conservatism: it has strains of individualism, populism and optimism that would have flummoxed Burke or Churchill. These downright "liberal" enhancements have made it far more appealing and lively, but they bring problems in their wake, not least the tension between libertarianism and traditionalism. Libertarians put individual choice at the heart of their thinking; traditionalists cite received wisdom. Libertarians criticize mainstream liberals for putting too many shackles on the individual—primarily through big government. Traditionalists criticize mainstream liberals for giving individuals too many choices. These two schools have been trading blows ever since Russell Kirk and Hayek did battle in the 1950s.

The most common casus belli is inevitably abortion. Traditionalists abhor abortion as a sign of a sick society that values individual choice even above the life of an unborn child. Libertarians support abortion as part of their general support for individual rights. In 1994 Barry Goldwater, explaining why social conservatives such as Jerry Falwell deserved "a swift kick in the ass," insisted that the decision to have an abortion "should be up to the woman involved, not the pope or some do-gooders or the religious right. It's not a conservative issue at all."[4] Goldwater's wife, Peggy, helped to found Planned Parenthood in Arizona and their daughter had an illegal abortion in the mid-1950s. Goldwater accused Pat Robertson of trying to turn the GOP into a religious organization, and he even backed a Democratic candidate for Congress against a Christian conservative. Many Schwarzenegger Republicans feel the same way. The abortion debate is likely to get sharper in the future, thanks to the relentless march of biotechnology. Virtually every advance in reproductive technology will divide business conservatives, who see yet another opportunity to make money, from social ones who worry about mankind perverting God's will.

If you burrow down to the precinct level of the Republican Party, you often discover that the battle between libertarians and traditionalists is about class as well as values. In particular, it is a battle between business conservatives and social conservatives. These two categories often overlap: many social conservatives are small-business owners (and vice versa). But there is also often a difference of emphasis. Business conservatives are focused on making money. Social conservatives are worried about what sort of society America is becoming. Business conservatives are instinctive deal makers. Social conservatives are natural absolutists. Business conservatives belong to country clubs. Social conservatives wear plaid trousers and read the Bible literally. This tension is most marked in the Northeast and the Midwest. In St. Charles, Illinois, members of the town's business elite certainly go to church every Sunday, but they also complain about extremists being "cannibals" eating their own party. Even in the South, where most businesspeople are socially conservative, they often shy away from ideological controversies—not least because they are bad for business. It was Southern business conservatives who tried to find compromises in the rows about states flying the Confederate flag and in the kerfuffle that followed Alabama's chief justice displaying the Ten Commandments in the state's main court building.

Less noticed is the logical contradiction between trying to be the party of both the free market and the heartland. Just as capitalism famously has its cultural contradictions, so does conservatism. In particular, the Republican Party regards itself as the party of business and growth, but it gets more of its support from the slow-growing heartland than from the faster-growing coasts. Worse, the more successful the party is at implementing its economic creed, the more quickly it devours its own demographic base.

George W. Bush embodies this contradiction every time he summers at his ranch near Crawford. Dressed in cowboy gear and roasting in 110-degree heat, the president is lorded as a man who is at "home in the heartland," in the White House's saccharine phrase. Americans regard the heartland as more than just a geographical expression (the country's central and rural areas). Rather, it is a moral condition: an embodiment of the authentic American tradition of self-reliance, family values and community spirit, a place where people do proper work—by wrestling with nature rather than shuffling symbols on a screen. The Democrats may be able to rely on celluloid America. Heartland America will always tend to vote Republican.

It is celluloid America, however, that does better in the free market. The worst poverty in America is not in the inner cities, but in rural Mississippi, Arkansas, West Virginia and Kentucky. In 2001, the government dished out $25 billion in direct subsidies to farmers, and billions more indirectly through water, power and infrastructure. Far from buttressing rugged individualism, this money has created a sort of state-funded feudalism, where a handful of landowners preside over vast armies of ill-educated and poorly paid migrant workers. Paul Krugman, a *New York Times* columnist, has calculated that the "blue" states (i.e., the coastal ones that Democrats win) subsidize the "red" Republican states to the tune of $90 billion a year.[5] The red states secure this largesse by old-fashioned political clout, particularly in the Senate, where each state has two senators: just 16 percent of the population elects half the Senate. As for the heartland's much-vaunted moral qualities, the states that Bush won in 2000 boast slightly higher rates of murder, illegitimacy and teenage childbirth than the supposedly degenerate states that voted for Gore.

THE BUSH DEFICIT

Bush's willingness to throw money at problems like the heartland could be a time bomb for his party. Economic management should be one of the Republicans' strongest suits, along with defense. The Republicans are supposed to be the "daddy party" (bringing home the bacon and warding off attackers) while the Democratic "mommy party" cares for the poor and sick. For much of their history—with the notable exception of the 1980s—the Republicans have loathed deficits. In *The Conscience of a Conservative* Goldwater argued that you should cut taxes only if you are willing to cut spending. In the 1990s Newt Gingrich made a balanced budget a centerpiece of the Contract with America. Now Bush has created a monster. Back in 2000, he was asked during a presidential debate what he planned to do with the projected budget surpluses if he won the presidency. He said he would use half to shore up Social Security, a quarter for "important projects," and a quarter for tax cuts. This he has patently not achieved. When Bill Clinton left office the cumulative surplus over the next ten years was projected to be $5.6 trillion; by August 2003, the Congressional Budget Office was predicting a ten-year deficit of $1.4 trillion.[6]

The deficit numbers are both better than they first appear and much worse. On the positive side, there is nothing wrong with running deficits during a downturn: indeed that is what governments are supposed to do to cushion the effects of recession. It is also more fair to look at the figures in terms of proportion of the economy. By these standards, the Bush 2004 deficit, projected at 4.3 percent of GDP, is still smaller than the 6 percent racked up by Reagan in 1983. And, despite Democratic complaints about the surplus being dissipated on tax cuts, the new tax cuts account only for around a quarter of the total fiscal reversal, according to the Office of Management and Budget; extra spending accounts for another quarter and the rest comes from the economic downturn which made a hash of the OMB's economic projections.[7]

Yet the numbers are also much worse, for two reasons. First, they are not real numbers. The only way the Bush administration could get its second big tax cut through Congress in 2003 was by indulging in Enronesque accounting. Officially, many of its tax cuts are temporary. But the idea that the taxes will ever be brought back is laughable. No politician would allow such tax rises (for that is what they will feel like) to happen. Get rid of these phantom sunsets, and the deficit jumps by $1.9 trillion over ten years. Add in other reasonable expectations—a change in the Alternative Minimum Tax, more money on Medicare and so on—and the official number is $5 trillion short over the next decade.[8] Rather than easing back into credit, America will see deficits that average 3 percent of GDP over the next decade.

The second worry is bigger. Starting in 2010, the baby-boom generation will begin to retire—and to place huge burdens on Social Security and Medicare. The numbers here are staggering. One 2003 study from the American Enterprise Institute put the total unfunded liabilities at $44 trillion (four times America's GDP); Medicare alone could eat up $20 trillion.[9]

Rather than prepare for this challenge, the Bush administration has run away from it; indeed, in 2003, it massively extended Medicare, subsidizing drugs for retired people, without any fundamental reforms. The same AEI paper claims that waiting till 2008 to try to fix the problem of entitlements will increase the total liability to $54 trillion.

Fundamentally, the issue of mismanagement and what will come to be known as the "Bush deficit" boils down to one thing: spending. Spending has bounded along at around 8 percent—well above the level under Bill Clinton. Of course, September 11, homeland security and the Iraq War have had an effect, but less than you might imagine. They explain no more than half the total rise in spending. Some conservatives comfort themselves with the fact that Ronald Reagan also cut taxes and increased spending. But the more you look at the comparison, the less it flatters Bush. Reagan did not have the baby boomers to worry about, and he made a real effort to make government smaller, wielding his veto pen fifteen times in his first two years; by contrast, George W. Bush did not veto anything in his first three years.

The Republican Party's incontinence is not limited to the White House. Congress egged Bush on to splurge more money on Medicare. Outside Washington, Republican politicians are bigger spenders than the Democrats are. In the five years running up to 2002, state legislatures controlled by Republicans increased spending an average of 6.54 percent a year compared with 6.17 percent for legislatures run by Democrats. State spending rose slowest—by "just" 6 percent a year—when legislatures were split, and each party controlled one chamber, confirming that divided government is often the best brake on spending.[10]

Why have the Republicans squandered their reputation for fiscal prudence? One excuse on the Right is that the Republicans want to build up big deficits in order to put a long-term constraint on the growth of government: any future Democratic administrations would have nothing to spend. Even if this were true, would this be sensible policy? It is rather like saying that, because your brother-in-law drinks too much, you're going to drink all the alcohol in the house before he visits for the Memorial Day weekend. People who believe in limited government should not try to introduce it by the back door—as an unwanted consequence of a fiscal crisis.

K Street conservatism and Red George

One big reason for this economic mismanagement is George W. Bush's instinctive tendency to side with Big Business. There is nothing inherently wrong with being probusiness in a probusiness country. But there is something wrong about pandering to particular businesses—about rewarding your friends rather than promoting competition.

Few parts of Washington have been as happy during the Bush administration as K Street. This is the home of the corporate lobbying community, of tasseled loafers and ingenious ways to transfer money from the state to a few select clients. The tariffs on steel and soft lumber, introduced in 2002, were extremely popular with the industries concerned, but hardly bolstered the Republican image as the party of free trade. The 2002 farm bill actually reversed previous attempts to get the government out of the farming business, even adding price controls (on the Soviet-like grounds that they were "counter-cyclical"). All in all, the farm bill separated taxpayers from some $180 billion over the next ten years, most of which will end up with big agribusinesses of one sort or another.

Worst of all has been the cozying up to the energy industry. Leave aside all the theoretical debates about global warming, where Bush sometimes has reasonable arguments. Seen from K Street, energy policy has been one long boondoggle. Dick Cheney's energy plan was largely written by the energy industry, hardly an ideal recipe for good policy making (particularly if some members of the energy industry happen to work for Enron). The final bill under discussion in early 2004 included perks for every energy company in the land, from lower charges for fossil-fuel companies using federal land to loan guarantees for the nuclear industry merely for building and operating plants. Trying to get this pork through Congress, the Republicans bribed the Democrats by pouring money into green subsidies, doling out more cash in the name of energy efficiency, alternative energy and all the other code words K Street has embraced. As Jerry Taylor of the Cato Institute pointed out, this was a "Leave No Lobbyist Behind" bill.

There is more to K Street conservatism than just delivering favors to business. The Republican Party is in the process of turning K Street into part of its political machine. Until the middle of the 1990s K Street was a bipartisan place. Lobbying firms bent over backward to employ both Republicans and Democrats. Democrats had the better pickings simply because their party had dominated Capitol Hill for most of the postwar period. But this changed with the Republican takeover of Congress in 1994. Tom DeLay, then the Republican whip, and Grover Norquist decided to consolidate this advantage by launching the "K Street project." They told lobbyists in no uncertain terms that they should hire more Republicans or risk being snubbed on the Hill.

The lobbying industry is now intertwined with the Republican Party. The party chairman, Ed Gillespie, was a leading lobbyist. So was Haley Barbour, its new governor of Mississippi. Almost all new appointments on K Street are Republicans. Every Tuesday morning Rick Santorum, the junior senator from Pennsylvania, holds a meeting with a dozen or so Republican lobbyists to discuss jobs on K Street. This intertwining is happening at a time when lobbyists are getting ever more influential. In 1968, there were only 62 of them; now there are 21,000 — and they have taken to raising money for legislators as well as just trying to influence them.[11]

Nicholas Confessore argues that the Republican Party is bent on using K Street in much the same way that Franklin Roosevelt and his heirs once used government to Democratic advantage.[12] In its glory days, the Democratic Party used its grip on the machinery of government to dole out largesse to loyal constituencies (the poor, the old and, eventually, racial minorities) and also provide jobs for its own footsoldiers. Now the Republican Party is using its sway over both K Street and the wider business community to build a private-sector equivalent to Roosevelt's machine. It hands out government contracts to businesses that fill its coffers: look at the way the pharmaceutical industry should gain from the new prescription-drug benefit in Medicare. It provides its most loyal footsoldiers, from congressional aides to congressmen, with a pot of gold on K Street when they retire.

This may pay plenty of political dividends in the short term. But what about the longer term? The GOP's vitality depends upon its willingness to think radical thoughts. At his best Reagan was a successful president not because he went down well in the boardrooms — most CEOs would have felt more at home with Gerry Ford—but because he succeeded in harnessing the creative energy of so many idealistic free-marketers. The Republican Party is also supposed to be the party of small government and light regulation. But lobbyists can flourish only in a world of government meddling and back-room deals. This reinforces our second big worry about the direction of the Republican Party: that under George W. Bush, the Republicans have moved from being the party of small government to the party of big government (as long as it isn't run by Democrats).

Even conservatives who come to office determined to lop big chunks off government usually end up shaving just a tiny fraction: look at the experience of Ronald Reagan and Margaret Thatcher. But Bush arrived in office with a bouquet of flowers, not an axe. "Government has a role and an important role," he told Congress on February 27, 2001, in a nice counterpoint to Bill Clinton's declaration to the same body that "the age of big government is over." Now "Red George," as conservatives may yet come to call him, is engaged in a bold experiment: to see whether programs that were created by liberals from the 1930s to the 1970s can be reshaped in a conservative direction.

The clearest example is education. Conservatives have long argued that the federal government should stay out of schools. In 1995 House Republicans made noises about closing down the Department of Education. Under Bill Clinton education expenditure rose fairly modestly, from $30 billion in the 1993 financial year to $36 billion in the 2001 financial year. Under George Bush, it skyrocketed to $56 billion in 2003 and is heading for $70 billion in 2008. The department has acquired Gosplan-like responsibilities—monitoring the performance of schools across the entire country and then cajoling poorly performing schools into doing better.

Bush has also displayed a marked penchant for what might be called "neopaternalism"—using social policy to prod people's behavior in a more conservative direction. The man who personifies neopaternalism is Wade Horn, who is responsible for families and children at the Department of Health and Human Services. Horn was a child psychologist by profession who, while working at the Children's Hospital in Washington, D.C., encountered large numbers of inner-city children who had clearly been psychologically damaged by the absence of a father—and created the National

Fatherhood Initiative in order to encourage men to become more involved with their children. Now he is pumping hundreds of millions of dollars into programs to strengthen marriage—such as teaching "relationship skills" to unmarried couples who are expecting a baby, and providing "marriage skills training" to married people who want to get along better.

Horn argues that his work "is not about expanding government; it is about doing it better." Family breakdown plays a role in a whole roster of social problems that cost the American government a fortune. What could be more pragmatic than trying to preempt these problems?

This sounds sensible—but so did many of the schemes that liberal social engineers advanced in the 1960s. And from a conservative viewpoint, government is usually an institution that cuts to the Left. Bureaucrats inevitably modify programs to suit their own purposes. Just as the expansion of school testing will allow the Department of Education to impose its theories on the country's schools, Horn's successors may take a less virtuous approach than he does. At some point the Right Nation will once again become grumpy about the size and ambition of the state; it may revolt against a party that talked small but governed big.

Big-Brother Conservatism

The most significant impact on the scale and scope of government stems from September 11. The Bush White House has spawned the biggest new government bureaucracy in years—Tom Ridge's Department of Homeland Security—and it has given much more power to John Ashcroft, the hyperactive attorney general. At first sight, this seems reasonable enough. Few people would dispute that the boundary between security and liberty needed to be redefined in the light of September 11. Even fewer mourn the passing of the good old days when private security companies were in charge of airport security. Bush initially tried to stop Ridge from having a department, arguing that a broom cupboard in the White House was all he needed, but Ridge plainly lacked the necessary clout to upgrade domestic security. And the American people seem to understand the need for bigger government.

"One of the things that's changed so much since September 11," Dick Cheney observed, "is the extent to which people do trust the government— big shift—and value it, and have high expectations for what we can do."[13]

All very pragmatic. But this approach becomes much harder to justify, especially for conservatives, once you take a closer look at what Ashcroft has been up to. Big-government conservatism has developed an even less appealing twin: big-brother conservatism. Ashcroft's desire to turn himself into the country's moralizer-in-chief has led him to engage in all sorts of meddling that has nothing to do with fighting terrorism. He has prosecuted "medical marijuana" users in California despite a state initiative legalizing the practice (which has since been partly upheld by the Supreme Court). He has tried numerous ploys to challenge Oregon's assisted-suicide law (including encouraging the Drug Enforcement Administration to revoke the licenses of participating doctors) despite the fact that Oregonians have passed the law not once but twice—and despite the fact that the Supreme Court has explicitly left policy making in this area to the states. He has repeatedly tried to bully local federal prosecutors into seeking the death penalty despite a long tradition of local discretion in death penalty cases.

This downright Gallic reverence for centralization could have long-term ramifications. One reason conservatives have generally welcomed federalism is that it allows for both experimentation and variety. It means, as Justice Louis Brandeis put it in 1932, "that a single courageous state may, if its citizens choose, serve as a laboratory; and try novel social and economic experiments without risk to the rest of the country."[14] It also means that a huge country with a richly diverse population can try lots of different approaches to moral issues. People in rural Nebraska can regulate lap dancing (if they must) in a different way from people in San Francisco; Vermont can demonstrate its uniqueness by favoring both rights for gay partners and tight controls on Internet pornography. In the 1990s the GOP owed many of its biggest successes—from welfare reform to school vouchers—to its enthusiasm for federalism.

From this perspective, Ashcroft's conversion into a centralizer is both hypocritical and dumb. It is hypocritical because Ashcroft was once a leading critic of big government. As attorney general and then senator from

Missouri, he resisted a federal injunction to desegregate St. Louis's schools so vigorously that the *Southern Partisan,* a neo-Confederate magazine, singled him out for praise. It is dumb because, as an Evangelical who refrains from smoking, drinking, dancing and looking at nude statues, Ashcroft represents a minority in his own party, let alone the country at large. The best he can hope for is a live-and-let-live attitude that gives minorities like his room to flourish. Ashcroft may well come to rue his Faustian bargain with big-brother government the next time a Democrat sits in his office.

SOUTHERN CAPTIVITY?

Ashcroft's big-brother conservatism is a good way of introducing what is perhaps the greatest danger on the road ahead for the Republicans: the prospect of seeming intolerant. At the risk of caricaturing a region that takes up a third of the union, that reputation for intolerance is entwined with the party's Southern strategy. For the party of Lincoln, capturing the South has been a remarkable electoral achievement, but it has come at a price. There is a recurring fear that an overdominant Southern wing will drag the GOP onto the cliffs of extremism in the same way that the McGovernite wing pulled the Democrats too far to the Left during the 1970s.

Southern extremism comes in two forms: race and religion. The politics of race are particularly complicated. For Bush and Rove, ousting Lott had probably less to do with winning black votes than with holding on to moderate white votes. That is not to deny that there are plenty of independent voters (of all colors) who moved to suburbs to escape things rightly or wrongly associated with black America, including crime, high taxes and a penchant for choosing appalling mayors (nobody did more for house prices in Maryland and Virginia than Marion Barry, the mayor of Washington, D.C., from 1978 to 1990 and then again, after serving a prison sentence for cocaine possession, from 1994 to 1998). So the reservoirs of goodwill toward black America are hardly limitless, but a lot has changed since George H. W. Bush ran the Willie Horton ad in 1988, let alone since the movie *Guess Who's Coming to Dinner?* came out in 1967. The smarter schools, churches and country clubs contain black and brown faces. Respectable people fear the charge of racism just as keenly as they used to fear the charge of loose morals. This is a problem for a party with deep roots in the South. Karlyn Bowman of the American Enterprise Institute points out that only 59 percent of Southerners approve of marriage between whites and nonwhites; by contrast, 75 percent of non-Southerners do. Had the Trent Lott saga continued, it might not have cost the Republicans many votes in Mississippi but it would have done so on Long Island and in Denver.

On the credit side for the GOP, George W. Bush's Republican Party is very different from the one that Trent Lott joined. The two most suspect members of the party, Strom Thurmond and Jesse Helms, have left the land of the living and the Senate, respectively. In the South, the GOP certainly has some good ol' boys who want to keep blacks in their place. But it is also the party of the New South—of entrepreneurs, professionals and suburbanites. Bill Frist, the new majority leader, comes from this forward-looking wing of the party. No black in American history has held such an elevated position as Colin Powell, and none has exercised as much day-to-day influence over a president as Condoleezza Rice. Bush's first cabinet included two blacks, three women, one Latino and two Asian-Americans, as well as six white men. In contrast, the first Bush cabinet in 1989 contained ten white males, two Latinos, one female and one black.

Yet if the Republicans are daily improving their reputation on race, it is less clear whether they can control their religious wing. As we have seen, the Republicans' stands on various social issues have brought them a legion of Christian footsoldiers in the South. But Southerners are atypically culturally conservative. Forty-four percent of Southern households keep a gun in the house compared with a national average of 35 percent and only 26 percent in the Northeast.[15] Forty-one percent of Southerners attend church at least once a week compared with 33 percent of non-Southerners. Sixty-five percent of Southerners say that they have had a religious experience that has changed the direction of their life compared with 48 percent of non-Southerners. Almost one in four Southerners wants to reintroduce prohibition.[16] This Puritanism is not universally observed in the region. New Orleans, Memphis and Nashville all have their fair share of honky-tonk women:[17] driving through Cajun country in 2003, one of us saw a sign advertising that a "New shipment of girls arrived yesterday." But on the whole, Southerners also have sterner views about sex, and the most culturally conservative Southerners have gravitated to the Republican Party, where they have made a point of putting moral issues like abortion and school prayer at the heart of Republican politics—often in the most confrontational style possible. It was the party's Southern wing that roared loudest for impeaching Bill Clinton. It is the party's Southern wing that is laboring to put God back into the classroom and prevent gays from getting married.

Most Americans may share some of these prejudices, but take a much less judgmental approach. They would prefer their children not be gay, but they resent any attempt to hound the ones who are. They dislike abortion, but don't want to sanction government-imposed limits on a woman's freedom to choose. They think that education needs to be based on morality. They admire religious leaders, but get nervous the moment prayers become obligatory. They thought that Bill Clinton behaved disgracefully, but recoiled from the hanging party of prigs who masterminded his impeachment.

The Southern wing's aggressive moralism does not scare off just independents; it also alienates other Republicans. The most appalled are probably the country-club Yankees in the Northeast. (If you take away alcohol and adultery, there isn't a whole lot for stockbrokers in Connecticut to do.) But the influence of the Religious Right has also lost the Republican Party a number of otherwise safe seats in the Midwest, the plains and the West. To take just one example: in 1996, Vince Snowbarger, a conservative Republican backed by the Christian Coalition, won Kansas's third congressional district. He proceeded to support the teaching of creationism in the state's public schools, and subsequently lost his seat to a Democrat in 1998.[18]

THE GUBERNATOR

Fundamentally, the Republicans' Southern problem is one of balance. The dominance of the Southern wing prevents the GOP from presenting itself as a big-tent national party. The obvious missing counterweight is the West—

and California in particular. Under Nixon and Reagan, the Sun Belt was firmly buckled up: Southern moralism was balanced by a more relaxed Western individualism. But as we saw in Chapter 4, the Sun Belt unbuckled in the 1990s when the Republicans lost control of California—thanks to the suicidal Dixification of the state party. Now suddenly hope has returned in the strange shape of an erstwhile cyborg with an Austrian accent.

To understand how important the election of Arnold Schwarzenegger to the governorship of California in October 2003 might be for the Republicans, it is worth describing another event in the state one year earlier. One of us visited the 2002 California Republican Convention in Anaheim shortly before covering another apparently doomed gathering, the British Conservative Party's conference in Bournemouth, England. The Tories at the time were down in the dumps—a sad array of past memories, preoccupied by subjects like Gibraltar and foxhunting. But in terms of dysfunctionality, Europe's most suicidal right-of-center party had nothing on the California Republicans. The Tory delegates might all have been close to seventy years old, but at least the party made an effort to put young people and nonwhite people on the podium. In contrast, the California Republicans in 2002 heroically eschewed the sort of multicultural marketing that had worked so well for George W. Bush in Philadelphia, presumably thinking that the fact that their gubernatorial candidate, Bill Simon, had arrived to the incongruous sound of James Brown's "I Feel Good" showed quite enough diversity, thank you. A podium consisting entirely of elderly whites might still work in Alabama; in Anaheim, with the melting pot bubbling all around, it looked suicidal. At the back of the hall, a telegenic young black running for the state assembly from south Los Angeles confessed that he had gotten zero help from the party. Offstage, George W. Bush's people seemed to have gone past the stage of crying about it all, and were already talking about the 2004 Senate race.

This despair was understandable. In 2002, Gray Davis, the Democratic governor, looked ripe for sacking, thanks to a stuttering economy, the electricity crisis and a looming budget deficit. Karl Rove had prodded the state party to choose Richard Riordan, a moderate former mayor of Los Angeles, who led Davis in the polls. Social conservatives, nevertheless, rallied behind Simon, a rich businessman with little political experience whose main recommendation was that he was against abortion. To jolt them further, Davis ran ads in the Republican primary questioning Riordan's record on abortion. You would think that Davis's obvious preference for Simon would have tipped off the California Republicans that something was wrong. But no. Simon won the GOP primary by 18 points and then succeeded in losing the general election to one of the most unpopular governors in the state's history.

The Republicans' path back to power in 2003 was so bizarre that it is hard to claim any definitive lessons from it. In retrospect virtually everything to do with the recall was skewed to Schwarzenegger's advantage. The list begins with the fact that a recall initiative got on to the ballot at all: the mechanism was supposed to be used only in extremis, and Davis had done nothing obviously criminal. The two-part structure of the ballot was also odd: to stay in office, Davis needed to persuade half the voters to back him in the first part of the ballot, but if he failed, whoever got the most votes in the second ballot would win. There was an extraordinary list of 135 possible candidates, including only one Democrat, Cruz Bustamante, Davis's lieutenant governor. And the oddly stunted campaign shielded Schwarzenegger from prolonged analysis of his "bimbo eruptions" (he admitted to being "playful" with women) and, far more important, prevented a Republican primary, where Schwarzenegger would have fallen foul of the social conservatives, just as Riordan had.

Yet even when you take all these oddities into account, Schwarzenegger's victory was still impressive. He won 48 percent of the vote compared with 32 percent for Bustamante and 13 percent for Tom McClintock, a die-hard Republican. The actor even confounded critics of the recall system by getting more votes than Davis, who got only 45 percent on the first part of the ballot. Moreover, Schwarzenegger ran as a Western Republican: he railed against big government, but his concept of freedom extended to people's personal lives. Merely by supporting abortion choice, the actor removed from the contest the weapon with which Davis had spiked his two previous challengers. In prior elections, suburban women had deserted the Republican cause, but despite his groping past, Schwarzenegger beat Bustamante solidly among women (43 to 36 percent). In fact, in 2003, it was the California Democrats who began to look like the extremists. For instance, in a last-minute attempt to round up Latino votes, Davis approved a bill to grant driver's licenses to illegal immigrants, something that he had opposed just a year before. Schwarzenegger opposed this, making it clear that he did so on the grounds of national security, not race. In Los Angeles County, America's biggest urban county, Schwarzenegger beat Bustamante by 45 percent to 37 percent: add in McClintock's vote and Republicans won 56 percent of the total, a remarkable number in a county where Davis had beaten Bill Simon by 50 percent to 35 percent only eleven months before.

None of these things mean that Schwarzenegger will make a success of it all. His governorship could easily get mired in more allegations about his past "playfulness" and furious arguments about the budget. If Schwarzenegger is forced to raise taxes, it will infuriate a right wing which already loathes his social views. But he can't cut services without alienating many ordinary voters. Similarly, it will take more than Schwarzenegger to de-Dixify the California Republicans. The 2001 redistricting process, which was run by the Democrats, cleverly carved out a minority of heavily Republican seats; these are mostly filled by social conservatives who have little need to appeal to independent voters.

However, the presence of such a well-known moderate Republican must have an effect on the GOP nationally. If things go well, Schwarzenegger will be wheeled out at the 2004 convention to show what a broad church the party is; he may even campaign to change the party's antiabortion platform, just as Pete Wilson, his campaign manager, did at the 1996 convention. Moderate Republicans will point out that their creed has national appeal: there is a Republican mayor in New York City and Republican governors in three of the Democratic Party's biggest strongholds, New York State, Massachusetts and Maryland.

FEEDING THE MOB

Schwarzenegger brings the argument about managing the mob full circle. The dividing line between being a contradictory, self-consuming rabble and a broad governing coalition is a narrow one. The challenge for the Republican Party is to present itself as a "both . . . and" party: the party of both social conservatives and libertarians, of both God and Mammon, of both the heartland and Wall Street, of both Arnold Schwarzenegger and Trent Lott.

Two things should give the Republicans some confidence in this. The first is that in recent times their party has shown considerable talent for being different things to different people. In Sugarland, Texas, or Cobb County, Georgia, it is the party of the booming suburbs. The mainly white families who live there are separated from America's manifold problems by barriers that are far more effective than legal segregation, including distance, zoning regulations and real estate prices. The Republicans stand for keeping it that way. By contrast, in West Virginia, the appeal is not to optimism but to anxiety. Republicans play on the fears of miners and steelworkers who are threatened by globalization, and they demonize outsiders preying on blue-collar life: Hollywood producers who undermine religion; gun regulators who threaten to outlaw hunting and prevent people from defending themselves; liberal environmentalists who want to regulate the coal and steel industries out of existence.

This ability to be all things to all men does not just change with geography. The Republican Party has demonstrated an impressive ability to reinvent itself. In the 1990s it was the party of antigovernment rebellion. In the 2000 election it repackaged itself as the party of compassionate conservatism. By 2002, it had transformed itself once again in the wake of September 11 into the party of national defense and national greatness.

This brings us to the second reason for Republican optimism. The key to managing the mob is finding it something to think about killing other than the people who are supposed to be leading it. And now the Republican Party has something. All political parties can keep themselves together if they have something big enough to hate. For most of the postwar period the glue that held the Right together was anticommunism.[19] Conservatives loathed communism for different reasons: free-marketers because it was anticapitalist, religious conservatives because it was anti-God, and mainstream conservatives because it was anti-American. But they all loathed it. They supported building up America's defenses and rolling back communism's ill-gotten gains abroad. Anticommunism allowed conservatism to drape itself in the flag. It is no coincidence that the conservative movement was at its most fratricidal after the fall of the Berlin Wall.

At the risk of sounding cynical about an atrocity that took the lives of three thousand people, September 11 has provided just such a cause for Bush the younger. The war on terrorism unites almost all conservatives (apart from the isolationist fringe) behind a great global struggle against the forces of darkness, and puts patriotism at the heart of politics. The resolution authorizing force in Iraq won the support of 48 out of 49 Republicans in the Senate; in the House, the margin was 215 to 6. It was the war on terrorism that made the difference between the electoral tie in 2000 and the conservative victories in 2002. According to Stanley Greenberg, a Democratic pollster, the Democratic Party remained more popular on taxes and Social Security than did the Republican Party in 2002. But the Republicans had a 40-point advantage (59 percent to 19 percent) over Democrats on the question of which party does a better job of keeping America strong.

Of course, events in Iraq since November 2002 have confused this picture. But so long as terrorism remains a serious threat to the United States—and there is little sign of al-Qaeda disappearing anytime soon—the Republicans, as the party that is toughest on terrorism, enjoy a strong advantage, an advantage that brings them the added bonus of providing them with something to unite around.

CHAPTER II

BEHIND ENEMY LINES

A FEW YEARS AGO Woody Allen wrote and directed a musical comedy called *Everyone Says I Love You*. One of the film's young characters suffers from a terrible affliction: compulsive conservatism. He cannot resist the temptation to annoy his liberal parents by ostentatiously reading the *National Review* and expounding "virile modern ideas" such as "a strong America and the right to bear arms." "Welfare does not work," he says near the beginning of the film. "It is the same outmoded liberal fantasy as affirmative action, not allowing school prayer and coddling criminals." Everything ends happily, however: the parents discover that their son is suffering from a tumor that has been depriving his brain of oxygen. The tumor eventually dissolves—and the boy soon resigns from his Young Republican Club and starts espousing left-wing liberalism.

These days more and more young Americans are suffering from a lack of oxygen to the brain. The College Republicans have tripled their membership in the past three years, increasing their chapters from 409 to 1,148 and recruiting 22,000 new members in 2002 alone. They now have more than 100,000 members. Nor are young people the only "natural liberals" who are falling victim to the strange affliction of conservatism. America now boasts a thriving black conservative intelligentsia. There are prominent conservative gays, conservative Latinos, conservative environmentalists, conservative actors, conservative columnists at the *New York Times* (well, two). Look wherever you want in "liberal America" and you can find conservative footsoldiers deep behind enemy lines.

These footsoldiers are a particularly tough breed, isolated in hostile territory and constantly ridiculed by their peers. Yet they are vital to the wider conservative movement—living refutations of the liberal jibe that conservatives are nothing more than a bunch of stupid white men. Who better to explain the way that family breakdown is damaging black Americans than somebody who has a black face? Who better to champion sexual abstinence than a pretty conservative student? At the very least, the behind-the-lines conservatives force the Democrats to devote resources to defending territory that they would like to be able to take for granted; at best, they are preparing (as they would no doubt see it) to liberate huge chunks of the population from enemy occupation. We have decided to focus on three groups: blacks, because they threaten the Democratic Party's claim to moral superiority; the young, because they bring so much energy to conservatism; and women, because they make up more than half the population.

A WHITER SHADE OF PALE

Despite George W. Bush's many concessions to multiculturalism, from his employment of Colin Powell and Condoleezza Rice to his sacking of Trent Lott, the Republicans plainly have a problem with blacks. In 1960 a third of the black electorate voted for Richard Nixon.[1] In 2000, scarcely one in ten of a much richer black population voted for Bush. The retirement of J. C. Watts in 2002 deprived the Republican Party of its only black face on Capitol Hill. All the same, there are black conservatives all across America.

The most influential is probably a small group of black intellectuals. The best known are the much maligned Clarence Thomas, the Supreme Court justice, Shelby Steele, a contrarian commentator on affirmative action, and Thomas Sowell, who has been a darling of the movement ever since he published *Race and Economics* in 1975, which argued that, since racial discrimination is economically irrational, the best way to combat it is through increased competition rather than government regulation. Many of these black conservative intellectuals are strikingly similar to the first generation of neoconservatives: cerebral types who started their lives as Democrats but broke with their party over issues such as identity politics and racial preferences. Like the neocons, they are strong supporters of Israel; like the neocons, they are sharply hostile to paleoconservatives like Pat Buchanan; and like the neocons, they are clustered in think tanks.

It is significant that the one black conservative who has made a run for the presidency is an intellectual. Alan Keyes's presidential run in 2000 is perhaps best remembered for the enthusiasm with which he threw himself into a "mosh pit" and went body surfing to the music of Rage Against the Machine. But Keyes, on paper at least, was by far the brainiest of the six Republican presidential candidates, with a Ph.D. in political theory from Harvard University (where he studied with Harvard's leading Straussian, Harvey Mansfield, and shared a room with a future conservative pundit, Bill Kristol). He regards the time he spent studying political theory with Allan Bloom as a life-transforming experience, and the spirit of the author of *The Closing of the American Mind* can be detected in almost everything Keyes says. Most politicians like to relate abstract questions to concrete problems. Keyes is incapable of hearing a concrete problem without thinking about its abstract significance.

This hyperintellectualism is sometimes illuminating, sometimes downright eccentric. Keyes is a fervent opponent of abortion (he wears a gold lapel pin in the shape of a ten-week-old fetus's feet), but he rests his case not just on the Bible but also on the Declaration of Independence, arguing that you need to apply the declaration to unborn children in exactly the same way as Lincoln applied it to slaves. In a similar vein, he calls for the complete abolition of the "slave" income tax (why bother with half measures like the flat tax?). And he argues that the division between church and state has no basis in the constitution. At times, Keyes is reminiscent of some of the eccentric conservatives of the 1950s. He did surprisingly well in the early stages of the 2000 Republican primary, attracting four thousand volunteers and beating two senators in the Iowa caucuses. Yet he is hardly an easy figure to get along with. Ask him some trite question about his favorite dessert and he is likely to accuse you of moral and intellectual bankruptcy before revealing that it is apple pie with a crumbly crust. Praise him for his silver tongue and he is likely to accuse you of racism. Keyes can even be tough on his supporters. At one rally, he ordered his fans to stop applauding. "I've seen it all before," he thundered. "People stand up and applaud for things and say they believe them. And then they go out and they cast their vote in ways calculated to do God knows what."[2]

Keyes, like many black conservative intellectuals, is a man of contradictions: a Roman Catholic who draws much of his support from Evangelicals; an opponent of multilateral institutions who puts great store on being called ambassador, a title he earned while working at UNESCO; and a conservative who plays the race card with even more enthusiasm than Jesse Jackson. In the December 1999 primary debate he addressed George W. Bush as "Massa Bush" to ridicule his "timidity" on taxes. When a talk-show host praised him for his eloquence he likened the compliment to saying "Oh, he dances real well."

Keyes is one of a kind. Yet the qualities he personifies are perhaps necessary psychological qualifications for a career spent operating in hostile territory. Few people in American politics endure quite as much ridicule as black conservatives. Mainstream blacks usually regard them as traitors. Benjamin Hooks, a former head of the NAACP, denounced black conservatives as a "new breed of Uncle Tom . . . some of the biggest liars the world ever saw." Jesse Jackson likened Clarence Thomas to a Ku Klux Klan member ("At night, the enemies of civil rights strike in white sheets, burning crosses. . . . By day, they strike in black robes"). Julianne Malveaux, a black journalist, even wished Thomas an early death at the hands of his white wife. No wonder black conservatives like Keyes can be a little bit touchy. And no wonder some of their best writing (notably Shelby Steele's) deals with the subject of being isolated in a world that puts a huge premium on social solidarity.

Two causes sit at the heart of black conservatism: abolishing affirmative action and introducing school vouchers. The main proponent of the former is Ward Connerly, a black businessman from Sacramento, California, who runs the American Civil Rights Institute. This "house slave," as Jesse Jackson called him, was a defender of positive discrimination himself until Governor

Pete Wilson appointed him to the University of California's Board of Regents in 1993. There he says he was shocked to find that a scheme for giving a helping hand to the disadvantaged had degenerated, in his view, into a full-blown system of race-based preferences. In 1994, Connerly persuaded Wilson, a close friend since the late 1960s, to change his mind on positive discrimination; in 1995, triumphing over bitter opposition, he pulled off the same trick with the Board of Regents; and in 1996, he took over Proposition 209, an initiative to ban affirmative action in public universities, from the two academics who had dreamed it up. He transformed a floundering campaign, which could not even collect enough signatures to get on the ballot, into a streamlined political movement. It passed with 55 percent of the vote.

Since then Connerly has taken his crusade around the country, suing academics and bureaucrats who try to impose affirmative action, and helping to plot initiatives in other states. In 2003, he suffered two reverses. First, the Supreme Court issued a convoluted ruling that allowed affirmative action to continue, but banned universities from doing it overtly through points-based systems. Second, in the same election that brought Arnold Schwarzenegger to power, the voters in California rejected Connerly's initiative banning the state from identifying its citizens by race or ethnicity. Connerly was not helped by Schwarzenegger, who opposed the initiative, but it is hard to believe that history is not on Connerly's side in a state where race is getting ever harder to define. One of Connerly's own grandparents was white, another was a full-blooded Choctaw Indian, and he has added to the racial mixture by marrying a white woman.

A perennial difficulty that black conservatives face in rallying fellow blacks to their battle against affirmative action is that they are fighting against self-interest. Why should blacks forsake the immediate benefits that spring from affirmative action (easier access to universities and jobs) in return for the long-term benefits that come from sticking to a principle (meritocracy) and testing yourself against the highest standards out there? No such problem exists with school vouchers—giving parents more choice over what schools their children attend. School vouchers were the brainchild of a white economist, Milton Friedman, who first advanced the idea in 1957. Many black conservatives, most notably Thomas Sowell, have been arguing for vouchers for years. But increasingly the main supporters are black parents. Opinion polls repeatedly show majorities of blacks—particularly those with school-age children—supporting school choice. And no wonder: the National Assessment of Educational Progress, America's equivalent of a national report card, reveals that the average black seventeen-year-old is four years behind his white counterpart in math and reading and five years behind in science.

The unlikely laboratory for the country's most radical free-market reform of education is Milwaukee—a city that elected a succession of social-ist mayors and once helped to give birth to the Progressive movement, which radically expanded government. Vouchers took off in Milwaukee because of an improbable combination of circumstances. First, the city is home to one of the country's leading conservative foundations, the Bradley Foundation, which has been pushing for vouchers for years. Second, the local black population was tired of watching its children being bussed to the other side of the city so that white neighborhoods could achieve the court-mandated goal of racial balance. Two prominent local blacks, Polly Williams, a state legislator, and Howard Fuller, a former basketball star who became superintendent of schools, argued that the solution to black educa-tional problems was not court-mandated schemes but parental choice. Third, voucher activists reached out to politicians of both parties. Both Tommy Thompson, the state's Republican governor, and John Norquist, the city's Democratic mayor, supported the idea.

The city's voucher experiment was small when it started in 1990: only 1 percent of schoolchildren were eligible and religious schools were excluded. But black parents approved of vouchers by overwhelming margins. Valerie Johnson, a mother of five, became a provoucher activist because she had seen her brothers destroyed by the Chicago school system (one was mur-dered for refusing to join a gang, one dropped out of school and is now homeless in California) and she was determined that her own children avoid the same fate. Activists such as Fuller argued that the voucher movement was nothing less than the modern equivalent of the civil rights movement. "Did we sit down at a lunch counter at Woolworth's in Greensboro, North Carolina, to arrive at another lunch counter today where we can't read the menu?" Over the past decade, the authorities have gradually removed restrictions from the scheme. By 2003, Milwaukee's "parental choice program" distributed vouchers to ten thousand students from poor families. Studies in Milwaukee and also in Cleveland and Florida, two other pioneers, show not only that voucher children did well, but also that the reforms seem to have sparked an improvement in local public schools—particularly the ones that faced the most competition.[3]

Buoyed by these results, and a 2002 Supreme Court ruling that vouchers could be used in parochial schools, the voucher movement is continuing to spread around black America, prompted by organizations like the Black Alliance for Educational Options (BAEO), activists like Queen Sister Afrika from We Are the Village People, and a rising generation of black leaders. Cory Booker, a young black Democratic politician, argues that the only way to fix the educational system is to return power to parents. Omar Wasow, who runs a web site called BlackPlanet.com, sees school choice as a direct outgrowth of *Brown v. Board of Education,* the Supreme Court decision of 1954 that desegregated public schools. None of these activists is a conservative; but all of them are willing to borrow conservative ideas and form alliances with conservative organizations to improve the desperate state of black schools.

Indeed, there has been something of a break in the Democratic coalition between its most loyal constituents, blacks, and its main source of activists, the teachers' unions. One of the most poignant moments in the 2000 Democratic primary came during a debate between Al Gore and Bill Bradley at the Apollo Theatre in Harlem, one of black America's hallowed sites. Tamela Edwards, a young black journalist, asked the then vice president why he so adamantly opposed school vouchers while sending his own children to private schools. "Is there not a public or charter school in D.C. good enough for your child?" she asked to loud applause from the predominantly black audience. "And, if not, why should the parents here have to keep their kids in public schools because they don't have the financial resources that you do?"[4]

Seeing their tormentors in the Democratic Party pull themselves apart over vouchers is all very well; but black conservatives also have a problem persuading white Republicans to embrace the cause. The picture is not entirely gloomy: Jeb Bush, a more cerebral type than his older brother, has long supported school choice in Florida. The White House has persuaded Anthony Williams, the mayor of Washington, D.C., to come out in favor of vouchers in the nation's capital. It is noticeable how many young conservatives, such as Maura and Dustin (with whom we began this book), are passionate about vouchers. On the other hand, George W. Bush dropped vouchers from his mammoth education bill at the first whisper of protest from Ted Kennedy. And there remains the suspicion that many white Republican suburbs would be extremely nervous about giving poorer children the choice to come to their schools.

This underlines the gulf that still exists between blacks and Republicans. Despite all George Bush's overtures, the Republicans remain a white party. (It is not just a question of having no blacks on Capitol Hill: the Republicans can muster only four Latinos; in contrast the Democrats have sixty-four minority faces).[5] The fact that the party is rooted in the white suburbs means that Republican politicians seldom have to deal with black constituents. Redistricting is only deepening the problem. In the various carve-ups of congressional seats, Republican incumbents have let Democratic incumbents create "majority-minority" districts in exchange for letting the Republicans have even whiter districts. The result has been to increase still further the number of GOP House members who have almost no blacks in their constituencies.

This gap is accentuated by the fact that basic Republican policies often carry, from a black point of view, at least, a racial edge. For instance, a Republican can say there is nothing inherently racist in favoring tax cuts over government expenditure, but blacks to a disproportionate degree both rely on government programs and work in the public sector. Meanwhile, the more the Republicans woo black voters the more fiercely the Democrats defend their patch, often accusing their rivals of racism. Bob Dole was able to get 12 percent of the black vote while largely ignoring black America; George W. Bush got only 9 percent after wooing it intensively. Black interest groups responded to Bush's wooing with a plethora of negative advertising—even accusing him of insensitivity to James Byrd, a black man who was horribly murdered in Jasper, Texas. Bush avoided going to the NAACP conference in each of his first three years in office.

THE TIMES THEY ARE A CHANGIN'

If the Republicans are still struggling with blacks, they seem to be doing much better with the young. In July 2003, the College Republicans held what was probably the most successful convention in their organization's 111-year history. About a thousand young Republicans—more than twice as many as the previous year—descended on Washington to hook up with one another, buy paraphernalia with politically incorrect slogans ("Democrats are evil doers" and "Bring back the blacklist") and listen to conservative firebrands demonizing liberals. "The life of a liberal is hell," explained Paul Erickson, the head of the Daschle Accountability Project (which tracks the Senate minority leader). "It is not possible to have a debate, a discussion, with someone who at their root . . . hates everything this country stands for but doesn't hate it enough to leave."

The College Republicans were once little more than a social club: the sort of organization that men in blue blazers and loafers joined in order to pad their résumés and meet girls from good families. One old CR recruitment poster featured an elephant inside a champagne glass under the words "Join the best party in town."[6] These days the College Republicans are the conservative movement's farm team. They may continue to party, but their organization is also part of the conservative machine, and even when they are very drunk they show a (surely unhealthy) disposition to babble on about the evils of liberalism and the wonders of tax cuts.

One of the first of the new breed of young Republicans was actually Karl Rove. He was appointed executive director of the College Republicans in 1971 after demonstrating outstanding skills as a young activist. (He once forged a letter from a Democratic senatorial candidate advertising "free beer, free food, girls and a good time for nothing" and distributed it in homeless shelters.) At the 2003 meeting, he returned to receive the Lee Atwater Award in front of hundreds of CRs in tuxedos and ball dresses. Dressed in a light gray suit and mint green striped tie, Rove looked like the school nerd among the chunky Midwesterners. But he was greeted like a football star. The proceedings started with the pledge of allegiance and a prayer thanking God (among other things) for the fact that George W. Bush was president. Then Rove launched into a speech devoted to a detailed account of the machinations that had brought him the leadership of the CRs three decades before, replete with asides about the disasters that have since befallen his then opponents. Just as Rove was getting into his flow, a small group of scrawny leftish infiltrators jumped up, brandishing signs and screaming "Rove lies, people die!" The demonstrators, it later emerged, were protesting about AIDS research, but most of the CRs seemed to assume that they were complaining about the war in Iraq—and they reacted to the protest much as a pack of hounds might react to the sight of a fox in their kennel. They flew at the intruders and drove them to the exits. The room erupted in choruses of "Karl, Karl, Karl" and "U.S.A., U.S.A.," and Rove returned to his monologue.

These days, however, it is normally young Republican foxes who are venturing into Democratic kennels. At the University of California at Berkeley, conservative students have established both a college newspaper (the *California Patriot*) and a chapter of the College Republicans (with five hundred members). The California College Republicans held their 2003 convention (entitled "Behind Enemy Lines") in Berkeley. A couple of hundred of them marked the thiry-fourth anniversary of the People's Park riots by descending on the park to mount a noisy display of patriotism (which awakened the local homeless from their midday naps, according to the participants). They waved flags, chanted "U.S.A." and sang the "Star-Spangled Banner" and "America the Beautiful." "Like the Marines rolled into Baghdad a few weeks ago to liberate the city, we rolled into Berkeley ready for a fight," one of them boasted.

This outbreak of conservative activism coincides with a general rightward shift in young people's views. Bob Dole lost the eighteen-to-twenty-nine age group's vote by nineteen percentage points; George W. Bush lost it by just two points. More eighteen-to-twenty-nine-year-olds now identify themselves as Republicans (30 percent) than Democrats (24 percent), according to a CNN/*USA Today*/Gallup poll conducted in October 2003, though the biggest political grouping is independents (45 percent). There are also deeper shifts in attitudes. American students are surprisingly skeptical about income redistribution: in 2002 only 50 percent of students believed that wealthy people should pay more taxes, compared with 66 percent in

1995. Despite the vivid evidence to the contrary from Spring Break activities (let alone those *Girls Gone Wild* videos), they are also nervous about the *Absolutely Fabulous* values of the sixties generation. In 2002, the UCLA Higher Education Research Institute discovered that only 42 percent of students were in favor of casual sex, compared with 51 percent in 1987, and only 54 percent of students believed that abortion should be legal, compared with 66 percent in 1989. A survey of undergraduates conducted by Harvard University's Institute of Politics in 2003 found that 60 percent opposed the legalization of marijuana, slightly more than the percentage of people in the general population. And they are increasingly sympathetic to America's use of its military might. The UCLA poll found that 45 percent of freshmen supported an increase in military spending, more than double the percentage in 1993. The same Harvard poll found that three-quarters of students trusted the military "to do the right thing" either all or most of the time. In 1975 the figure was about 20 percent.

Why this uptick in conservatism? One reason is a desire to tweak the noses of America's leftish academic establishment. On many faculties, Naderites outnumber Republicans. One form of professor baiting has been to set up gun clubs. The Harvard Law School's gun club boasts some 120 members, 5 percent of the student body. Alexander Volokh, who founded the club in 2001, takes members shooting on a range in New Hampshire—a journey not just across the state line but also across a cultural chasm. Guns are banned on the Harvard campus; the New Hampshire range displays a sign saying "Children under 13 shoot for free." Volokh has also held a wide range of gun-themed events on campus, including screenings of films that feature "regular people using guns as a force for good." Another student wrote an article in the *Harvard Law Record* entitled "Discovering the Joy of a Semi-Automatic." Over at Mount Holyoke, an all-women's college more readily associated with Betty Friedan than with Charlton Heston, students have formed the first college chapter of the Second Amendment Sisters, a national organization of progun women.

Rather more seriously, a gap seems to have opened up between the September 11 generation of students and their Vietnam-era professors. The Harvard poll found that two-thirds of students were in favor of going to war with Iraq. Prowar groups sprouted at such liberal campuses as Brandeis, Yale and Columbia. At the University of Wisconsin at Madison—a stronghold of antiwar protests in the Vietnam era—one columnist for a student newspaper reprimanded a professor for canceling classes to go on an antiwar demonstration.[7] At Amherst many students were vocally annoyed when forty professors paraded into the dining hall with antiwar slogans.

The conservative movement, which sees the September 11 generation as its brightest prospect for years, has always devoted a lot of energy to recruiting the young. The CR's meeting in Washington coincided with a meeting of the Young Americas Foundation, a distant descendant of William Buckley's Young Americans for Freedom. YAF now organizes conferences and seminars, and brings promising conservative students to Rancho del Cielo, Reagan's ranch in California (which the organization "saved for the nation"). The Federalist Society provides young conservative lawyers with a social network. The Collegiate Network distributes some $200,000 a year to fifty-eight student newspapers, and sends aspiring conservative journalists to Washington to receive instruction from such high priests of conservative journalism as Fred Barnes. Its sister organization, the Intercollegiate Studies Institute, publishes a campus magazine that ridicules political correctness, sells conservative classics on the cheap (Barry Goldwater's *Conscience of a Conservative* is a steal at $2) and sends aspiring George Wills to a summer school in Oxford to sit at the feet of such conservative sages as Roger Scruton.

The movement is not just interested in breeding conservative leaders for the future; young activists are useful vote gatherers now. When the GOP discovered that it had lost the ground war in 2000, one of the people it turned to was Morton Blackwell. Blackwell (who was the youngest Goldwater delegate to the 1964 convention at the Cow Palace) has been an advocate of "high-touch politics" for years: in 1979 he founded his Leadership Institute to train young conservatives how to speak in public, appear on television and, above all, run political campaigns. Now "high-touch politics" is all the rage in Republican headquarters. In 2002, College Republicans provided their party with frontline troops, registering voters in college and getting them to the polls (their chairman claims that they pestered 300,000 people). Another group, Generation-GOP, says it increased turnout among the young in Arkansas by twenty thousand people. This is not mere youthful bravado. Norm Coleman, who won a fiercely contested Senate race in Minnesota against Walter Mondale (after Paul Wellstone died in a plane crash), claims that the College Republicans "provided the energy and the bodies that put him over the top."

These young activists are changing the GOP as well as revitalizing it. For the most part they are middle-class and hard-working—the very antithesis of the comfortable preppies who used to define Republicanism. Most of them have to work to afford the $25,000 that it costs to attend college for a year: hence their enthusiasm for tax cuts. They usually have a pretty irreverent attitude to authority. These are Beavis-and-Butthead Republicans, not barbershop-quartet Republicans like Prescott Bush at Yale. And despite antics like the invasion of Berkeley, they are a more tolerant lot than older conservatives—open-minded on gay marriage and liberal on race. Whatever its problems, the Grand Old Party is doing a good job of rejuvenating itself.

RED-HOT WOMEN

For many liberals, "conservative women" are almost as much a contradiction in terms as "conservative students." How can women support a party that opposes abortion choice or that elevates such macho figures as Tom "the hammer" DeLay to leadership positions in Congress? Such surprise reflects more than just prejudice: since the 1950s women as a sex have been drifting away from the Republican Party. Many women think that the party has failed to adapt to a changed world, in which women earn their own paychecks and control their own lives.

The change in women's voting is remarkable. In 1956, women preferred Eisenhower to Adlai Stevenson by a margin of twenty-six percentage points. In 1960, women supported the scowling Richard Nixon against the dashing John F. Kennedy by seven points. Yet ever since the Beatles released their first LP, women have marched smartly to the left. In 1980, when men gave Ronald Reagan a nineteen-point lead, women gave him a two-point advantage over Jimmy Carter. Bill Clinton won the female vote easily. In the 2000 presidential race, men supported George Bush 53 to 42 percent, but women supported Al Gore 54 to 43 percent.[8] John Judis and Ruy Teixeira point out that in twelve of the nineteen states that Gore won, it was only because female votes made up for the male deficit.[9]

All the biggest women's organizations are left-of-center. Most well-known feminists accuse conservatives of having Neanderthal views on abortion and women's role in society. The money raised by Emily's List, which supports women candidates, goes almost entirely to Democrats. As for academia, in all our peregrinations around American campuses, we have yet to meet a conservative women's studies professor, and suspect that we never will.

Yet conservative women patently exist, in huge numbers. Fifty percent of women with children voted for Bush, as did 56 percent of women who earned more than $70,000; and, most interestingly of all, slightly more women under age thirty-four voted for Bush than for Gore (49 percent to 46 percent), the first time the gender gap has disappeared in any age group since 1980.[10] Women of all ages are more likely to adopt liberal positions on abortion, health care and gun control than men, but they also take conservative positions on crime and punishment, with strong support for curfews for teenagers. One in three women owns at least one gun. Much of the elbow work in any Republican precinct is done by women volunteers. The National Federation of Republican Women boasts 100,000 members and 1,800 local organizations. In every category of conservative America, there is a female of the species, from Evangelicals to neocons. Nevertheless, we have chosen to focus on five types of conservative women: the politicians, the Tory Ladies, the social conservatives, the think tankers and the media vixens.

First, consider the politicians. In terms of raw numbers, the Republicans generally do less well than the Democrats. The GOP has five female senators (compared with the Democrats' nine) and twenty-one female members of the House (compared with the Democrats' thirty-eight). On the other hand, there are more Republican statewide officeholders than Democrats (forty-one compared with thirty-six), and the conservative movement is trying hard to "breed" more conservative women, through organizations like the Clare Boothe Luce Policy Institute, which provides young conservatives with training in speaking, and offers prizes and scholarships. "Our girls are going to have to fight their girls," as the *National Review*'s Kate O'Beirne puts it.

George W. Bush has arguably given women as much prominence as Bill Clinton did (though a lot depends on how much weight you give to the unappointed but extremely potent Hillary). Bush women include Elaine Chao at Labor, Ann Veneman at Agriculture, Gale Norton at Interior, Christine Todd Whitman (for a while) at the Environmental Protection Agency, and, most important of all, Condoleezza Rice at the National Security Council. Karen Hughes may have returned to Texas but looks sure to help in the 2004 campaign. Margaret La Montagne, a single mother of two, followed Bush from Texas to act as his chief policy advisor on education, health care and crime.

For years women have generally been a force for moderation in the upper ranks of the Republican Party. Female Republican senators and congresswomen often give the impression that they are too firmly grounded by the twin demands of family and career to have time for zealotry of any sort. Olympia Snowe, the senator from Maine, is as close to a Rockefeller Republican as exists in today's GOP. Whitman, who was a successful governor of a relatively liberal state, New Jersey, before taking the EPA job in Washington, took a moderate tack on all sorts of subjects, particularly abortion. She was closer to Bush socially than politically, in line with their shared preppie backgrounds: for example, she gave him his beloved Scottish terrier, Barney (whose mother, uncle and sister live with the Whitmans in New Jersey).

Over the past decade, a more strident group of female conservatives has begun to break into national politics, women who claim to be fighting for a new generation of women's issues—cutting taxes, downsizing government, fighting crime and supporting the family. In 1994, for example, the Gingrich revolution brought seven new women Republicans to the House, the largest number ever elected in a single year. The group included Barbara Cubin, who boasted about not being a "Femi-nazi" and once treated her male colleagues in the Wyoming state legislature to homemade cookies baked in the shape of penises;[11] Helen Chenoweth, who advocated the abolition of the Internal Revenue Service and insisted on being called "congressman"; and Linda Smith, who dubbed the League of Women Voters the League of Women Vipers. Cubin is the only one of the class of seven to remain in Congress, but her career flourishes. In 2000 she was elected to the NRA's board of directors. A more recent addition to the conservative regiment is Katherine Harris, the former Florida secretary of state, who helped decide the 2000 election and recount. Despite her Whitmanesque background (she comes from one of Florida's most prominent families) she has embraced hard-line conservative positions and is often to be seen around the Heritage Foundation.

The growing conservatism of national politicians reflects a similar change among activists, where the term "social conservative" is acquiring a distinctly new meaning. In the old days, the term had more to do with socializing than with saving society, and for many Tory Ladies, as we shall call them, it still does. The epitome of country club Republicanism, they are still to be found at fund-raisers, lunch clubs and the National Federation of Republican Women. The classic Tory Lady is the thoroughly respectable type: the wife of a successful local worthy who spends some of her spare time and energy (particularly after her children have grown up) on fund-raising and organization. Their models are the two Mrs. Bushes, Barbara and Laura, and their inclination is also to be one-nation Tories: moderate in style and quite often in substance, too. Both Barbara and Laura Bush have been quiet supporters of abortion choice.[12] When Laura thinks that her husband is going over the top, she is apt to tell him "Rein it in, Bubba."

Over the past thirty years, the Tory Ladies have been challenged by another, more ideological, sort of "social" conservative. Women have had a strong presence among social conservatives ever since Phyllis Schlafly penned *A Choice, Not an Echo* in 1964. Schlafly's Eagle Forum can mobilize social conservatives in every state in the country. Large numbers of women are swept into the conservative movement by their fierce opposition to abortion. Most decent-sized towns boast a prolife chapter, staffed mostly by women, as well as at least one other social conservative organization, protesting, say, against Hollywood or pornography. In Evangelical megachurches, many of the daytime committees meeting to discuss homeschooling, reconverting gay family members, and so on seem to be run by mothers.

The *rive droite* has the Independent Women's Forum, a loose association of women who are too right-wing to join traditional women's organizations but too secular to join the Eagle Forum and its siblings. Rather, the stance of its members, mostly Washington insiders, might be described as postfeminist. To hell with all that nonsense about women as victims, the organization claims; today's women are quite capable of making their own way in the world. The institute supports positions that would be radioactive if men were to advance them, such as opposing the Violence Against Women Act or Take Our Daughters to Work Day. Despite having only 1,600 members and a quarterly periodical with a circulation of 16,000, the Forum packs a pretty big punch. Leading members include Christina Hoff Sommers of the American Enterprise Institute, who has made a career out of undermining women's studies, Diane Ravitch, an education expert, and Lisa Schiffren, who wrote Dan Quayle's diatribe against Murphy Brown (a sitcom journalist who decided to have a child out of wedlock). Its past directors include the vice president's wife, Lynne Cheney. Bush named Nancy Mitchell Pfotenhauer, the Forum's president, as U.S. delegate to the United Nations Commission on the Status of Women. The president also brought in Diana Furchtgott-Roth to his Council of Economic Advisors and, as we have already seen, chose as his marriage czar Wade Horn, one of several men to serve on the Forum's advisory board.

The final group of women conservatives are the media vixens. Fox News has been remarkably successful at placing strident right-wing females in front of television viewers. The blondest and sharpest-tongued is Ann Coulter, who has the extraordinary distinction of having been sacked by the *National Review* for being too right-wing. (On September 13, 2001, she wrote of the Islamic world that "we should invade their countries, kill their leaders and convert them to Christianity"; today, she dismisses the people who sacked her as a bunch of "girly boys.") Coulter started her career as a lawyer, but she was always a lawyer with a very political edge: she helped represent Paula Jones when she sued Bill Clinton for sexual harassment. Today her strident views and tart tongue have turned her into a celebrity whose real talent is provocation. She packs university debating societies, reducing liberal students to little balls of rage. People at the annual Conservative Union queue for hours to get her to sign their copies of her books. *Slander: Liberal Lies About the American Right,* topped the nonfiction best-seller list in 2002; a year later it was followed by *Treason,* which seemed to argue (presumably nonslanderously) that most Democrats are traitors. She said that her only dilemma during the Lewinsky affair was whether Clinton deserved impeachment or assassination. Listen to her on terrorism: "Even Islamic terrorists don't hate America like liberals do," she complained once "[The Islamists] don't have the energy. If they had that much energy, they'd have indoor plumbing by now." Or on guns: "God made man and woman; Colonel Colt made them equal." Like most of the other vixens, she is considerably less forthright on abortion, but it is hard to complain that she does not give value for money.

The interesting thing about Fox's vixens is that they seem to be an entirely conservative phenomenon. The Democrats may own Hollywood and the hinterlands of American journalism. But they seem unable to come up with an equivalent to Coulter. This failure may not be entirely to the detriment of the liberal cause: it is hard to believe that Coulter does not drive away moderates as quickly as she rallies the faithful. But people like Coulter have given conservatism a different public face.

THE FEMALE CONUNDRUM

Will the conservatives improve their ratings among women? Once again, it is worth issuing the standard disclaimer that women vote for all sorts of reasons. But in the end the spread of conservatism among women depends on those two thorny arguments, abortion and the wider role of women in society. Both are moving slightly in the conservatives' favor.

Interestingly, two-thirds of American women now refuse to call themselves feminists. Many equate feminism with the idea that women can only really fulfill themselves in the workplace—an interpretation that feminists dispute but which has some foundation (Betty Friedan described the life of the educated housewife as a "waste of a human self," Helen Gurley Brown of *Cosmopolitan* called a housewife "a scrounger, a sponger" and Gloria Steinem called homemakers "dependent creatures who are still children").[13] Of all Hillary Clinton's gaffes, the one that may cause her the most trouble if she decides to run for president may be her caustic remark about women who stay home and bake cookies. This was always going to offend those women who never wanted to have a career in the first place, but it also may have put off the increasing number of professional women who started careers but then chose to stay at home all or part of the time, normally to be with their children. Only 67 percent of white American women with MBAs work full time, compared with 95 percent of men.[14] No doubt the glass ceiling is responsible for driving some women away from office life, but many decided to become a "waste of a human self" because they thought "second shifting" offered a more meaningful life. "Question: Why Don't Women Get to the Top?" asked the cover of a lengthy study in the *New York Times Magazine* in October 2003: "Answer: Because They Don't Want To."[15]

Ironically, one thing that is making conservatism more attractive to women is the success of feminism. The assumption, still common in much of the literature from the main left-of-center feminist organizations, that women are victims and men are victimizers chafes with many women. These days women encounter far fewer gender-related obstacles to their success than their mothers did. Girls do better than boys at school. More women than men graduate from college. In 2003, 63 percent of the graduating class at Berkeley Law School were women; at Harvard the figure was 46 percent, at Columbia 51 percent, at Yale 50 percent.[16] Most women believe that the only limit to their ambitions is their own individual talent—and they don't any longer feel beholden to the feminist establishment. The sort of individualism that the Independent Women's Forum preaches has its appeal.

Yet just when the path seems clear for the conservative women's movement, two huge obstacles present themselves. The first is that there are plenty of social conservatives who genuinely want to turn back the clock, who think that women's liberation was a mistake and that women would be better off in the home. The second is abortion. Social conservatives regard the abolition of abortion as the great crusade of our age: the equivalent of the struggle against slavery or fascism. In one way they are winning the argument: support for abortion rights is falling among younger women. Yet most women are still prochoice—and they regard the bitter battle within the Republican Party over abortion as off-putting. They may be attracted to conservative ideas of individual responsibility, but they do not want to be forced to engage in a relentless argument with social conservatives about the ethics of abortion.

PART IV

EXCEPTION

CHAPTER 12

AMERICA THE DIFFERENT

IN THE LAST SECTION of this book we turn to the subject of American exceptionalism. Why is America increasingly the odd man out among rich nations? Why does America arouse so much scorn and fury among its former allies? And what role does the conservative movement play in amplifying American exceptionalism? The story of the Right Nation within America is part of an even more significant story. That is the story of why America is itself something of a Right Nation.

The differences between America and its allies can be found in a wide variety of areas, from foreign policy to crime and punishment, from welfare to the war on terror; and they have become much more obvious since the end of the Cold War. These differences are not just differences of policy. At its root American exceptionalism is based on an explosive combination of two things: different underlying values, many of which date back centuries, and the political clout of the American Right. America's default position on most subjects is somewhat to the right of the default positions of other rich countries. And over and over again, the conservative movement has succeeded in exaggerating these differences still further.

THE SUPERPOWER IN YOUR FACE

How exceptional is America? Before answering our question, we need to deal with a couple of caveats. The first is that the United States includes millions of people who would rather die than vote Republican. There are plenty of prominent Americans—particularly in places like Manhattan, San Francisco and Los Angeles—who pride themselves on being just as "liberal" as their peers in Europe. The *New York Times* is often just as leftish as the British *Guardian* or the French *Le Monde*. The *New York Review of Books* marketed itself in Europe in 2003 with a cartoon of George W. Bush in the garb of a Roman emperor, next to the slogan "There is another America—and we need to hear from it." Similarly, America can sometimes look strikingly more liberal than Europe. American women can get abortions up to twenty-six weeks into their pregnancies (the limit in many European countries is twelve). In 2003 the American Episcopalian Church in New Hampshire appointed a gay bishop, Gene Robinson, at almost exactly the same time that its Anglican sister, the Church of England, backed down from doing the same thing. Another Northeastern state, Vermont, was one of the first places on the planet to accept a form of gay marriage in 2000.

The second caveat is that there are plenty of respectable people who think that Europe and America are actually converging. Over the past fifty years, living standards have moved closer together and shops, offices and factories have become more alike. Trade between Europe and America is now worth $400 billion a year. More important, the Europeans have largely abandoned socialism, closing the gap between the two political systems. As late as 1981, François Mitterrand's socialist government took over France's banks and many of its large industrial companies, vastly increased social spending, reduced the amount of time people had to work and hired another 100,000 government workers.[1] Nowadays, the main debate in Paris is how American the French economy should be. The same argument also applies to foreign policy. During the Cold War, America was confronted by a rival communist superpower and its satellites. It faced gigantic protest movements, most dramatically over Vietnam but also over the deployment of cruise missiles.

Despite the fury over Iraq, most countries these days are happy to go along with America's leadership. When George W. Bush revoked the Anti-Ballistic Missile Treaty, Russia and China essentially gave their consent. America has 725 military bases beyond its borders — all of them by permission of its allies. As Bush told his allies in Prague in 2002: "We share common values — the common values of freedom, human rights and democracy."[2]

The transatlantic optimists argue that America is still a widely admired country that many people want to imitate. You can measure this by the people jostling for American citizenship, by people queuing up for American films and products or by opinion polls. For instance, a huge audit of world opinion by the Pew Research Center in 2003 (which went over the same ground as an even bigger survey a year earlier) found that majorities of people in twenty-one countries out of forty-four still looked upon the American people favorably. The same poll showed that most of America's allies support the war on terror; that most admire many of the fundamental values that America has long promoted, such as globalization, the free market and democracy; and that nearly all of them would feel less safe if there were another superpower to challenge it.[3] With so much in common, and so much to admire in each other, the current difficulties will pass, the optimists insist — just as the difficulties over Suez and cruise missiles passed.

The trouble with these arguments is that they stretch some facts too far and ignore others. The same Pew survey which shows that most foreigners still have a favorable opinion of the American people and American values also shows that favorable opinions of America as a whole have declined in almost every country for which historical data were available. In fifteen countries surveyed in June 2003, favorable opinions of America were between fifteen and twenty points lower than they had been in 2000. Three-quarters of the population in France (76 percent) and solid majorities in Turkey (62 percent), Spain (62 percent), Italy (61 percent) and Germany (57 percent) believed that Europe should have a more independent relationship with the United States on matters of diplomacy and security.[4] Another survey in 2003 found that 64 percent of Europeans (including 81 percent of Germans and 82 percent of French) disapproved of George W. Bush's handling of foreign policy. Eighty-three percent of Americans and 79 percent of Europeans agreed that Europeans and Americans have different social and cultural values.[5] Who would have believed that, two years after September 11, nearly one in five Germans would tell *Die Zeit* that the American government might have been behind the atrocity?[6]

Of course, non-Americans admire many things about America; and, of course, Jacques Chirac is less of an ideological opposite than Joseph Stalin was. But the end of the Cold War was not the end of history. The defeat of the Soviet Union has given both sides of the Atlantic a chance to study their erstwhile allies in a new light—and has prompted talk of differences as much as similarities. It is rather like two relative strangers who fight off muggers and then go off for a celebratory meal only to discover that they don't have as much in common as they thought. The problem with the common values that George W. Bush hailed in Prague—"freedom, human rights and democracy"—is that they are so vague. Apply them to, say, the Middle East or the treatment of the poor, and Europeans and Americans reach very different conclusions.

From this perspective, the general economic convergence is a mixed blessing. The closer that America and Europe get in terms of economy and trade, the more they realize how different they are in terms of their deeper values. America is different from Europe on many of the fundamental questions of life—such as patriotism, criminal justice and religiosity—and what is more, conservative America is damned proud of these differences. This different America is much keener on using force abroad and harsh punishment at home. It is much keener on business and risk. And it is much less willing to allow the state to solve society's problems. George W. Bush didn't create these differences, of course: they have their roots deep in American history, as we shall see in the next chapter. But the differences are becoming increasingly galling for many non-Americans, because America is suddenly the superpower in your face.

Thanks precisely to the gathering pace of globalization, America is no longer just the "indispensable power," as Madeleine Albright called it in 1998, but the inescapable power.[7] Thomas Jefferson once said that "every man has two countries—his own and France." Today every man has two countries—his own and America. American culture is so omnipresent that everybody has, as it were, a virtual American buried inside their brains. American power is so overwhelming that people everywhere watch America's politicians just as closely as they watch their own. And with this familiarity has come a growing sense of powerlessness. People around the world feel that they are citizens of the United States in the sense that they are participants in its culture and politics. They watch Bush and Co. make all sorts of decisions on subjects about which they feel passionately. Yet Bush and Co. are plainly not accountable to these non-Americans; indeed, they often treat them with contempt. It is not surprising that the mantra of the protesters about the Iraq War was "We have the right to be heard."

This is compounded by the growing self-confidence—Europeans would call it arrogance—of America. The postwar generation of American leaders, Prescott Bush's generation, was still somewhat in awe of Europe—particularly of Great Britain. Anglo-Saxon by origin and Anglophile by prejudice, they half agreed with Harold Macmillan when he said that Britain needed to play Greece to America's Rome. They were also admirably sensitive to Europeans' national pride: they made every effort to cloak American power (and make no mistake, cloaking was all it was) in a framework of multilateral institutions. But the Bush people have no such sensitivities. Many of them, as we have seen, hail from the Sun Belt rather than from the more "European" Northeast. They regard Europe as a sclerotic continent—a prejudice brilliantly captured in Donald Rumsfeld's aside about "old Europe." And they regard the idea of Europe playing Greece to America's Rome as a farrago of nonsense. Rather than wanting to push America in a European direction, Bush wants to push America—and the world—further in what he would no doubt regard as an "American" direction.

These differences have reappeared throughout this book. Now it is time to dig a little bit further behind them. We will look at American exceptionalism in five broad areas—foreign policy, crime and punishment, the extent of the state, capitalism and inequality, and abortion and religiosity.

DIFFERENT AND PROUD OF IT

When Europeans think about American exceptionalism, the first thing they turn to is American foreign policy. In fact, George Bush's diplomacy (which we discussed in Chapter 8) is harder to depict as straightforwardly "right-wing" than his stance on some domestic issues. When he came to power, Europeans accused him of being an isolationist; now they worry that he's an imperialist. However, two things stand out from this muddle. First, America is much less predisposed to share power than other countries are; and, second, the Right has responded to two cataclysmic events—the end of the Cold War and September 11—by giving American foreign policy an unusually unilateralist slant.

Some of the most glaring examples of American exceptionalism have to do with policies toward particular regions or states. No other country supports Israel so adamantly or condemns Cuba so utterly. America's critics argue that these positions have more to do with domestic lobbies than principle; but many Americans plainly feel differently. Israel—the most contentious transatlantic issue—has become an emotional cause for the Right, and, arguably, for the American people as a whole. In May 2002 pro-Israeli resolutions, including $200 million for the Israeli military, passed the House by 352–21 and the Senate by 94–2, with almost all the opposition coming from Democrats.[8] Polls show Americans backing Israel by roughly the same margins that most non-Americans back the Palestinians; indeed support for hard-line policies is higher in America than it is in Israel itself. No leader in the world other than George W. Bush would have described Ariel Sharon as "a man of peace."[9]

The underlying case for American exceptionalism, however, rests on its attitude toward the multilateral order. Once again, optimistic Atlanticists have a point. In historical terms, America can still claim to be the most multilateralist superpower in history: over the past fifty years it has surrendered power to international organizations on a scale that would have been inconceivable for Britain in the nineteenth century or Spain in the sixteenth. Yet the plain fact is that no other country currently seems to have so many problems with international treaties. This is partly a matter of process: treaties require ratification by a two-thirds vote in the Senate and, under the constitution, remain subject to domestic law. But it also reflects American skepticism about the need for such entanglements in a unipolar world.

That skepticism predates George W. Bush. His critics often forget that the Senate rejected the Kyoto Protocol in a unanimous vote in 1997, and that

Bill Clinton did next to nothing to take America into the global-warming treaty. Still, Bush's unilateralism has been particularly aggressive. The Kyoto Protocol was junked without a Clintonian pretense of an apology: it was simply proclaimed, wrongly, as it happens, to be "dead." The White House has fought tooth and nail against the establishment of the International Criminal Court, rejected bits of the Biological Weapons Convention and refused to support the Comprehensive Test-Ban Treaty and the Ottawa Land Mine Convention. To build its national missile-defense system, it shredded the Anti-Ballistic Missile Treaty as fast as it could and tried to persuade Vladimir Putin to accept a "gentleman's agreement" on nuclear weapons before acceding to a formal pact. [10]

The war on terrorism has exaggerated American exceptionalism still further. America was attacked on September 11; Europe was not. America is engaged in a "war on terror." Many Europeans, although they did invoke NATO's Article Five (affirming that an attack on one of them was an attack on them all), have not decided whether "war" is anything more than a metaphor. America sees the conflict as one of good versus evil. Many Europeans reject such "simplistic" terms. "We're living through the battle of the born-agains," complained one French expert: "Bush, the born-again Christian, bin Laden the born-again Muslim." [11] As the wrangles over Iraq demonstrated, the war on terrorism has pushed America toward a policy of preemption rather than just containment and deterrence, the creeds its allies prefer. Even if Bush or his heirs reject the moral imperialist arguments of the neoconservatives, which we covered in Chapter 8, America clearly wants to be an unchallenged hegemon—comfortably more powerful than any other power. Even Howard Dean, the great "liberal" antiwar candidate, boasted about his willingness to "send troops anywhere, anytime" and railed against Bush for treating the Saudis so delicately. [12]

So American foreign policy is exceptional, and it is likely to remain so for three fundamental reasons: power, population and patriotism. In terms of power, America is the only country that can project military might globally. Both the French and the neoconservatives are right to sense that "super-power" is too weak a word to capture America's current dominance. At its height Britain was probably as powerful as the next two countries combined. Today America is as powerful as the next twenty countries combined.

America spends 40 percent (and rising) of the world's total military expenditure. The European Union's total spending on military equipment is barely half the American figure; in terms of research and development it is closer to a quarter.[13]

For a while the Clintonites were seized by a European fear that there was something wrong about the degree of America's preeminence. They didn't object to Europe and the United Nations trying to bind Gulliver down. This strategy soon frayed. America found that European multilateralism couldn't deal with the Balkans. The European Union may one day have a common foreign policy—or pieces of one—but it certainly does not have one at the moment: witness the failure of France, Germany and Britain to form a common policy on Iraq because of profound disagreements, or even on Israel, where they cannot translate their underlying agreements into a coordinated strategy. One day, China will be a rival to America, but for the moment its entire official military budget is less than the annual increase in America's.

Military power is not everything. America is rediscovering, as it labors to rebuild Iraq, the importance of both allies and "soft power." ("Even if America has the biggest hammer, not every problem is a nail," observes one European foreign minister.) But America's preeminence in hard power means that it will inevitably be called in to deal with failing states (particularly where they are linked to terrorist networks). It means that America will inevitably be the arbiter in intractable conflicts (like the Middle East) or in the worst humanitarian crises. It means that America inevitably has different considerations from other powers. As Robert Kagan points out in *Of Paradise and Power*, small powers have always sought protection in international rules, just as great powers have always worried about the constraints of such rules: in the eighteenth century, it was the United States that wanted international law to apply to the high seas, and the British navy, "Mistress of the Seas," that opposed it.[14] For the foreseeable future, America will be the world's policeman—and policemen are not noted for taking a liberal view of the world. Americans are much more inclined than Europeans to seek military solutions to problems. Fifty-five percent of Americans "strongly agree" that war is sometimes necessary to obtain justice; the figure in Europe is just 18 percent.[15]

The second reason America will remain exceptional is demography. In the 1780s Benjamin Franklin noted that "the increase of inhabitants by natural generation is very rapid in America, and becomes still more so by the accession of strangers." The same remains true today. America is perhaps the only advanced country with a young and growing population. The most recent census showed that immigration is proceeding faster than most people thought and that America's birth rate is surprisingly buoyant. With present trends, America's population will rise from 280 million to 350–400 million over the next twenty-five years and to 400–550 million Americans by 2050. Western Europe's population looks set to fall, in some places dramatically. In Estonia, the prime minister has been reduced to pleading with his countrymen to have sex more often. This imbalance has a huge effect on foreign policy. America is bound to focus more on the countries that supply most of its immigrants—on Mexico and the rest of Latin America rather than on Old Europe. More important, America, where the median age will remain about thirty-five for the next half-century, is bound to be more "youthful" in its approach to the world than Europe, where the median age will jump from thirty-eight to fifty-three, and Japan, where it will rise from forty-one to fifty-three.[16] The Europeans and the Japanese will have to devote ever more of their resources to the elderly. They will also find their cultures dominated by people who are set in their ways and averse to risk.

The last reason why America is destined to be different from Europe (though not from Japan or China) has to do with nationalism. Europeans have embarked on a grand experiment in dissolving their national identities in a European superstate: understandably so, since nationalist wars have destroyed Europe repeatedly in the past few centuries. America has no such qualms about its national identity. Indeed, many of its difficulties with the European Union stem from the fact that Americans assume that the EU is nothing more than an economic unit. As far as Washington is concerned, Brussels is a place where you go to discuss trade, not foreign policy. Americans cannot understand why the EU won't admit Turkey, just as America "admitted" Mexico into NAFTA.

American patriotism runs deep. No other developed country displays its flag more obsessively or sings its national anthem more frequently. It is not just a matter of being very proud of their country (though the proportion that are—80 percent—is well above the figures for West European countries);[17] six in ten Americans believe that American culture is superior to other cultures, compared with three in ten French people and four in ten Britons and Germans.[18] Bernard-Henri Lévy, one of France's most celebrated intellectuals, boasts about the growing number of his fellow countrymen being able to say, "I am no longer French, but European of French origin."[19] An American who renounces his nationality has difficulty in getting back into the country.

Firing up that patriotism has been one of the Right's hallmarks: since September 11, members of the Bush administration have never appeared on television without a flag pin on their lapels. But even if the Democrats recapture the White House, we should not expect America to start signing treaties and giving away its sovereignty. You can argue about the degrees of exceptionalism, but for the foreseeable future, America's view of the world will be substantially different from everybody else's.

RIGHTEOUS PUNISHMENT

In diplomacy, it is sometimes difficult to depict policies as straightforwardly right- or left-wing. No such problem exists with crime and punishment. Thanks to following an overtly conservative agenda on law and order, America has quadrupled its imprisonment rate in just thirty years. It now has 700 people in every 100,000 under lock and key, five times the proportion in Britain, the toughest sentencer in Western Europe. One in twenty American men has been to jail, and one in eight has been convicted of a felony. The average is much higher among some groups. Nearly one black man in five has been to prison, and one in three has been convicted of a felony. At current incarceration rates, an American male born in 2001 will stand a one in ten chance of going to prison during his life.[20]

The high imprisonment rate is partly related to the high crime rate, but it also reflects the Right's determined policy to increase the number of mandatory sentences, particularly for drug offenses. For most of the twentieth century, America's imprisonment rate—at around 100 people per 100,000—

was broadly in line with that of Europe. Since the 1980s, however, conservatives have successfully pushed for laws to limit the discretion both of "liberal" judges to make the punishment fit the crime and of "liberal" parole boards to determine when prisoners are fit to be released. In the ten years after 1986, the average term in federal prison rose from thirty-nine to fifty-four months; it seems to be rising further, spurred on by laws like California's "three strikes and you're out" law and by the sheer number of prisons. In 1997 the Corrections Corporation of America announced that it was building three prisons in California entirely on speculation: "If you build it in the right place," explained a spokesman, "the prisoners will come."[21]

Meanwhile, the "war on drugs" has been used as an excuse both to expand police forces and to militarize them. In Europe, it is still rare to hear of policemen using weapons. In Fresno, California, the SWAT team has night-vision goggles and two helicopters and patrols the streets seven days a week; in Boone County, Indiana, it has an amphibious armored personnel carrier. In one recent two-year accounting period, the Department of Defense sent local SWAT teams more than 1 million pieces of military hardware, including seventy-three grenade launchers.[22]

The most notable feature of America's justice system is its unforgiving nature. Prisons everywhere are pretty ghastly, but America's make less effort to rehabilitate inmates than any others in the first world do. Throughout the 1990s, as conservative lawmakers built more and bigger prisons, they tended to cut back on soppy "European" programs, like drug treatment. They also disenfranchised "liberal" parole boards: mandatory sentences mean that prisoners have no obligation to prove that they are ready for outside life. Outside prison, the after-care system is even weaker. Many ex-cons are simply presented with a one-way bus ticket. Felons are banned from many jobs, in some cases they are denied housing benefits and nearly 5 million of them are not allowed to vote (in ten states, more than 20 percent of black men of voting age are thus barred from voting). This year, some 600,000 inmates will be let out of prison—more than the population of Washington, D.C. Two-thirds of them will be rearrested within three years.[23]

The Right defends its approach to crime on two commonsense grounds: it works and it's popular. America's crime rate has come down over the past decade, even if all those released prisoners are now helping push the rate back up a bit. New York is by some measures safer than London (although those measures ignore murder). Liberal criminologists may argue that the drop in crime has less to do with heavy sentences than with population trends and improved policing. But how many Democratic politicians are willing to make the case for lighter sentences or more money for rehabilitation? That bolsters the Right's second boast: Americans like their tough crime policies. That old joke about every conservative's favorite lady being "Laura Norder" rings true; law and order is a reliable vote-getter. Implying that Democrats are soft on crime has been the oldest Republican trick in the book—which is one reason Democrats have embraced the death penalty so willingly.

America's unforgiving attitude even touches people who, by European standards, haven't actually committed crimes. Americans are far more censorious than Europeans, not just when it comes to illegal drugs but also to alcohol. Most European countries regard alcohol as a normal part of civilized life: parents introduce their adolescent children to wine with meals. In America, however, Puritanism survives. During the 1980s most American states raised the drinking age from eighteen to twenty-one. This almost turned one of the president's daughters into a martyr: in the first summer of her father's presidency the nineteen-year-old Jenna Bush was booked for trying to buy alcohol twice in just one month in Texas, a state that imposes a mandatory prison sentence for a third offense. One school principal in suburban Colorado was briefly suspended for permitting junior high school students to taste a "thimbleful" of wine during a three-hour meal in France. "They tasted wine," said a spokesman for the school. "They may have ingested alcohol."

To European eyes, it sometimes looks as if Americans are determined to criminalize, pathologize, regulate or legislate out of existence almost every hazard. No country treats smokers (or indeed tobacco companies) with such vindictiveness as the United States. No country creates more rules to try to keep the petty disorders of human life at bay. Most school districts in America now have a policy of zero tolerance of misdemeanors. Children as young as five have been kicked out of school for possessing cough drops, for wearing Halloween costumes that include paper swords and fake spikes or for possessing rubber bands or toy guns. A five-year-old was expelled for bringing to school a razor blade that he found at a bus stop, and a six-year-old was suspended for kissing a classmate.[24]

THE NONHELPING HAND

Another big difference can be found in what people expect from the state. Put simply, Americans are exceptionally keen on limiting the size of the state and the scope of what it does. Government spending accounts for around 30 percent of GDP—considerably lower than in Britain (39 percent) and half the level of that in Scandinavian countries. This figure seems even smaller when you remember that America spends so much more on defense than other countries: $1,138 per person in 2002 compared with $590 in Britain (and much less in most other European countries).[25]

In many European countries there is a lively debate about whether higher levels of taxation might be justifiable in exchange for better services. Some 62 percent of Britons told pollsters in 2001 that they felt that way; in America only one person in one hundred agrees that taxation is too low.[26] Indeed, one of the most familiar mantras of American political life is that it's the people's money, not the government's—and that if you don't get it back as a tax cut, it will only be wasted in Washington. George W. Bush likes to remind his staff of a woman he met on the campaign trail in Iowa who told him, "I've learned that if you leave cookies on the plate, they always get eaten."[27] In 2002, with the budget surplus disappearing and the biggest tax cut in American history still fresh in the memory, you would think that it would be foolhardy to campaign for more tax cuts. Yet that is just what George W. Bush did in the midterm elections—and the Republicans won handsomely. When he unveiled a plan to cut taxes by $670 billion in January 2003, Milton Friedman said the cut was justified purely on the grounds that it would make government smaller. There is only one way to cut government down to size, he said—"the way parents control spendthrift children, cutting their allowance."[28]

For many Americans—and particularly conservatives—there is a fundamental principle involved in keeping government small. This is the principle that power rests with the individual and not the state. In pretty much every other country in the world, the word "devolution" is part of the political vocabulary. In America, the idea that power can be devolved from the center is an oxymoron. Power rests first with individuals, then with local communities and then with the states; the federal government comes last in the pecking order. Americans are nervous even about handing over power to their elected representatives. It is the only developed country apart from Switzerland where referenda are common.

Indeed, ballot initiatives have been one of the Right's most powerful weapons: tax-cutting measures such as California's Proposition 13 play the same role in the iconography of the Right as general strikes once played in the iconography of the socialist movement. A huge number of these propositions have been used to curtail the power of politicians—whether through "term limits" or through spending limits. The governor of California, America's biggest and richest state, controls only about a fifth of the money that the state spends. And, of course, he can be recalled at whim.

Europeans are much keener on using the state to fight poverty than Americans, and much less inclined to draw a line between the deserving and the undeserving poor. According to the Pew survey, 74 percent of Russians, 71 percent of Italians, 62 percent of the French and 62 percent of Britons think that it is more important for the government to ensure that nobody is in need than it is to allow individuals to be free to pursue their goals. A mere 34 percent of Americans favor government safety nets over their own freedom—a ratio equaled only by countries with a long tradition of governmental incompetence and corruption such as Venezuela, Honduras, Guatemala, Ghana, Nigeria and Pakistan. Only three in ten Americans (29 percent) *completely* agree that government has a responsibility to help the poor (the figure in Britain is twice as high).[29] Americans worry that state welfare rewards people for self-destructive behavior and reduces their incentive to get back onto their own feet. When Bill Clinton's welfare reform cut America's already relatively ungenerous subsidies to single mothers still further, Phil Gramm, a Republican senator, remarked that the 40 million people who had been getting a free ride would now "get out of the wagon and help the rest of us to push."[30]

Another vivid example of America's hostility to the welfare state is provided by health care. Europeans often libel America as being a country where poor people are left to die in the lobbies of hospitals because they don't have any credit cards; in fact there is a public system, Medicaid, precisely for such emergencies. All the same, America is the only rich country without a national health service or a system of free child support, and some 44 million Americans lack health insurance. A decade ago, the Clintons tried to bring these people into the fold, thereby making America a bit more European. But as we have seen, Republicans managed to demonize the scheme as a semisocialist plot to nationalize a seventh of the economy, and Hillary care never got off the ground. Most Americans like the country's system of private provision—and they are willing to tolerate expensive care and millions of uninsured in order to keep it.

The cost of sticking to that principle has been high. A survey by the World Health Organization in 2000 placed America first in terms of total spending on health (at $3,700 per person per year), but only thirty-seventh in terms of service. America's top 10 percent were the healthiest in the world, the middle bulge got "a mediocre deal" and the bottom 5–10 percent got an abysmal one. The result is that average life expectancy of people in the world's richest country is well below that in Canada, Japan and every major nation in Western Europe. The average American doesn't live as long as the average Greek; the average American male doesn't live as long as the average Puerto Rican. Despite this, the talk is not of fundamental reform, only of tinkering—such as the introduction of the prescription drug benefit for the elderly in 2003.

CAPITALISM AND THE CHARM OF INEQUALITY

If Americans are unusually hostile to government, they are also unusually enthusiastic about capitalism. Despite the past twenty-five years of deregulation, most European societies see the gospel of "creative destruction" (or what the French call *le capitalisme sauvage*) as a necessary evil. This distrust is a mixture of compassion, egalitarianism and snobbery (the first act of any

English millionaire who made his money in trade was to buy a country estate and pretend to be a farmer). European politicians have tried to shackle capitalism, and to civilize it, by imposing high minimum wages, by making it difficult to fire people, by making business look after the environment, by making bankruptcy a painful process and by forcing companies to be accountable to all their stakeholders, not just their shareholders.

The American government does most of these things too—but to a far lesser extent. Free-marketers may complain about the proportion of corporate income tied up by rules (10 percent, according to Friedman), or about intrusive regulations, such as California's air quality initiatives or the Americans with Disabilities Act. But it is much easier to go about the basic business of business—hiring, firing, investing, borrowing and even going bust—in America than in any other big developed country; and there is a much clearer chain of accountability, with companies being primarily answerable to their shareholders. This stems from an exceptional faith in capitalism. Witness the bookshops packed with tomes about how to run businesses, or the way children are encouraged to run lemonade stands. Where else could a rap musician make a record called "Get Rich or Die Trying?"[31] Americans have sought to rein in business only under fairly dire circumstances—typically after stock market crashes—and the laws that have emerged have aimed to strengthen shareholder capitalism. Thus Teddy Roosevelt's campaign against the "malefactors of great wealth" at the beginning of the last century helped bring in antitrust laws, Franklin Roosevelt's New Deal in the 1930s set up the Securities and Exchange Commission, and the post-Enron fracas in 2002 produced the accountant-patrolling Sarbanes-Oxley Act.

Nothing typifies America's idiosyncratic approach better than its tolerance of inequality. The past three decades have seen an extraordinary growth in inequality—in many ways, a return to the world of the Gilded Age. Census Bureau data clearly show a rising share of national income going to the top 20 percent of families. But as Paul Krugman has pointed out, that probably understates the rise in inequality: within this elite group, the top 5 percent have done better than the next 15 percent, the top 1 percent have done better than the next 4 percent and so on.[32] In 1970, for example, the top 0.01 percent of taxpayers earned 0.7 percent of total income. But in 1998 the top 0.01 percent earned more than 3 percent of all income. That meant that the 13,000 richest families had almost as much income as the 20 million poorest households. In 1980, the average American chief executive was paid around forty times as much as the average worker; now the multiple is above four hundred. In terms of assets rather than income, the disparity is even larger; the wealthiest 1 percent of households controls 38 percent of the national wealth, double the amount held by the bottom 80 percent.[33]

Unsurprisingly, by most measures, America is the most unequal of the world's developed countries. One study by the Economic Policy Institute found that the gap between the top 10 percent and the bottom 10 percent in terms of income was bigger in America than in any other country; indeed it was more than twice as large as the ratio in several Nordic countries.[34] Interestingly, the reason America was so unequal by this measure was not because its poorest 10 percent were particularly badly off (indeed, in purchasing power parity terms, they were narrowly ahead of similar groups in Britain and Australia); it was because America's richest tenth had far higher median incomes.

This may explain why the huge surge in inequality has produced little populist backlash. In 2000 Al Gore's attempt to campaign on behalf of "the people versus the powerful" arguably did him more harm than good. In 2002, Americans fumed at their corporate bosses for their excesses (such as the $2,000 shower curtain the head of Tyco ordered for himself at the company's expense), and there was certainly criticism of huge pay packets for people who did not perform, but it never translated into the sort of visceral dislike of big gulfs in income that it might have in Europe. For the most part Americans associate success with merit rather than with luck, birth or criminality. For one thing, they admire success. "Money is how we keep score in life," is Ted Turner's phrase. When Robert Goizueta, the veteran boss of Coca-Cola, tried to justify his $80 million annual pay package at a shareholder meeting in the 1990s, he was interrupted four times—with applause. For another, Americans are extraordinarily optimistic about their own chances in life. One poll in 2000 found that an extraordinary 19 percent of Americans thought they belonged to the richest 1 percent—and another 20 percent thought they would be in the richest 1 percent at some point in their lives. This was a fantasy, but not an outrageous one. Social mobility is higher in America than other countries, with 50 percent to 80 percent of the people in America's bottom quintile pushing themselves out of that bracket within ten years.[35]

George W. Bush's tax cut in 2003 would have been unthinkable in most other countries. Its main proposal was to abolish the taxation of dividends at a personal level. Half the proceeds from this elimination would flow to the richest 1 percent of taxpayers, another 25 percent to the rest of the top 5 percent, according to Citizens for Tax Justice. Bush talked about the average American keeping $1,083 of his or her own money, but that average is boosted by people like Bill Gates. The median taxpayer kept only a couple of hundred dollars, and anybody in the bottom fifth got next to nothing. Bush himself stood to gain $44,500, Dick Cheney more than $327,000 (a sum greater than the pretax incomes of forty-nine out of fifty American households).[36] When people protested, Bush pointed out forcefully that "class warfare" was not the American way. Congress gave him most of what he asked for.

ABORTION AND RELIGIOSITY

Every January, tens of thousands of antiabortion protesters, many carrying gruesome placards, descend on Washington, D.C., to mark the anniversary of *Roe v. Wade,* the Supreme Court decision that effectively made abortion a constitutional right in 1973. Since that date, about seventy-five other countries have liberalized their abortion laws, and in most other places, that was enough to settle the debate. This has plainly not happened in America. Opponents of abortion regularly appear on television comparing the practice to the Holocaust or slavery. For a time, prolife extremists took to blowing up clinics and shooting abortion doctors. More often, the battle is political, with, for instance, Congress voting to ban partial-birth abortion in 2003 or conservative state legislatures passing laws preventing minors from obtaining abortions without parental consent. But the battle over abortion also stretches into court appointments, schooling, stem cells and even obscure lawsuits. The Center for Reproductive Law and Policy has filed lawsuits against the states of Florida and Louisiana for allowing the sale of "choose life" license plates but not "pro-choice" ones.

Why does abortion remain so much more controversial in America than in the other countries that have legalized it? After all, most Americans have broadly similar views on abortion to those held by the majority of Canadians or Britons: they don't like the practice, and they recoil at partial-birth abortion, but they do not want the practice to be forced into the back streets. Their attitude was perfectly captured by Bill Clinton when he said that he wanted abortion to remain "safe, legal and rare."[37] Indeed, it is partly for this reason that Republican presidents, including George W. Bush, remain nervous about pushing the issue too hard.

Yet this similarity only goes so far. The people who want to ban abortion in America may be in a minority, but they are a much bigger minority than in other countries: 46 percent oppose unfettered abortion, compared with 17 percent in Britain. Abortion also embodies the war between liberal and conservative America: between the America of individual rights and the America of traditional values, between the America of the courts and the America of the Evangelical churches. "Abortion is today the bloody crossroads of American politics," argues Bill Kristol, in language that is typical of the debate. "It is where judicial liberation (from the constitution), sexual liberation (from traditional mores) and women's liberation (from natural distinctions) come together. It is the focus of liberalism's simultaneous assault on self government, morals and nature."[38]

Extreme stuff perhaps, but conservatives have a point when they cite *Roe v. Wade* as an example of liberal triumphalism. European countries liberalized abortion through legislation and, occasionally, referenda. This gave legalization the legitimacy of majority support, and allowed countries to hedge the practice with all sorts of qualifications. In America, the Supreme Court—or, as conservatives like to describe them, five unelected liberally minded judges—decided that reproductive rights are included in a fundamental right to privacy which, rather like freedom of speech and freedom of religion, is guaranteed by the constitution; and they allow abortion up to about twenty-six weeks. This was provocative, to say the least, as abortion rights are clearly not enshrined in the constitution in the same plain way that free speech is, and the Right has been trying to change the composition of the court ever since. By going down the legislative road, the Europeans managed to neutralize the debate; by relying on the hammer blow of a Supreme Court decision, the Americans institutionalized it.

The abortion issue exemplifies three American traits. The first, once again, is religiosity. In America 95 percent of people believe in God, against 76 percent of Britons, 62 percent of the French and 52 percent of Swedes. More than three out of four Americans belong to a church, 40 percent go to a church once a week and one in ten goes several times a week. One out of four own five Bibles or more.[39] The Pew Global Attitudes Project revealed that six in ten Americans say that religion plays a "very important" role in their lives. This is roughly twice the percentage of self-avowed religious people in Canada and an even higher proportion when compared with Japan and Europe. To find comparable numbers, you need to look at developing countries. When Americans say "very important," they mean it: 39 percent of them describe themselves as born-again Christians.[40] Nowhere else do Evangelical Protestants carry such great weight: in America they account for one out of every three voters, compared with just below a quarter in 1987. While European churches are trying to hang on to the few parishioners they can muster, American churches seem to be in a state of almost permanent boom. The churches that are doing best are those that insist on passionate commitment to Christ more than their more moderate competitors.

One focus for American fundamentalists is "the Rapture"—the moment when true Christians, it is believed, will be taken up to heaven. This is based on a passage in Thessalonians: "First the Christian dead will rise, then we who are still alive shall join them. Caught up in clouds to meet the Lord in the air."[41] Fundamentalists see this not as a metaphor, but as an imminent fact. In Florida you come across bumper stickers warning that the car may become driverless should the Rapture arrive. In parts of southern Texas, there seem to be only two sorts of radio stations: Spanish-language ones and those featuring Evangelicals going on about the Rapture. The *Left Behind* series of books, which deal with the world after the Rapture, have sold 55 million copies since the first one was published in 1995.

These sorts of facts are the ones that Europeans jump on when they depict Americans as Bible-crazed zealots. Europeans like to see themselves as rational heirs of the Enlightenment: how can they deal with a country where three times as many people believe in the virgin birth as in evolution?[42] Yet the same differences also help to explain many Americans' contempt for what they see as Europe's unholy secularism. Here is one American conservative writer on Europe:

> Europeans are materialistic: the EU has a low profile on strategic issues because it was designed by bureaucrats obsessed by trade and money. Europeans care more than we do about physical pleasure; they traffic in titillation (to judge from the nightly offerings on television or such best-sellers as *The Sexual Life of Catherine M*). To many American eyes it's tough to have family traditions in a region where so many prefer to be childless (its fertility rate is 1.47 births per woman), tough to have religious values when less than 20 percent of Europeans attend church.[43]

The second American trait that the abortion debate typifies is the fondness for arguing about fundamentals. Europeans routinely turn moral issues into technical ones—and then hand them over to technocratic elites. America is a country of fundamentalists of all sorts, secular as well as religious, thanks to its constitutional tradition, its legal culture and perhaps its Puritan heritage. In Europe the debate about abortion is conducted in medical rather than moral terms. Ditto the debate about stem cells. For Americans, abortion can seemingly never be just about health. It has to be a clash of absolutes: the right to choose versus the right to life.

The third trait is the exceptional role of the Right itself. Democrats have been no slouches when it comes to using *Roe v. Wade* to mobilize their troops. But conservatives were the first to turn abortion into a wedge issue in the South, as values trumped class in American politics. Abortion was not the first issue that redefined modern cultural politics: that honor goes to civil rights. But it was certainly one of the most powerful. In 1972, Republicans dubbed George McGovern the triple-A candidate (amnesty, acid and abortion) and they have used the issue to round up Southern Evangelicals and

Northern Catholics ever since. There are still prochoice Republicans such as Colin Powell and Arnold Schwarzenegger, but they have been swimming against the tide. Some 88 percent of state Republican platforms oppose abortion, and none support it. In the 2000 election, 74 percent of those who said abortion should always be illegal voted for Bush, while 70 percent of those who said it should always be available voted for Gore. America might always have been more flustered about abortion than other countries, but the Right has certainly worked very hard to raise the temperature. There is no chance of America becoming "European" in its attitude toward abortion.

VALUES AND THE RIGHT

The abortion example is symptomatic of American exceptionalism because it shows how its two main ingredients complement each other: a distinctive set of values and an unusually powerful conservative movement that nourishes, accentuates and exploits those values. Both require a little more explanation.

Examine American values and you are immediately confronted with an apparent paradox. Americans are both more individualistic than continental Europeans and also more traditional. The individualism goes much deeper than just disdain for safety nets. Americans are also far more inclined to trust their own abilities: 65 percent of them in the Pew survey rejected the proposition that "success in life is pretty much determined by forces outside our control." In Europe majorities in every country except Great Britain and the Czech and Slovak Republics accepted this dismal proposition, and even in these three European exceptions opinion was equally divided. The percentage of Americans who believe that success is determined by forces outside their control has fallen from 41 percent in 1988 to 32 percent today; by contrast, the percentage of Germans who believe it has risen from 59 percent in 1991 to 68 percent today.

However, if Americans are self-interested individualists, they are also church-going patriots. This comes out best in a regular survey by the University of Michigan, which now covers seventy-eight countries. It charts two broad battles. One test has to do with priorities, with people being asked about how important basic things like food and safety are to them as against more ethereal values such as self-expression, tolerance and so on. Americans, like the inhabitants of most rich countries, tend to be at the self-expressive end of the spectrum. The other test tries to measure traditionalism (devotion to country, God and family) against "secular-rational values" (for example, support for euthanasia, divorce and abortion). Here, America parts company with the rest of the wealthy world, emerging as a far more traditional place than any European country with the single exception of Ireland. Americans were the most patriotic people in the survey: 72 percent say they are very proud of their country (even though this bit of the poll was taken before September 2001). Four out of five Americans said they held "old-fashioned" views about marriage and family. In terms of religiosity, Americans were closer to Nigerians and Turks than Germans or Swedes. Interestingly, Americans have also become more traditional in these respects since the first survey in 1981.

How did America get to be so exceptional? One reason, of course, is its extraordinary conservative movement. But why is America such fertile soil for conservatism? We need to go back and look at the conservative traits America has always carried with it—the ones that predate modern American conservatism and may well outlive it too. Dustin, the young activist from Colorado Springs whom we met at the beginning of this book, describes some of his friends as being "conservatives who don't know it." Much the same could be said for the United States as a whole.

CHAPTER 13

RIGHT FROM THE BEGINNING: THE ROOTS OF AMERICAN EXCEPTIONALISM

T HE LIFE SPAN of the American conservative movement is comparatively short. The life span of America's exceptional conservatism, on the other hand, stretches back to the country's birth. The United States has always had conservative instincts: suspicion of state power, enthusiasm about business and deep religiosity. But for most of its history America has been so comfortable with its innate conservatism that it has had no need of a political movement to articulate conservatism's principles or harass its enemies.

The idea that America had conservatism encoded in its DNA might strike some people as a little odd. Wasn't America the Enlightenment made flesh? The world's first "new nation"? The very model of a young country? "The Utopia of radicals and the Babel of Conservatives"?[1] The United States deliberately swept away the Old World of monarchy, aristocracy and established church, and guaranteed its people the right to life, liberty and the pursuit of happiness. In the decades after its birth the new republic sided with revolutionary France against the assembled powers of the old order. Indeed, when the French revolutionaries stormed that ancient symbol of despotism and oppression, the Bastille, the Marquis de Lafayette sent the key of the prison to George Washington.

There is no doubt that America's conservatism is an exceptional conservatism: the conservatism of a forward-looking commercial republic rather than the reactionary Toryism of old Europe. But it is conservatism nonetheless. If America is a new nation, it is getting rather long in the tooth. If America is the product of a revolution, it is a very different revolution from the French one. And there have been elements in American society from the very beginning—religiosity, capitalism and even geography—that have put a brake on any drift to the Left. America is the only developed country in the world never to have had a left-wing government.

YOUNG AT HEART, OLD IN YEARS

Start with the idea that the United States can no longer really be regarded as a "new nation." There is no doubt that America is singularly lacking in ancient *châteaux* and *schlossen* (though it has no shortage of more recent McChâteaux and McSchlossen). But this scarcely constitutes evidence of youth. The first settlers arrived when James I was on the throne and England was not yet Britain. Galileo was offered a chair at Harvard University, which was founded in 1636, before Charles I had his head cut off. The Declaration of Independence was signed a century before the unification of both Germany and Italy (supposedly part of Old Europe). The historical hearts of Boston and Washington feel as old as many European capitals (older, in some ways, because they weren't bombed in the Second World War). Many of the traditions that define Britain as an old country in the minds of admiring Americans—the pomp and circumstance of empire, the rituals of Charles Dickens's Christmas, Sherlock Holmes's deer-stalker hat—were invented a century after the American constitution. "The youth of America is their oldest tradition," Oscar Wilde quipped more than a century ago. "It has been going on now for three hundred years."

In fact, America has a good claim to being one of the oldest countries in the world, in the sense of possessing one of the oldest constitutional regimes.[2] The United States is the world's oldest republic, its oldest democracy and its oldest federal system. The country possesses the world's oldest written constitution (1787); the Democratic Party has a good claim to being the world's oldest political party. France has had five republics since 1789, not to mention monarchies, empires, directories, consulates and a collaborationist-fascist dictatorship. New Labor has thoroughly revamped one of the oldest parts of the British constitution, the House of Lords. But America has done little more than tinker with its constitutional arrangements, such as allowing voters rather than state legislatures to choose senators. Even the Thirteenth Amendment, which abolished slavery, was an attempt to force America to live up to its original constitutional ideals, rather than a departure from those ideals.

The past feels eternally present in American life. Americans routinely make monumental decisions—such as whether women can have abortions or children can say prayers in school—with reference to the designs of a group of eighteenth-century gentlemen who wore knee breeches and powdered wigs. Politicians happily describe themselves as Jeffersonians and Hamiltonians. Even cyberlibertarians, hardly the most historically minded of people, like to describe themselves as "Jeffersonians with laptops." With the exception of the amendments after the Civil War which dealt with equality for all American citizens, the constitution remains very much as the founders intended it: a complicated system of checks and balances designed to prevent any politician from becoming a latter-day George III. "Our history has fitted us, even against our will, to understand the meaning of conservatism," Daniel Boorstin observed back in 1953. "We have become the exemplars of the continuity of history and of the fruits which come from cultivating institutions suited to a time and place, in continuity with the past."[3]

It is true that the American past is punctuated by the Civil War, the bloodiest conflict of the nineteenth century. But the Civil War was in many ways a very conservative war. Both sides loudly proclaimed that they were fighting to defend the constitution: the North to defend the federal system and, later, the vision of individual equality that stands at the heart of the document, the South to defend the rights of states guaranteed in that same federal system. The United States has been singularly free of the sort of revolutionary wars that are so common in Europe: wars that are designed to sweep away the old regime and replace it with something new.

One reason why Americans are obsessed by history and tradition is that they have little need to bury the past like the Germans or Japanese. They lustily celebrate Memorial Day and Independence Day. They regularly send books on the Founding Fathers to the top of the best-seller lists. They form historical societies to reenact the Civil War. They dutifully troop to the country's great monuments. The Capitol is always full of schoolchildren being given reverential lessons on the nation's constitution. (It is impossible to think of Italian teachers speaking with such awe of the Italian constitution.) One of America's most popular children's television programs, *Liberty's Kids,* lovingly retells the heroic deeds of the Revolution.

But because they conceive of themselves as a new nation, Americans don't feel any need to make a cult of newness in the way that some Britons and French do. They have not disfigured the center of Washington with aggressively new buildings, as modernists have felt the need to update London. Many parts of Europe give the impression that they are divided into two parties: an "old party" that regards everything new as suspect and a "new party"— now very much in the ascendant in Britain—that hates the Old World and regards newness as a virtue in and of itself. Ironically Old Europe is currently engaged in a radical experiment to create a New Europe. The Maastricht Treaty is not yet a teenager, the common currency is barely out of its diapers, a new constitution is being debated, ten new members are due in 2004, there is talk of creating a common foreign policy. In America everybody but a radical fringe is happy with the constitutional arrangement.

A CONSERVATIVE REVOLUTION

How conservative was the American Revolution? We should begin by admitting that it was plainly a revolution. As Gordon Wood demonstrated in *The Radicalism of the American Revolution* (1993), the rebels didn't just kick out the British; they kicked out the legal trappings of the feudal social order—primogeniture, entail, titles of nobility, the established church and the rest of it. They based their republic on two revolutionary principles—that all men are created equal and that power ultimately derives from the will of "the people."

There was nevertheless a conservative subtext in everything the revolutionaries did. The revolution began as a colonial rebellion rather than an attempt to remake the world anew like its French equivalent.[4] The revolution was the work of landed gentlemen rather than alienated intellectuals or enraged peasants: prudent and prosperous men who initially argued that they were fighting on behalf of the principles of the British constitution, not against them. They invoked historical English party names, calling themselves "Whigs" and their opponents "Tories," and claimed that they were fighting to preserve ancient British rights (trial by jury, due process, free assembly and no taxation without representation, for example) rather than to establish new ones.

The resulting revolution was a remarkably restrained affair. The worst the American Tories suffered was exile and dispossession. There were no show trials and executions in Philadelphia in the way that there were in Paris. Instead, the revolution unleashed a wave of constitution making. In the wake of the Declaration of Independence in 1776 every state drew up its own constitution, and the states bound themselves together in the limited Articles of Confederation (1783). The states then met together in Philadelphia in 1787 to draw up a national constitution that could reconcile a degree of central control with the ancient rights of the states. The Founding Fathers lived on to contemplate their handiwork in serene old age.

There was undoubtedly more to the American Revolution than defending ancient British liberties. The Founding Fathers gradually realized that something more creative was demanded of them than a defense of the status quo—that, as John Jay of New York declared, they were "the first people whom heaven has favored with an opportunity of deliberating upon and choosing forms of government under which they should live."[5] And they were more interested in securing liberty in general than in merely defending their rights under the ancient British constitution. They read Locke and Montesquieu as well as Blackstone. However, the liberty they sought was a very moderate sort of liberty: the freedom for individuals as far as possible to pursue their own ends unconstrained by government interference. It was this overriding commitment to civic liberty that gave the American Revolution its conservative edge. It put a limit on the ambitions of government. Government was to be judged not by its ability to promote virtue or prosperity but by its ability to leave people alone to pursue their private ends.

The Founding Fathers had no truck with old ideas about virtuous aristocratic elites, but they had no illusions about the innate goodness of the masses either.[6] "If men were angels," Madison wrote in *Federalist* number 51, "no government would be necessary. . . . If angels were to govern men, neither external nor internal controls on government would be necessary."

In that spirit, the Founding Fathers regarded democracy as a means to a higher end rather than an end in itself—the higher end being liberty. They were careful to design a system that guarded against democracy's "turbulence and follies." They used the division of powers (among other things) to prevent the most common dangers of democracies: majorities oppressing minorities, minorities hijacking the government, and elected representatives putting their own interests before the people's. They created a Senate, with senators being initially appointed by the states rather than directly elected, in order to provide "an anchor against popular fluctuations." They used the principle of federalism to make sure that decisions were made at the lowest possible level. And, of course, they had a somewhat limited idea of who constituted "the people": women, non-landowners and slaves, for example, were not allowed to vote. The intricacy of the founders' design was remarkable. While senators sat for six years so that they could take a long-term view of things, representatives sat for two years in order to be closer to the will of the people. Presidents were elected by an electoral college, rather than crude majorities, in order to make sure that they paid attention to smaller states.

It is hardly surprising that Edmund Burke, the patron saint of British conservatism, admired the American Revolution as much as he hated its French stepsister. The French ended up producing disaster, he argued, because they were fighting for freedom in the abstract ("the wild gas of liberty," as he put it)—and because they wanted to use the government to remake human nature. The Americans produced a successful revolution because they were fighting for the real freedoms of real people, for the established way of life in America against the growing ambitions of an arbitrary power, and they tempered their government to suit human nature. They never lost sight of the fact that the task of government is to protect the individual in his private pursuit of happiness.

A BLUEPRINT FOR THE RIGHT

Burke was right to see the conservative essence behind the revolutionary words. Through accident or design, the constitution has helped push America toward conservatism (and ultimately away from socialism) in two ways — by putting a limit on the power of the centralized state and by giving disproportionate power to rural states.

Distrust of government came over to America on the first English ships. The Puritans who settled in New England were fugitives from Anglican hegemony — and they were soon followed by other kinds of religious dissenters, including Catholics. The colonists got used to ignoring rules that were made in London. Sir Robert Walpole, the first British prime minister, described British rule of the thirteen colonies as a system of "salutary neglect"; and it was the attempt to transform that into a real system of imperial rule that precipitated the revolution. Even during the revolution, the Continental Congress was unwilling to provide George Washington with the men and materials that he needed to fight the British.[7]

Americans repeatedly reasserted their preference for "salutary neglect." During the republic's early years, the battle between small-government Republicans and Federalists was eventually solved in the Republicans' favor. In his first inaugural address in March 1801, Jefferson reaffirmed his commitment to "a wise and frugal government which shall restrain men from injuring one another, shall leave them otherwise free to regulate their own pursuit of industry and improvement, and shall not take from the mouth of labor the bread it has earned." The Democratic platform of 1840, the first document of its kind, begins with the words: "Resolved, That the federal government is one of limited powers. . . ." Twenty years later, in their own first platform, the Republicans sounded a similarly anarchistic note: "Resolved . . . That the people justly view with alarm the reckless extravagance which pervades every department of the Federal Government. . . ."[8]

The second way that the American political system reinforced conservatism was that it gave a disproportionate amount of power to America's most conservative elements. The American South — a region originally controlled by a plantation aristocracy and rooted in slavery—was the dominant political force in the country between the Revolution and the Civil War. Jefferson, Madison and Washington were all slaveowners. In the seventy-two years between 1789 and 1861, Southerners accounted for ten of sixteen presidents, twenty-four of thirty-six House Speakers and twenty of the thirty-five Supreme Court justices.[9]

The Civil War and Reconstruction put a violent end to the South's power. But the Southern genius for politics nevertheless reasserted itself in the first half of the twentieth century. The fact that the South was so solidly Democratic meant that the region's senators could turn themselves into "human institutions with southern accents," reelected term after term and, thanks to the chamber's rigid seniority system, appointed to the chairmanships of all the most important committees.[10] When Lyndon Johnson arrived in the Senate in 1949, only one of the Senate's thirteen committees was not chaired either by a Southerner or somebody closely allied to the South. Conservative Southern Democrats formed a powerful voting block with Northern Republicans to protect the region's peculiar racial practices and to frustrate ambitious liberal reforms.

The practice of giving every state two senators, regardless of population, has also reinforced America's conservative tendency. Sparsely populated rural states like Wyoming and Montana have as much say in the Senate as California and New York. This inevitably magnifies the influence of rural voters in the West and Midwest and limits the influence of urban voters on the coasts and in the industrial belt. Throughout American history senators from small states have acted to frustrate federal programs favored by the House. And the electoral college system gives a conservative bias to presidential races for the same reason, as Al Gore discovered in 2000 when he won the popular vote by a decent margin, but still lost the White House.

It didn't happen there

If the constitution strengthened the more conservative forces in the country, it also weakened the more radical ones. Socialist parties blossomed in every important country in Europe in the second half of the nineteenth century, mobilizing mass support for expanding the power of the state, both to provide welfare services (such as pensions) and to restrain the power of the market. But in America socialists cast their seed on barren ground.

This failure was partly for mechanical reasons. The first-past-the-post electoral system, the focus on the presidency and the separation of powers made it all but impossible for third parties to challenge the duopoly. The fact that universal male suffrage was introduced for whites as early as the 1820s in some states prevented socialists from linking their demands for economic change to demands for universal suffrage, as they did in Europe.

Yet the socialists' failure was also ideological: in America, they ran into a working class that showed far less enthusiasm for socialist ideas. Back in 1890 Friedrich Engels fumed that "America is so purely bourgeois, so entirely without a feudal past and therefore proud of its purely bourgeois organization." Interestingly, the left-wingers that America did eventually manage to produce clung to individualism, unlike their European equivalents. Prior to the Great Depression the entire gamut of American labor, from the mainstream unions in the American Federation of Labor to the radical Industrial Workers of the World, opposed programs that extended the role of the state. The AFL opposed state provision of old-age pensions, compulsory health insurance, minimum-wage legislation, unemployment compensation; and from 1914 onward it was even against legislating maximum hours for men.[11] Most American leftists were more interested in getting their fair share of the American dream than creating a socialist society.

By 1929 Joseph Stalin was so impatient with the progress of socialism in America that he summoned Jay Lovestone, the head of the American Communist Party, to Moscow to explain the lack of success. Lovestone duly came up with much the same sort of excuse as Engels, blaming the absence of a European class system, aristocracy and so on.[12] In fact, the Great Depression did eventually "Europeanize" American politics a little. The New Deal led to a huge expansion in the state's powers to tax, spend and regulate, including a Social Security system to help the aged and government agencies to monitor the affairs of business. The membership of unions exploded from a little more than 3 million in 1927 (11.3 percent of the nonagricultural workforce) to more than 8 million in 1939 (28.6 percent of the nonagricultural workforce).[13] The unions also deepened their relationship with the Democratic Party.

For all that, the most striking thing about the New Deal, considering the extent of the calamity that America was facing, was its moderation. The American Fabians who flocked to Roosevelt's Washington with the dream of establishing central planning were sorely disappointed. Roosevelt preferred regulation to outright state control, resisting calls to nationalize the disintegrating banking system. Congressmen fought to preserve the power of local government. Everyone hesitated to make the safety net too cushy. The Social Security Act of 1935 specifically excluded agricultural workers and domestic staff, thus leaving many poor blacks out in the cold. In September 1935, the newly created Gallup polling organization asked Americans what they thought about the amount of money the government was spending on relief and recovery. Twice as many respondents said that the government was spending too much as said it was spending the right amount. Scarcely one in ten said it was spending too little. After Roosevelt's reelection, 50 percent of Democrats said that they hoped that his second administration would be more conservative than his first, and only 19 percent said that they wanted it to be more liberal.[14]

This lack of a socialist party put the United States on a very different path from its European competitors. Before the Second World War social spending was no smaller in the United States than in Europe. In 1938 the Roosevelt administration spent 6.3 percent of GDP on social programs like employment assurance and public employment—a higher proportion than governments in Sweden (3.2 percent), France (3.4 percent), the United Kingdom (5.5 percent) and Germany (5.6 percent).[15] But after the war things diverged dramatically. In Europe the socialist parties that had been gathering strength for years seized the opportunity of postwar reconstruction to impose far-reaching social programs. In America the government hesitated to introduce free child health care, let alone a full-blown national health service. America's two main attempts at providing health coverage—Medicare and Medicaid—did not appear for another quarter century. When Ronald Reagan rode into the White House in the 1980 election on a wave of conservative resentment against "big government," the United States had a lower tax rate, a smaller deficit as a proportion of GNP, a less developed welfare state and fewer government-owned industries than any other western industrialized nation.

Put in these terms, it can sound as if America was tricked out of having a proper socialist movement. But there have always been three other forces keeping America on the Right well before it discovered a conservative movement—religion, capitalism and, most fundamental of all, geography.

IN GOD'S NAME

Why are Americans so religious? The obvious reason is that religion played such a prominent role in both the creation and shaping of the country. The earliest American colonies were settled by Puritans, dissenters who saw the new land as an opportunity to escape from religious persecution and practice their religious faith as vigorously as they could. The constitution's First Amendment specifically guaranteed the "free expression" of religion. By and large, the new country lived up to this promise, but those who did still feel discriminated against, notably the Mormons, helped to spearhead the move westward in the nineteenth century.

The other reason for America's religiosity is perhaps more surprising: it is the fact that America was founded as a secular state. The same First Amendment that guarantees the free exercise of religion also prohibits Congress from making any law "respecting an establishment of religion." The separation of church and state distinguishes America from European "confessional states." Many religious conservatives complain that this separation unjustly excludes religion from the public square. Many of the most vigorous supporters of the separation are liberals. But in fact the separation of church and state has done more than anything else to preserve religion as a vigorous (and usually conservative) force in American life.

The disestablishment of religion injected market forces into American religious life. Religious organizations could not rely on the state for subsidies in the same way as, say, the Church of England. They had to compete to survive. This was exactly as Jefferson, one of the most vigorous supporters of disestablishment, predicted. In his notes for a speech to the legislature in 1776 he argued that religious freedom would strengthen the church because it would "oblige its ministers to be industrious [and] exemplary."[16] American religion was always throwing up new churches that could market the Word better than the competition. During the Great Awakening of the 1840s, for example, revivalists dispensed with Latinate sermons ("all *hic haec hoc* and no God in it") and invented rousing gospel songs.[17] Disestablishment also lifted a huge burden from religion. What better way to distort faith than to make it dependent on the whims of politicians? And what better way to debilitate faith than to link it to the pursuit of sinecures and preferments? America was mercifully free from the local equivalents of Trollope's parsons, who were constantly maneuvering for official preferment. It was also free from the power struggles that debilitated the Catholic Church: remember that Lord Acton's injunction that power corrupts and absolute power corrupts absolutely comes from his description of the medieval papacy. American churches had nothing to rely on to ensure their survival other than their own spiritual strength.

The religious groups that survived best in America's competitive environment were the most "enthusiastic": the ones that took their faith most seriously and preached it most vigorously. Even today, Americans swap religions quickly: around 16 percent of the population has changed denominations and the proportion rises the more fundamental the creeds get, with one study showing that half the pastors in megachurches having moved from another denomination.[18] Some people think America is currently in the middle of its Fourth Great Awakening;[19] but the truth is that these great awakenings have been so frequent and prolonged that there has never been a period of sleep from which to awake. Revivalism does not need to be revived; rather, it is a continuous fact of American life.

America's penchant for religion hasn't exclusively benefited conservatives. One of the most religious groups in the country is also one of the most Democratic: African-Americans. Two of the most prominent left-wing politicians, Jesse Jackson and Al Sharpton, are both reverends (Sharpton was ordained at the tender age of ten). Throughout American history, protest movements have had a religious component. The underground railway, which helped slaves to the North and freedom, was run by holy criminals. The father of populism, William Jennings Bryan, was a lay preacher. Religious people were in the forefront of the struggle for civil rights for women and blacks. During the 2000 election campaign Al Gore talked about using "faith-based organizations" to help solve America's social problems almost as enthusiastically as George Bush.

But throughout its history America's religiosity has encouraged Americans to see problems in terms of individual virtues and vices. It has also encouraged Americans to try to solve society's ills through voluntary activity rather than state action. Calvin Colton, a Briton who visited America in the 1830s, noted that the separation of church and state had given rise to "a new species of social organization before unknown in history."[20] In America voluntary organizations took on functions that, in Europe, were performed either by the state or by state-financed churches. Religious groups set up elaborate systems of voluntary welfare. The Catholic Church, for example, established a separate welfare state, a parallel universe with its own schools, hospitals and provisions for the indigent and unfortunate. Many of these voluntary groups were highly suspicious of government interference. In 1931 the chairman of the Red Cross's central committee went before Congress to discuss a proposed federal appropriation of $25 million for relief of drought victims. "All we pray for," he said, "is that you let us alone and let us do the job."[21]

Religion has also reinforced America's patriotism. From the first the religious groups who fled to America had a strong sense that they were settling in a special place with a special role in God's plan—a city on a hill, a beacon to the rest of the world. America has long regarded itself as a redeemer nation. "Nation after nation, cheered by our example, will follow in our footsteps till the whole earth is freed," said Lyman Beecher, a nineteenth-century cleric. Patriotism and religion are mutually reinforcing. This is why, during Eisenhower's presidency, religious groups got the phrase "under God" (Lincoln's phrase from the Gettysburg address) added to the Pledge of Allegiance, whose original version, conservatives note, was written by Francis Bellamy, a socialist educator.[22]

THE MIGHTY DOLLAR

If God has predisposed America to conservatism, then so has Mammon. Why throw in your lot with radicals when you can simply move farther West? Why agitate for revolution when you are doing so well out of the established system? As Werner Sombart famously put it, the ship of American socialism ran aground on "shoals of roast beef and apple pie."

America has always been a feast of plenty. From the sixteenth century onward, visitors have waxed lyrical about the country's abundance of everything: abundance of space which allows people to own their own homes and support their own families; abundance of food that makes them the most generously fed people in the world; and abundance of opportunities for upward mobility. In Europe, too many people were always chasing too few opportunities. In America, there were always too few people to exploit everything the country had to offer. In the 1780s J. Hector St. John de Crèvecoeur, a visiting Frenchman, noted that "there is room for everybody in America. . . . I do not mean that everyone who comes will grow rich in a little time; no, but he may procure an easy, decent maintenance, by his industry." In 1817, William Cobbett, a British critic of the establishment, commented on American dietary excesses: "You are not much pressed to eat and drink, but such an abundance is spread before you . . . that you instantly lose all restraint." In 1831 Alexis de Tocqueville, the first person to meditate at any length on American exceptionalism, remarked that fortune offered "an immense booty to the Americans."[23]

These differences became more marked with the invention of mass production. Americans simply possessed more *stuff* than anybody else: more cars, more telephones, more radios, more vacuum cleaners, more electric lights, more bathtubs, more supermarkets, more movie theaters, more of any new invention or innovation that would make life more endurable. In *The Future in America* (1906), H. G. Wells noted that even in the "filthy back streets of the East Side" of New York people were much better off than their peers in London.[24] During his stay in New York in 1917, Leon Trotsky was astonished by the facilities in his cheap apartment in the East Bronx: "electric lights, gas cooking-range, bath, telephone, automatic service elevator, and even a chute for the garbage." All this won his children over to New York.[25] Franklin D. Roosevelt said that if he could place one American book in the hands of every Russian, he would choose the Sears, Roebuck catalogue.[26]

Just as important as the abundance of material goods was the abundance of opportunity. For most of America's history, most of its inhabitants could expect to get richer during their lifetimes—and expect that their children would get richer still. In 1909–1929 consumer expenditure per head rose almost 45 percent in real terms, and then rose another 52 percent from 1929–1960.[27] The twin engines of economic expansion—geographical expansion into new lands in the West and technological expansion into new realms of production—created a constant supply of new opportunities. And at the same time a relentless supply of new immigrants stood ready to take the places that were being vacated at the bottom of the ladder. Everybody in the country— old or new, immigrant or settled, middle class or lumpen proletarian, Italian godfather or WASP patrician—seemed to be moved by the same motives: the desire to make a profit, to accumulate dollars, to get ahead in the world and flaunt your wealth as a sign that you had got ahead.

It was only fitting that a people of plenty should put their trust not in the state, but in the providers of plenty—the businessmen. Capitalism came to America with the first settlers. The country was founded by profit-obsessed corporations: the Virginia Company, the Massachusetts Bay Company and, more darkly for the country's future, the slave-trading Royal African Company (New York was named after the latter's president, James, Duke of York).[28] The Puritans, who came for religious rather than commercial reasons, also had a distinctly capitalist frame of mind. There have always been exceptions to this enthusiasm for capitalism, such as the Southern Agrarians, the Populists and Michael Moore, but in general America has had little use for the European contempt for business. Americans celebrate the creative genius of businesspeople in much the same way that the French celebrate the creative genius of artists and intellectuals. Ronald Reagan captured this attitude perfectly when, as a flack for General Electric in the 1950s, he liked to say that the company's primary product was progress.[29] American school textbooks recounted tales of the practical genius of men like Henry Ford and Thomas Edison (and will no doubt one day celebrate the practical genius of Bill Gates). The first instinct of policy makers has generally been to stand back and give businesspeople the room that they need to exercise their creative genius.

America has been much more inclined to let public work be covered by private philanthropy than Europe has. The country's landscape is littered with monuments to business philanthropy: great universities like Stanford and Chicago; great galleries like the Getty and the Frick; great medical research centers like Rockefeller University. Every one of these monuments is the product of a large private fortune translated into a large public good. And for each of these great monuments there are a thousand small-scale charities bent on repairing the fractured raiment of society. Andrew Carnegie, John D. Rockefeller Sr. and the rest of the robber barons were hard-faced men who destroyed their competitors and crushed trade unions. But they were also great philanthropists. Carnegie talked about the religion of philanthropy. His dictum that "the man who dies rich dies disgraced" created a fashion among his fellow robber barons for pouring money into universities, art galleries and medical schools, a fashion that survives with today's new tech billionaires.

The idea that wealth entails responsibility went much deeper than billionaires. Americans of all degrees of wealth have been unusually generous with their money. Even while he was a poor clerk in Cleveland, Rockefeller gave away a fixed proportion of his income. More important still, Americans have been unusually generous with their time. Voluntary organizations designed to solve society's problems have flourished more lavishly in the United States than perhaps any other country. Today American philanthropic contributions account for about 1 percent of national income, compared with between 0.2 percent and 0.8 percent in Europe.[30] Crucially, Americans much prefer to give away their money themselves, rather than let their government do it: foreign aid is a pathetic portion of government spending.

This tradition of philanthropy encouraged America to tackle its social problems without building a European-style welfare state, and to embrace modernity without abandoning its traditions of voluntarism, decentralization and experiment. The country did a remarkable job of creating a national infrastructure before the introduction of the federal income tax in 1913. And, even as the federal government grew in the 1930s and 1940s, boosted by war, depression and idealism, America took the conservative attitude that the public sector should not be allowed to crowd out the voluntary one.

The lure of the West

The roots of American conservatism are embedded in the most fundamental thing about any country: its geography. America is the world's fourth largest country, and, unusually for such a large place, two-thirds of it is habitable. It is a land of wide-open spaces—a place where rugged individualism can become a philosophy rather than just a hopeful cliché, where reinvention is always possible and where conservatism can become a much more optimistic—even sometimes utopian—creed than it has been anywhere else.

Geography helps to explain why immigration, so often a source of discontent in more crowded places, has usually had the opposite effect in America. The history of every big city in America has been littered with fights between the established inhabitants and new arrivals. But immigrants have repeatedly replenished the supply of devotees to the American capitalist dream. (An old Ellis Island motto: "The cowards never came, and the weak died on the way.") Most immigrants saw—and still see—America as a land of milk and honey compared with their old homelands. Most have embraced their new country with the enthusiasm of converts and followed the path of upward mobility: starting off in ethnic enclaves (which also had the effect of diluting working-class solidarity) and then eventually making it into the suburbs and the great American middle class. It cannot be a mere coincidence that the most consistently left-wing group in America has been blacks—the only people who did not come to the country voluntarily.

And once people arrived in America, they kept on moving. Internal migration has been one of the secrets of America's economic success. One of Margaret Thatcher's cabinet ministers once famously exhorted Britain's unemployed to "get on their bikes" to look for work; that advice has never been needed in America, where there has always been somewhere better to go. The Left is correct to point out that some economic migrations have been desperate affairs: think of Tom Joad and the hapless Okies in *The Grapes of Wrath*. But the truth for most migrants over time has been more enriching. "The western wilds, from the Alleghenies to the Pacific, constituted the richest free gift that was ever spread out before civilized man," Frederick Jackson Turner wrote in his paper, "The Significance of the Frontier in American History" (1893). "Never again can such an opportunity come to the sons of men." A senior Republican in California, surveying the prosperous elderly white faces at his party's state convention, says that one word comes to his mind: Okies. (He means it as an insult, but it also shows that Tom Joad's descendants have not done badly.)

The migrants left their past behind, along with all the accumulated traditions of the Old World. Many migrants were identified not by their family names but by their given names and preferably by their nicknames—a tradition that still thrives in Texas (and can be seen in George W. Bush's habit of giving everybody he knows a pet name).[31] Daniel Boorstin produces a wonderful quotation from a Texas pioneer: "Truly this is a world which has no regard for the established order of things, but knocks them sky west and crooked, and lo, the upstart hath the land and its fatness."[32]

The modern equivalent of this homestead is the suburb. Ask Americans where they want to live, and only 13 percent say they would like to live in a city; the biggest number—37 percent—say a small town, and 25 percent say the suburbs.[33] Most Americans seem to expect, in their heart of hearts, that they will end up living in a sun-blessed subdivision.[34] And they are right to do so. More than half the population now lives in a suburb of some sort; by contrast, two-thirds of the population in Europe is categorized as urban. And American suburbs are different: the new Edge cities include far more offices and workplaces, far more immigrants, far more space and far more variety in terms of rich suburbs and poor suburbs than the standard middle-class dormitory "commuter belts" of the sort you see round big European cities.

The New World's capacity to reinvent itself—to summon up ever newer worlds from its vast expanse of space—has reinforced the odd mixture of individualism and traditionalism at the heart of American conservatism. The Sun Belt that burst into prominence in the Reagan era might almost be regarded as a new nation. Its towns began without any of the palaces, cathedrals, archives and monuments that weigh people down with memories of the past. It is a nation of sprawling cities, a slash-and-burn social policy and incessant reinvention, a nation of strip malls and megachurches, of country-and-western music and NASCAR racing.

Yet many of the rootless people of the new frontier combined this reinvention with a fierce thirst for the solace of religion. This religion was much more hard-edged than the sort that flourished back on the East Coast, let alone back in Europe. It saw money not as something that needed to be apologized for but as a sign that you had worked hard and earned the Lord's blessing—an idea that survived long after wagon trains gave way to Jeep Cherokees. In June 1981 Ronald Reagan's deputy counsel, Herbert

Ellingwood, told a "financial success seminar" in Anaheim, California, that "economic salvation and spiritual salvation go side by side."[35] One of us once rather merrily suggested to a group of Christian conservatives in Colorado that Jesus Christ was really something of a socialist—and then had to spend the next half hour in what might be described as emergency Bible study. In the South in particular this religion can be fiercely judgmental. The mystical visions of the New Testament about forgiving people their trespasses has held less appeal than Old Testament pragmatism; if you do bad things, bad things happen to you. As T. R. Fehrenbach, Texas's leading modern chronicler, observes, the passages in the Bible that made more sense to his state were "the parts in which the children of Israel saw the sweetness in a harsh land and piled up the foreskins of their enemies."[36]

Meanwhile, the frontier also inured Americans to violence. Guns were essential to people who were taming a wild frontier. Frontier societies easily turned to the ultimate punishment—execution—to preserve a precarious order or indeed to grab the land in the first place. The people who built Texas, such as Jack Hays and L. H. McNelly, saw themselves as warriors, not murderers. In the spirit of the West, writes Fehrenbach, "Hays, who shot many a squaw outside her teepee, was no more a killer than a bombardier who dropped his armaments on crowded tenements in World War II."[37] Even once the land was grabbed, the burden of self-defense in disputes lay with the individual. (If they were too wimpish to do so, tough luck: they should have stayed at home.) The prospect of prosperity and the permanent threat of anarchy: what could be more conducive to conservative thinking than that?

So America has always had conservative elements. But it did not really have a Right Nation until the mid-twentieth century. Since then a set of conservative inclinations and prejudices have hardened into something more substantial. For most of its history, America didn't need a conservative movement because it was a fundamentally conservative nation. This movement sprang up in the 1950s when conservative Americans began to react against the advances that "big government liberalism" had made in the past two decades, and it roared into life in the 1960s when Johnson's Democrats tried to drag the country dramatically to the Left. Even today hostility to liberalism—be it Southern churchgoers protesting against gay marriage or Bill O'Reilly harrying the European axis of weasel on Fox News—forms a strong part of American conservatism. But American conservatism plainly has metamorphosed into something far more formidable than knee-jerk reaction; at home and abroad it is an ideology that is characterized as much by aggressive preemption as by defensive reaction. It is to this modern conservatism, and its own exceptional nature, that we now turn.

CHAPTER 14

HERESY AND REFORMATION: AMERICA'S EXCEPTIONAL CONSERVATISM

A N EASY WAY TO DISCOVER how much more right-wing conservative America is than even its closest European cousins is to compare John Ashcroft with Oliver Letwin. You might expect the two to have a lot in common. Ashcroft is Bush's attorney general. Letwin, a rising star in the British Conservative Party, was the shadow home secretary for most of Bush's first term. In that job his portfolio was close to Ashcroft's: crime, prisons, drugs, terrorism and justice. American conservatives have closer ties to the British Tory Party than to anybody else. Thatcherism and Reaganism may have taken their place in history, but there is a genuine sense of shared identity—that together they changed the world. The brighter British Tories date Thatcherism back to the 1964 Republican Convention in San Francisco's Cow Palace that nominated Barry Goldwater. For their part, even youngish Republicans still talk about the influence of Sir Keith Joseph, the Institute for Economic Affairs and free-market Tory intellectuals in the 1970s. "They were crucial," argues Bill Owens, the governor of Colorado.

Letwin knows this common ground better than most. He is the son of Shirley Robin Letwin, an American academic who studied with Friedrich Hayek at the University of Chicago, sat at Michael Oakeshott's feet, and became one of the leading luminaries of the Institute of Economic Affairs. Letwin himself did a spell teaching at Princeton, and still turns to America for ideas. Indeed, he argues that, in the long run, British politics will become even more like America's. The big issue will be the role of the state in a market economy, with the Democrats and the Labor Party favoring an active central government, and the Tories and Republicans (and "half of Tony Blair") trying to devolve control to the local level—giving people more power over their schools, hospitals and policemen.

Yet, for the time being, two stark differences between the two men dwarf any possible similarities. The first difference is obvious enough: power. Ashcroft is in office, born aloft by a vibrant conservative movement; Letwin's party was until recently in danger of self-destruction. On November 5, 2002, the day that George W. Bush led the Republicans to victory in the midterm elections, Iain Duncan Smith, the Tory's lackluster leader, was reduced to warning his squabbling party to "unite or die." Within a year, they had ditched him, in favor of the more substantial Michael Howard, who promoted Letwin to shadow chancellor in December 2003.

Political fortunes rise and fall, but the second difference between Letwin and Ashcroft is more fundamental: their idea of what conservatism means. Both, it is true, generally favor smaller government. However, Letwin's idea of a smaller state is dramatically larger than Ashcroft's, including, for example, a state-run health service and generous grants for all students. Ashcroft has always been in favor of the death penalty and harsh mandatory sentences; he has always opposed abortion, gun laws, drug liberalization, flag burning and virtually anything that smacks of the 1960s. Letwin supports abortion rights, opposes the death penalty and repeatedly disassociates himself from illiberalism of all sorts. In foreign policy, the Jewish Letwin is a far less hardline supporter of Israel than the Pentecostalist Ashcroft is. He is also far better disposed to the United Nations, an organization from which Senator Ashcroft once tried to withdraw American support.

One small incident epitomizes the gulf. In late 2002 Letwin hinted casually on the BBC's early-morning *Today* radio program that the Tories might consider backing gay marriages: "Whilst we attach a huge importance to the institution of marriage, we do recognize that gay couples suffer from serious particular grievances."[1] Ashcroft is a vigorous supporter of the federal marriage amendment. But the difference is deeper. The *Today* program, where Letwin appears regularly, is the epitome of the leftish media that Ashcroft shuns. Most mornings, far from talking to the media, he does not even get around to looking at the "liberal press" until he has finished his Bible study and prayers.

The war on terrorism, which you would imagine might bring conservatives together, seems only to highlight their differences. For Ashcroft, it has become a personal crusade. When he heard about September 11, he immediately told his staff that "this will change the world as we know it," and he has since characterized it as a battle against a "conspiracy of evil." That has justified passing ever tougher laws to smite terrorist suspects—secret military tribunals, designating American citizens as enemy combatants, wiretapping mosques and the rest of it. It is said that Kennedy's Justice Department was so set on fighting organized crime that it would arrest a mobster for spitting on the sidewalk; Ashcroft wouldn't let an Islamic terrorist even get the phlegm ready to spit. Letwin, by contrast, has taken a more nuanced approach: as shadow home secretary, he too called for tougher sentences, but he has also spoken about civil liberties and agonized about the underlying causes of terrorism. For Ashcroft, the overriding priority is to protect Americans from another devastating attack. He has no more interest in the social causes of Islamic unrest than Oliver Cromwell did in the social causes of Catholicism in Ireland; what matters is that the enemy should be driven off a cliff.

A DIFFERENT SORT OF CONSERVATISM

It is tempting to dismiss these differences as a matter of personalities. Ashcroft is the most socially conservative member of Bush's cabinet; Letwin is a cuddlier figure than some previous Tory home secretaries have been (including Michael Howard). But this adds a matter of a few inches on either side, when the political gulf between the different sorts of conservatism on both sides of the Atlantic needs to be measured in yards, if not miles. That gulf is partly a matter of organization and partly a matter of belief.

The difference in political organization has been such a consistent theme throughout this book that it deserves only the briefest summary here. The sort of mass movement that has borne Ashcroft to his current heights, the movement whose rise we have chronicled in these pages, simply does not exist anywhere else, at least on the Right. In the rest of the world, conservatism is the creature of a political party—or a faction of a political party. In America, it is a populist movement, vital and self-confident, prepared to work with the Republican Party if it is willing to toe the conservative line, but otherwise willing to spend as long as it takes in the wilderness.[2]

For instance, if you were to install Karl Rove in the Conservative Party's headquarters in Smith Square in London and tell him to recreate an American-style conservative movement, he would not know where to begin. In terms of a *rive droite,* there are only a handful of small conservative think tanks. Their budgets are all well below $2 million. It is a world of scrimping and saving, of cash crises and last-minute fund-raising, a world where many people work for nothing rather than dream of climbing a conservative career ladder to riches.[3] He might be heartened by the presence of a conservative press in the shape of the *Daily Mail* and the *Daily Telegraph* (the Murdoch papers having defected at least for the moment to Tony Blair) but there are no proper conservative talk radio stations and nothing to match Fox News. Indeed, Rupert Murdoch would not be able to Foxify his British Sky News without breaking various broadcasting rules about objectivity. As for the footsoldiers, there is a lobby for big business—the Confederation of British Industry—but no antitax movement to compare with Grover Norquist's outfit; there is a prohunting lobby, but no progun lobby to compare with the NRA; there is an anti-European movement but it never quite knows whether to run against the Conservatives or to help them.

Rove might imagine that he could call on the Church of England—"the Tory Party at prayer"—to rouse up some people. This might prove even more dispiriting. The Anglicans, like the Catholics, tend to be a force on the left, harrowing the government about not spending enough on the poor rather than campaigning for moral virtue. In recent British public life, only one prominent politician has been consistently identified with trying to put Christian ethics at the center of politics—the late Lord Longford—and he interpreted Christ's teaching to mean that society should be trying to free murderers, rather than speeding up their execution. Otherwise, there is a small antiabortion movement, a marginal and unpoliticized Evangelical

Christian community and a few people who complain about nudity on the BBC.

Britain's secularism is par for the course in Europe, a continent that is not so much Christian as post-Christian. The sort of moralistic conservatism of many in George W. Bush's administration has no real equivalent within the Gaullists in France or the CDU in Germany either. In most European Christian Democratic parties, the "Christian" bit is usually said sotto voce: there is certainly no link to Evangelical moralism, and no question of the cabinet holding impromptu religious ceremonies on foreign trips, as Bush's team did on the plane back from El Salvador.

And remember where this comparison began: the Tories are the closest the Republicans have to foreign partners. In most countries outside Britain and America, Letwin's enthusiasm for shrinking the state would mark him out as an extreme right-winger. Most continental conservatives prefer the sort of Toryism of Peregrine Worsthorne, who argued that conservatives should "staunchly" defend the welfare state on the grounds that it is a bulwark of social stability: "only if the many are spared economic hardship can the few expect to enjoy economic and social privilege."[4] Most continental conservatives would frown on Letwin's enthusiasm for Rudy Giuliani's zero-tolerance policing methods, redesigning social policy or waging war against Iraq. Look around the richer developed countries and radical conservatism is either on the ropes (as in Canada) or never managed to climb into the ring in the first place. In Japan, France and Germany, there is hardly a politician—let alone a party— whose philosophy could be described as conservative in the American sense of the word. Italy has Silvio Berlusconi, who is undoubtedly pro-American, but who focuses a disproportionate amount of his procapitalist energies on getting rid of cumbersome media-ownership rules. Spain and Portugal have also recently been run by pro-American governments that have seemed conservative compared with what went on before, but their philosophies would still put them on the left of the Democratic Party in America.

This brings the argument back to the second gulf—the one to do with principle. The Right Nation we have described in this book believes in a fundamentally different sort of conservatism from the one that the old conservative parties of Europe still cling to.

AN OLD RELIGION, REBORN

How different is "American conservatism"? Plenty of people question whether either the adjective or the noun is accurate. On the question of its "American-ness," the creed has actually derived a good deal of its inspiration from the Old World. Two Austrian imports, Friedrich Hayek and Ludwig von Mises, did as much as any native-born Americans to reenergize America's instinctive faith in the free market after the Second World War, providing the words that justified the prejudices of many American businesspeople. David Stockman, Reagan's budget director, spoke of wielding the sword "forged in the free-market smithy of F. A. Hayek." Many of the people who reinvented conservatism in the 1950s revered Europe. Russell Kirk worshipped Edmund Burke. James Burnham cowrote a book with André Malraux.[5] William Buckley was partly educated in England, traveled abroad frequently and deliberately gave the *National Review* a "European" emphasis, complete with articles by members of the Hapsburg royal family. Irving Kristol recalls that as a young man he only got to know conservatives—as opposed to ex-radicals with budding right-wing opinions—when he moved to England in 1953. He was fascinated "by the fact that they felt perfectly at ease with themselves as conservatives, neither apologetic nor unduly contentious."[6]

This tradition of looking overseas for inspiration continues to this day. As we have seen, Leo Strauss is one of the most revered figures in George W. Bush's Washington. George Will, one of America's most widely read conservative commentators, has claimed that "the conservatism for which I argue is a 'European' conservatism."[7] Contemporary American conservatism has attracted so many eloquent immigrant supporters (such as our fellow countrymen John O'Sullivan and Andrew Sullivan, or the Canadian-born David Frum) that Michael Lind has even coined a term for them: "immicons."

Nor is it just a question of disputed ancestry. For many critics, the real problem with defining "American conservatism" is the noun. Can the diverse group of sometimes contradictory beliefs and often feuding people that we have catalogued in this book really be pushed into one distinct creed? At the very least, American conservatism is a house with many mansions.

Americans who describe themselves as "conservatives" nevertheless disagree on almost all the most fundamental questions of life. Paleoconservatives lament the passing of tradition. Libertarians celebrate capitalism's creative energy. Religious conservatives want to put faith at the heart of politics. Business conservatives command an economic system where, in Karl Marx's phrase, "all that is holy is profaned." The Straussians at the *Weekly Standard* are philosophical elitists who believe that the masses need to be steered by an educated intelligentsia. The antitax crusaders who march behind Grover Norquist are populists who believe that pointy-headed intellectuals need to be given a good ducking. "What is the difference between conservatives and cannibals?" goes one Democratic joke. "Cannibals eat only their enemies."

Equally plainly, American conservatism has shown remarkable ability to mutate over time. Newt Gingrich demonized government. George W. Bush believes that government can be an instrument of conservative reform. Ronald Reagan put "liberty" at the heart of his administration. Many of Bush's supporters are more interested in "virtue." American conservatism has also been a reactive creed: it was sired as much by the radical liberalism in the 1960s as it was by the writings of Hayek and Mises. Even today, American conservatives are often more motivated by an all-consuming loathing of their instinctive enemies, from Yasser Arafat to Paul Krugman, than they are by maintaining and defending a particular set of intellectual beliefs.

American conservatism is a practical, flexible creed, refashioned to deal with the shock of great events, rather than a fixed ideology written down in a conservative equivalent of Mao's *Little Red Book*. In his masterly intellectual history of American conservatism, George Nash even argued that American conservatism was such a mutable creed that it was pointless trying to define it: American conservatism is simply what American conservatives say and do.[8]

So does it make any sense to talk about "American conservatism"? We believe that it does for two reasons. First, for all its wild tributaries, American conservatism clearly has a mainstream. This is the faith that Ronald Reagan and George W. Bush tap into so effortlessly: the faith of Dustin and Maura, our two young Republicans in Colorado, and millions of conservative footsoldiers. This faith is not just a positive creed (it is about more than just reacting to American liberalism); it also has raw political power. It is the faith that gets the eccentric army of tax cutters and religious fundamentalists onto the battlefield—and onto the same side. As we pointed out before, the members of this army may wear the livery of different causes and disagree about all sorts of things, but they have enough in common to constitute a vibrant political movement.

The second reason is that the mainstream of American conservatism is clearly different from the mainstream of conservatism elsewhere. No other conservative movement can marshal the same array of tax cutters and religious conservatives. No other conservative movement can produce institutions such as Focus on the Family, Patrick Henry College and the Heritage Foundation. Like many issues in which it is worth separating the forest from the trees, it all depends on your perspective. Wander around the annual meeting of CPAC, among the assembled monarchists, flat-taxers and religious activists, and you can soon become fixated on the differences that divide American conservatives. Stand back a little and look at George W. Bush's army from the perspective of London or Paris and you are struck by the distinctiveness of the faith that holds them together.

We think that the best way to understand the exceptional nature of American conservatism is through a religious metaphor—as a reformation. Not unlike the religious upheaval that Luther began five hundred years ago, American conservatism combines renewal with heresy. The established faith the Right Nation has reinterpreted is classical conservatism, and the heresy it has introduced is classical liberalism (or at least a good chunk of it). The result may not be a clean break with conservatism elsewhere, because most other forms of conservatism have had minireformations and counterreformations of their own, but it is nevertheless a very singular creed.

The starting point was the old established, unreformed church. Classical conservatism, as defined by Burke, was built upon six pillars: a deep suspicion of the power of the state; a preference for liberty over equality; love of country; a belief in established institutions and hierarchies; skepticism about progress; and elitism. As we explained in our introduction, American conservatism exaggerates the first three of these attributes, and subverts the last three. The result is a distinctive mixture of über-traditionalism and classical liberalism.

Begin with the traditionalism. This plays a galvanizing role in the Right Nation. Conservative footsoldiers, not to mention generals like Ashcroft and Bush, relish the manifestations of tradition in all its various forms, from religious worship to patriotic ceremonies, from voluntary organizations to family occasions. Visit a family meal in the red states and listen to the solemnity with which grace is said; or watch the way that families dress up for church. At the AEI dinner in 2003 where George Bush announced his plans to democratize the Middle East, he began the evening by asking his attorney general to sing the national anthem. Ashcroft obliged in a lusty baritone. Ashcroft's performance was followed by a trooping of the color, before Bush unveiled his grand strategy.

This would have delighted Burke for many reasons. He believed that individuals only flourish when they are enmeshed in a network of traditions and institutions. Weaken the social fabric, he argued, transform man into a mere atom of egoism, and he could well return to a primitive state. Yet American conservatives celebrate very different traditions from their European counterparts, traditions that are marinated in the egalitarianism and optimism of American culture. In Sinclair Lewis's *Main Street,* set in the Midwestern town of Gopher Prairie, one of his characters, Vida Sherwin, gives a good sense of what American traditionalism is all about:

> I'm afraid you'll think I'm a conservative. I am! So much to conserve. All this treasure of American ideals. Sturdiness and democracy and opportunity. Maybe not at Palm Beach. But, thank heaven, we are free from such social distinctions in Gopher Prairie. I have only one good quality—overwhelming belief in the brains and heart of our nation, our state, our town. . . .

Modern America has never had either an established church or a titled aristocracy—and the handful of American conservatives, like Russell Kirk, who hanker after the trappings of feudalism are barking (however eloquently) up the wrong tree. Real American conservatives put huge store on the symbols of the egalitarian nation that emerged from that revolution: on flags, pledges of allegiance and military ceremonies. American conservatives have an almost sacramental conception of their country. They regard it as a "promised land," a "sanctuary on earth for individual man," "the last best hope of man on earth" and, of course, "a city on a hill." For American conservatives America is not just a geographical reality; it is the material expression of a spiritual ideal. Ronald Reagan was perhaps the most articulate exponent of this elemental conservative belief. He believed that God had chosen America as the agent of His special purpose on earth. Because America embodied the democratic ideal, because it hoped to bring that ideal to the rest of the world, it was not condemned to decay, in the way that the Roman and British Empires had decayed.[9]

This highly nationalistic conservatism may be different from its European parent, but it is patently recognizable to classical European conservatives both in Britain and on the continent. Didn't the French and the British once argue that their countries were the manifestations of God's will on earth—and that they would defy all previous laws of political gravity? From a European perspective, American traditionalism has a bit too much democratic millenarianism and not quite enough noblesse oblige. But what can you expect from such a young version of an old religion?

We are all liberals now?

The difficulty for traditionalists comes when the faith of this young church moves from novel interpretations of old traditions to embracing heresy. Whichever way you look at it, American conservatism has embraced a great chunk of classical liberalism—so much of it in fact that many observers have argued that American conservatism was an oxymoron; that it was basically classical liberalism in disguise.

Classical liberalism has traditionally been the sworn enemy of conservatism, because it places the unfettered individual at the heart of its philosophy. Classical liberalism regards freedom as the ultimate good: classical conservatism is more interested in virtue. Liberalism is resolutely prochoice: conservatism worries about the sort of choices that people will make unless they are shaped by tradition and guided by wisdom. Liberalism is rooted in the Enlightenment: conservatism is rooted in a critique of the Enlightenment. "The age of chivalry is gone," lamented Edmund Burke. "The age of economists, sophists and calculators has arrived."

Here we have to be careful not to stereotype European conservatism as a stuck-in-the-mud philosophy. Lord Hugh Cecil compared his version of conservatism to a great river that draws its waters from many converging streams. In the nineteenth century the great river of British Toryism drew at least some of its water from liberalism. Conservatives abandoned the aristocratic argument that great landowners were the bulwark of liberty for the much more democratic argument that a property-owning democracy was the best bulwark of liberty. Conservatives such as Disraeli relentlessly labored to put liberal means to conservative ends—to reconnect property with responsibility and privilege with duty. The electoral genius of the British Conservative Party in the twentieth century was to identify itself with a sort of bourgeois "individualism lite," conceding what was necessary to the middle classes while ensuring that the landed elite continued to punch well above its weight. Most of the continental Christian Democratic parties have ended up in a similar place.

American conservatives did not so much make strategic concessions to individualism as embrace it with the lust of a young lover. Hayek, the John Calvin of the American conservative reformation, wrote an essay entitled "Why I am not a conservative," cursing the creed for worshiping the state and trying to constrain individuals. If the heroes of classical conservatism are usually defined by their relationship to tradition and community (what makes a gentleman a gentleman is a combination of his ancestry and his willingness to serve his local community as employer, justice of the peace and patron of charities), the heroes of modern American conservatism are usually rugged individualists: businesspeople who turned dreams into companies, homesteaders who brought civilization to a barren land and, once again, the cowboy. The late conservative academic Max Beloff and Irving Kristol once engaged in a debate about the use of titles that captured the difference between British Toryism and American conservatism. Kristol argued that Britain "is soured by a set of very thin, but tenacious aristocratic pretensions" which "foreclose opportunities and repress a spirit of equality that has yet to find its full expression." The result is that British life is both "cheerless" and "abounding in resentment." Beloff, who was intensely proud of being a life peer, retorted that what threatens conservatism in Britain "is not its remaining links with the aristocratic tradition, but its alleged indifference to some of the abuses of capitalism. It is not the dukes who lose us votes, but the 'malefactors of great wealth.'" He wondered why Kristol regarded himself as a "conservative" because he is "as incapable as most Americans of being a conservative in any profound sense." Conservatism must have an element of Toryism in it, Beloff concluded, or else there is nothing to it but "the Manchester school [of classical liberalism]."[10]

That element of Toryism is strikingly lacking in America's conservative movement. Look round the Right Nation and a remarkable number of conservative footsoldiers are obsessed with removing government's constraints on the individual. Gun enthusiasts dislike gun laws. Antitax activists want to take the government's hands out of people's pockets. Religious conservatives want to help people escape from the intrusion of the secular state—particularly when it comes to the education of their children. "What I really need," croons Montgomery Gentry, a country music duo who are hugely popular in the Right Nation, "is an open road and a whole lot of speed."

The most striking thing to an outsider about both Ronald Reagan and George W. Bush is their overwhelming sense of purpose and self-confidence, a purpose and self-confidence that come from a firm conviction that the future is on their side. The great preoccupations of classical conservatism have been managing decline and staging dignified retreats. Twentieth-century Britain's greatest Tory novelist, Evelyn Waugh, set off on his honeymoon with Oswald Spengler's *Decline of the West* in his suitcase, called his first novel *Decline and Fall* and got ever more pessimistic with age. Enoch Powell, a Conservative politician, once stated flatly that "all political lives end in failure, because that is the nature of politics and of human affairs."[11] Over the past quarter century, only one European conservative could proclaim that "There is no alternative" and really mean it. And Margaret Thatcher increasingly looks like an aberration—an American conservative who happened to be born in Grantham rather than Houston.

Many European conservatives have been resolutely opposed to the "spirit of innovation," both in the trivial sense of the worship of change for its own sake and in the more profound sense of the belief that the world can be remade anew. Disraeli said that "there are so many plans and so many schemes—and so many reasons why there should be neither plans nor schemes."[12] R. A. Sayce, an Oxford don of the old school, argued that "all change is for the worst, even change for the better."[13] Lord Percy of Newcastle, a conservative minister of education in the 1930s, once explained his opposition to new-fangled ideas for improving education: "nonsense, nonsense; a child ought to be brought up to *expect unhappiness.*"[14] More recently, Michael Oakeshott, that quintessentially Tory philosopher, derided innovation as "almost always an equivocal enterprise, in which gain and loss are so closely interwoven that it is extremely difficult to forecast the final upshot: there is no such thing as an unqualified improvement."[15]

European conservatism is as permeated with nostalgia as *Brideshead Revisited.* Sages such as Burke and Louis de Bonald saw the good society not in some utopian future but in the medieval past, with its feudal code of chivalry, its cult of the gentleman and its pervasive religiosity. These days practical politicians no longer mourn the passing of feudalism, of course. But they are nevertheless inclined to nostalgia. The best-known slogan of John Major, the circus acrobat's son who fought his way to the top of the Tory party, was "Back to Basics." When asked to talk about England, he waxed lyrical about rural cricket matches and "the spinster cycling to communion through the morning mist."[16]

American conservatism certainly does not despise history. Lou Cannon, Reagan's best biographer, has pointed out that one of the secrets of the fortieth president's appeal was his ability to talk about the future in the accents of the past. George W. Bush returns to Crawford, Texas, every summer to remind people that he is in touch with eternal American values. Yet American conservatism is nevertheless suffused with optimism. Ronald Reagan (who hardly ever looked glum in his life) was fond of quoting Tom Paine's adage that "We have it in our power to begin the world over again." Newt Gingrich believed that what made Republicans unbeatable was their willingness to embrace the future (leaving Democrats clinging to the old economy). Conservatism flourishes most luxuriously not in the historical centers of America but in the newest bits: in the suburbs and exurbs that spring up on the edges of America's cities, particularly in the Sun Belt. It is fitting that

Paul Weyrich came up with the name of the Heritage Foundation when he noticed a sign on a vacant lot: "Coming Soon: Heritage Town Houses."[17]

In Waugh's world, technology was the enemy: the only gadget he seemed to have warmed to was an ear-trumpet—and that only because it gave him a chance to dispense with it conspicuously, when bored. By contrast, Gingrich condemned the Left for rejecting "any hope of salvation through technological innovation." This obsession with technology goes into overdrive when it comes to outer space. American conservatives' willingness to spend public money on projects seems to be inversely related to those projects' distance from the surface of the earth. In the same week that Walter Mondale, an eat-your-spinach Democrat if ever there was one, questioned the costs of the manned space program, Reagan called for its continuance: "The American people would rather reach for the stars than reach for excuses why we shouldn't."[18] George W. Bush has not allowed the little matter of a deficit to stop America planning to send a man to Mars.

American conservatism has a downright Promethean edge. The English Tory Oakeshott argued that "to be conservative . . . is to prefer the familiar to the unknown, to prefer the tried to the untried, fact to mystery, the actual to the possible, the limited to the unbounded, the near to the distant . . . the convenient to the perfect, present laughter to utopian bliss."[19] American conservatism is almost the opposite of Oakeshott's creed: an activist philosophy tinged with utopianism. Forget about learning to live with present imperfection; American conservatives cannot see an imperfection without trying to fix it. Gingrich once reminded people that the phrase "the pursuit of happiness" includes an active verb. "Not happiness stamps, not a department of happiness, not therapy for happiness. Pursuit."[20]

American conservatives believe in man's ability to transform the world for the better. They have no sympathy with old-fashioned conservatism's preoccupation with constraints and scarcity. At a campaign stop on Ohio in 1984, Reagan denounced Mondale for offering "a future of pessimism, fear and limits."[21] (Almost all intelligent argument about how you deal with limited resources takes place on the Left in America). Some of the most Republican parts of America are also some of the least welcoming—rescued from a harsh and unforgiving nature by the sheer force of human will. If he had lived in a godforsaken place like Waco, Texas, rather than London, Oakeshott might have had second thoughts about preferring present laughter to utopian bliss. Irving Kristol points out that, when he published an American edition of Oakeshott's *Rationalism in Politics,* the book from which the passage is quoted, it sold a mere six hundred copies.[22]

Trying to claim American conservatism as a subset of one Old World creed or another misses the point, which is that they have all got mixed up into something new and American. The main ingredients of American conservatism—the übertraditionalism and individualism—are, we would argue, pretty exceptional. But what really makes American conservatism distinctive from other creeds is the way these two elements have mixed together.

THE LACK OF A HARD RIGHT

It is also worth adding one final aspect of conservative exceptionalism for which even liberal Americans should be grateful: the marginalization of the Far Right. In many ways mainstream American conservatism is more extreme than European conservatism: more hard-edged, more populist, more willing to flirt with gun enthusiasts and antigovernment activists. Yet America has been much more successful than Europe—particularly continental Europe—at keeping the radical Right under control.

In the 1950s Richard Hofstadter wrung his hands about "the paranoid style in American politics." Yet this "paranoid style" never produced a fascist movement comparable with the one in Europe. Europeans habitually accuse George W. Bush of being a right-wing extremist. Yet Bush has never had any truck with the standard fare of radical right-wing ideology. He is pro-immigration (insanely so by the standards of even moderate European conservatives). In his first major speech on foreign policy he warned that giving in to the temptation "to build a proud tower of protectionism and isolation" would be a shortcut to chaos and stagnation.[23] Far from being tinged with anti-Semitism, his party has been criticized for being passionately pro-Israel.

It is undoubtedly true that America has produced a vigorous militia movement that carries the country's hostility to government and infatuation with firearms to lunatic extremes. It is also true that some elements in the Republican Party have periodically been seized by paranoia: think of McCarthyism or the wilder shores of Clintonophobia. Yet, in general, America's two-party system has been as successful at marginalizing the Far Right as it has been at emasculating the Far Left.

The most violent component of the American hard Right—the militia movement— is in steep decline. The number of militias fell from a high of 858 in 1996 to 143 in 2003, according to the Southern Poverty Law Center (which follows their activities), and the remaining groups are mere shadows of their former selves, weak, disoriented and disorganized. In 2001, for example, the Northern Michigan Regional Militia (which once attracted Timothy McVeigh and Terry Nichols to its meetings) was dissolved because it didn't have any members with enough military experience to lead training exercises in the woods. Many militia members simply got tired of waiting, surrounded by automatic weapons, tins of canned food and bottles of water, for a revolution that never came. The failure of Y2K to bring about the collapse of western civilization was a particularly heavy blow.

The rapid decline in the militias seems to have coincided with a small rise in neo-Nazi activity. The Southern Poverty Law Center reckons there are now 700 hate organizations, with more than 100,000 members, the highest count for 20 years.[24] Yet the American neo-Nazi movement is less bloodcurdling than it sounds: its leaders are old and frail, and it has faced a string of legal assaults. By most estimates the neo-Nazi movement has proportionately more supporters in Germany, Hungary, Poland, the Czech Republic and Sweden than in the United States. One in ten young Swedes reportedly listens to "white power" music. There are similar movements—skinheads, nativists, anti-Semites—in virtually every European country.

The Far Right "Preachers of Hate," to borrow the title of a recent book, have enjoyed much more electoral success in Europe than they have in the United States.[25] In 2003, the Swiss People's Party won 26.6 percent of the popular vote, giving it more seats in the lower house of parliament than any of the three mainstream parties. One of the party's election posters showed a black face with the caption "The Swiss are becoming Negroes." Jean-Marie Le Pen's National Front remains a considerable force in French politics: in the first round of the 2002 presidential election it won 18 percent of the vote, propelling Le Pen into a runoff against Jacques Chirac, who won easily. In 1999 Jorg Haider's Freedom Party came second in Austria's general election, with 27 percent of the votes, and became part of the governing coalition in Austria. In Holland Pim Fortuyn, a maverick right-winger who worried that Muslims were undermining his country's traditions of tolerance, finished second in the polls as well—albeit posthumously. Silvio Berlusconi has made room in his government for Gianfranco Fini, the leader of the former Fascists. By contrast, Pat Buchanan, the most right-wing candidate to run for the American presidency in recent years (and certainly mild stuff when compared with either Le Pen or Haider), got only 0.5 percent of the vote in 2000.

A Utopia of their own

"What matters most about political ideas is the underlying emotions," Sir Lewis Namier once wrote, "the music to which ideas are a mere libretto, often of a very inferior quality." One can go on forever pointing out ideological reasons why American conservatism is different from its equivalents around the world. But in many ways conservatism is a matter of instincts, not reason. One of the hallmarks of modern American conservatism is the tendency of conservative-minded Americans to stumble across structures that epitomize their creed, without even realizing the radicalism of their actions. There is no better place to hear the music of American conservatism than in the country's fast-proliferating planned communities.

Head north out of Phoenix, Arizona, up the I-17 interstate. Drive past the signs for Happy Valley Road and Carefree Highway and, less auspiciously, one advising you not to pick up hitchhikers because you are passing a federal prison. Eventually you come to one for "Anthem by Del Webb." Anthem feels more like a luxury holiday resort than a town. It includes a water park with Disneyesque waterslides, a children's railway, hiking trails, tennis courts, a rock-climbing wall, two golf courses, several spotless parks, a supermarket mall, two churches, a school and, for those who want a little more security, the Anthem Country Club, a gated (and guarded) community.

Anthem, which is planned to have 12,500 homes, opened in 1999. Its houses and roads look spotless. One reason for this is that everybody who buys a house in Anthem has to follow certain covenants, conditions and restrictions (CC&Rs), governing everything from the color of your house to whether you can put your car on blocks outside it (you can't). Everybody in Anthem seems to be white, with the obvious exception of the construction workers, but it is certainly not an exclusive enclave for the rich. Far from it: homes start at a distinctly modest $155,000. Even the residents of the Anthem Country Club hardly seem posh. They tend to laugh at the rules, regarding them, like the long commute to Phoenix, as part of the price. Why did one young mother come here? "Because it's safe, because there are activities, because it's, well, like us."

Indeed, Anthem is not bucking a trend, but joining it. In many of the fastest-growing parts of America, particularly the South and the West, development is being driven by "master-planned communities" of one sort or another. In big cities half the new home sales are in association-managed communities. Altogether, some 47 million people—one in six Americans— live in 18 million homes in 230,000 communities and pay around $35 billion in fees every year. Now the industry is preparing itself for some 70 million retiring baby boomers.

It would be wrong to claim that all such associations are conservative. There are gated communities that prove inviting for black rap stars (in Baton Rouge, Louisiana) and for gays (in Manitoba Springs, Florida). Even retirement communities can be racier than they first appear: in 2000 there were two dozen complaints about couples having sex outdoors at one of Anthem's Arizonan neighbors, Sun City West, the average age of the offenders being seventy-three.[26] And despite the common image of dogs and fences, only around 8 million people live in communities that have gates. But the prevailing tone is conservative. Planned communities tend to be Republican strongholds (Anthem votes that way by margins of close to two to one). They also embody a certain hostility to government. Sometimes this is transparent. In Nevada, a fifty-five-acre community called Front Sight, featuring streets with names like Second Amendment Drive and Sense of Duty Way, is being built for gun enthusiasts (people who buy an acre plot get lifetime use of the twenty-two planned ranges, an Uzi machine gun and a safari in Africa). But more generally the motive is secession: the desire to set up a society within a society. Many of the people who live in planned communities are deeply distrustful of government. The most common worry is security (hence all those gates, though there is not much evidence that gated communities are safer than nongated ones). But there are also concerns about education, health care, transport: everything the public sector is supposed to provide. The residents often tax themselves to provide services that are usually provided by the state. Some residents have to cough up for maintaining the roads, pavements and streetlights, looking after the parks and providing security.

It cannot be coincidental that community associations took off in California in the 1970s, the same decade as the passing of Proposition 13, which cut taxes for local government. And their growth has also coincided with that of private schools and private security guards; the latter now outnumber the "public" police by four to one in Southern California. A growing part of the American middle class is abandoning the state: living on private roads, sending their children to private schools, paying for their own private police force, playing golf at private clubs. Why bother supporting public services when you get all yours delivered privately? Some elderly gated communities have voted not to let public schools within their walls. The CC&Rs represent a form of privatized legal system. Many just govern how you sell your house. But the lists of rules seem to be getting longer. A maximum size for dogs—usually thirty pounds—is increasingly common. The CC&Rs trump a good deal of municipal law (for instance, in terms of property-sales contracts). Even more powerful, a community can set rules about who is allowed to live in it. Many of the retirement towns require at least one person in each house to be fifty-five or older, and exclude children.

The spread of the secessionist utopias like Anthem may cause America all sorts of social problems. What about all those poorer people, stuck with public housing, public schools and public transport? But they are also breeding grounds for conservative footsoldiers. It is not just a case of self-interest (why pay for public schools if your children go to private ones), but of ideology. American liberalism is entwined in government; yet the fastest-growing part of the housing market is based on the idea of secession from the government. That is a conspiracy to keep America conservative that should make Hillary truly despair.

AN ALL-AMERICAN CREED

The fundamental fact about American conservatism is not just that it is conservatism but that it is *American*. Conservatism in the United States is like an immigrant who has been so thoroughly assimilated that his European relatives can hardly recognize him any longer. In particular, American conservatism has absorbed three of the most pervasive characteristics of the country: its optimism, its individualism and its uncomplicated faith in capitalism. And in absorbing these ideas it has rejected—or forgotten—some of the most essential beliefs of European conservatism: skepticism, pessimism and belief in social hierarchy.

In 1890 Friedrich Engels argued that the success of American conservatism lay in its freedom from the trappings of feudalism. Americans, he argued, "are born conservatives—just because America is so purely bourgeois, so entirely without a feudal past and therefore proud of its purely bourgeois organization."[27] Today's European conservative parties are more likely to be decked out in the trappings of social democracy than feudalism. But today's American conservatives remain just as "purely bourgeois" and just as proud as they were in the 1890s of the bourgeois organization of society. That accounts for both their difference from European conservatives and their continued success.

America is in a particularly partisan mood at the moment, with the bestseller lists dominated by partisan screeds and political leaders all but calling their rivals traitors. But it is important to remember that these raging partisans have more in common than they think. We have already seen that conservatism has been transformed by what might be called Americanism. Now we need to look at the way that liberalism is being transformed by the same force.

CHAPTER 15

THE MELANCHOLY
LONG WITHDRAWING ROAR
OF LIBERALISM

In his great poem, "Dover Beach," Matthew Arnold lamented that although Victorian England was full of people who paid lip service to the Christian faith, religion itself was in retreat.

> The Sea of Faith
> Was once, too, at the full, and round earth's shore
> Lay like the folds of a bright girdle furl'd
> But now I only hear
> Its melancholy, long, withdrawing roar.

The sound that we have been hearing in the background of American political life for the past thirty years is the melancholy, long, withdrawing roar of liberalism. Lest there be any confusion, we do not mean the classical liberalism we talked about in our last chapter, but the big-government American variety. Such leftish liberals exist in the modern United States, to be sure, but their creed has lost its sway over the country; indeed, it is the absence of any cogent left-wing movement that does as much as anything else to make America such an exceptional place. The victory of the Right only becomes fully apparent once you look at what has happened to the Left.

There are still a heck of a lot of leftish people in America. In 1984, even the feeble Walter Mondale managed to capture 41 percent of the vote.

Moreover, liberals still dominate many of the most prominent bits of the country, including the universities, the media and the coastal cities that attract the most foreign visitors. As even some conservatives admit, liberals hold court in most of the nicer bits of urban America from Brentwood to Bleecker Street, plenty of the more desirable vacation spots from Sausalito to Cape Cod and almost everywhere where the waist is an identifiable part of the body (the red states are against a lot of things, but second helpings are not among them). Liberals powered Michael Moore to the top of the best-seller list and, for a while, Howard Dean to the front of the Democratic pack in the 2004 presidential race.

And in one significant political arena, the Democrats have got more lib-eral. Just as congressional Republicans have become more conservative since the mid-1970s, congressional Democrats have tipped the other way. In 1972, the American Conservative Union gave the Democrats in the House of Rep-resentatives an average score of 32; by 2002 it was just 13 (see Appendix). In 1972, Dixiecrats in Georgia (average score 83), Virginia (84) and Mississippi (90) had higher conservative scores than most Northeastern Republicans. Now only one state—Kentucky—has an average Democratic score higher than 41, and that is because Kentucky's lone Democrat, the progun, prolife, protobacco Ken Lucas, who gets an 84 rating, is a Republican in everything other than name (he nobly skipped the Democratic Convention in Los Ange-les in 2000, because he didn't want to be a distraction from "party unity").[1]

As recently as the 1980s, Southern conservatives still hogged many of the most powerful positions in the Democratic Party hierarchy by dint of sen-iority. Today they have been replaced by card-carrying liberals from the left and right coasts, such as Nancy Pelosi, the House minority leader, whose San Francisco district we look at in our conclusion. In the Senate, that lion of lib-eralism, Ted Kennedy, is probably the most powerful Democratic senator. He was first elected to the Senate in 1962, and is now its most senior mem-ber, after Robert Byrd, another veteran Democrat. Having analyzed the vot-ing behavior of the 106th Congress, which ended in 2002, Gary Jacobson of the University of California, San Diego, calculated that it was the most ideo-logically divided since before the First World War.[2]

This growing partisanship in Congress reflects a growing divide in the country at large. If the Right has its hate figures, like Hillary Clinton, so too does the Left. Many modern Democrats do not simply disagree with George W. Bush: they loathe everything about him from (as they see it) his Neanderthal views to his self-satisfied smirk. Bush's average approval rating among Democrats, based on 111 polls up till September 2003, was 51.7 percent, compared with a Republican figure of 94 percent, but this was skewed by the September 11 effect. Before that date, his average score with Democrats was a paltry 30 percent, against 89 percent from Republicans.[3] And once the September 11 sheen wore off, the gap returned with a vengeance: by the summer of 2003 Bush was still regularly scoring more than 90 percent from Republicans, but his Democratic figure had fallen to as low as 16 percent—leaving a partisan gap between the two figures far wider than even that achieved by Bill Clinton.[4]

So there is no doubt that there are plenty of *liberals* in America. There is equally no doubt that those liberals are desperate to get the Republicans out of power. But *liberalism* as a governing philosophy is dead. The success of American liberalism was based on its ability to solve problems. The New Deal not only tackled the Depression, it created a constituency for activist government. By 1952 registered Democrats outnumbered Republicans by two to one. According to Harry Hopkins, one of FDR's closest advisors, his party had discovered the perfect formula for perpetual power: "tax and tax, spend and spend, elect and elect." But for the past thirty years this formula has been failing. Americans no longer rally to the standard of activist government, in the way that they did in the 1960s, or in the way that Europeans continue to do. Witness the ever-declining numbers of Americans who think the government can be relied upon to do the right thing. (In 1994 one Democratic official in Montgomery County, Maryland, even announced a plan to drop the word "government" from official usage because it was "off-putting" and "arrogant.")[5] Witness the way that Bill Clinton helped to dismantle government programs.[6]

Any hope of liberal America breaking out of that stranglehold is limited by what might be called the rule of the two-thirds: only one-third of the population these days wears the Democratic label, and only one-third of those Democrats describe themselves as liberals.[7] (By contrast, two-thirds of Republicans describe themselves as conservatives.) New Democrats have captured the governorships of conservative states such as New Mexico, Arizona and Kansas, but they have done so only by dint of sacrificing their ancestral liberalism—by sounding as tough as General Patton and as mainstream as Wal-Mart. Janet Napolitano (in Arizona) and Kathleen Sebelius (in Kansas) produced tough-minded solutions to educational and fiscal problems. In New Mexico, Bill Richardson cut the state's income tax and capital gains tax. Up in Michigan, Jennifer Granholm has stuck to her "no new taxes" pledge and struck a robust pose when confronted by civil disorder. The reaction of Phil Bredesen, the new governor of Tennessee, to his state's budget deficit in 2003 was typical: round up all the department chiefs, tell them to cut spending by 9 percent and make them explain their policies in a public forum.

WHY KERRY AND DEAN ARE ON OUR SIDE

There is a stock rejoinder to this death-of-liberalism pessimism on the Left: What if the Democrats win the presidency in 2004? Well, that is certainly possible, given the daily slaughter of American troops in Iraq and widespread worries about economic insecurity. But would a Democratic victory really invalidate our overall point about conservatism sitting at the heart of American exceptionalism? To the contrary, we think it would swiftly be seen to underscore it. Even with a Democrat in the White House, America would remain a more conservative place than any of its peers in the West.

The battle for the 2004 Democratic nomination was in itself something of "a long withdrawing roar." A good place to begin is a hot Saturday afternoon in August 2003 at Falls Church, Virginia. The roads around the suburb were clogged with cars—and nobody was happier than Joe Trippi. Seven months before, the veteran consultant was running a presidential campaign with seven volunteers and a mere $150,000 in the bank. Trippi often had to dispatch his candidate unaccompanied to speaking engagements, to save airfares. Now 4,500 people had turned up at short notice in a Virginia suburb—and $350,000 had just come in over the Internet that morning.

The meteoric rise of Howard Dean, the former governor of Vermont, was one of the most exciting things in American politics in years. It is not unusual for some maverick to cause unexpected turbulence for the front-runner in the primaries: John McCain did it spectacularly in New Hampshire in 2000. But this time Dean transformed himself into the front-runner. By August, he led the main establishment candidate, John Kerry, by twenty-one points in New Hampshire, and he was raising far more money than any other candidate. By December he had collected $40 million, not to mention the endorsements of Al Gore and several of America's largest unions.

The Dean rebellion was testament to two forces. The first is the power of the Internet, which he used to gather volunteers and money. The second is the power of liberal activists in the Democratic Party. Dean purloined a slogan from the late Paul Wellstone, claiming that he represented "the Democratic wing of the Democratic Party"—the wing that was furious with its leaders, like Senator Kerry, for going along with everything George Bush did. This went down well with hard-core Democrats, who to put it simply were pig-wrestling mad. They were mad about the "stolen" election, mad about tax cuts, mad about the USA Patriot Act and mad, above all, about the Iraq War. No sooner had Dean sounded his trumpet against that conflict than he had an army at his back.

Howard Brush Dean was in fact a fairly odd champion for American liberalism. He came from a similar background to that of George W. Bush (indeed Bush's grandmother acted as a bridesmaid to Dean's grandmother). His father was a Wall Street banker and loyal Republican (the young Dean's first experience of national politics was visiting the 1964 national convention that nominated Goldwater). He grew up on Park Avenue and Long Island. He was educated at St. George's, Prescott Bush's old school, and Yale University.

As the governor of America's most liberal state, Vermont, for eleven years, the doctor-turned-politician was hardly a left-winger by European standards: a pragmatic New Democrat who resisted irresponsible spending increases, consistently backed business interests, denounced welfare recipients for lacking self-esteem and devoted a great deal of energy to muzzling the local Far Left (Vermont is one of the few states where such an entity is a real political force: it has the only socialist congressman, Bernie Sanders). Dean was equally conservative on cultural issues: he won the top rating from the National Rifle Association for championing Vermonters' right to carry concealed guns and became a convert to the death penalty at a time when even Republican governors were expressing doubts about it.

Even during his insurrectionary presidential campaign, he remained loyal to some of his conservative principles. He sold himself as a "deficit hawk" and "balanced budget fiend." He proudly proclaimed that he wanted to be the candidate of "guys with Confederate flags in their pickup trucks," although he later withdrew the remark after a barrage of criticism from his rivals. His health care plan was much more market-driven than Hillary Clinton's 1994 scheme, and much cheaper than Dick Gephardt's 2004 plan ($88 billion compared with $214 billion). On foreign policy, he reminded his supporters that, yes, he opposed the war in Iraq, but he quickly added that he supported both the first Gulf War and the Afghanistan campaign, and at Falls Church promised he would "never hesitate" to send American troops "anywhere in the world to defend our country." America, said Dean, has a right to launch a preemptive attack against the threat posed by a rogue regime that possesses weapons of mass destruction; he just didn't think that Iraq possessed such weapons.

The man who got left-wing America on the march held views on all sorts of controversial subjects that would have disqualified him from left-of-center politics in Europe. He was a firm supporter of Israel.[8] He opposed the Kyoto Protocol. He supported the intervention in Liberia, and he mocked Bush for not being tough enough on Saudi Arabia. Indeed, Dean said that thirty years ago, he would have been an Eisenhower Republican. "It's kind of a sad commentary that I'm the most progressive candidate running, out here talking about a balanced budget and a health care system run by the private sector," he told the *New York Times.* "I was a triangulator before Clinton was a triangulator. In my soul, I'm a moderate."[9] A young Swedish Deaniac who one of us came across working for Dean in Iowa protested that, back home in Sweden, his candidate would be regarded as a "middle-of-the-road conservative."

Dean succeeded in turning himself into a champion of the Democratic Left not by renouncing his middle-of-the-road views across the board but by butting heads with the Bush administration on two polarizing issues—his opposition to the war in Iraq and his determination to repeal all the Bush tax cuts. Dean's Goldwaterish determination to offer a choice, not an echo, dragged most of the establishment Democratic candidates smartly to the left. Kerry, the very embodiment of establishmentarianism, said that the last thing the country needed "was a second Republican Party." John Edwards, a senator from North Carolina, revived Al Gore's Dixified populism with an added dose of protectionism. Nice old Bob Graham, normally a model of senatorial civility, suddenly started talking about Bush's impeachment, before he dropped out due to lack of cash. Wesley Clark joined the clamor over the Iraq War. Only Joe Lieberman stood firm against the left-wing wind.

For a while the nomination looked as if it was Dean's for the asking. Thousands of young volunteers tramped the highways and byways of Iowa and New Hampshire rallying supporters and spreading the message of resurgent liberalism. "Please nominate this man," pleaded the cover of the *National Review.* But when the voters turned their attention from venting their anger to choosing a candidate who could beat Bush they pulled back sharply from Dean's brand of angry liberalism. In mid-January, a Gallup poll found that only one in four Democrats wanted their party to nominate a "liberal."[10] As the Iowa caucuses approached, Dean's unyielding opposition to Bush's foreign policy began to count against him. His refusal to admit that Saddam Hussein's capture had made America any safer combined with his insistence that Osama bin Laden could only be pronounced guilty after a (possibly international) trial gave new weight to the idea that the Democrats were in the process of repeating the mistake of 1972—and choosing a second McGovern.

The Iowa caucuses turned out to be a humiliation for the "Democratic wing of the Democratic Party." Dean finished third, behind not just Kerry but also Edwards who, like Kerry, had voted in favor of the Iraq War and refused to cancel the bulk of Bush's tax cuts. After all the sound and fury, four in five Iowa caucus-goers endorsed candidates who voted at least to authorize the American strike against Iraq. The second casualty of the evening was the other prominent liberal—though this time a representative of the blue-collar rather than the college-campus Left. Dick Gephardt had stood on a populist message of erecting protectionist barriers, jacking up public spending on health care and introducing a higher minimum wage. The congressman retired from politics after coming in a humiliating fourth.

Dean's setback in Iowa was compounded by a bizarre speech after his defeat, ending in a banshee-like scream of defiance, which only solidified the impression that he was more interested in venting than in governing. Suddenly, the campaign was dominated by the question of "electability"—with liberal America trying to guess which candidate would be least offensive to the more conservative population at large. Kerry repeated his success in New Hampshire, winning more than half the votes of those people who tried to pick the man most likely to beat Bush. Dean finished twelve points behind a notoriously wooden senator whom he had been leading by twenty points only a few weeks earlier—and promptly sacked Trippi as his campaign manager.

Wesley Clark's dismal third-place performance was also a blow to the party's liberal wing. A newcomer to politics, the previously Republican general had tried to present himself as an electable version of Dean, parading his military credentials ("I won a war") while relentlessly pandering to the party's liberal base. He garnered the endorsements of activists such as Ted Danson and Michael Moore (and he pointedly failed to repudiate Moore's assertion that Bush was a deserter from the American army). He agreed with the principle of a woman's right to choose even up to the "head coming out of the womb." Yet this failed to translate into votes. For all its anger at Bush, the Democratic electorate wanted to choose an electable moderate rather than an ideological firebrand—or a facsimile of an ideological firebrand. And that electable moderate was clearly John Kerry.

Naturally, political afficionados, particularly conservative ones in the White House, have rushed to point out that the junior senator from Massachusetts actually possesses a much more "liberal" political record than Dean (at least until the Vermont governor started running for president). Kerry burst on the political scene as a leader of the antiwar movement in the early 1970s, when the Nixon White House collected "opposition" material on him. He was Massachusetts's lieutenant governor under Michael Dukakis. As a senator, he has espoused liberal views on every subject under the sun, from partial-birth abortion to the death penalty, offending even against Americans' God-given right to cheap gas by advocating a fifty-cent increase in the gas tax; he has also called for "unpatriotic" cuts in funding for the FBI and

362 • THE RIGHT NATION

restrictions on the CIA. Americans for Democratic Action, the leading liberal rating organization, gave Kerry a higher approval rating (93 percent) than Ted Kennedy (88 percent). "Who would have guessed it?" crowed Ed Gillespie, the chairman of the Republican National Committee, "Ted Kennedy is the conservative senator from Massachusetts!" Other Republicans stress that Kerry is another representative of the European wing of the Democratic Party, even thinking that he is suspiciously "French-looking." "Good morning," the House majority leader, Tom DeLay, told a group of delighted College Republicans in August 2003. "Or as John Kerry would say, 'Bonjour.'"

Rove's minions will hurl such accusations—and much, much more—at Kerry in the 2004 campaign in an effort to depict him as Dukakis reborn, and they may very well succeed. But Kerry's long voting record needs to be set against two things. The first is that he presented himself as the centrist alternative to Dean: a man who had voted in favor of the Iraq War and who believed in preserving at least some of the Bush tax cuts. He savagely attacked Dean's fitness for the position of commander in chief when the Vermonter said that America wouldn't always have the world's most powerful military. He claimed that his politics owed more to the Teddy Roosevelt "let's make the market fair" tradition than to left-wing populism.[11] If Dean, the former centrist, exploded onto the scene by pulling the party to the Left, Kerry, the Massachusetts liberal, won the nomination by pulling it back to the center.

Second, far from accentuating his past as a war protester, Kerry won the nomination in large part by stressing his record as a warrior. He constantly reminded people that he was a decorated Vietnam veteran who risked his life for his fellow soldiers in the Mekong Delta. This was partly a criticism of the Bush administration: Kerry argued that one reason the administration was so keen on going to war was that it was full of "chicken hawks" who had run away from Vietnam. He got some of his loudest applause on the stump when he boasted how he knew "something about aircraft carriers for real." But it was about more than just Bush-bashing. Kerry wanted to show that he was tough enough to deal with a difficult world of terrorism and rogue states. He would not send men to war precipitously, as the Bush administration had; but he would never hesitate to do so if he thought it was necessary for America's security.

Kerry rammed this point home by surrounding himself on the stump with firefighters and veterans, the very embodiments of all-American masculinity, and by emphasizing his enthusiasm for macho sports such as ice hockey, wind-surfing and killing wildlife with a gusto that even the Nicholas Soames wing of the Tory Party might find a little adventurous.[12] "I love dove," he enthused to the *Washington Post*. "You clean them. Let them hang. It takes three or four birds to have a meal. You might eat it at a picnic, cold roasted."[13] He then launched into a detailed description of how to prepare a deer (you carve out the heart, pull out the entrails and then cut out the meat).

Indeed, far from recognizing a kindred spirit, as DeLay implied, it is hard to imagine any European mistaking Kerry for a left-winger (or, indeed, for a Frenchman). Kerry wasted no time in telling people that he would not hesitate to execute terrorists, and he too has a list of countries that Bush was not nearly nasty enough toward. Kerry has supported most American military actions since the Vietnam war—Bosnia, Kosovo, Panama, Somalia, Haiti and, of course, the Iraq War.

European liberals would also be struck by another thing about Kerry: his extreme personal wealth. Kerry is the richest member of a Senate that is stuffed full of rich men and women: a New England blueblood (his middle name is Forbes) whose wife, Teresa Heinz, inherited a fortune of more than half a billion dollars from her first husband, John Heinz III, a Republican senator and heir to the ketchup fortune. Kerry was educated at a Swiss boarding school before going on to St. Paul's boarding school and to Yale University (where he joined the Skull and Bones Society, just like three successive Bushes). During the darkest days of his presidential campaign he kept himself afloat by mortgaging his house in Boston for more than $6 million. Most European socialist parties have come a long way from the days when they consisted solely of horny-handed sons of toil. But few of them are led by preppie semibillionaires.

This background may explain why Kerry is actually an odd form of liberal. On closer examination of his voting record, his enthusiasm for the cause has often seemed similar to George H. W. Bush's enthusiasm for conservatism: it has been a means to an end. Kerry has ticked the right, or rather left, boxes, without much sign of engagement. He has neither tried to rethink liberalism, in the way that candidate Clinton tried to do in the early

1990s, nor identified himself passionately with any particular liberal cause. Rather his relationship with the main interest groups on the Left has been rather like that of Bush senior: unemotional loyalty, punctuated by an occasional yelp of protest, which is followed by rapid backtracking. For instance, at one point in the 1990s Kerry criticized the teachers' unions for blocking reforms, calling for an end to tenure "as we know it"; at another he suggested to minorities that affirmative action was no longer a great progressive crusade. On both occasions the ambitious senator retreated with his tail between his legs.

Indeed, the more you look at the nation's prominent Democrats from an international perspective, the less left-wing they seem. Dean's remark that he was more of an Eisenhower Republican than a red-blooded liberal might have been made by any of the leading candidates in 2004. None of them proposed any dramatic extension of government; most of them pushed positions that were firmly to the right of Michael Dukakis, let alone George McGovern. Edwards, another multimillionaire, got most of his financial support from his fellow trial lawyers—and stressed his appeal to white Southerners. Lieberman was even further to the Right—a religious moralist who condemned Bill Clinton's adultery, supported the Iraq War and, for a while, even made friendly noises about education vouchers. Clark had been a Republican before morphing into a left-wing Democrat in the frosts of New Hampshire. He boasted about voting for Reagan and, as recently as 2002, gave a speech praising Bush and encouraging people to back the GOP. (It is hard to imagine any left-of-center party in Europe turning to the army for its leader.)

Even the last great hope of American liberalism, Hillary Clinton, seems to have begun a voyage back to the center. She may remain La Pasionaria of the American Left, but ever since she has entered politics in her own right, she has quietly changed her tune, dropping her pro-Palestinian stance, speaking out in favor of tough welfare policies and decking herself in hawk's plumage. In the Senate, she cleverly joined the Armed Services Committee rather than sticking to her old stomping ground of health and welfare; and she has used that position to support rather than undermine the war on terrorism. When Donald Rumsfeld testified behind closed doors before the committee during the darkest moment in the Iraq War, he got some of his strongest support from the former first lady. She has also made highly publicized visits to see the troops in Afghanistan and Iraq. Even her mawkish memoir can be interpreted as a complicated piece of centrist politicking: the erstwhile derider of cookie-baking wives went out of her way to establish that the Clinton marriage was a traditional affair, not just some union of political convenience, and talked about her Methodism and even her teenage affection for Barry Goldwater. Like Kerry and the rest of them, she knows the importance of electability.

AND ONCE IN POWER?

To judge by his campaign, John Kerry is hardly a "European" president in the making. But once again, let's indulge the idea that he might try to lurch to the Left. What could a truly liberal President Kerry actually achieve? The answer surely is very little.

The most obvious constraint for an old-style liberal president would be the power of Congress, which looks likely to remain under Republican control. The Senate, where the Republicans hold only a 51–49 majority, will be a close call, but the Democrats are trying to defend nineteen seats, four more than the Republicans. Ten of the Democratic seats are in states that George W. Bush won in 2000, and in five of them the incumbent Democrats are retiring (Georgia's Zell Miller, North Carolina's John Edwards, South Carolina's Fritz Hollings, Florida's Bob Graham and Louisiana's John Breaux). By contrast only three of the Republican seats are in states that Al Gore won. In the House, most incumbents are pretty well protected thanks to yet another bout of gerrymandering after the 2000 census. The few new competitive seats look more likely to become Republican ones.

The second constraint on any Democratic president veering to the Left is money. In the 2000 election cycle an estimated $3 billion was spent on presidential and congressional races, and another $1 billion on state contests. No other country remotely comes close. The average cost of winning a single Senate seat, now $7.7 million, is half the amount the entire Labor

Party spent getting reelected in Britain in 2001.[14] The Democrats are marginally less addicted to corporate largesse than the K Street conservatives at the helm of the Republican Party, but only in the way that a cokehead is in less trouble than a heroin junkie. There are occasions—as with the Dean insurgency—when politicians can raise impressive sums of money from small donations. But insurgencies by their very nature can only happen when you break the normal rules of politics. As a machine, the Democratic Party relies on bigger contributions. The Democrats certainly get money from trade unions, but unions rank only about fifth on the list, behind a host of business interests: movie moguls, trial lawyers, real estate companies and investment bankers. And, Dean aside, the trend is to dig deeper into corporate pockets. One of Bill Clinton's great contributions to his party was to prove that the people's party could ransack business just as effectively as the Republicans. For instance, in the old battle of *Insurers v. Trial Lawyers,* Clinton milked the trial lawyers just as efficiently as the Republicans drained the insurers.

All this political money inevitably drags the Democrats to the Right. In most other countries, politics usually makes at least a bow to the classic Marxist struggle between capital and labor; in America, politics is, for the most part, about the struggle of one bit of capital against another. That is not to deny that politicians will occasionally vote against their better financial interests—as when the Congress voted to allow the reimportation of cheaper drugs from abroad in July 2003, despite a torrent of pharmaceutical money on the other side—but in the end the corporate givers need to get their nickel's worth. In 1996, the Clinton administration rewarded one of its biggest donors, the telecommunications industry, with $70 billion worth of free broadcasting spectrum—a gift that John McCain described as "one of the greatest rip-offs since the Teapot Dome Scandal."[15] The only time that Democrats seem able to break the grip of corporate money is when they find people rich enough to run with their own money. Thus Jon Corzine, a former head of Goldman Sachs, spent around $60 million of his fortune in his successful bid to become a senator from New Jersey. Tony Sanchez, whose money came from the energy business and banking, spent almost as much in his unsuccessful bid to become governor of Texas. People who make that sort of money are seldom inclined to redesign capitalism.

The third force that would frustrate any liberal president is what might be called the permanent Washington establishment: the people who live by the Potomac regardless of who occupies the White House. Howling about the liberal Beltway establishment has been a staple of right-wing life for years. But the days when conservatives left the capital for their businesses and ranches whenever they lost office are long gone. Washington is now home to a permanent conservative establishment powered by money and steeled by ideology: think tanks that can produce clever critiques of any policy at the drop of a hat; pundits to howl about liberal overreach in the *Washington Times* and on Fox. This conservative establishment was relentless in its persecution of Bill Clinton, a centrist Democrat; just imagine what it would do to a real liberal.

THE LINO PARTY

Most center-left parties have moved to the Right over the past decade or so: witness the transformation of Labor under Tony Blair. Yet the Democratic agenda is still downright conservative compared with any of their peers outside America. America's left-wing party still takes a more cavalier attitude to multilateral conventions abroad, and at home it would involve dramatically less government, less welfare and less taxation, and dramatically more religion, more punishment and more guns. These days, American politics is a sport played between the center Right against the Right. From an international perspective, Democrats are now LINOs—Liberals in Name Only.

The most vivid example of the exceptionalism of the American Democratic Party is its position on capital punishment. In most of the civilized world support for the death penalty is the prerogative of the lunatic fringe (and the lunatic Right at that). The European Union refuses to admit countries unless they renounce the practice. Capital punishment is banned (except in extreme cases such as treason) in 110 countries. The only countries to execute people on the American scale are China, Iran, Saudi Arabia and Congo; and the only other advanced country to sanction the death penalty is Japan. Fledgling democracies routinely ban it as a way of proving their fitness to join the commonwealth of respectable nations: when Nelson Mandela came to power in South Africa, one of the first things he did was to abolish the practice. America's penchant for executions has long been a source of friction with other advanced countries—not least because of the lousy defense that many accused are offered. One prominent Swiss newspaper marked George W. Bush's inauguration by printing all the photographs it could find of the 152 prisoners who were executed in Texas during his governorship. Jack Lang, one of France's best-known politicians, even called Bush "a murderer."

Why doesn't Democratic America feel the same way? After all, opposing capital punishment could be seen as part of a great American tradition. Michigan outlawed the practice in 1846 when it was common in European countries. Getting rid of this supposedly barbaric Southern practice was one of the great aims of the liberal establishment in the 1960s. Moreover, by many objective standards, America's machinery of death is badly broken. The system is hopelessly capricious, something that ought to scandalize a party that contains so many lawyers. A Texan criminal is far more likely to pay the ultimate price than a Californian. More than one hundred people who were put on death row since the death penalty was reintroduced in 1976 have been exonerated. The system is also biased against the poor and minorities, the very people that Democrats claim they are in politics to help. Poor defendants are much more likely to have incompetent lawyers. In one notorious case in Texas, the defense lawyer fell asleep on the job; in another, the counsel for the defense turned out to be a part-timer who also ran a bar, Buster's Drinkery.

Yet there is precious little sign of the Democrats changing their mind. Granted, the most unambiguously liberal thing about John Kerry is that he opposes the death penalty, except for terrorists. But as a presidential candidate he has made rather more of the exception than of the principle. More typical is the example of Rod Blagojevich, who became governor of Illinois in 2003—and promptly denounced the decision by his maverick Republican predecessor, George Ryan, to commute 167 life sentences (Ryan had been worried by the faultiness of the trial system). George W. Bush is always linked with the death penalty, but Bill Clinton oversaw the most dramatic increase in killing of any president. During the 1990s, the number of executions in the

United States climbed almost fivefold, and the number of states conducting executions more than doubled, from thirteen to thirty-two. In 1996, in the wake of the Oklahoma City bombing, Clinton signed something called the Antiterrorism and Effective Death Penalty Act. In the 1998 California governor's election, Gray Davis chided his Republican opponent, Dan Lungren, with insufficient zeal in death penalty cases. "If your people had done a better job," he said, "we wouldn't have fifteen-year delays for death penalty appeals." He made support for the death penalty a prerequisite for his appointments to the bench. Other recent Democratic governors, such as Alabama's Don Siegelman, have tried to speed up executions. Out of twenty-four Democratic governors in 2003, we have struggled to find any who oppose the death penalty.

In most cases, this has more to do with electoral calculation than principle. The Democratic Party is still haunted by the defeats of its most outspoken abolitionists—notably Michael Dukakis and Mario Cuomo, who lost the 1994 governor's election in New York to George Pataki in part because he had vetoed capital punishment bills twelve times. Seventy percent of Americans support the death penalty, according to Gallup, up from just 42 percent in 1966. Even self-described moderates support the death penalty by a margin of 52 percent to 46 percent. A plurality of Americans believe that the death penalty is not imposed often enough. (Seventy-one people were executed in 2002 out of the 3,700 people on death row.) More Democrats say that the death penalty is not imposed often enough (40 percent) than say it is imposed too often (36 percent).

Executions are such good vote-getting issues that states are 25 percent more likely to conduct executions in years when gubernatorial elections are held than in other years. Executions are becoming so associated with "closure" that they are becoming semipublic once again. When Timothy McVeigh was executed in 2001, almost three hundred people, most of them relatives of the victims of the Oklahoma City bombing in 1995, chose to witness the execution "live": about thirty of them in prison, through a glass screen, the rest on closed-circuit television. Together, they constituted the largest audience for an American execution since the last public hanging in 1936 (when twenty thousand people had a nice day out watching the execution of Rainey Bethea in Owensboro, Kentucky).

The reaction to George Ryan's mass commutation showed how right the Democrats are to be wary of the issue. Instead of adding momentum to the abolition movement, as Ryan had hoped, it woke the sleeping giant of victims' rights. Critics of Ryan's grand gesture were quick to point out that it was also "arbitrary and capricious" to take everyone off death row, even those who are clearly guilty. Two of the beneficiaries of Ryan's hand-wringing were Fedell Caffey and Jacqueline Williams. In 1995 they decided they wanted another baby (Williams already had three), so they stabbed a pregnant woman to death and extracted the nearly full-term fetus from her body. For good measure, they also murdered the pregnant woman's ten-year-old daughter and eight-year-old son.

Acceptance of the death penalty is only one part of Democratic America's move to the Right. Liberals correctly point out that they have won the argument in their party over abortion and affirmative action. But there are plenty of liberal causes that the party steers clear of: gay marriage is the love that dares not speak its name. Despite all the unfairness of the drug war, you hear more about legalizing drugs from the Cato Institute than you do from the Democratic Party. The Democrats have beat a strategic retreat on welfare, and put up a weak fight over Bush's huge tax cuts.

As for religion, the Democrats are certainly the more secular of the two parties; in 2000, Al Gore picked up 61 percent of the votes of Americans who don't go to church.[16] And yet Gore himself was an avowedly religious sort. He studied divinity at Vanderbilt University, and, having been born again with Tipper in the 1970s, he always regarded religion as the cornerstone of his life.[17] "I believe in serving God and trying to understand and obey God's will for our lives," he told Harvard students on commencement day in 1994. In *Joined at the Heart,* Al and Tipper wrote that "our deeply held beliefs form the very core of the values we hold in common, and the rituals of our faith tradition have always provided a reassuring and stabilizing rhythm to family life." Grace before meals was as necessary as the food itself, they argued. Bedtime prayers were indispensable. Going to church on Sunday morning was the "most important family activity every week."[18] Gore was almost as enthusiastic as George W. Bush about using religious organizations to help solve social problems. Plenty of other Democrats also wear their faith on their sleeves. The Clintons are both enthusiastic churchgoers, Hillary being a Methodist like Bush. The Clintons' spiritual advisor, Jesse Jackson, is never shy about bringing God into public life. Perhaps the first thing that the American public discovered about Joe Lieberman was that he was a particularly observant Jew. Dick Gephardt, John Edwards and John Kerry all regularly mention the Lord. Even Howard Dean, the most secular Democratic candidate since Michael Dukakis, discovered a surprising enthusiasm for attending church once the primaries hotted up.

OF HOLLYWOOD AND HARVARD

So where on earth are unreconstructed liberals to be found? The great hold-outs, if you talk to conservatives, are those twin corrupters of the young: academia and Hollywood. In fact neither is quite as European as you might expect.

Academic towns are invariably centers of liberal activism. In some cases, like Berkeley, Harvard or Columbia, the university fits into the local leftish culture. In many more—such as Austin, Athens and Boulder—the university is an angry little island of bearded and pony-tailed revolt, usually surrounded by a sea of Texan, Georgian or Coloradan Republicanism. But that does not stop liberal American academia from often seeming more American than liberal—at least to anyone who has spent any time in European academic life.

In Europe, universities are not just financed by the state, but often run by it too. In France, universities don't bother to compete for staff because the academic hierarchy is fixed by tradition and state decree. In Germany, the state both decides which students universities will admit (all students who pass a state examination can go to their local university) and fixes the professors' salaries. By contrast, America's 4,100 universities, whether nominally public or private, are creatures of the market. They relentlessly compete with each other for everything from star faculty to promising students. Most universities are also ruthless money-making machines, forever looking for ways to expand their revenues and maximize their endowments. Academic fees have grown much faster than inflation (in 2002 public colleges raised their fees by almost 10 percent). The fact that Harvard is floating on a sea of money does not deter it from begging its alumni for ever more donations (and giving their children a slight advantage on admissions applications to spur on their generosity).

Students who cannot swim in the university's competitive environment are left to sink. Only half of America's students graduate within five years. The proportion is a mere one in four when you look at students from families with the lowest incomes. When it comes to their professional lives, professors are ruthless practitioners of the economics of inequality. Universities try to improve their position in the academic hierarchy by hiring star professors. And star professors relentlessly try to improve their salaries and perks by flirting with rival institutions. The bidding wars for academic stars have become so frantic that universities have to offer a lot more than just generous salaries to net their prey: super-sabbaticals, research assistance, even jobs for spouses. Columbia University even installed Jeffrey Sachs—a development economist who specializes in studying poverty—in an $8 million town house.[19]

Tinseltown also regards itself as a temple of liberalism. Lew Wasserman remained a Democratic power broker for half a century. Bogie and Bacall did their bit for Adlai Stevenson; Marilyn Monroe and the Rat Pack turned out for Kennedy; Warren Beatty stumped for Robert Kennedy in 1968, strategized for George McGovern in 1972 and worked as a key advisor for Gary Hart in 1988; Clinton had a pack of Hollywood supporters from the beginning of his national career, led by Mike Medavoy, who became head of Tri-Star; Rob Reiner helped keep Howard Dean's campaign afloat.[20] Liberal philanthropists, such as Stanley Sheinbaum and Norman Lear, are an essential call for any aspiring Democrat candidate. The Right likes to jeer at these thespians for being shallow. The truth is that Hollywood opinion comes in different degrees of cogency. At the top, there is something close to a left-wing salon. Beatty is a surprising font of knowledge on American politics, and even once flirted with the idea of running for president. Lauren Bacall can rip into George W. Bush in a way reminiscent of Ann Richards's savaging his father. Yet these skills do not seem to have been inherited by the younger generation. One Democratic presidential candidate from the 1980s who happened to have run a decent-sized state once complained to one of us about having to take lectures from Whoopi Goldberg about fiscal policy. Alec Baldwin threatened to leave the United States if George W. Bush was elected, failed to carry out his threat, and went on to compare the 2000 election to the September 11 attacks in their impact on American democracy.[21]

But look at the way that Hollywood is actually organized and you discover a very different picture. The European entertainment industry is swaddled by a web of government subsidies and protections, all justified by the need to preserve culture and educate the masses. Hollywood, by contrast, was founded by immigrants who merely dreamt of putting bums in seats. The studios sit at the center of a highly decentralized industry built upon speed and flexibility and dedicated to the great god of profit maximization. Hollywood films dominate almost every market in the world. Successful Hollywood stars can take home $20 million from a single film. The unsuccessful eke out a marginal existence in low-wage jobs. The whole thing is remarkably free of any government involvement.

Far from being a civilizing outlet, Hollywood is looked on by most European liberals with a mixture of terror and disgust. No matter how much money Tinseltown raises for the American Left, no matter how often it pours scorn on George W. Bush, most of the rest of the world thinks it represents exactly the same sort of culture that he does—the greedy, violent colossus that has far too much sway over the world's affairs. Like so much of Democratic America, Hollywood is, in its bones, a much more conservative place than most of its denizens are prepared to admit.

CONCLUSION:
LIVING WITH THE RIGHT NATION

G AZING INTO THE FUTURE of any nation is a hazardous business. In a country as large and magnificently contradictory as America, it is arguably an exercise in hubris. The United States may be steered by the Right Nation, but it contains myriad potential futures. All the same, a good place to begin the quest is with the arm of government that was designed by the founders to be closest to popular opinion—the House of Representatives—and with the two people who, in other countries, would be the nation's prime minister and its leader of the opposition: Dennis Hastert, the Republican Speaker, and Nancy Pelosi, the Democratic minority leader.[1]

The two typify the political clash that we have followed throughout this book. Hastert, a hulking former wrestling coach, is a fairly straightforward conservative: antiabortion, anti–gay marriage, anti-Kyoto, pro–invading Iraq, pro–death penalty. Pelosi, a tiny birdlike woman, is at the other end of the political spectrum. Hastert got a 100 percent rating from the American Conservative Union in the days when he voted regularly. (American Speakers are in an odd position: they head their party in the House while serving as the bipartisan leader of the House.) Pelosi got an 8 percent rating from the same organization in 2000 and a 0 percent rating in 1999. Both of them are genuinely liked by their colleagues on Capitol Hill, but it is hardly surprising that their relationship is little more than polite.

Revealing even more of the country's political differences are the districts these individuals represent. Pelosi's district (California's eighth) is more or less coterminous with San Francisco, the "bluest," most liberal city in America. Until the 1960s, such a state of mind did not preclude Republicanism: indeed, all San Francisco's mayors from 1912 to the mid-1960s were members of the GOP. But nowadays only 13 percent of the registered voters are Republicans, and there are no GOP elected officials. The current president of the city's board of supervisors is a member of the Green Party, as are three of the seven members of the school board. In 2003, the city nearly elected Matt Gonzalez, a Pablo Neruda–reading Green, who seemed to possess neither a car nor a watch, as its mayor; but he was narrowly defeated by the supposedly conservative Democrat, Gavin Newsom, who duly started issuing marriage licenses to gays.[2]

Compared with other "red" districts, Hastert's (Illinois's fourteenth) is deep scarlet. It begins in the suburbs thirty miles west of the Chicago Loop and then stretches out through miles of cornfields to a point just forty miles short of the Iowa border. To drive across it takes a good three hours. Hastert's district can claim to be the most Republican in the country, at least if you factor in length of loyalty to the party. Unlike *nouveaux droites* such as Texas, Illinois has been full of Republicans since the party's founding in 1854. The district contains many of the GOP's greatest landmarks—from memorials erected to Union soldiers killed in the Civil War to Ronald Reagan's birthplace.

The differences between the two places are so striking that it is difficult to know where to begin. San Francisco is part of vertical America—a land of soaring skyscrapers and high-density living. Hastert's district is part of horizontal America. The same arguably goes for the people: in Illinois, a broad girth is a sign of health. In San Francisco, even the chefs are thin. San Francisco is as edgy as America gets—a peculiar mix of blue bloods and gays, dotcom millionaires and aging hippies. Hastert's district is resolutely "normal." The local citizens think of themselves as typical Americans, and their geographical vision is often bounded by the Great Plains that surround them.

The most important difference lies in attitudes to growth. San Francisco is one of the most beautiful places on earth: look out over the Golden Gate Bridge when it is enveloped in mist and you can imagine that you have arrived in paradise. It also has all the amenities of civilized life, from fine restaurants to fine museums. All the same, the city is stagnating. Its share of the Bay Area's population has fallen from 30 percent in 1950 to 13 percent today. Whenever it looks as if the place is beginning to pick up—as it did in the 1970s and the 1990s—antigrowth activists come up with ballot initiatives to hold it back. They say that the city can't grow without sacrificing its legendary beauty; that 777,000 people is enough for a bit of hilly property that is just forty-seven miles square and surrounded on three sides by water. But you don't have to be a property developer to see that this is hooey. Back in 1950, the city burghers were talking about a population of 1 million. As for beauty, parts of San Francisco remain stunning, but much of the city's housing consists of nondescript houses and some districts (particularly south of Market Street) are downright tawdry. A good deal of the antigrowth lobby seems to be about thumbing its nose at business. "Conservationists" recently celebrated stopping a developer from refurbishing the city's old armory, which is becoming increasingly decrepit.

In contrast, Hastert's flat, boring district is in love with growth. New houses march like a vast army resolutely westward across the Great Plains from Chicagoland to rural towns such as Yorkville (where Hastert was a teacher) and even to Dixon (where Reagan spent much of his boyhood). And behind the houses are all the accoutrements of suburban boom time, particularly huge schools and "mega" shopping malls. The high school where Hastert once taught has doubled in size since he entered politics in 1980. The main roads are lined by row upon row of shopping malls, each one of them filled with superstores that seem to be bent on testing the principle of economies of scale to the limit.

The second big difference between the two districts lies in the relative importance of family life. Most of the people flocking to Hastert's district are doing so for one reason: to raise their children. They want space to build big houses—many cover more than four thousand square feet—and freedom from the downside of urban life, particularly crime. In upmarket St. Charles, 85 percent of the residents own their own homes; even in meat-and-potatoes Elgin, home ownership stands at 70 percent to 75 percent.

San Francisco has a much different focus. In the first half of the twentieth century, it was one of the most family-friendly cities in the country, with magnificent parks and schools and an abundant supply of family houses. The popular midcentury radio program *One Man's Family* was a hymn to the joys of raising a family in the shadow of the Golden Gate Bridge. But the city now has one of the lowest proportions in the country of families with children (the local joke is that San Francisco has more dogs than children). Almost 70 percent of the population is single. This is not just because the city is the capital of gay America; it also has a disproportionate number of young singles and older people living alone. Both the property market and the school system discourage families. Only 35 percent of San Franciscans own their own homes. At the same time, rent control both freezes the rental sector and institutionalizes an antigrowth mentality. The public school system is strained by a combination of high immigration—half the city's schoolchildren speak a language other than English at home—and poor management. Middle-class parents either send their children to private schools or move out of the city.

There is also a somewhat surprising class difference between the two districts. Hastert's is as resolutely middle class as it is cheerfully middle American. A few senior executives live in multimillion-dollar houses and send their children to private schools, but most people belong to the vast American middle class. They shop in the same giant shopping malls, eat in the same chain restaurants (such as Chili's and IHOP) and send their children to the same giant public schools. Sue Klinkhamer, the mayor of St. Charles, points out that her local school district is so big that fairly modest people can send their children to the same schools as millionaires.

San Francisco, by contrast, looks more like an aristocratic society. The city is home to some of the wealthiest people in the country, many of them, like the Gettys, the heirs rather than the creators of huge fortunes. It also has a disproportionate number of single professionals with enough disposable income to live like the characters in *Sex in the City*. Yet the city also hosts one of the country's biggest concentrations of homeless people, with between 8,000 and 16,000 people, many of them drug-addicted or mentally ill, living on the streets. "A mixture of Carmel and Calcutta" is the pungent verdict of Kevin Starr, California's state librarian, on his native city.

The contrast between middle-class Illinois and aristocratic San Francisco extends to their representatives. Hastert taught history and politics and coached wrestling at Yorkville High School for sixteen years (and his wife, Jean, taught physical education there for thirty-six years). He is passionate about old cars, sports and farming. Pelosi, by contrast, is more blue-blooded. Both her father and brother were mayors of her native Baltimore. She was taken under the wing of another political dynasty—the Burtons of San Francisco. Her husband is one of the city's leading businessmen, and the Pelosis are a fixture on the San Francisco social and cultural scene.

Less surprisingly, the political cultures of the two congressional districts are like oil and water. Hastert's district is a place where even Democrats profess affection for George Bush. Pelosi's district is a place where Mark Leno, the state assemblyman for the city's eastern half, can find himself labeled a "conservative" despite the fact that he is a homosexual who favors both "transgendered rights" and the legalization of cannabis for medical use. But the political differences between the two districts go beyond mere ideology. San Francisco is a city of political activists. Cecil Williams, a self-styled "minister of liberation" who runs Glide Memorial Church in the heart of the Tenderloin, boasts that "we don't just do one kind of demonstration here, man. We do them all." The city saw some of America's biggest demonstrations against the Iraq War. Activists tend to attribute this involvement to the city's high level of education: more than half the population has either a college or postgraduate degree. Government is the city's biggest employer, and San Francisco is also a mecca of nonprofit foundations.

Alas, an obsession with politics does not necessarily make for a well-run polis. San Francisco's political arrangements are dysfunctional. Power is divided between a mayor and a board of supervisors who are frequently at loggerheads. The eleven supervisors are elected by separate districts rather than by the whole city, an arrangement that institutionalizes parochialism. Add to this the city's fondness for ballot initiatives, and you have a recipe for urban gridlock.

The situation in Illinois is exactly the reverse. Hastert's constituents will turn up for the occasional rally to, say, commemorate September 11, and plenty of them are angry about the high level of property taxes, but they don't obsess about politics. The people who look after Hastert's two-hundred-acre farm while he is away have so far refused all his invitations to make their first visit to Washington, D.C. Yet local politics seem to work pretty well: the streets are clean; the schools are successful. The mayors of blue-collar Aurora and Elgin have done a great deal to regenerate their cities.

Two other differences in values are particularly striking. The first is attitudes toward religion. Hastert's slice of the Right Nation does not have the same fire-and-brimstone feel as, say, Sugarland, Texas (where his sidekick, Tom DeLay, rules the roost), but religion matters. New churches are being built, old ones expanded. In the Chicago suburbs some churches have thousands of members. Out in the sticks some small towns have one bar and seven churches. San Francisco, by contrast, has been closing churches for years. There was a time when the Catholic archbishop was one of the most powerful political figures in the town. Now, in a largely secular city, he is a marginal figure, one among a cacophony of religious voices that range from Buddhists to members of the Church of Satan.

The second difference in values is attitudes toward social disorder. Hastert's district is meticulously well kept and relatively free of urban ills such as vagrancy. Klinkhamer, the mayor of St. Charles, says she recently received a telephone call complaining about cobwebs on a local bridge. She had them removed that day. In Pelosi's district, beggars line the streets and live in doorways. The United Nations fountain in the Civic Center recently had to be walled off because the homeless used it as a public lavatory. Yet the left-leaning city has defiantly resisted aping the heartless conservative tactics of Rudy Giuliani in New York City. Far from being shown zero tolerance, homeless people in San Francisco get a monthly stipend from the government and free food from religious organizations. A recent ballot initiative suggesting that the homeless be given care rather than cash was struck down on a legal technicality.

HAS CONSERVATISM WON?

Looking at "Pelosiville" and "Hastertland," it is not difficult to see why American politics has shifted to the Right. If American politics is a seesaw, it is an unevenly balanced one. Imagine Dennis Hastert at one end of the seesaw and Nancy Pelosi on the other end, and you have some idea about which party is sitting with its legs dangling in the air. In the war between the two Americas, Hastertland has been winning.

It is worth admitting that the "victory" of American conservatism remains far from complete.[3] Despite having a Republican president, a Republican Congress and more Republican state legislators than any time in living memory, the American government is spending money "like a drunken sailor," as John McCain puts it. As for the culture wars, the divorce rate is more than double what it was at the start of the swinging sixties while the proportion of single-parent families is triple. Even wholesome hotel chains, such as Holiday Inn, provide hard-core pornography on demand. And, of course, America remains a polarized nation which could well dispense with its conservative president at the next election.

Yet even when you include these caveats and qualifications, something rather remarkable has happened in American politics. Who would have imagined that the 2004 presidential election would represent something of a last chance for the Democrats? But conservatism's progress goes much deeper than the gains that the Republican Party has made over the past half century or the steady decline in Democratic registration. The Right clearly has ideological momentum on its side in much the same way that the Left had momentum in the 1960s. Back in Prescott Bush's era, when J. K. Galbraith decided that everyone who was anyone was a liberal, "conservatism" was variously dismissed as a "paranoid style," a "political pathology" or a "status anxiety." Confronted by Barry Goldwater in the 1960s, the great Richard Hofstadter was reduced to rhetorical spluttering: "When, in all our history, has anyone with ideas so bizarre, so archaic, so self-confounding, so remote from the basic American consensus, ever got so far?" Yet the peculiar movement that Goldwater fashioned out of Southern resentment and Sun Belt optimism has kept widening and deepening. Nowadays, spluttering about a candidate being remote from the American consensus might just as easily come from Harvard MBAs discussing John Kerry's presidential race. When the *New York Times* announced in January 2004 that it was appointing a journalist to cover "conservatives" and to "examine conservative forces in religion, politics, law, business and the media," one could argue that it was a tacit admission by the nation's paper of record that it had somehow missed the biggest story in American politics of the past half century.[4]

The extent to which the center of gravity in American politics has moved to the right has been clearly illustrated by the current president and his predecessor. First came the first two-term Democratic president since the Second World War, who only achieved that feat by governing like an Eisenhower Republican. Now the grandson of Prescott Bush has cut taxes, catered to the Religious Right and generally governed like a Sun Belt business tycoon. This certainly annoys more than just the liberal quarter of America: George W. Bush probably provokes as much hostility as any president since 1945. But what is striking is how far Bush has reduced the Democratic Party into merely the anti-Bush party: the party of the moon rather than the sun. If Bush wins the election, he will continue with a radical conservative agenda, redesigning Social Security, solidifying his tax cuts, pouring more money into America's military might. If John Kerry wins, he will be reduced to trying to reconstruct the status quo ante, cutting back on tax cuts for the superrich and repairing relations with foreigners (up to a point), but generally coping with an agenda dictated by the Right.

Back in 1955, the *National Review* looked merely quixotic when it urged its readers to stand athwart history and put a stop to the two greatest trends of the time—collectivism and secularization. Yet today both these insidious European imports are being fought with enormous vigor. America is the most religious country in the rich world, with churches full, Evangelicals on the march and the Almighty popping up all over public policy. As for collectivism, it is all but vanquished. It is not just that everybody in American politics sings from the free-market hymnbook. As Hastertland amply illustrates, private property has become ever more widespread: ever more Americans own their homes and, thanks to suburbanization, the size of those homes has doubled since the 1950s.[5] Compared with their peers overseas, Americans have much more control over their educations, medical spending, retirement plans and investments than their contemporaries abroad. Government spending may be increasing; but so too is the capacity of American conservatives to opt out of the state: witness the growth of homeschooling or of secessionist planned communities.

In the 1950s and 1960s, when the conservative movement was getting off the ground, it looked as if America was set to become more European, with a bigger welfare state, tighter restrictions on firearms and a moratorium on the death penalty. Today, thanks in large part to the strength of the Right Nation, American exceptionalism is reasserting itself with a vengeance. The big trends in everything from demography to military expenditure suggest that the gap between Europe and the United States is set to grow in the next few decades.

So how did conservatism make so much headway? The simple answer is that, like all the most successful products, it answered a need that nobody quite realized was there. In retrospect, American conservatism had both history and sociology on its side. The United States has always been a conservative country, marinated in religion, in love with business and hostile to the state. Most of the population growth since the 1950s has been in the conservative parts of the country—in the South and suburbia rather than in the Democratic cities or the liberal Northeast. All it took was for the Democratic Party to lurch to the Left for the sleeping giant of conservatism to be awakened. Yet there was also plainly more to the success of conservatism than just responding to latent demand; the conservative movement helped to create its own market.

There is something almost Hegelian about the modern conservative movement. First came the thinkers who talked about the importance of markets or religion. Then came the legions of tax cutters and Evangelical Christians who gave those ideas political voice. Looking back at F. A. Hayek and William Buckley or more recently at Paul Weyrich and Edwin Feulner, it is amazing both how organized conservatives have been and how focused on the importance of ideas. Conservatives laboriously built a counterestablishment of think tanks, pressure groups and media stars that was initially intended to counterbalance the liberal establishment but has now turned into an establishment in its own right—and one with a much harder edge than its rival. The Democrats have only just got round to setting up their own version of Heritage. The relentlessness of conservative America can be unedifying—the treatment of Bill Clinton springs to mind. But over the long term, it has made for effective politics, particularly as the conservative movement has tightened its hold on the Republican Party.

In strategic terms, the change has been overwhelming. A philosophy that had once "lost its voice," as Russell Kirk put it, now speaks with a thousand voices. It has its contradictions and eccentricities, to be sure. But for the moment, the Right seems to be winning the argument at both ends of the market. Among the elites, it has been making the intellectual weather for most of the past two decades; it is remarkable how far the best liberal thinkers have been reduced to reacting to conservative arguments. Meanwhile, the American Right has also mastered the art of populism, redefining a force that used to be driven by economic discontent and left-wing demagogues like William Jennings Bryan as a howl of cultural protest—the fury of ordinary Americans at the nattering nabobs of the liberal elite.

If our story has been one of conservative success, it has also been one of liberal failure. American liberalism, as both a body of ideas and a political coalition, is a shadow of its former self. In the 1960s liberals acted as if they were in the process of refashioning the country. Yet the Great Society, for all its undoubted benefits, turned into a gigantic exercise in overreach, creating a populist backlash in its wake. Nowadays, American liberalism has fragmented into two remnants: a collection of single-issue pressure groups (the teachers' unions, abortion rights activists, etc.) and an inchoate leftist protest movement, furious about the Right Nation's advances. It is no longer a self-confident governing philosophy capable of rising above the self-interest of those pressure groups or the self-indulgence of the angry Left. That is why Clinton, the most talented Democratic politician of his generation, ended up governing like an Eisenhower Republican; and why his wife, if she ever gets the chance, will probably end up doing the same thing.

This victory is reflected in Hastertland and Pelosiville. The relationship between the relentless suburbanization in Illinois and Republicanization is not as automatic as the GOP likes to claim. For instance, as Hastertland sucks ever more immigrants and young professionals out of Chicago, it also increases the number of Democrats. Reagan's boyhood hometown, Dixon, has a Democratic mayor—albeit one who voted for Reagan and who describes George W. Bush as "a great human being." Yet the national picture, where polls show suburbanites preferring Republican policies by margins of around fifteen points, is replicated in Hastertland. Some soccer moms may dislike

Hastert's "Southern" views on abortion, and some businesspeople may rail about the Bush deficit. But most voters rally to the Republican message of low taxes, tough sentences for criminals, strong families and a hard-hitting approach to national security.

And once again, it is important not to be mesmerized by party labels. While Hastertland will embrace the odd Democrat who adjusts his or her message to the priorities of people who own their own homes and go to church every Sunday, it is hard to see it ever being lured back to the old-style "European liberalism" that the San Francisco branch of the Democratic Party stands for. The flat land of McMansions, malls and megachurches is not going to start yearning for bigger government, sending its sympathies to the French consulate, tolerating an invasion of sturdy beggars or doing any of the other things that San Francisco regards as normal.

Whether America becomes more Republican remains to be seen; but it has plainly become a more conservative, less European country. Like it or not, we all have to live with the Right Nation. The question is: How?

AN ANSWER AT HOME

Consider, first, the problem for nonconservatives within America. For many liberals the prospect of living with the Right Nation must seem insurmountable. To put it bluntly: liberals hate George W. Bush. They think that the accidental president had no right to turn such a close election into a launchpad for such radical conservative policies, no right to go to war against Iraq, no right to build up huge deficits, no right to ban partial-birth abortion and no right to be so damn Texan. In a cover story for the *New Republic* in 2003, Jonathan Chait reveled in the fact that he didn't just hate Bush for his policies, he hated everything about him, from the way he walked ("shoulders flexed, elbows splayed out from his sides") to the way he talked ("blustery self-assurance masked by a pseudo-populist twang"). "I even hate the things that everybody seems to like about him," he wrote.[6] Bush hating is arguably America's fastest-growing business, with Michael Moore, Al Franken and Paul Krugman as its robber barons and every leftish author in the land desperate to break into the market. There is even a Bush-hater's handbook written by a Canadian who took up American citizenship just to vote against the president.[7]

The similarity between today's Bush hatred and yesterday's Clinton hatred is striking. Remember the way right-wingers accused Clinton of drug running and murder? The web site Bushbodycount.com has compiled a list of people it says the Bush family has rubbed out, starting with JFK. Remember all the cash Richard Mellon Scaife poured into his "Arkansas project" to get rid of Clinton? George Soros is pouring millions into getting rid of Bush, a cause he describes as "the central focus of my life."[8] Counterpunch.com compares Bush with Hitler, conceding only that "Bush is simply not the orator that Hitler was."

In electoral terms, this strategy for dealing with the Right Nation is almost certainly self-defeating. Most polls show Americans like Bush more than his policies. The more you demonize the man, the more you consolidate his base and alienate floating voters. Underlying liberal America's fury is fear: fear that the Democratic Party is relentlessly becoming the minority party, fear that Bush is in the business of fundamentally changing America, fear that the argument of this book is correct. In the 1930s FDR used his solid majorities in Congress (and slim majority in the Supreme Court) to lay the foundation of the welfare state. Thirty years later LBJ used the shock of Kennedy's assassination and his crushing victory over Goldwater to build the Great Society. In the 1980s, Ronald Reagan seized on memories of "the Carter malaise" to shift the balance of public spending from providing welfare to strengthening American power. Bush, in the eyes of many liberals, has used September 11 to thrust his country in a more conservative direction. That is why Bush-hatred comes across as even more intense than Clinton hatred—and even more desperate.

Are American liberals doomed to spend the rest of their lives convulsed by anger or despair, or can they find a way of living with the Right Nation? Paradoxically, two of the things that have served conservatism so well in the past—America's constitution and its huge size—today give liberals reasons for hope. Liberal America is protected by the separation of powers. The Supreme Court, for instance, may have put Bush into the White House, but since then, it has delivered a number of notably liberal judgments, permitting affirmative action, striking down bans on gay sex and even agreeing to hear a case brought by the prisoners held at Guantánamo Bay.

More generally, the federal system allows liberalism to flourish at a local level. Liberal mayors can still rule liberal cities, like San Francisco, just as liberal governors can still rule liberal states, like Vermont. The federal system also provides a refuge for moderate Republicans. For instance, George Pataki and Arnold Schwarzenegger would both have a tough time rising in the current hard-line congressional party, but as governors of New York and California, they wield considerable political clout. In most other countries, there is only one political ladder worth climbing—within the parliament at Westminster, for example—so the party bosses are all-important. In America, an ideological rebel can build a successful career on the state level.

This flexibility is powerfully reinforced by geography. In such a big country, it is hard for any faction—even one as coordinated as the modern conservative movement—to run roughshod over the wishes of others. This is partly a matter of realpolitik: despite the growth in partisanship, there is still a moderate middle in America that no Republican president can ignore. Bush may have signed a bill outlawing partial-birth abortion, but even as he did so he mumbled about the will of the country being not to ban all types of abortion.

Looking back over America's past, the historian Robert Wiebe once noted that "what held Americans together was their ability to live apart. Society depended upon segmentation." People who disagreed with their neighbors could simply move elsewhere and live as they pleased. The Quakers left Puritan Boston for Philadelphia. The Mormons trekked across the country to settle in Utah. More recently, gays have migrated to cities such as San Francisco and even to gay gated communities. Technology is now reinforcing this world of choice. Not that long ago, Americans had only three television stations to choose from—and social conservatives raged that they were all controlled by liberals. Today the proliferation of cable channels and the explosion of the Internet mean that nobody has reason to feel disenfranchised. Liberals and conservatives have a good chance of living together by living apart.

America has long cherished a tradition of moral federalism that has made such "living together" relatively easy. The Founding Fathers labored mightily to keep the federal government out of the business of civic virtue. James Madison noted (in *Federalist Paper* 56) that different groups progress at different speeds. Alexander Hamilton (in *Federalist Paper* 17) argued that any attempt to impose a centralized morality would be "as troublesome as it would be nugatory." This tradition of moral federalism has never been more relevant. One of the reasons we have been so critical of John Ashcroft in this book is because he has ridden roughshod over America's instinctive commitment to diversity—something that will ill serve the causes he cherishes. That is not to deny that the federal government should sometimes step in to protect individual—and constitutional—rights. Few now question the idea that the federal government was right to use its might to dismantle segregation in the South. But in general the federal government should err on the side of caution on issues where reasonable people can disagree including surely gay marriage. It should recognize that different communities have different views on both politics and morals (note how large cities voted for Gore by a 71 percent to 26 percent margin while small towns and rural areas voted for Bush by 59 percent to 38 percent).[9] And it should try, as far as possible, to allow those communities to make decisions for themselves, rather than forcing them to bow to Washington. Agreeing to disagree offers the country the best chance of avoiding an endless culture war in which each side uses the federal government to force its views on the other.

THE VIEW FROM ABROAD

The problem of living with the Right Nation at home is challenging enough, but it is nothing compared with the problem it poses beyond America's borders. For one thing, hardly anyone abroad has a good thing to say about the Right Nation's hold over America. If Bush has divided opinion at home, he has united it abroad—pretty much all against him. A mere 10 percent of the people in France and 15 percent in Germany approve of American foreign policy.[10] Tony Blair stood by Bush during the Iraq War in the teeth of fierce domestic opposition. In November 2003, tens of thousands of Britons marched to protest against George Bush simply visiting their country. Asked which characteristics they associated with their guest and ally, 60 percent of Britons said "a threat to world peace," 37 percent said "stupid" and 33 percent said "incoherent." Only 10 percent found him "intelligent," and 7 percent called him a good world leader—and this from the country that Bush hailed as America's "closest friend in the world."[11]

For another thing, hardly anyone outside America understands that conservatism is here to stay. The prevailing view abroad is quite the opposite: that the Right Nation will simply go away when America comes to its senses and Bush is defeated in 2004. Most foreigners are thus in much the same state of mind as Pauline Kael was in 1972. "I don't know how Richard Nixon could have won," the *New Yorker's* film critic said. "I don't know anybody who voted for him."[12] In America, most liberals have finally woken up to the idea that there is a vast conservative country hidden away in the uncivilized wilderness between the Hudson River and Pasadena. By contrast, most foreigners know only Kael's and Pelosi's America. San Francisco is familiar from films or even personal experience (tourism has been the city's biggest industry since the early 1960s). To Europeans, San Francisco's compact structure, leftish politics and permissive atmosphere feel just like home. Hastert's America is one that they do not visit and probably barely understand. They thus assume that Bush is an aberration—an electoral fluke. It is as if an otherwise sensible friend had taken a highly unsuitable mistress. It will pass, they say. The current foreign policy of France and Germany might be subtitled "Waiting for the nightmare to end."

As the rest of the world comes to understand America's conservative core, the tensions will surely grow. If advancing technology is allowing liberal and conservative America to live apart, it is also making America an ever more omnipresent force in the rest of the world. Wherever you travel, Washington, D.C., dominates the news. The rest of the world feels that it is becoming ever more tangled up in the red, white and blue—and, if the polls, demonstrations and diplomatic rows are anything to go by, the rest of the world does not much like it. As Tom Friedman, the *New York Times's* foreign affairs columnist, puts it, the more his country gets in the world's face, the more "radioactive" it becomes.

Is it really that bad? There is a danger of falling for what one of our colleagues has dubbed the "illusion of prelapsarian innocence."[13] There was no pre-Bush golden age when the Parliament of Man dealt with the world's problems with measured wisdom. The 1990s are littered with examples of the West failing to intervene when it should have (for instance, to stop the genocide in Rwanda), of interventions that failed (Srebrenica, Somalia) and of successes that were only retrospectively blessed by the UN Security Council (Kosovo). The West singularly failed to deal with Saddam Hussein, North Korea and the Middle East.

Hardly prelapsarian. Yet before Bush came along the Western alliance was nevertheless more united than it is today. There are still plenty of subjects on which Europe and America work comfortably together: look at all those intelligence subcommittees and intellectual-property working parties. There is still a vast body of issues in which the Western world has a common interest. But there must be more to an international alliance than allies simply doing together what they would each happily do separately. You can argue whether Bush had a right to expect France or Germany to go along with him over Iraq in the same way that Blair did, but at the very least the president had the right to expect his allies to refrain from lobbying against him on an issue that, wrongly or rightly, mattered so much to America. As Blair told the House of Commons in arguably the best speech of the whole drama, "Partners are not servants, but neither are they rivals."[14] By the same token, from a European viewpoint, the Bush administration may not like the International Criminal Court that the Europeans so cherish, but, having secured its opt-out, it hardly becomes an ally to go around trying to bully other countries into not joining, as America has tried to do. "All we need from the United States is benign neglect," one European diplomat puts it. "Is that too much to ask?"[15]

What can be done? A starting point would be more grown-up behavior on both sides, particularly when it comes to rhetoric. It is hard to imagine what Donald Rumsfeld thought he could gain from belittling his allies by calling them "Old Europe," as he did on January 22, 2003, let alone comparing Germany with Libya and Cuba, as he did a few days later. It is all very well for Texas congressmen to hurl insults at the French, but in places like Lebanon the French have proved their expertise and bravery as peacekeepers. On the other side of the Atlantic, European newspapers such as the

Guardian and *Le Monde* now regularly print cartoons that are the equivalent of depicting blacks with bones through their noses: Americans are always fat, boorish and bloodthirsty. There is also prelapsarian ignorance so willful that it borders on spite. In Europe, Bush is regularly attacked for not signing the Kyoto Protocol and rejecting the International Criminal Court without any mention of the fact that Bill Clinton was also hardly a fan of either. Europeans seldom acknowledge Bush as a man who has increased America's aid budget by 50 percent or as the first American president to formally endorse a Palestinian state. In conservative America, opposition to American policies is repeatedly blamed on the perfidious Jacques Chirac without note that the vast majority of America's allies disapproved of the Iraq War. Even in Rumsfeld's supposed loyal "New Europe," 70 percent to 80 percent of Hungarians, Czechs and Poles opposed an American war in Iraq.[16]

Look beyond the mudslinging, and the condition of the Western alliance is both much better than it first appears and much worse. It is better because the sad drama in Iraq has taught the Right Nation a tough lesson about the importance of soft power. The philosophy of *oderint dum metuant* (let them hate us so long as they fear us) makes no sense for a country trying to wage a global war on terrorism. Fighting terrorism is about winning "hearts and minds." For all its might, America contains only 5 percent of those hearts and minds: it does not help to have most of the rest regarding you with suspicion. America's radioactivity is one reason Iraq has proved so difficult to pacify. America's radioactivity has also made it harder to rally international support. Chastised (not that it will admit it), the Bush administration has since pursued a more multilateral approach in managing the peace. It is also reemphasizing multilateralism in dealing with Iran and North Korea.

Yet if pragmatism may push the Western partners together in the short term, two other things will pull them apart in the longer term. The first is the gap in hard power between America and its allies, which is likely to be even bigger when the next crisis comes along. Just as the Right Nation is gaining strength within America, America is gaining strength in the world at large. We have already mentioned the enormous gap in defense spending among the world's nations; but this is supported by economic might and demography. America, which already accounts for more than 30 percent of

GDP and 40 percent of global spending on research and development, seems to be the only large advanced country whose economy is capable of fast growth and the only one with a young population.[17] By 2050, America's median age will still be around thirty-six, while Europe's will have risen from thirty-eight to fifty-six. Any global problem will continue to be an American problem.

The second reason for pessimism about the state of the Western alliance is, perversely, the war on terrorism. For all the rhetoric about the war on terror being a shared struggle, there is now a basic asymmetry. During the Cold War, the Atlantic alliance was united by an acknowledged common threat of shared destruction. No longer. Winston Churchill defined an appeaser as someone who hopes that the crocodile will eat somebody else first. But Europeans do not feel in al-Qaeda's sights to the same extent that Americans do; and many think they would be safer if their leaders did not confront radical Islam in the same way that America has done. When al-Qaeda struck in Madrid in March 2004, it helped change the election result, in part because some Spanish voters decided that their government had made their country more vulnerable by backing George Bush's invasion of Iraq. Many Europeans see no reason to toe the line behind America in a new war that they believe America has brought upon itself.

Two of the biggest sores in the Atlantic alliance provide convenient "principles" for the Europeans to hide behind when it comes to explaining their reluctance to follow America's lead on global terrorism. The first is the Iraq War. Washington's mistakes—its exaggerations about the weapons of mass destruction, its failure to plan the reconstruction and so on—have provided Europeans with another excuse to stand back. The other far more potent excuse is the plight of the Palestinians. Many Europeans argue that as long as America takes such a one-sided view of the deepest Arab grievance, it is hard to get anywhere in the region. After all, the same plucky Israel that the Right Nation reveres is for most of the rest of the world a land-hungry monster, throwing up settlements on other peoples' land, firing rockets into crowded cities and denying basic human rights. In 2003 Israel was deemed the biggest threat to world peace in one poll in Europe, and the Middle East is a prompt for much of the more poisonous private rhetoric in the Western alliance. While one side of the Atlantic complains about a Jewish cabal running American foreign policy, the other side lobs back charges of anti-Semitism. It is not surprising that Tony Blair, the politician who has fought hardest to keep the alliance together, has devoted so much time and capital to pushing Bush on the Israeli-Palestinian dispute. "I do not believe," he announced in the same impassioned Commons speech about rivals and partners, "there is any other issue with the same power to reunite the world community than progress on the issues of Israel and Palestine."[18]

EUROPE'S CHALLENGE

What can Europeans do to make it easier to live with the Right Nation? Four priorities suggest themselves—three positive, the other negative. The first is to close the gap in hard power. Europeans and Americans will be able to establish a mature relationship only when the Europeans begin to take more responsibility for their own defense. During the Cold War, Western European military spending was around 60 percent of the American level; now it is closer to 40 percent.[19] At the moment, Europe is a freeloader on American military might. This breeds resentment in America and irresponsibility in Europe.

The point about strength should not be limited to tanks and battleships. In the period between 1945 and 1990, Europe's economies basically caught up with America's: average incomes in Western Europe rose from 50 percent of American levels in 1950 to above 80 percent (with the richer countries at basically the same level).[20] But the continent's failure to address structural reform has cost it dearly. Since 1995, some 60 percent of the world's economic growth has come from America. American workers are more productive than Europe's—and they work on average three hundred hours more a year than their European equivalents. For every five hours a German works, an American works more than six.

The second priority has to do with ambition. Europe's lack of hard power has fed a deeper malaise in foreign policy. In some way, the partners' roles have gotten muddled up. A quarter century ago, it was the idealistic European Left that came up with dreamy schemes for changing the world, and fumed about Kissingerian realpolitik. Now it is the American Right that has the dreamy schemes about democratizing the Middle East, and the European Left that talks about the necessity of not interfering in other sovereign states' affairs.[21] This preference for the "devil-you-know" was crystallized in Jacques Chirac's promise on March 10, 2003, to veto an Iraq War resolution at the UN Security Council, "whatever the circumstances."[22]

The third priority is the need to redesign the United Nations. If Europeans are to insist that America stick to the multilateral system, then they must make sure that these multinational institutions are redesigned to deal with the threat of global terrorism. In particular, they must help to create a credible multilateral mechanism for using preemptive force. It is all very well to warn, as Kofi Annan did in October 2003, that "if nations discount the legitimacy of the UN, and feel they can and must use force unilaterally and preemptively, the world will become even more dangerous."[23] But it is hard to ignore two things: first, the traditional policies of containment and deterrence do not make sense when dealing with stateless terrorists like al-Qaeda or rogue states like North Korea; and second, preemption is hard to do within the UN system. At present, force is permissible in only two circumstances—self-defense as defined in Article 51, and by sanction of the Security Council. Some new guidelines, perhaps embodied within Article 51, need to be agreed upon. The Europeans also have to face up to the need to redesign that relic of the Second World War, the Security Council—for instance by giving permanent seats, if not vetoes, to the likes of Japan, Germany, India and Brazil.

The fourth and last priority applies as much to America as to Europe: to prevent the political disagreements within the Western alliance from spilling over into economics. When the political arguments are about war and nuclear weapons, import tariffs on steel, lumber and bras might seem somewhat mundane. But there is a danger of the growing gap between America and the rest of the world threatening the political underpinnings of the global free-trading order. The risk is of disagreements about politics creating trading blocs, of Fortress Europe turning against Fortress America—a tragedy not just for the people within those battlements but for those in the developing world who would probably be kept out of both castles.

The Righteous Nation

What about the Right Nation itself? Can it make itself easier to live with? There are grounds for compromise, but fewer perhaps than the rest of the world wants.

The list of occasions when the Bush administration has been needlessly abrasive is a long one. The mistakes began early: Was it really necessary to profess no regret whatsoever about the death of the Kyoto Protocol? Wouldn't it have been better to blame it all on the impossibility of getting an agreement in the Senate? But the real damage was done in the two years after September 11. By any measure, the Bush administration spent—many would say squandered—an enormous amount of international goodwill in a remarkably short time. Whatever the shortcomings of Old Europe, the rift in the Western alliance was not inevitable. After September 11, Europe instinctively rallied to America. *Le Monde* declared, "We are all Americans now." NATO invoked Article Five, proclaiming for the first time that the whole organization had been attacked, only for its offers to help in Afghanistan to be brushed aside.

Even when it came to dealing with Saddam, there was considerable agreement among the allies about the need to do something: witness the unanimous decision by the Security Council to back America's first resolution in November 2002. There are all sorts of reasons why things went wrong in the next few months, many of them, as we have already pointed out, to do with European countries being needlessly obstreperous. But America's radioactivity counted against it. By the time it came to selling the second Iraq resolution in February and March 2003, the United States was seen as so high-handed that it could not even persuade allies like Mexico and Chile to back its stance on removing Saddam: of the fifteen other members of the Security Council, America managed to attract only Britain, Spain and Bulgaria to its side.

Was it politic of the administration to demand "regime change" in Iraq even before going to the UN? Was it clever of Cheney and Rumsfeld to dismiss the inspections as a sham even before they had been given a chance to work? Would another thirty days of UN inspections have been enough to win a majority on the Security Council? "If we are an arrogant nation, they will resent us," Candidate Bush famously warned in the second presidential debate in Winston-Salem. Yet, as Fareed Zakaria points out, the favorite verb of President Bush has come to be "expect"—as in he expects the Palestinians to dump Arafat or expects Turkey to fall in line.[24] This approach has not only conspicuously failed to persuade the expectees, it goes down particularly badly with people who would normally warm to America. "Most officials in Latin American countries are not anti-American types," says Jorge Castañeda, Mexico's foreign minister until 2003. "We have studied in the United States or worked there. We like and understand America. But we find it extremely irritating to be treated with utter contempt."[25]

It is significant that the Right Nation still provokes the most virulent hostility overseas when it abandons the basic American principles that it wants to trumpet. For instance, it is hard to think of anything that has done more harm to America's image abroad than its treatment of the "enemy combatants" in Guantánamo Bay. The idea that suspects—even ones caught in Afghanistan— can be denied access to lawyers and forced into a trial system where the ultimate appeal is only to Bush (who has already declared everybody at Guantánamo Bay to be "very bad men") has outraged even conservative Britain—not least because the "American Taliban," John Walker Lindh (a white Californian), was accorded a proper civilian trial. Donald Rumsfeld can claim the unique achievement of devising a judicial system so blatantly unjust that he drove Britain's right-wing *Daily Mail* to scream for justice on behalf of two black British Muslims whom in other circumstances it might have been keener to forget.

Yet there is plainly a limit to the Right Nation's willingness to appease its critics. Instinctively, as we saw in our chapter on the neoconservatives, conservative America leans toward unilateralism. It has always been skeptical about the fancy-pants sophisticates who run the foreign policy establishment in Washington, and about the organs of international diplomacy—particularly the United Nations. One State Department insider describes Rumsfeld as pursuing a deliberate policy of antagonism not only toward America's allies but also to large chunks of his own administration.

But it is not just stubbornness; the refusal to compromise ties into something slightly nobler. Arthur Schlesinger Jr. once remarked that "foreign policy is the face a nation wears to the world."[26] He noted that Americans have always been two-faced. On the one hand, they are a practical people, who have favored fact over theory, trial and error over deductive logic. On the other hand, they have always had a strong strain of idealism. This strain of idealism has been at work from the country's Puritan beginnings to John Foster Dulles's invocation of a holy war against communism. The moralistic edge to the Bush administration's foreign policy—dividing the world into those who are "with us or against us," taking on the evil-doers, trying to bring democracy to the Middle East and so on—fits into this long pedigree.

Moreover, for all the problems it causes the rest of the world, American exceptionalism is a major reason for the nation's success. Look at the values that the rest of the world sneers at—and they help explain why America is out in front. America's brash keenness on capitalism, for instance, helps to explain why American productivity is pulling ahead of Europe's. Twenty years ago, the European model, with its emphasis on social solidarity and high levels of public education, seemed to have a lot going for it. Now the American model is better at dealing with the quicksilver markets of the postindustrial economy. And what about that exceptional religiosity? A century ago Max Weber posited a connection between the Protestant ethic and the spirit of capitalism. Today the triumph of secularization in Europe seems to be going hand in hand with the decline of the work ethic, just as the survival of religion in the United States is going hand in hand with the survival of the work ethic.[27] Between 1979 and 1999, the average American working year lengthened by fifty hours, or nearly 3 percent. The average German working year shrank by 12 percent. Europeans also retire earlier, spend longer on the dole, go on strike more frequently. Niall Ferguson, a hard-working Scotsman who teaches at Harvard University, points out that northern Europe's decline in working hours coincides almost exactly with steep declines in religious observance.[28]

The more time you spend in the Right Nation, the more you are struck by its sense of certainty. Billy Graham, the man who rescued the young George W. Bush from his dissolute life, once said simply: "I know where I've come from. I know why I'm here, and I know where I'm going." The same confidence resounds from so many of the people we have met in this book—

from Dustin and Maura in Colorado Springs to the inhabitants of Hastert-land. It sits at the heart of the Right Nation: conservative America is "Right" not just in the sense of being conservative, but also in the sense that it is sure that it is right. That righteousness helps to explain the paradox of the United States that we mentioned in our introduction: why America is often both the most admired country and the most reviled, why it is hailed as a symbol both of success, opportunity and progress and also of intolerance, injustice and inequality. That paradox will endure as long as the Right Nation itself.

APPENDIX

Conservative ratings of Members of the House of Representatives

State	1972	1986	2002	Dems '72	Dems '86	Dems '02	Reps '72	Reps '86	Reps '02
Alabama	70	62	80	64	51	37	80	90	98
Alaska	11	65	86	11	na	na	na	65	86
Arizona	66	69	79	11	5	0	93	85	95
Arkansas	52	51	43	53	41	25	67	82	96
California	38	39	38	12	6	6	66	88	90
Colorado	54	62	67	32	12	2	77	88	100
Connecticut	29	19	37	35	0	7	16	40	67
Delaware	70	27	76	na	27	na	70	na	76
Florida	66	56	66	52	39	13	82	85	94
Georgia	83	68	76	83	63	16	86	86	99
Hawaii	0	5	11	0	5	11	na	na	na
Idaho	58	59	94	na	32	na	58	86	94
Illinois	43	34	53	12	10	14	74	69	92
Indiana	49	48	63	16	10	18	76	86	93
Iowa	42	34	71	0	7	32	59	48	81
Kansas	65	57	78	40	30	20	71	76	97
Kentucky	45	53	91	33	31	84	75	82	93
Louisiana	70	56	79	70	46	33	na	85	98
Maine	0	45	0	0	na	0	na	45	na
Maryland	38	37	37	33	24	3	48	76	71
Massachusetts	6	5	4	3	4	4	17	14	na
Michigan	38	30	46	9	6	12	56	68	90
Minnesota	28	31	46	3	6	15	53	72	97
Mississippi	90	60	65	90	45	41	na	83	100
Missouri	41	40	60	36	19	11	90	81	98
Montana	46	48	100	17	10	na	75	86	100
Nebraska	75	72	80	na	na	na	75	72	80
Nevada	50	59	54	50	32	16	na	86	91
New Hampshire	78	86	86	na	na	na	78	86	86
New Jersey	21	28	42	6	8	7	44	55	82
New Mexico	64	56	56	60	18	0	67	75	84
New York	25	29	35	8	6	7	48	58	78
North Carolina	71	59	62	68	35	15	77	87	95
North Dakota	34	27	32	0	27	32	67	na	na
Ohio	49	42	55	14	10	7	63	78	90
Oklahoma	50	45	86	35	36	40	80	85	95
Oregon	41	41	28	37	10	11	45	89	96
Pennsylvania	35	38	55	21	17	14	49	64	92
Rhode Island	0	5	8	0	5	8	na	5	na
South Carolina	77	60	65	78	39	8	70	82	93
South Dakota	21	18	88	21	18	na	na	na	88
Tennessee	62	41	71	47	24	37	82	74	98
Texas	61	57	53	58	35	22	88	93	95
Utah	50	94	78	33	na	40	67	94	98
Vermont	60	14	0	na	na	0	60	14	na
Virginia	81	62	74	84	39	15	80	78	97
Washington	22	33	39	9	12	13	100	66	92
West Virginia	31	14	41	31	14	24	na	na	76
Wisconsin	41	36	42	10	10	5	74	69	87
Wyoming	0	100	100	0	na	na	na	100	100
Averages:*	45	43	53	32	20	13	63	75	91
Medians:*	47.5	43.5	58	31	17.5	13	70	81	93

*Averages and medians are for the full 435 members of Congress.

Each year, the American Conservative Union (ACU) gives a rating to each congressman that is meant to indicate his or her level of support for conservative issues (http://acuratings.com). The rating ranges from 0 (indicating a very liberal position) to 100 (a very conservative position) and is based on the way that each House member has voted in a set of 10 to 20 votes. The ACU looks for classic ideological "cleavage" issues: missile treaties and the Jane Fonda bill (which sought to stop Americans visiting countries in military conflict with the United States) in 1972; sanctions against South Africa and support for the Contras in 1986; banning partial-birth abortions, support for tax cuts and opposition to the International Criminal Court in 2002. We have analyzed the ratings for those three years, entered each representative's score in a database, and averaged the scores of party and state. We have also given overall averages and medians for the entire Congress.

We think that the ratings provide a good general indicator of ideology, but they are not perfect. A Republican congressman will happily call for less government intervention in the morning, and then try to add amendments to an appropriations bill that benefits his district in the afternoon. Also, the ratings for small states are unreliable. For example, Wyoming's ACU rating was 0 in 1972, and 100 in both 1986 and 2002. This was the result of Wyoming having only one congressional seat. In 1972 it was occupied by Teno Roncalio, a Kennedy Democrat who voted for the SALT treaty and court-ordered desegregation but against the Jane Fonda bill. In 1986 it was held by Dick Cheney, who followed the conservative line unflinchingly, as has the current occupant, Barbara Cubin, who supported the withdrawal from the ABM Treaty and the extension of the welfare reform act. For a rather sophisticated analysis of the use of ideological ratings see Keith Poole and Howard Rosenthal, *Congress: A Political-Economic History of Roll Call Voting* (Oxford: Oxford University Press, 1997), pages 165–83. A more straightforward explanation is provided by Linda Fowler in her article, "How interest groups select issues for rating voting records of members of the U.S. Congress," *Legislative Studies Quarterly*, 1982, pages 401–13.

ACKNOWLEDGMENTS

THIS BOOK would not have been possible without the cooperation of its subject matter. Just imagine the hullabaloo if two American conservatives were to set off to write a book about the state of British journalism. By contrast, the Right Nation seldom objected to us prodding our stethoscope around its rib cage. There have been some unfortunate incidents—the Southerner who misheard our employer's name and thought we worked for *The Communist* being one—but most people have exhibited nothing but patience and kindness to two inquisitive Brits, welcoming us into their churches and colleges, exposing the inner workings of their think tanks and pressure groups, and letting us in on their plans to mobilize the voters of Alabama or to build an anti-Clinton library. Thank God we weren't French.

And, lest we be accused of bias, we should add that we have received just as much hospitality from the numerous liberals who have tried to persuade us that our thesis is dead wrong. In our introduction, we claimed the advantage of impartiality; certainly the vast majority of Americans whom we have talked to paid us the compliment of treating us as objective witnesses rather than as partisan ax-grinders or sinister foreign spies.

Many people read the manuscript of this book. John Dickerson, Gillian Peele and Simon Green all pointed out errors, both large and small. We would particularly like to thank our colleague, Ann Wroe, and our British editor, Stuart Proffit, for reading the manuscript when it was still in a horribly wretched state—and for providing sound advice on how to improve it. This book would not have been possible without Mark Doyle, who corrected many of our facts and drew up the ratings for the conservativeness of different Congresses. We would also like to thank Sophia Bradford for her help with pictures and Peter Winfield for his help with the maps. Needless to say, none of the mistakes in this book are theirs. We would also like to thank Mario and Ariadne Platero, Zanny and Sebastian Mallaby, Charlotte and John Duthie and, in particular, Richard and Jane Micklethwait for providing us with board and lodging when they assuredly had more amusing things to do with their time.

We have been extremely lucky once again to have Scott Moyers as our editor. He has been a consistent source of advice and enthusiasm, tempered only by a growing horror that we might just be correct. We would also like to thank Sophie Fels and Ann Godoff for all their help. And for the fourth time we are grateful to our agent, the peerless Andrew Wylie.

We would also like to thank the people who have had to put up with us most. Bill Emmott has been an exceptionally generous editor; we would also like to thank him for allowing us to reuse some pieces we have written for the *Economist*. We are also grateful to Lucy Tallon, Rachel Horwood, Venetia Longin, John Parker, Zanny Minton Beddoes, Dominic Ziegler and Brian Beedham for tolerating two authors at close quarters. Carol Howard, John Peet, Clive Crook, Johnny Grimond, John Smutniak and Barbara Beck have all helped on specific questions. Once again Gideon Rachman has provided unceasing inspiration from his Brussels backwater.

Our biggest debt remains to our families. It would be misleading to describe our wives as diehard supporters of *The Right Nation;* Fev and Amelia celebrated our decision to write another book with much the same enthusiasm as the Gore family celebrated George W. Bush's inauguration. Our children—Tom, Guy, Edward, Ella and Dora—have all duly been press-ganged into this semiloyal opposition, tempted over to our project only by gross acts of bribery on our part. However, now that it is finished, we can freely admit that many of the complaints about the time wasted on "Daddy's book" were all too justified. Yet again, we promise to be better in the future.

The Right Nation is dedicated to Adrian's daughter, Dora Wooldridge, and to John's niece and nephew, Tessa and Joshua Micklethwait—all of whom are under four. By the time they read this book, our thoughts about the Right Nation and its opponents may well seem quaint. But we hope that one thing at least comes through: our enthusiasm for America in all its varied forms, blue, red and rainbow. We have spent much of our adult lives living in the United States or writing about it in some guise or other; we also have four children who were born in the country. This book is written by two Britons, who will always remain foreigners; but it is also a belated thank-you note to a country that has given us both so much.

NOTES

INTRODUCTION

1. "Income in the United States 2002," U.S. Census Bureau, September 2003; *UK National Statistics, Social Trends* 33 (London: HMSO), p. 106.
2. "Too Many Convicts," *Economist*, August 10, 2002.
3. Nigel Hamilton, *JFK: Reckless Youth* (New York: Random House, 1995), pp. 141–43.
4. Quoted in Steven Hayward, *The Age of Reagan: The Fall of the Old Liberal Order, 1964–1980* (New York: Forum, 2001), p. 11.
5. Jacob Weisberg, *In Defense of Government: The Fall and Rise of Public Trust* (New York: Scribner, 1996), p. 42.
6. Voter News Service poll, 2000; CNN exit poll, 2000 presidential election, November 2000, http://edition.cnn.com/ELECTION/2000/epolls/us/2000.html.
7. Quoted in Robert Nisbet, *Conservatism, Dream and Reality* (New Brunswick, N.J.: Transaction Publishers, 2002), p. 116.
8. This is a favorite rallying cry of Grover Norquist.
9. Quoted in Nisbet, *Conservatism, Dream and Reality*, p. 41. Mrs. Thatcher believed this profoundly. See John Campbell, *Margaret Thatcher: The Iron Lady* (London: Jonathan Cape, 2003), p. 639ff.
10. Douglas Davis, "What Might Be Called One-Year-Out-Madness Is Sweeping Through Our Nation," *Newsday*, August 19, 1999.
11. The Mars example was from an Americans for Tax Reform meeting on August 27, 2003.
12. Andres Duany, quoted in "Live with TAE," *The American Enterprise*, October/November 2002, p. 18.
13. Based on census figures for 1980, 1990 and 2000, www.census.gov/Press-Release/www/releases/archives/census_2000/000717.html.
14. James A. Morone, *Hellfire Nation: The Politics of Sin in American History* (New Haven: Yale University Press, 2003), p. 4.
15. Ibid.
16. The cheese-eating phrase was originally used on *The Simpsons*.

CHAPTER 1: FROM KENNEBUNKPORT TO CRAWFORD

1. Lewis Namier, *England in the Age of the American Revolution* (London: Macmillan, 1963), p. 19.
2. Bill Minutaglio, *First Son: George W. Bush and the Bush Family Dynasty* (New York: Times Books, 1999), p. 19.
3. Ibid.
4. Walker and Bush's business dealings are scrutinized in Kevin Phillips, *American Dynasty: Aristocracy, Fortune and the Politics of Deceit in the House of Bush* (New York: Viking, 2003).

5. Mickey Herskowitz, *Duty, Honor, Country: The Life and Legacy of Prescott Bush* (Nashville, Tenn.: Rutledge Hill Press, 2003), p. 81.

6. Ibid.

7. Elizabeth Mitchell, *W: Revenge of the Bush Dynasty* (New York: Hyperion, 2000), p. 82.

8. Minutaglio, *First Son,* p. 41.

9. Herskowitz, *Duty, Honor, Country,* p. 127.

10. Stephen Mansfield, *The Faith of George W. Bush* (New York: Jeremy P. Tarcher/ Penguin, 2003), p. 9.

11. Pamela Colloff, "The Son Rises," *Texas Monthly,* June 1999.

12. Ibid.

13. Earl Black and Merle Black, *The Rise of Southern Republicans* (Cambridge, Mass.: Belknap Press, 2002), p. 41.

14. Michael Lind, *Made in Texas: George Bush and the Southern Takeover of American Politics* (New York: Basic Books, 2003), pp. 34–35.

15. T. R. Fehrenbach, *Lone Star: A History of Texas and the Texans* (New York: Da Capo, 2000), p. 672.

16. Interview with authors, January 24, 2003.

17. Theodore H. White, *America in Search of Itself: The Making of the President 1956–1980* (New York: Harper and Row, 1982), p. 238.

18. Minutaglio, *First Son,* p. 82.

19. Ibid., p. 132.

20. Ibid., p. 77.

21. Herskowitz, *Duty, Honor, Country,* p. ix.

22. Mitchell, *W: Revenge of the Bush Dynasty,* p. 81.

23. Ibid., p. 124.

24. David Frum, *The Right Man: The Surprise Presidency of George W. Bush* (New York: Random House, 2003), p. 47.

25. Minutaglio, *First Son,* p. 85.

26. Lou Dubose, Jan Reid and Carl Cannon, *Boy Genius: Karl Rove, the Brains Behind the Remarkable Political Triumph of George W. Bush* (New York: PublicAffairs, 2003), p. 15.

27. Minutaglio, *First Son,* p. 187.

28. Ibid., p. 191.

29. Mitchell, *W: Revenge of the Bush Dynasty,* p. 16.

30. Dubose, Reid and Cannon, *Boy Genius,* p. 5.

31. Minutaglio, *First Son,* p. 279.

32. Dubose, Reid and Cannon, *Boy Genius,* p. 25.

33. Dan Balz and Ronald Brownstein, *Storming the Gates: Protest Politics and the Republican Revival* (New York: Little, Brown, 1996), p. 228.

34. Interview with author, January 1998.

Chapter 2: The Conservative Rout, 1952–1964

1. Stephen Ambrose, *Eisenhower: The President,* vol. 2, *1952–1969* (London: George Allen and Unwin, 1984), p. 220.

2. Ibid., p. 43.

3. Rick Perlstein, *Before the Storm: Barry Goldwater and the Unmaking of the American Consensus* (New York: Hill and Wang, 2001), p. 13.

4. H. W. Brands, *The Strange Death of American Liberalism* (New Haven: Yale University Press, 2001), pp. 74–75.

5. Perlstein, *Before the Storm,* p. 5.

6. Brands, *The Strange Death of American Liberalism,* p. 78.

7. Ambrose, *Eisenhower: The President,* p. 23.

8. U.S. Office of Management and Budget, Budget for Fiscal Year 2004, historical tables, p. 21.

9. Brands, *The Strange Death of American Liberalism,* p. 59.

10. George H. Nash, *The Conservative Intellectual Movement in America Since 1945* (Wilmington, Del.: Intercollegiate Studies Institute, 1998), p. 317.

11. Ibid., p. 128.

12. Lionel Trilling, *The Liberal Imagination* (New York: Viking, 1950), p. ix.

13. Louis Hartz, *The Liberal Tradition in America* (New York: Harvest, 1955), p. 57.

14. Whittaker Chambers, *Witness* (New York: Random House, 1952), p. 793.

15. Quoted in James A. Morone, *Hellfire Nation: The Politics of Sin in American History* (New Haven: Yale University Press, 2003), p. 393.

16. Justin Martin, *Greenspan: The Man Behind Money* (Cambridge, Mass.: Perseus Publishing, 2000), p. 49.

17. Ibid., p. 149.

18. Nash, *The Conservative Intellectual Movement in America,* p. 66.

19. Ibid., p. 183.

20. Quoted in ibid., p. 8.

21. Steven Hayward, *The Age of Reagan: The Fall of the Old Liberal Order, 1964–1980,* (New York: Forum, 2001) p. xxii.

22. William Rusher, *The Rise of the Right* (New York: William Morrow, 1984), p. 38.

23. Perlstein, *Before the Storm,* p. 73.

24. John Judis, *William F. Buckley, Patron Saint of the Conservatives* (New York: Simon & Schuster, 1988), p. 184.

25. Whittaker Chambers, "Big Sister Is Watching You," *National Review* 4 (December 28, 1957), pp. 594–96. Quoted in Nash, *The Conservative Intellectual Movement in America,* p. 144.

26. Quoted in Nash, *The Conservative Intellectual Movement in America,* p. 145.

27. Rusher, *The Rise of the Right,* p. 81.

28. Earl Black and Merle Black, *The Rise of Southern Republicans* (Cambridge, Mass.: Belknap Press, 2002), p. 3.

29. Ibid., p. 40.

30. Ibid., p. 42.

31. Ibid., p. 207.

32. Perlstein, *Before the Storm,* p. 46.

33. Quoted in James T. Patterson, *Grand Expectations: The United States, 1945–1974* (New York: Oxford University Press, 1996), pp. 392–93.

34. Thomas Byrne Edsall and Mary D. Edsall, *Chain Reaction: The Impact of Race, Rights and Taxes on American Politics* (New York: W. W. Norton, 1991), p. 36.

35. Ibid.

36. Ibid., p. 61.

37. Richard Reeves, *President Kennedy: Profile of Power* (New York: Simon & Schuster, 1993), pp. 655–56.

38. Lewis L. Gould, *Grand Old Party: A History of the Republicans* (New York: Random House, 2003), p. 360.

39. Perlstein, *Before the Storm,* p. 374.

40. Ibid., p. 224.

41. Ibid., p. 459.

42. Ibid., p. 392.

43. Theodore H. White, *The Making of the President, 1964* (New York: Atheneum, 1965), p. 352.

44. Perlstein, *Before the Storm,* p. 444.

45. White, *The Making of the President, 1964,* p. 110.

46. Perlstein, *Before the Storm,* p. 337.

47. Ibid., pp. 337–38.

48. White, *The Making of the President, 1964,* p. 352.

49. Perlstein, *Before the Storm,* p. 333.

50. Theodore H. White, *The Making of the President, 1968: A Narrative History of American Politics in Action* (New York: Atheneum, 1969), p. 31.

51. White, *The Making of the President, 1964,* p. 406.

52. White, *The Making of the President, 1968,* p. 32.

53. Michael Barone, *Our Country: The Shaping of America from Roosevelt to Reagan* (New York: Free Press, 1990), p. 315.

54. Quoted in Lisa McGirr, *Suburban Warriors: The Origins of the New American Right* (Princeton: Princeton University Press, 2001), p. 132.

55. White, *The Making of the President, 1964,* p. 220.

56. James Q. Wilson, "A Guide to Reagan Country: The Political Culture of Southern California," *Commentary* 43 (May 1967), p. 39.

57. White, *The Making of the President, 1964,* p. 68.

58. Ibid., p. 230.

59. McGirr, *Suburban Warriors,* p. 54.

60. Lee Edwards, *The Conservative Revolution: The Movement That Remade America* (New York: Free Press, 1999), p. 132.

61. Robert Lekachman, "The Postponed Argument," *New Leader,* November 23, 1964, p. 314. Quoted in Hayward, *The Age of Reagan,* p. 52.

62. Perlstein, *Before the Storm,* p. 421.

63. Ibid., p. 472.

64. Jerome Himmelstein, *To the Right: The Transformation of American Conservatism* (Berkeley: University of California Press, 1990), p. 67.

CHAPTER 3: THE AGONY OF LIBERALISM, 1964–1988

1. Theodore H. White, *The Making of the President, 1964* (New York: Atheneum, 1965), p. 365.

2. Rick Perlstein, *Before the Storm: Barry Goldwater and the Unmaking of the American Consensus* (New York: Hill and Wang, 2001), p. 303.

3. Quoted in James T. Patterson, *Grand Expectations: The United States 1945–1974* (New York: Oxford University Press, 1996), pp. 587–88.

4. Daniel P. Moynihan, *Maximum Feasible Misunderstanding: Community Action in the War on Poverty* (New York: Free Press, 1969), pp. 128–66; Tom Wolfe, *Radical Chic and*

Mau-Mauing the Flak Catchers (New York: Bantam, 1999), originally published in 1970 by Farrar, Straus and Giroux.

5. Thomas Byrne Edsall and Mary D. Edsall, *Chain Reaction: The Impact of Race, Rights and Taxes on American Politics* (New York: W. W. Norton, 1991), pp. 45–46.

6. Christopher Lasch, *The True and Only Heaven: Progress and Its Critics* (New York: W. W. Norton, 1991), p. 505.

7. Steven Hayward, *The Age of Reagan: The Fall of the Old Liberal Order, 1964–1980* (New York: Forum, 2001), p. 302.

8. Theodore H. White, *The Making of the President, 1968: A Narrative History of American Politics in Action* (New York: Atheneum, 1969), p. 346.

9. Edsall and Edsall, *Chain Reaction,* p. 95.

10. Ibid., p. 52.

11. Ibid., pp. 111–12.

12. Hayward, *The Age of Reagan,* p. 154.

13. Michael Elliott, *The Day Before Yesterday: Reconsidering America's Past; Rediscovering the Present* (New York: Simon & Schuster, 1996), p. 175.

14. National Elections Studies database, University of Michigan, http://www.umich/edu/_nes/nesguide/nesguide.htm.

15. George H. Nash, *The Conservative Intellectual Movement in America Since 1945* (Wilmington, Del.: Intercollegiate Studies Institute, 1998), p. 319.

16. White, *The Making of the President, 1968,* p. 143.

17. Jerome Himmelstein, *To the Right: The Transformation of American Conservatism* (Berkeley: University of California Press, 1990), p. 100.

18. David Reinhard, *The Republican Right Since 1945* (Lexington: University of Kentucky, 1983), p. 222.

19. Nash, *The Conservative Intellectual Movement in America,* p. 319.

20. Richard Viguerie, *The New Right: We're Ready to Lead* (Falls Church, Va.: The Viguerie Company, 1980), pp. 51–52.

21. National Elections Studies database, University of Michigan.

22. Lou Cannon, *Governor Reagan: His Rise to Power* (New York: Public Affairs, 2003), p. 394.

23. Hayward, *The Age of Reagan,* p. 448.

24. Lewis L. Gould, *Grand Old Party: A History of the Republicans* (New York: Random House, 2003), p. 403.

25. Quoted in Lee Edwards, *The Conservative Revolution: The Movement That Remade America* (New York: Free Press, 1999), p. 188.

26. Gary Dorrien, *The Neo-Conservative Mind: Politics, Culture, and the War of Ideology* (Philadelphia: Temple University Press, 1993), p. 2.

27. Irving Kristol, *Neo-Conservatism: The Autobiography of an Idea* (New York: Free Press, 1995), p. 25.

28. "The Negro Family: The Case for National Action," U.S. Department of Labor, Washington, D.C., 1965.

29. Godfrey Hodgson, *The World Turned Right Side Up* (New York: Houghton Mifflin, 1996), p. 130.

30. Kristol, *Neo-Conservatism,* p. 6.

31. Quoted in Nina J. Easton, *Gang of Five: Leaders at the Center of the Conservative Crusade* (New York: Simon & Schuster, 2000), pp. 41–42. Easton provides the best short

summary of Strauss's arguments we have come across. For a less accessible account by influential Washington Straussians, see Steven Lenzner and William Kristol, "What Was Leo Strauss Up To?" *The Public Interest,* Fall 2003.

32. Robert Kaiser and Ira Chinoy, "How Scaife's Money Powered a Movement," *Washington Post,* May 2, 1999.

33. Himmelstein, *To the Right,* p. 141.

34. Ibid., pp. 144–45.

35. William J. Lanouette, "The New Right—'Revolutionaries' Out After the Lunchpail Vote," *National Journal,* January 21, 1978, p. 88.

36. Quoted in Lee Edwards, *The Power of Ideas: The Heritage Foundation at 25 Years* (Ottawa, Ill.: Jameson Books, 1997), p. 38.

37. William Rusher, *The Rise of the Right* (New York: William Morrow, 1984), p. 228–29; Himmelstein, *To the Right,* p. 86.

38. Himmelstein, *To the Right,* p. 82.

39. Gillian Peele, *Revival and Reaction: The Right in Contemporary America* (Oxford: Clarendon Press, 1984), p. 3.

40. Himmelstein, *To the Right,* pp. 82–83.

41. James A. Morone, *Hellfire Nation: The Politics of Sin in American History* (New Haven: Yale University Press, 2003), p. 453.

42. Himmelstein, *To the Right,* pp. 116–17.

43. Ibid.

44. Ibid., p. 118.

45. Morone, *Hellfire Nation,* p. 453.

46. David Maraniss, *First in His Class: A Biography of Bill Clinton* (New York: Simon & Schuster, 1995), p. 282.

47. Earl Black and Merle Black, *The Vital South: How Presidents Are Elected* (Cambridge, Mass.: Harvard University Press, 1992), p. 279.

48. Earl Black and Merle Black, *The Rise of Southern Republicans* (Cambridge, Mass.: Belknap Press, 2002), p. 154.

49. Ibid., pp. 102–11.

50. Hodgson, *The World Turned Right Side Up,* pp. 210–11.

51. Edsall and Edsall, *Chain Reaction,* pp. 130–131.

52. Hodgson, *The World Turned Right Side Up,* p. 206.

53. Lou Cannon, *President Reagan: The Role of a Lifetime* (New York: Simon & Schuster, 1991), p. 160.

54. Hayward, *The Age of Reagan,* pp. xix–xx.

55. Cannon, *President Reagan: The Role of a Lifetime,* pp. 15–16, 85.

56. Black and Black, *The Rise of Southern Republicans,* p. 224.

57. Cannon, *President Reagan: The Role of a Lifetime,* p. 43.

58. Quoted in Hayward, *The Age of Reagan,* p. xxix.

59. Ibid., p. 100.

60. Cannon, *President Reagan: The Role of a Lifetime,* pp. 493–94.

61. Sidney Blumenthal, *The Rise of the Counterestablishment: From Conservative Ideology to Political Power* (New York: Harper and Row, 1986), p. 142.

62. Rusher, *The Rise of the Right,* p. 314.

63. Cannon, *President Reagan: The Role of a Lifetime,* p. 363.

64. Christopher Lasch, *The True and Only Heaven: Progress and Its Critics* (New York: W. W. Norton, 1991), p. 515.

65. For these figures, see Appendix.

CHAPTER 4: THE FIFTY-FIFTY NATION, 1988–2000

1. Joe Klein, *The Natural* (New York: Broadway, 2003), p. 14.

2. For a vigorous defense of George H. W. Bush, see Jonathan Rauch, "Father Superior," *New Republic*, May 22, 2000.

3. Quoted in Dan Balz and Ronald Brownstein, *Storming the Gates: Protest Politics and the Republican Revival* (Boston: Little, Brown, 1996), p. 131.

4. Interview with Grover Norquist, August 27, 2003.

5. Balz and Brownstein, *Storming the Gates*, p. 71.

6. John Podhoretz, *Hell of a Ride: Backstage at the White House Follies, 1989–1993* (New York: Simon & Schuster, 1993), p. 153.

7. Ibid., p. 157.

8. Linda Feldmann, "Economy Struggles, but War May Still Buoy Bush," *Christian Science Monitor*, April 16, 2003.

9. Podhoretz, *Hell of a Ride*, p. 30.

10. Ibid., p. 89.

11. Ibid., p. 94.

12. Ibid.

13. E. J. Dionne, *They Only Look Dead: Why Progressives Will Dominate the Next Political Era* (New York: Simon & Schuster, 1998), p. 197.

14. Balz and Brownstein, *Storming the Gates*, p. 144.

15. Ibid., p. 134.

16. Larry J. Sabato, *Feeding Frenzy: How Attack Journalism Has Transformed American Politics* (New York: Free Press, 1991), p. 20.

17. Sidney Blumenthal, *The Clinton Wars* (New York: Farrar, Straus and Giroux, 2003), p. 88.

18. Balz and Brownstein, *Storming the Gates*, p. 136.

19. Eric Schneider, ed., *Conservatism in America Since 1930* (New York: New York University Press, 2003), p. 396.

20. Ibid.

21. Balz and Brownstein, *Storming the Gates*, p. 68.

22. Klein, *The Natural*, p. 35.

23. Bill Clinton's keynote address to the Democratic Leadership Council in Cleveland, May 6, 1991.

24. "Like Father, Like Son," *Economist*, April 19, 2003.

25. Blumenthal, *The Clinton Wars*, p. 36.

26. Balz and Brownstein, *Storming the Gates*, p. 147.

27. Blumenthal, *The Clinton Wars*, p. 44.

28. Balz and Brownstein, *Storming the Gates*, p. 79.

29. Ibid., p. 89.

30. Adam Clymer, "The 'Teacher of the Rules of Civilization' Gets a Scolding," *New York Times*, January 26, 1997.

31. Blumenthal, *The Clinton Wars*, p. 86.

32. Ibid., p. 67ff.
33. George Stephanopoulos, *All Too Human* (Boston: Little, Brown, 1999), p. 228.
34. Klein, *The Natural*, p. 80.
35. Dionne, *They Only Look Dead*, pp. 82–83, 118–50.
36. Balz and Brownstein, *Storming the Gates*, p. 199.
37. Ibid., p. 56.
38. Ibid., p. 318.
39. David Plotz, "Ralph Reed's Creed," *slate.com*, May 4, 1997.
40. Quoted in Balz and Brownstein, *Storming the Gates*, p. 320.
41. Plotz, "Ralph Reed's Creed."
42. Balz and Brownstein, *Storming the Gates*, p. 311.
43. Blumenthal, *The Clinton Wars*, p. 120.
44. Hillary Rodham Clinton, *Living History* (New York: Simon & Schuster, 2003), p. 230.
45. All the figures in this paragraph come from Balz and Brownstein, *Storming the Gates*, p. 257.
46. See also George Kelling, Catherine Coles, and James Q. Wilson, eds., *Fixing Broken Windows: Restoring Order and Reducing Crime in Our Communities* (New York: Free Press, 1998).
47. Charles Murray, "The Coming White Underclass," *Wall Street Journal*, October 29, 1993.
48. Balz and Brownstein, *Storming the Gates*, p. 114.
49. A longer version is published as a book, edited by Ed Gillespie and Bob Schellhas, *Contract with America: The Bold Plan by Rep. Newt Gingrich, Rep. Dick Armey and the House Republicans to Change the Nation* (New York: Times Books, 1994).
50. David Maraniss and Michael Weisskopf, *Tell Newt to Shut Up* (New York: Touchstone, 1996).
51. Klein, *The Natural*, p. 145.
52. Dick Morris, *Behind the Oval Office: Winning the Presidency in the Nineties* (New York: Random House, 1997), pp. 81–88.
53. Klein, *The Natural*, p. 149.
54. Michael Barone, ed., *Almanac of American Politics, 1998* (Washington, D.C.: National Journal, 1997), p. 25.
55. Morris, *Behind the Oval Office*, pp. 300–5.
56. Barone, ed., *Almanac of American Politics, 1998*, p. 39.
57. Quoted in Godfrey Hodgson, *The World Turned Right Side Up* (New York: Houghton Mifflin, 1996), p. 283.
58. Stephanopoulos, *All Too Human*, p. 411.
59. Dionne, *They Only Look Dead*, p. 32.
60. Bill Clinton, State of the Union Address, January 27, 1998.
61. Balz and Brownstein, *Storming the Gates*, p. 321.
62. Ibid., p. 305.
63. Lou Cannon, *Governor Reagan: His Rise to Power* (New York: Public Affairs, 2003), p. 213.
64. "Not Extinct," *Economist*, July 13, 1991.
65. Bill Clinton, remarks at the Democratic National Convention, Los Angeles, August 14, 2000.

CHAPTER 5: FOR TEXAS, BUSINESS AND GOD

1. Quoted in John Kenneth White, *The Values Divide: American Politics and Culture in Transition* (New York: Seven Bridges Press, 2003), p. 187.

2. Ibid., p. 188.

3. Ibid.

4. Bob Woodward, *Bush at War* (New York: Simon & Schuster, 2002), p. 13.

5. Quoted in Eric Alterman, *What Liberal Media? The Truth About Bias and the News* (New York: Basic Books, 2003), p. 193.

6. Roxanne Roberts, "Lone Star Cosmos: At Their Ball, Texans Draw Washington into Their Vast, Expanding Universe," *Washington Post,* January 20, 2001.

7. Michael Lind, quoted in "The Future of Texas," *Economist,* December 21, 2002.

8. Michael Lind, *Made in Texas: George Bush and the Southern Takeover of American Politics* (New York: Basic Books, 2003), pp. 120–21.

9. Lou Dubose, Jan Reid and Carl Cannon, *Boy Genius: Karl Rove, the Brains Behind the Remarkable Political Triumph of George W. Bush* (New York: Public Affairs, 2003), p. 73.

10. George W. Bush, *A Charge to Keep* (New York: William Morrow, 1999), p. 97.

11. Bill Minutaglio, *First Son: George W. Bush and the Bush Family Dynasty* (New York: Times Books, 1999), p. 19.

12. Ibid., p. 109.

13. Bob Sablatura, "George W. Bush: Wealth Produced via Stock Swaps and Bailouts," *Houston Chronicle,* May 8, 1994.

14. Gerry Fraley, "Rangers Plan New Stadium in Arlington," *Dallas Morning News,* October 25, 1990.

15. Terrence Samuel, "Does Money Talk?" *U.S. News & World Report,* September 15, 2003.

16. David Frum, *The Right Man: The Surprise Presidency of George W. Bush* (New York: Random House, 2003), p. 283.

17. Speech by George W. Bush to UN General Assembly, November 10, 2001.

18. Remarks by George W. Bush on global HIV initiative, April 29, 2003.

19. See http://www.press.uchicago.edu.Misc/Chicago/481921.html.

20. Frum, *The Right Man,* p. 3.

21. Stephen Mansfield, *The Faith of George W. Bush* (New York: Jeremy P. Tarcher/Penguin, 2003), pp. 117–19.

22. Frum, *The Right Man,* pp. 101–3.

23. John Parker, "Survey of America," *Economist,* November 8, 2003, p. 12.

24. Ibid.

CHAPTER 6: THE *RIVE DROITE*

1. Quoted in Gertrude Himmelfarb, *Marriage and Morals Among the Victorians* (New York: Vintage Books, 1987), p. 202.

2. David Carr, "White House Listens When Weekly Speaks," *New York Times,* March 11, 2003.

3. Full disclosure: One of us once wrote an article for the *Weekly Standard* (predicting dire times ahead for Tony Blair shortly before he won a landslide victory).

4. Franklin Foer, "After Meritocracy," *New Republic,* February 5, 2001.

5. Eric Alterman, *What Liberal Media? The Truth About Bias and the News* (New York: Basic Books, 2003), pp. 35, 39.

6. Ken Auletta, "Vox Fox," *New Yorker,* May 26, 2003, p. 63.

7. Ibid., p. 58.

8. David Kirkpatrick, "Shaping Cultural Tastes at Big Retail Chains," *New York Times,* May 18, 2003.

9. Quoted in Alterman, *What Liberal Media?* p. 29.

10. See, for example, Terry M. Moe, *Schools, Vouchers and the American Public* (Washington, D.C.: Brookings Institution Press, 2001).

11. Matt Bai, "Notion Building," *New York Times Magazine,* October 12, 2003, p. 86.

CHAPTER 7: THE BRAWN

1. Adam Liptak, "Defendants Fighting Gun Charges Cite New View of Second Amendment," *New York Times,* July 23, 2002.

2. See www.pbs.org/wgbh/pages/frontline/shows/choice2000/bush/wead.html.

3. See http://family.org/fmedia/misc/a0027564.cfm.

4. See http://family.org/cforum/extras/a0027493.cfm.

5. Joan Didion, "Mr. Bush and the Divine," *New York Review of Books,* November 6, 2003.

6. Kimberly Conger and John Green, "Spreading Out and Digging In: Conservatives and State Republican Parties," *Campaigns and Elections,* February 2002.

7. Robert Kaiser and Ira Chinoy, "The Right's Founding Father: Fighting a War of Ideas," *Washington Post,* May 2, 1999.

8. David Low, *Low's Autobiography* (London: M. Joseph, 1956), p. 120.

9. Hillary Rodham Clinton, *Living History* (New York: Simon & Schuster, 2003), p. 446.

10. Dan Balz and Ronald Brownstein, *Storming the Gates: Protest Politics and the Republican Revival* (Boston: Little, Brown, 1996), p. 163.

CHAPTER 8: WITH US OR AGAINST US

1. George W. Bush, acceptance speech, Republican National Convention, August 3, 2000.

2. Frank Bruni, *Ambling into History: The Unlikely Odyssey of George W. Bush* (New York: HarperCollins, 2002), p. 4.

3. Ramesh Ponnuru, "Getting to the Bottom of This Neo Nonsense," *National Review,* June 16, 2003, pp. 29–32.

4. Ivo H. Daalder and James Lindsay, *America Unbound: The Bush Revolution in Foreign Policy* (Washington, D.C.: Brookings Institution, 2003), p. 18.

5. Ibid., p. 112.

6. Ibid., p. 15.

7. Ron Suskind, *The Price of Loyalty: George W. Bush, the White House, and the Education of Paul O'Neill* (New York: Simon & Schuster, 2004), pp. 70–75.

8. Stephen Fidler and Gerard Baker, "America's Democratic Imperialists," *Financial Times,* March 6, 2003, p. 17.

9. David Plotz, "Paul Wolfowitz: Bush's Testosterone Man at Defense," *Slate,* Friday, October 12, 2001.

10. Charles Krauthammer, speaking at the American Enterprise Institute. Quoted in Julie Kosterlitz, "The Neo-Conservative Moment," *National Journal,* May 17, 2003.

11. "Lindbergh Lives," *Economist,* March 15, 2003.

12. John Vinocur, "In Private, French Talk Differently About Veto," *International Herald Tribune,* March 6, 2003.

13. John Vinocur, "What Does Europe Want?" *International Herald Tribune,* January 20, 2004.

14. Michael Lind, "The Weird Men Behind George W. Bush's War," *New Statesman,* April 7, 2003.

15. See http://www.israeleconomy.org/strat1.htm.

16. Fidler and Baker, "America's Democratic Imperialists," p. 17.

17. Elizabeth Drew, "The Neo-Cons in Power," *New York Review of Books,* June 12, 2003, p. 20.

18. Bob Woodward, *Bush at War* (New York: Simon & Schuster, 2002), p. 98.

19. Daalder and Lindsay, *America Unbound,* p. 33.

20. Carl Cannon, "Memory and More in the Middle East," *National Journal,* June 7, 2003, p. 1779.

21. David Wurmser, quoted in Kosterlitz, "The Neo-Conservative Moment."

22. David Frum, *The Right Man: The Surprise Presidency of George W. Bush* (New York: Random House, 2003), p. 259.

23. Graham Turner, "The New Empire," *Daily Telegraph,* June 16, 2003.

24. George W. Bush, *A Charge to Keep* (New York: William Morrow, 1999), p. 239.

25. Jeffrey A. Krames, *The Rumsfeld Way: Leadership Wisdom of a Battle-Hardened Maverick* (New York: McGraw-Hill, 2002), p. 37.

26. Ibid., pp. 37–38.

27. Bush's speech at West Point is published in *America and the World,* a Council on Foreign Relations book (New York: W. W. Norton, 2002), pp. 364–71.

28. Quoted in Arthur Schlesinger Jr., "Eyeless in Iraq," *New York Review of Books,* October 23, 2003.

29. Ibid.

30. See www.whitehouse.gov/news/releases/2002/0620020614-8.

31. Irving Kristol, "American Conservatism, 1945–1995," *The Public Interest,* September 1, 1995; Pat Robertson, *The New World Order* (Dallas: World Publishing, 1991). On this subject see Michael Lind, *Up from Conservatism: Why the Right Is Wrong for America* (New York: Free Press, 1997), pp. 99–120.

32. Max Boot, "The Case for American Empire," *Weekly Standard,* October 15, 2001.

33. Max Boot, "Washington Needs a Colonial Office," *Financial Times,* July 3, 2003.

34. Daalder and Lindsay, *America Unbound,* p. 37.

35. The Pew Research Center for the People and the Press, Survey, October 15–19, 2003.

36. David Frum and Richard Perle, *An End to Evil: How to Win the War on Terrorism* (New York: Random House, 2003).

37. See Joseph Nye, *The Paradox of American Power: Why the World's Superpower Cannot Go It Alone* (New York: Oxford University Press, 2002).

38. See http://news.bbc.co.uk/1/shared/spl/hi/programmes/wtwta/poll/html/default.stm.

39. Max Boot, "All-Stars of Team Bush Fall Flat in Iraq," *Los Angeles Times,* December 14, 2003.

40. Daalder and Lindsay, *America Unbound,* p. 167.

41. Author interview with Jeane Kirkpatrick, August 11, 2003.

CHAPTER 9: THE ROAD AHEAD

1. "Dusting Off William McKinley," *Economist,* November 13, 1999.
2. Gary C. Jacobson, "The Bush Presidency and the American Electorate," *Presidential Studies Quarterly,* December 1, 2003.
3. "2004 Political Landscape," The Pew Research Center for the People and the Press, November 5, 2003.
4. Julie Kosterlitz, "On the Ropes," *National Journal,* September 6, 2003.
5. David Broder, "Political Steamroller," *Washington Post,* November 17, 2002.
6. "Fund-raising Gives GOP a Big Lead in Last Cycle," *New York Times,* March 19, 2003.
7. Elisabeth Bumiller, "Keepers of Bush Image Lift Stagecraft to New Heights," *New York Times,* May 16, 2003.
8. Kosterlitz, "On the Ropes."
9. Adam Clymer, "Buoyed by Resurgence, GOP Strives for an Era of Dominance," *New York Times,* May 25, 2003.
10. Our colleague was John Smutniak.
11. U.S. Bureau of Labor Statistics, Employment and Earnings, January 1983 and 2001 issues.
12. Michael Barone, "Life, Liberty and Property," *National Journal,* February 15, 2003, p. 508.
13. John Judis and Ruy Teixeira, *The Emerging Democratic Majority* (New York: Scribner, 2002), p. 50.
14. Ibid., p. 38.
15. See http://www.cis.org/articles/2002/back203.html.
16. Quoted in Michael Barone, *The New Americans: How the Melting Pot Can Work Again* (Washington, D.C.: Regnery, 2001), p. 182.
17. Ibid., pp. 161, 165.
18. Gregory Rodriguez, "The Emerging Latino Middle Class," a report for Pepperdine University Institute for Public Policy, October 1996.
19. Judis and Teixeira, *The Emerging Democratic Majority,* p. 39.
20. Mark Penn, "The Democratic Party and the 2004 Election," paper released by the Democratic Leadership Council, July 28, 2003.
21. Joel Kotkin, "Paths to Prosperity," *American Enterprise,* July/August 2003.
22. Michael Barone, ed., *Almanac of American Politics 2004* (Washington, D.C.: National Journal Group, 2003) Introduction.
23. Gallup poll, January 20–22, 2003.
24. Barone, ed., *Almanac of American Politics 2004,* Introduction, p. 31.
25. Cato Handbook for Congress: 108th Congress, p. 3.
26. Janny Scott, "The Changing Face of Patriotism," *New York Times,* July 6, 2003.
27. See http://www.abcnews.go.com/sections/politics/US/bush_sotu_poll_040119.html.
28. Katha Pollitt, "Pull Out No Flags," *Nation,* October 8, 2001.

CHAPTER 10: HOW IT COULD GO WRONG

1. "Good Ol' Strom?" *Economist,* November 30, 2002.
2. Thomas Edsall, "Lott Renounces White Racialist Group He Praised in 1992," *Washington Post,* December 16, 1998.
3. "I am large / I contain multitudes," from *Song of Myself.*

4. William Rentschler, "Barry Goldwater, Still in His Element as the Straightshooter from the West," *Chicago Tribune,* October 23, 1994.

5. Paul Krugman, *The Great Unraveling* (New York: Norton, 2003), p. 177.

6. "A Flood of Red Ink," *Economist,* November 8, 2003.

7. U.S. Office of Management and Budget, Mid-year Budget Review, released July 15, 2003.

8. For a detailed explanation, see "A Flood of Red Ink."

9. Jagadeesh Gokhale and Kent Smetters, "Fiscal and Generational Imbalances," www.aei.org/docLib/20030723_SmettersFinalCC.pdf.

10. Dennis Cauchon, "GOP Outspends Democrats in States: Both Far Outpace Inflation," *USA Today,* May 19, 2003.

11. Nicholas Dawidoff, "Mr. Washington Goes to Mississippi," *New York Times Magazine,* October 19, 2003.

12. Nicholas Confessore, "Welcome to the Machine: How the GOP Disciplined K Street and Made Bush Supreme," *Washington Monthly,* July/August 2003.

13. Quoted in Bob Woodward, "A Test of Government's Trustworthiness," *Washington Post,* October 25, 2001.

14. *New State Ice Co. v. Liebmann,* U.S. Supreme Court, 1932.

15. Tom Smith, "National Gun Policy Survey," National Opinion Research Center, December 2001.

16. Karlyn Bowman, ed., "Opinion Pulse," *American Enterprise,* March 2003, pp. 60–61.

17. See our colleague Suzi Parker's book, *Sex in the South: Unbuckling the Bible Belt* (Boston: Justin Charles, 2003).

18. John Judis and Ruy Teixeira, *The Emerging Democratic Majority* (New York: Scribner, 2002), p. 151.

19. These paragraphs owe much to John Fonte, "Homeland Politics," *National Review,* June 2, 2003, pp. 27–30.

CHAPTER 11: BEHIND ENEMY LINES

1. DeWayne Wickham, "Focus on Blacks: Voters of All Races Need to Go to the Polls," *USA Today,* October 24, 2000.

2. Anthony York, "America's Wake-up Call?" *Salon.com,* January 25, 2000.

3. Some of the studies are summarized in Marie Gryphon and Emily Meyer, "Our History of Educational Freedom," *Policy Analysis* 492, October 8, 2003.

4. "Blacks v. Teachers," *Economist,* March 10, 2001.

5. "The Color of Conservatism," *Economist,* January 23, 2003.

6. Nina J. Easton, *Gang of Five: Leaders at the Center of the Conservative Crusade* (New York: Simon & Schuster, 2000), p. 139.

7. Kate Zernike, "A Nation at War: Campuses," *New York Times,* April 5, 2003.

8. CNN exit poll, 2000 presidential election.

9. John Judis and Ruy Teixeira, *The Emerging Democratic Majority* (New York: Scribner, 2002), p. 50.

10. CNN exit poll, 2000 presidential election.

11. Elinor Burkett, *The Right Women: A Journey Through the Heart of Conservative America* (New York: Touchstone, 1998), pp. 15–16.

12. Helen Thomas, "Laura Bush Keeps Opinions to Herself," *Seattle Post-Intelligencer,* April 17, 2002.

13. Burkett, *The Right Women,* p. 41.

14. Lisa Belkin, "The Opt-Out Revolution," *New York Times Magazine,* October 26, 2003.

15. See *New York Times Magazine,* October 26, 2003.

16. Belkin, "The Opt-Out Revolution."

CHAPTER 12: AMERICA THE DIFFERENT

1. Daniel Yergin and Joseph Stanislaw, *The Commanding Heights: The Battle Between Government and the Marketplace That Is Remaking the Modern World* (New York: Simon & Schuster, 1998), p. 300.

2. Interview on Czech television, transcript released November 19, 2002, www.whitehouse.gov.

3. "Views of a Changing World 2003: War with Iraq Further Divides Global Publics," The Pew Research Center for the People and the Press, June 3, 2003.

4. Ibid., p. 29.

5. *Transatlantic Trends 2003: A Project of the German Marshall Fund of the United States and the Compagnia di San Paulo,* pp. 4–5.

6. Andrew Gimson, "A Sad Case of Schadenfreude," *The Spectator,* September 13, 2003.

7. Interview with Ted Koppel, *Nightline,* ABC, February 18, 1998.

8. Clyde Prestowitz, *Rogue Nation* (New York: Basic Books, 2003), p. 212.

9. Bush remarks, April 18, 2002.

10. Philip Gordon, "Bridging the Atlantic Divide," *Foreign Affairs,* January/February 2003, p. 77.

11. Pierre Hassner of the Center for International Studies and Research in Paris, quoted in J. F. O. McAllister, "Mad at America," *Time,* January 20, 2003, p. 23.

12. Dean rally in Falls Church, Virginia, August 23, 2003.

13. "Will a Quartet of Euro-Enthusiasts Undermine NATO?" *Economist,* May 3, 2003.

14. Robert Kagan, "Power and Weakness," *Policy Review,* June/July 2002.

15. *Transatlantic Trends 2003,* p. 14.

16. "A Tale of Two Bellies," *Economist,* August 24, 2002.

17. Allensbach Opinion Research Institute, 2002, quoted in John Parker, "Survey of America," *Economist,* November 8, 2003.

18. "Views of a Changing World 2003."

19. Bernard-Henri Lévy, "A Passage to Europe," *Time,* August 10, 2003.

20. See http://www.ojp.usdoj.gov/bjs/abstract/piuspo1.htm.

21. James A. Morone, *Hellfire Nation: The Politics of Sin in American History* (New Haven: Yale University Press, 2003), p. 460.

22. Ibid., p. 461.

23. "A Stigma That Never Fades," *Economist,* August 10, 2002.

24. "Jesse Jackson's Wrong Target," *Economist,* November 25, 1999.

25. "The Military Balance 2003–04," International Institute for Strategic Studies, 2003.

26. Both figures taken from table, "Tale of Two Legacies," *Economist,* Christmas special, December 21, 2002.

27. David Frum, *The Right Man: The Surprise Presidency of George W. Bush* (New York: Random House, 2003), p. 33.

28. Milton Friedman, "Tax Cuts = Smaller Government," *Wall Street Journal Europe,* January 20, 2003, p. A12.

29. "Views of a Changing World 2003."

30. Jason De Parle, "As Rules on Welfare Tighten, Its Recipients Gain in Stature," *New York Times,* September 11, 1999.

31. The artist in question is 50 Cent.

32. Paul Krugman, "For Richer," *New York Times,* October 20, 2002.

33. "Do You Like Your Class War Shaken or Stirred, Sir?" *Economist,* September 4, 2003.

34. Ibid.

35. Ibid.

36. Hendrik Hertzberg, "Dividends," Talk of the Town, *New Yorker,* January 20, 2003, pp. 29–30.

37. Cynthia Tucker, "Making Abortion Safe, Legal and Rare," *San Francisco Chronicle,* January 22, 1993.

38. Bill Kristol, "On the Future of Conservatism," *Commentary,* February 1997.

39. Morone, *Hellfire Nation,* pp. 22–23.

40. John Parker, "Survey of America," *Economist,* November 8, 2003, p. 11.

41. 1 Thessalonians 4:16–17.

42. Parker, "Survey of America," p. 11.

43. Christopher Caldwell, "No, Europe Needs to Get Real," *Time,* January 20, 2003.

CHAPTER 13: RIGHT FROM THE BEGINNING

1. Daniel Boorstin, *The Genius of American Politics* (Chicago: University of Chicago Press, 1953), p. 6.

2. Michael Lind, *The Next American Nation: The New Nationalism and the Fourth American Revolution* (New York: Simon & Schuster, 1995), p. 225.

3. Boorstin, *The Genius of American Politics,* p. 6.

4. Ibid., p. 70.

5. Gordon Wood, *The American Revolution: A History* (New York: Modern Library Chronicles, 2002), p. 65.

6. Martin Diamond, "The American Idea of Equality: The View of the Founding," in *As Far as Republican Principles Will Admit: Essays by Martin Diamond,* ed. William A. Schambra (Washington, D.C.: AEI Press, 1992), pp. 248–49.

7. H. W. Brands, *The Strange Death of American Liberalism* (New Haven: Yale University Press, 2001), pp. 1–2.

8. Jacob Weisberg, *In Defense of Government: The Fall and Rise of Public Trust* (New York: Scribner, 1996), p. 40.

9. Lind, *The Next American Nation,* p. 38.

10. Robert A. Caro, *Master of the Senate: The Years of Lyndon Johnson* (New York: Knopf, 2002), p. 90.

11. Seymour Martin Lipset and Gary Marks, *It Didn't Happen Here: Why Socialism Failed in the United States* (New York: W. W. Norton, 2000), pp. 98–99.

12. John Parker, "Survey of America," *Economist,* November 8, 2003, p. 5.

13. Lipset and Marks, *It Didn't Happen Here,* p. 203.

14. Brands, *The Strange Death of American Liberalism,* pp. 24–25.

15. Lipset and Marks, *It Didn't Happen Here,* p. 286.

16. Garry Wills, *Under God: Religion and American Politics* (New York: Simon & Schuster, 1990), p. 370.

17. James A. Morone, *Hellfire Nation: The Politics of Sin in American History* (New Haven: Yale University Press, 2003), p. 127.
18. Parker, "Survey of America," p. 14.
19. See Robert Fogel, *The Fourth Great Awakening and the Future of Egalitarianism* (Chicago: University of Chicago Press, 1999).
20. Quoted in Seymour Martin Lipset, "American Exceptionalism Reaffirmed," in *Is America Different? A New Look at American Exceptionalism,* ed. Byron Shafer (Oxford: Clarendon Press, 1991), p. 25.
21. Ibid., p. 26.
22. Gene Healy, "What's Conservative About the Pledge of Allegiance?" Cato Institute, November 4, 2003, http://www.cato.org/dailys/11-04-03.html.
23. David M. Potter, *People of Plenty: Economic Abundance and the American Character* (Chicago: University of Chicago Press, 1954), p. 80.
24. H. G. Wells, *The Future in America* (New York: Harper and Brothers, 1906), pp. 105–6.
25. Lipset and Marks, *It Didn't Happen Here,* p. 27.
26. Potter, *People of Plenty,* p. 80.
27. Seymour Martin Lipset, *The First New Nation: The United States in Historical and Comparative Perspective* (London: Heinemann, 1963), p. 325.
28. John Micklethwait and Adrian Wooldridge, *The Company: A Short History of a Revolutionary Idea* (New York: Modern Library, 2003).
29. Brands, *The Strange Death of American Liberalism,* p. 139.
30. "In Praise of the Unspeakable," *Economist,* July 20, 2002.
31. Daniel J. Boorstin, *The Americans: The National Experience* (New York: Vintage Books, 1965), p. 91.
32. Ibid., p. 113.
33. Gallup poll results cited in "Live with TAE," *The American Enterprise,* October/November 2002, p. 17.
34. Andres Duany, quoted in "Live with TAE," *The American Enterprise,* October/November 2002, p. 18.
35. Kevin Phillips, *Post-Conservative America: People, Politics and Ideology in a Time of Crisis* (New York: Random House, 1982), p. 141.
36. T. R. Fehrenbach, *Lone Star: A History of Texas and the Texans,* updated edition, (New York: Da Capo, 2000), p. 716.
37. Ibid., p. 711.

CHAPTER 14: HERESY AND REFORMATION

1. Paul Waugh, "New Rights for Gay Couples Divide Conservative Party," *The Independent,* December 7, 2002.
2. Irving Kristol, author of *Neo-Conservatism: The Autobiography of an Idea* (New York: Free Press, 1995), was one of the first people to point this out (pp. 377–78).
3. John Micklethwait is a (sadly unpaid) director of Policy Exchange, a right-of-center think tank.
4. E. J. Dionne, *Why Americans Hate Politics: The Death of the Democratic Process* (New York: Simon & Schuster, 1992), p. 173.
5. George H. Nash, *The Conservative Intellectual Movement in America Since 1945* (Wilmington, Del.: Intercollegiate Studies Institute, 1998), pp. 181–82.

6. Kristol, *Neo-Conservatism*, p. 25.

7. Quoted in J. Davis Hoeveler, *Watch on the Right: Conservative Intellectuals in the Reagan Era* (Madison: University of Wisconsin Press, 1991), pp. 54–55.

8. Nash, *The Conservative Intellectual Movement in America*, pp. xiv–xv.

9. Lou Cannon, *Governor Reagan: His Rise to Power* (New York: Public Affairs, 2003), p. 120.

10. Max Beloff, "Of Lords, Senators, and Plain Misters," *Encounter* 68 (April 1987), pp. 69–71; "An Exchange Between Max Beloff and Irving Kristol," *Encounter* 69 (June 1987), pp. 69–71.

11. Quoted in Simon Heffer, *Like the Roman: The Life of Enoch Powell* (London: Weidenfeld and Nicholson, 1998), p. 961.

12. Quoted in Roger Scruton, *The Meaning of Conservatism* (London: 1998), p. xiii.

13. Quoted in Michael Bentley, *Lord Salisbury's World* (Cambridge: Cambridge University Press, 2001), p. 253.

14. Eustace Percy, *Some Memories* (London: Eyre & Spottiswoode, 1958), p. 105.

15. Michael Oakeshott, *Rationalism in Politics and Other Essays* (Indianapolis: Liberty Press, 1991), p. 411.

16. "What a Lot of Old Tosh—Lyrical Certainties from John Major?" *Independent on Sunday*, April 25, 1993. The phrase, incidentally, was lifted from George Orwell.

17. Lee Edwards, *The Power of Ideas: The Heritage Foundation at 25 Years* (Ottawa, Ill.: Jameson Books, 1997), p. 10.

18. Cannon, *Governor Reagan: His Rise to Power*, p. 120.

19. Oakeshott, *Rationalism in Politics*, p. 409.

20. Quoted in E. J. Dionne, *They Only Look Dead: Why Progressives Will Dominate the Next Political Era* (New York: Simon & Schuster, 1996), p. 271.

21. George Will, *The New Season: A Spectator's Guide to the 1988 Election* (New York: Simon & Schuster, 1988), p. 61.

22. Kristol, *Neo-Conservatism*, p. 377.

23. George W. Bush, "A Distinctly American Internationalism," speech delivered at Ronald Reagan Library, Simi Valley, California, November 19, 1999.

24. "The Perils of Recycling," *Economist*, August 30, 2003.

25. From Angus Roxburgh, *Preachers of Hate: The Rise of the Far Right* (London: Gibson Square Books, 2002).

26. "Retirement Center Having Sexual Issues," *Dayton Daily News*, June 3, 2003.

27. Engels to Sorge, February 8, 1890, in *Selected Correspondence*, p. 467. Quoted in Seymour Martin Lipset and Gary Marks, eds., *It Didn't Happen Here: Why Socialism Failed in the United States* (New York: W. W. Norton, 2000), p. 21.

CHAPTER 15: THE MELANCHOLY LONG WITHDRAWING ROAR
OF LIBERALISM

1. Michael Barone and Richard Cohen, eds., *Almanac of American Politics, 2002* (Washington, D.C.: National Journal Group, 2001), p. 652.

2. Gary Jacobson, "Partisan Polarization in Presidential Support: The Presidential Connection," paper prepared for delivery at December 2002 Political Science Association meeting.

3. This is based on our analysis of 111 polls between January 2001 and September 2003.

4. Based on four polls in August and September 2003.

5. Jacob Weisberg, *In Defense of Government: The Fall and Rise of Public Trust* (New York: Scribner, 1996), p. 32.

6. H. W. Brands, *The Strange Death of American Liberalism* (New Haven: Yale University Press, 2001), p. ix.

7. "National Election Studies Guide to Public Opinion and Electoral Behavior," University of Michigan, 2002.

8. Michelle Goldberg, "Howard Dean's Israel Problem," *Salon.com,* September 23, 2003.

9. Matt Bai, "Dr. No and the Yes Men," *New York Times,* June 1, 2003.

10. CNN/*USA Today*/Gallup poll, January 9–11, 2004.

11. Harold Meyerson, "An Unexpected Powerhouse," *Washington Post,* January 29, 2004.

12. For the uninitiated, Nicholas Soames is a patrician Tory MP.

13. Laura Blumenfeld, "Hunter, Dreamer, Realist: Complexity Infuses Senator's Ambition," *Washington Post,* June 1, 2003.

14. Julian Glover, "Tories Win Election Spending Battle," *The Guardian,* December 17, 2001.

15. Kevin Phillips, "How Wealth Defines Power: The Politics of the New Gilded Age," *American Prospect,* May 1, 2003.

16. John Harwood and Sheilagh Murray, "The Constant Dividers in American Politics: Race and Abortion," *Wall Street Journal Europe,* December 19, 2002.

17. Bill Turque, *Inventing Al Gore* (New York: Houghton Mifflin, 2000), p. 94.

18. Al Gore and Tipper Gore, *Joined at the Heart* (New York: Henry Holt, 2002), p. 40.

19. Karen Arenson, "For Professor, a Town House Fit for a King," *New York Times,* November 20, 2002.

20. The best examination of Hollywood politics is Ronald Brownstein's *The Power and the Glitter: The Hollywood-Washington Connection* (New York: Pantheon, 1990).

21. Bill Cottrell, "Actor Compares 2000 Election to September 11," *Tallahassee Democrat,* March 8, 2003.

CONCLUSION: LIVING WITH THE RIGHT NATION

1. We accept that naming the Speaker as prime minister is a little bit of a stretch, because of the Speaker's partial neutrality. He is still, however, the de facto leader of his party there.

2. "Almost Green," *Economist,* December 13, 2003.

3. See, for example, James Pinkerton, "Is America Conservative?" *Tech Central Station,* December 2, 2003. http://remotefarm.techcentralstation.com/120203A.htm.

4. Sridar Pappu, "Off the Record," *New York Observer,* February 2, 2004.

5. David Brooks, "Americans Have Reasons to Be Grateful," *International Herald Tribune,* November 26, 2003.

6. Jonathan Chait, "Mad About You," *New Republic,* September 29, 2003.

7. Jack Huberman, *The Bush-Hater's Handbook: A Guide to the Most Appalling Presidency of the Past 100 Years* (New York: Nation Books, 2004).

8. Laura Blumenfeld, "Soros's Deep Pockets v. Bush," *Washington Post,* November 11, 2003.

9. CNN exit poll, 2000 presidential election, November 2000.

10. "America's Image Further Erodes, Europeans Want Weaker Ties," The Pew Research Center for the People and the Press, March 18, 2003.

11. *Sunday Times*/Yougov poll, conducted November 13–14, 2003.

12. Terry Teachout, "Republican Nation, Democratic Nation?" *Commentary,* January 2001.

13. Peter David: see "Over Here," *Economist,* November 22, 2003.

14. Blair speech to House of Commons, March 18, 2003.

15. "For Us or Against Us?" *Economist,* November 22, 2003.

16. Fareed Zakaria, "The Arrogant Empire," *Newsweek,* March 24, 2003.

17. Bill Emmott, "A Survey of America's Role in the World," *Economist,* June 29, 2002.

18. Blair speech to House of Commons, March 18, 2003.

19. Charles Grant, *Transatlantic Rift: How to Bring the Two Sides Together* (London: Centre for European Reform, 2003), p. 28.

20. John Parker, "Survey of America," *Economist,* November 8, 2003.

21. Ian Buruma, "Wielding the Moral Club," *Financial Times,* September 13, 2003.

22. The full text is: "My position is that, whatever the circumstances, France will vote no because it considers that this evening there are no grounds for waging war."

23. Kofi Annan, remarks to black American politicians, October 7, 2003.

24. Zakaria, "The Arrogant Empire."

25. Quoted in Zakaria, "The Arrogant Empire."

26. Arthur M. Schlesinger Jr., "Foreign Policy and the American Character," *Foreign Affairs,* Fall 1983.

27. Niall Ferguson, "Why America Outpaces Europe (Clue: The God Factor)," *New York Times,* June 8, 2003.

28. Ibid.

INDEX

PHOTOGRAPH CREDITS